Royal Irish A

TODD LECTURE SERIES.

VOL. IV.

CATH RUIS NA RÍG FOR BÓINN;

WITH

Preface, Translation, and Indices.

ALSO

A TREATISE ON IRISH NEUTER SUBSTANTIVES,

AND

A SUPPLEMENT TO THE INDEX VOCABULORUM OF ZEUSS' 'GRAMMATICA CELTICA.'

BY

EDMUND HOGAN, S.J.,

F.R.U.I., M.R.I.A.;

Royal Irish Academy's Todd Professor of the Celtic Languages.

DUBLIN:

PUBLISHED AT THE ACADEMY HOUSE, 19, DAWSON-STREET.

SOLD ALSO BY

HODGES, FIGGIS, & CO. (LTD.), GRAFTON-ST.;

AND BY WILLIAMS & NORGATE.

LONDON: 14, Henrietta-street, Covent Garden. | EDINBURGH: 20, South Frederick-street.

1892.

CONTENTS.

CONTENTS.

PREFACE.

THIS Battle of the Boyne, now printed and translated for the first time, was the second of those battles of the Seven Years War which are said to have been fought at the beginning of the Christian era. The battle-field, the manuscripts that contain a description of the fight, or make reference to it, the warriors and chiefs who figure in it, its date, causes, circumstances, and results will form the subject of some preliminary remarks.

I.—The Battle-Field.

It is called "Rosnaree on the Boyne" to distinguish it from Rosnaree in Island Magee or *Seimne*, where Aedán, King of Scotland, made submission to Baedán, King of Ulster, about the year 575.[1] About two miles below Slane the Boyne becomes fordable, and its course is broken by several islets. On its south-west bank is Rosnaree, and on its opposite swelling bank are seen Knowth, Dowth, New Grange, a series of raised mounds, raths, caves, circles, and pillar-stones.[2] This Ross or headland was the place of residence of King Dathi's mother,[3] the burial place of King Cormac son of Art,[4] the spot where Conn the Hundred-Fighter was slain,[5] where Saints Fintan and Finnian established cells, and St. Colum-Cille found the skull of Cormac, which he reverently put again into the grave.[6] The researches of the Ordnance Survey discovered

---

1 "L. Lecan," fol. 139 aa.

2 "Parliamentary Gazetteer of Ireland"; "Wilde's Boyne and Blackwater,' p. 188. Rosnaree is erroneously placed on the north bank in the map prefixed to Dr. Reeves' "Adamnan."

3 "O'Curry's MS. Materials," p. 286.

4 *LU.*, pp. 60 b, 51 a.

5 "Battle of Magh Lena," p. 98.

6 "Reeves' Adamnan," p. 236.

that tradition still pointed out as the grave of Cormac a *duma* or mound, which was near the site of the Catholic chapel, but has since been levelled.[1] A few days ago Mr. J. P. Johnson showed me Cormac's grave on a mound, and adjoining it a "pagan burial place," about five minutes walk to the west of his mill of Rosnaree; on these mounds human bones are found scattered about, and bones of great size have been dug up. The stream of the Boyne flowing by that place was called Linn Rois, or the Pool of the Ross.[2] Near it the Ulstermen came "across Dubid, across the Boyne into Mag Brég and Meath," and made their drunken raid into the South. According to Hennessy, Dubid is "apparently some little river north of the Boyne,"[3] but it is clearly Dowth, opposite Rosnaree, which is called *Dubad* in the "Four Masters," and *Duibḟid* in "Tigernach."[4]

In the "B. of Lismore," 205 a, Rosnaree is thus referred to: "What is yon wooded headland? saith Patrick, *i.e.* Rosnaree. It is Ros Caille, saith Caílte, and there are a thousand kinds of trees in it, and the king's sons had a great palace there." The place was called *Ros Caille*, or the Headland of the Wood, and also *Ross Finnchuill*, or the Promontory of the Fair-Hazel:—

> "Ross Finnchuill of Cluain Diothrach
> where youths and greyhounds used to be,
> was a dark wood, royal its gifts,
> for the hunting of Dathi, son of Fiachra.
> Beibhinn, the daughter of powerful Brian,
> was the mother of Dathi, son of Fiachra;
> it was she, as I have heard here,
> who obtained the meadows round the fair Ross.
> the Esgir of Brannan, son of Eochaidh,
> the grave of Conn of the hundred battles
> was a dark oak-forest until now."[5]

---

1 "Cambrensis Eversus," ed. Kelly, i. 483, 484.
2 "Four Masters," i. 462.
3 "Mesca Ulad," ix. 14.
4 "Four Masters," an. 238.
5 Reeves' "Adamnan," p. 374. Macniad took up a position there, "C. M. Lena," 144; to Rosnaree Baile Mac Buain went to meet Ailenn his *fiancée*.

II.—The Seven Manuscripts

which contain descriptions of the battle are:—

1. "The Book of Leinster," fol. 171, copied *circ.* 1150.
2, 3. Two MSS. belonging to Colgan, date uncertain, but before 1650.
4. "Egerton," 106, fol. 53, copied in 1715.
5. "MS. 23 k, 37 (pp. 198–219), R. I. Academy," copied in 1715.
6. "Stowe MS., R. I. Academy" (E. iv. 3, pp. 111–128), copied in 1727.
7. A MS. of Maynooth, date uncertain, but before 1795.

All are mentioned in M. de Jubainville's "Catalogue," p. 81, except the last, the existence of which I learned from my friend, Mr. John M'Neill, and the collation of which with M'Solly's MS. I owe to the kindness of the Rev. E. O'Growney, Professor of Irish at Maynooth. Colgan's copies are not in the Convent of the Franciscan Fathers, Dublin. The modern recensions of Egerton,[1] Stowe, the Royal Irish Academy, and Maynooth may be considered as identical.[2] They differ so much in matter, arrangement, and phraseology, from the *LL.* version, that collation would be difficult, and would involve very copious quotations; and as they are interesting and represent an ancient text different from that of *LL.*, and moreover preserve many rare archaic vocables, they merit substantive treatment, and are printed here with a translation.

Besides the MSS. or books that describe the battle, there are others that mention it, viz. "The Battle of Magh Rath," p. 210; "The B. of Fenagh," p. 328 (a MS. of year 1516); "The Stowe MS.," xxvi., fol. 62; "The R. I. Academy's MS.," 23 k, 44, &c.; and "Harleian, 5280," fol. 54 a.

---

[1] Father M'Swiney, S.J., transcribed for me some pages of "Egerton," which show that it is like M'Solly's copy.

[2] The Royal Irish Academy and Maynooth versions scarcely ever differ.

III.—The Warriors and Chiefs mentioned in our text.

Ninety of these figure in our tale, of whom only forty-five appear in M. De Jubainville's treatise on the "Epopée Celtique en Irlande."[1] The following is the traditional pedigree of the chief Ulster heroes; it includes the names of five women, and they seem to have been non-combatants, viz. Clothra, Dechtire, Fedelm, Findchaem, and Findscoth.

This pedigree of the Clann Rudraige is not quite as authentic as that of the descendants of the Godolphin Arabian; but it is here given as throwing some light on our story.

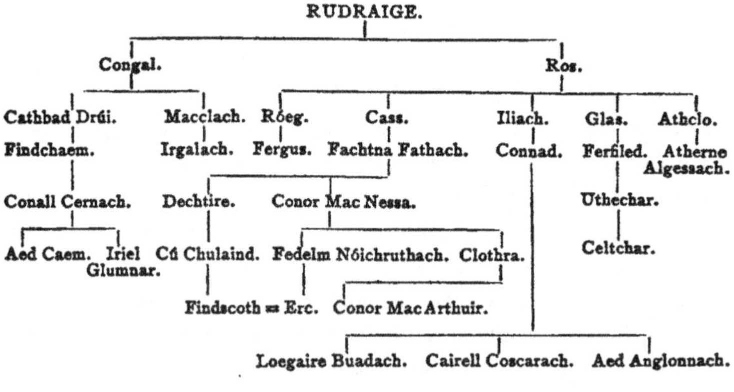

It will naturally be thought that these people are mere figments of bardic fancy; and incredulity is awakened by the wonderful things told about some of them in our text, such as that Conall Cernach[2] killed a thousand Leinster men with his own hand, and that Cairpre slew eight hundred, &c. Even seven hundred and fifty years ago such things were looked on

---

[1] The Index to that book gives a full list of the heroes of the Cycle of Conchobor, whose names appear in the tales edited by Windisch, Stokes, De Jubainville, and others.

[2] But here we must understand Conall and *his men*; cf. "bellum in Monte Badonis in quo corruerunt nongenti sexagenti viri *de uno impetu Arthuri* (Nennius in "Monum. Hist. Britonum," p. 74).

as "l'histoire véritable des temps fabuleux," as the scribe of the "Táin Bó Cualnge," in the "B. of Leinster," writes at fol. 104 b:—"A blessing on everyone who shall faithfully memorize the Táin in this form, and shall not put it into any other form. But I, who have transcribed this history, or rather fable, do not believe some things in this history or fable. For some things in it are delusions of demons, some are poetic figments, some seem true ['similia'], and some not; some were written to amuse fools."

This shows that the *LL.* scribe was "nae fool," and confirms what the poet Thomas Moore said of the Irish scribes in general. Of him O'Curry says[1]:—"Moore alternately scanned myself and the many dark and time-worn books by which I was surrounded, and he said, 'Petrie, these huge tomes could not have been written by fools or for any foolish purpose.' Doubtless under the hands of bards things were exaggerated and highly coloured, but yet may have had, and probably had, an historical basis; and we may say of them what a German critic, C. G. Schoell[2] (whose audacities of assertion in other matters are to be reprobated), says of the Briton "Nennius": "In the hands of this writer all things become fables; however, his writings may be useful as giving a picture of his times."

More competent men than Schoell, and as able and willing to apply the solvents of modern criticism, find a basis of facts in the sagas of the cycle of Conchobor. Such men as D'Arbois de Jubainville, Windisch, and Whitley Stokes think that, though much in these early tales is due to the fancy of writers, there is a foundation of facts which seem to date from about the time of the dawn of the Christian Era.[3] However,

[1] "Manuscript Materials," p. 154.

[2] "Inter istius manus scriptoris omnia in fabulas sunt versa. Usui esse possit ut ætatis illius indolem perspiciamus; quod haud parvi est ducendum."—"De Eccles. Britonum, Scotorumque Historiæ Fontibus," p. 37: Berlin, 1851.

[3] "D'Arbois' Introduction à l'Etude de la Littérature Celtique," p. 45. Windisch, in "Rev. Celt.," v. 77, says:—"Nous sommes amenés à attribuer ces légendes aux premiers siècles de notre ère. . . . Nous pouvons tenir pour certain que les

Dr. Windisch prudently says, "I don't see why there was not a King Conchobor and a Queen Medb," and the sceptical scribe of *LL.* does not deny it. But at the risk of being thought behind the times and the *fin de siècle*, I venture, with my countrymen of the eighth, ninth, tenth, eleventh, and twelfth centuries to salute them as real personages, though I do not admire them, and would make some uncomplimentary remarks about Medb were I not speaking in presence of some of her descendants who are members of the Royal Irish Academy. I do not go as far as O'Curry, who says of the "Táin Bó Cualnge," in which Conchobor and Medb figure so prominently, "though often exhibiting high poetic colouring in the description of particular circumstances, it unquestionably embraces, and is all through founded upon, authentic historic facts."[1] Yet will I go as far as I can in that direction, picking my steps in the very shaky bog of early Irish history, and taking care not to go farther than my documents will carry me.

Now, firstly, the triumphs of Conchobor and his Ulster heroes over the south and west of Ireland have been handed down to us by early Irish writers of the south and west kingdoms, without the slightest hint about the unreality of these things and persons. Assuredly, the Irishmen of these four kingdoms, who, according to Campion, "were greedy of praise and fearful of dishonour," would have denied, or called in question, stories so disparaging to their countries, if they did not believe them. 2ndly. The scribe who copied these sagas into the "Book of Leinster," *circa* 1150, though sceptical enough with

mœurs que ces légendes assignent à cette époque ont eu leur réalité, sauf les exaggérations de la fantaisie, en un temps qui n'est certainement pas postérieur au commencement de notre ère. . . . Je ne vois pas pourquoi il n'aurait pas existé un roi Conchobor, une reine Medb, qui chez les générations suivantes sont passés à l'état de héros légendaires." "Conor and the other persons mentioned are said to have lived in the first century of the Christian Era, and the possible incidents of the Saga may well have taken place at that period."—Stokes' Pref. to "Siege of Howth."

[1] "MS. Materials," p. 33.

regard to details, does not question the reality of those Ulster warriors. 3rdly. Maelmuire of Clonmacnois, the scribe of "L. na Huidre," slain in 1106, copied into that book many sagas[1] celebrating the triumphs of the Ulster warriors over his own countrymen, and never once calls their existence into question. 4thly. "The Tripartite Life of St. Patrick," compiled in the eleventh century from documents, many, if not all, of which were composed before A.D. 1000,[2] mentions "the reign of Coirpre Nia Fer,"[3] who was killed in the Battle of Rosnaree. 5thly. In the same century the conscientious and enlightened chronicler, Tigernach, treats of Coirpre, Conchobor, &c., as real kings. 6thly. The Bodleian fragment of "Cormac's Glossary," the language of which "shows it to have been written not much before the eleventh century,"[4] gives the name of Eochaid, son of Luchta, who is mentioned in our text. 7thly. Cinaed Ua Hartacáin, who died in 975, in a poem preserved in *LL.*, p. 31 b, mentions Eogan son of Durthacht, Gergenn son of Illad the son of Ross, and the sons of Uisliu. In another poem, *LL.* 161, Cinaed mentions the seige of Howth by the Leinstermen, and names Aithirne, Conchobor, Coirpre, the sons of Ross Ruad, Find Fili, and Mess Dead.[5] 8thly. Probus, author of the "Vita Quinta," in the tenth or ninth century,[6] mentions "the reign of Coirpre Nia Fer."[7] 9thly. Maelmura of Othan, who died in 884, mentions the name of Rudraige, Fachtna Fathach, Fergus son of Ross, or Fergus son of Róig,

---

[1] Pages 19–22, 55-82, 82–99, 90–112, 113–115, 121–121, 134.

[2] Whitley Stokes ed. of "The Tripartite Life," Introduction, p. lxxxix.

[3] "Tripartite Life," ed. by Whitley Stokes, p. 122.

[4] Stokes' edition of this "Fragment," pp. 1, 30.

[5] On this M. D'Arbois de Jubainville says: "Cette Légende était déja connue au dixième siècle, comme on peut le voir par un poème de Cinaed hua Artacain, mort en 275."—"Essai d'un Catalogue," &c., p. 142.

[6] "A work well ascertained to the tenth century."—Sir S. Ferguson in "Patrician Documents," p. 125. M. de Jubainville says he lived in the ninth century: I forget in what book he says so.

[7] The page of the "Trias Thaumaturga" where this is given may be found by reference to Colgan's Index.

LL., p. 135 a. 10thly. In the "Book of Armagh," which was copied in 807 from old and faded documents of the eighth century, or earlier, "the reign of Coirpre Nia Fer" is recorded at fol. 14 aa, and so are the names of Cass and Glass, which appear in our pedigree of the Ulster warriors. To this eighth century we may also perhaps refer the statement of the "Tripartite Life," as, to use the words of Sir Samuel Ferguson, "the first elements of almost all its matter may be found in the 'Book of Armagh,' either recorded at full length, or indicated in the rough index to names of persons and places at the end of Tirechan in that collection. There can be little doubt that, whatever be the date of its compilation in its present form, most of its substance is drawn from traditions, which were current before the compilation of the 'Armagh Codex.'"[1] 11thly. Cennfailid, son of Ailill, a poet of the seventh century, wrote some verses on the death of Cú Chulaind, which are cited in the "Book of Leinster," p. 121. He says that this hero was slain in his fight against Lugaid, son of Cúrúi.[2] "The time of Cennfailid was the golden age of Irish literature. To the reign of Guaire Aidne, who died in 659 or 662, the narratives of the Irish *file* refer the redaction of the épopée of the 'Táin Bó Cúalnge.' The greatest part of the old epic literature of Ireland appears to have been committed to writing during the hundred and fifty years which followed the dawn of Guaire's reign. In the seventh century died Dallan, son of Forgal, Senchan Torpeist, and Cennfailid, the most ancient, perhaps, of the Irish *file*, who may be considered as the real authors of the compositions which bear their names. At the same epoch the cultivation of Greek and Latin literature was carried on in Ireland with marvellous ardour and success."[3]

From those considerations which I have put forward, it

---

[1] Ferguson's "Patrician Documents," p. 127, and Hogan's "Documenta Patriciana," pp. 110-111.

[2] De Jubainville's "Cours de Litt. Celt.," v., pp. 829, 347.

[3] De Jubainville's "Introduction à l'Étude de la Littérature Celtique," p. 366.

seems that, from the twelfth backward to the seventh century, Coirpre Nia Fer and the other warriors of the cycle of Conchobor were looked on as real men of flesh and blood; and a strong presumption is created that they were not mere figments of bardic fancy.

IV.—The Date of the Battle and of the Saga.

It must have been before the end of the first century, as Marianus Scotus does not give the name of Conchobor Mac Nessa in his list of Ulster Kings from the beginning of the second century. It was fought about the first year of our era, if we are to believe O'Flaherty,[1] our best native guide, who founds his view on "The Annals of Tigernach," "The Synchronisms of Fland," "The Books of Clonmacnois and Lecan," and "The Chronicon Scotorum." In this view he is borne out by the old "Book of Fenagh," p. 32. It was fought in the summer which followed the beginning of the Seven Years War.

The Saga, such as we have it in the earliest and latest version, is non-Christian and pre-Christian in texture and tone. But from a linguistic standpoint the LL. text is Middle-Irish, as is shown by the total absence of the neuter article, except in the word *an-i*. There are also post-Danish interpolations of Norse names, such as Olaf,[2] Sigurd, Sciggire, Lochland, &c., which must have been inserted after the Irish had become acquainted, if not with the persons, at least with the names of some sea-rovers of the North. When that was we cannot tell, though we know that those rovers began to infest our shores about the year 795. We find, even in the older MS. of "L. na Huidre," Cu Chulaind speaking of his fighting against Lochland, "fri Lochlaind a túaid," p. 114 a, last line.[3]

---

[1] "Ogygia," pp. 128, 132.

[2] An Amlaip invaded Ireland in 852.—"Ann. of Ulster."

[3] In a "S. Gall MS.," written *circ.* 850, p. 112, we read "don laechraid lainn oa Loth-lind" (Lochlind?).

What seems to give to the tale a fabulous character is this: that the heroic "Red Branch Knights" of Ulster, including Cu Chulaind and Conchobor, under the advice of their chief druid, who was himself a brave soldier, sought for foreign aid as early as the first years of our era. That appears an interpolation due probably to a Lagenian hand. We learn indeed from Tacitus, that about the year A.D. 80 an Irish regulus found his way to the camp of the Roman general, Agricola, and tried to induce him to invade Ireland;[1] and we are told by the poet and historian, Thomas Moore, that "it would hardly be possible to find a picture more pregnant with the future, more prospectively characteristic, than this of an Irish prince, in the camp of the Romans, proffering his traitorous services to the stranger and depreciating his country as an excuse for betraying her."[2] That was the act of one defeated or disappointed man.[3] But it is scarcely credible that the warriors and chiefs of all Ulster would have called in the aid of "strangers," unless they really were what Cathbad calls them ("friends in absence") foreign friends, that is, I think, their kinsmen of Scotland and the Isles, and even of Britain. This view receives some countenance from the Irish "Nennius," p. 48, which says that the Firbolg seized upon Mann, Ara, Ile, and Rachra, the Galian seized the island of Orc, the Cruithne seized the northern part of Britain.

V.—Causes of the Battle.

Medb, the warlike and wise Queen of Connacht, being anxious to improve the breed of cattle in the West of Ireland, sent envoys to Dáre, chief of Cooley, in Louth, to ask a loan of his celebrated brown bull, offering him in return a chariot worth fifty cows, and a large tract of the best land in Roscommon. The envoys obtained Dáre's consent, and, in honour of

---

[1] "Tacitus' Agricola," cap. 24. [2] "Moore's Hist. of Ireland," i. 118.
[3] I retract this: Tacitus does not say so; *cf.* Livy, v. 26.

the event, were entertained at a great banquet. One of them drank to excess, and boasted that if Dáre had not given the loan of the bull, Medb would come and take that noble animal in spite of him. Whereupon the envoys were sent home without the bull. Medb was indignant, mustered her forces, crossed the Shannon at Athlone, met some Leinster and Munster allies at Kells, passed the Boyne in spite of the heroic resistance of Cu Chulaind, wasted Ulster up to the gates of King Conchobor's palace of Emain, near Armagh, and carried away the famous bull of Cooley. The Ulster warriors were taken by surprise, and had not time to line the ditches. It is said that they were then labouring under a mysterious disease[1] much more prostrating than our modern influenza. They soon recovered, however, went in pursuit of Medb, routed her army at Gairech, near Athlone, but suffered so heavily in the fight that they were unable to pursue the Connachtmen and secure the bull.[2] Thus cattle-lifting was the *teterrima belli causa* between Ulster and the other provinces, as it was of the strife between the Dioscuri and Apharetidæ.[3]

VI.—Summary of the Saga.[4]

After the Battle of Gairech Conchobor could not eat, drink, or sleep, &c. To Cathbad, who was deputed by the Ulaid to diagnose his malady, he says the memory of the invasion of his territory and the loss of the bull was undermining his life; and he vows immediate vengeance on Medb.—1-5 (1-4).

Cathbad seeks to comfort him by saying he had already inflicted heavy loss on his foes; counsels him to wait till

---

[1] The "cesnaiden Ulad," due to Macha's curse, *LL.* fol. 125 b.

[2] For these details see O'Curry's "MS. Materials, pp. 30-40, and Windisch in "Rev. Celt.," v. 70-79.

[3] See "Rev. Celt.," April, 1892, p. 287.

[4] The numbers refer to the paragraphs of the *LL.* version; the numbers and sentences in parentheses refer to the later version. Passages found only in the "B. of Leinster" are marked *LL.*; passages found only in the later versions are in parentheses.

summer, which was the best season for campaigning; to give his warriors time to heal of their wounds; and, meanwhile, to send for Conall Cernach, then warring away from Ireland, and to seek the assistance of foreign powers.—6, 7 (4–7).

(Conchobor says he will wait; but adds that, even if Conall and the foreign hosts do not come, he will ravage Leinster, Munster, and Connacht.—8.)

LL.—Envoys are sent, find Conall Cernach in the Isle of Lewis, are entertained by him, and Conall sends messengers to his friends in Gallic and foreign lands.—8.

LL.—The Ulstermen hear from Conall, and resolve to give a round of banquets in his honour.—9.

The foreign auxiliaries land in three divisions, viz. at Murlough Bay, and at Larne, Co. of Antrim, and at the mouth of the Castletown river, near Dundalk.—10. (All land together at Inis Oilella, near Dundalk.—12.)

LL.—Conchobor is at Dundalk, thinks the strangers are the Irish of the three provinces, suspects treachery; when Sencha reports that they are his auxiliaries, "the clot of gore that was on his heart came from his mouth."—11, 12. (Conchobor comes to meet them.—12.)

By Conchobor's request they are entertained at Cú Chulaind's castle (for a whole week).—13 (13).

LL.—Cú Chulaind is asked by Conchobor—firstly, to request the Ulster chiefs to entertain the auxiliaries; secondly, to invite the 150 veteran Ulster champions to join the campaign—Cú Chulaind refuses.—14.

LL.—Conchobar himself visits the veterans in their royal house, and brings them to the trysting place at Dundalk.—15.

LL.—The southern kings and Medb hear of Conchobor's resolve; the "three great waves" reverberate; the princes assemble their troops at their chief forts. Eochu King of North Munster sends a proposal to Medb that full reparation should be made; she refuses; then yields, on the advice of Ailill her Prince Consort; but, as if to defeat the pacific views of Eochu and Ailill, she sends as envoy to the Ulstermen Dorn Ibair, the man whom they most hated; the Ulster chief at her court protests against this; but adds that the Ulstermen would not harm an envoy.—16, 17, 18.

(Medb, hearing of Conchobor's preparations, of her own accord resolves to send Mac Róigh to Conchobor to ask him to put off the war for a year (!). Mac Róigh declines to go, as he had given good reason to the Ulstermen to dislike him. Medb says the Ulstermen never molest envoys.—9.)[1]

LL.—Find, King of Leinster, marches his army from Dind Ríg to join his brother Cairpre, King of Tara. They send a prudent envoy to Conchobor with offers of full reparation.—19.

(Mac Róigh visits the Leinster Kings and goes with their envoys to Conchobor.—10.)

Conchobor refuses the terms, and says he "will pitch his tent in every province of Ireland," and will encamp at Rosnaree *south* of the Boyne that night.—19, 20 (11, 14).

The envoys return and report this refusal to Cairpre and Find.—21. (Mac Róigh and the envoys report to Cairpre this refusal, and the arrival of Conchobor's auxiliaries at the strand of Eochaill, and at the strand of the daughter of Flidas, and Conchobor's march to Rosnaree.—15.)

LL.—The Leinster kings resolve to give him battle, and send word to Medb, promising help, if Conchobor marches to Connacht, and asking her aid if he attacked them.—21.

(Mac Róigh returns to Medb; description of him.—15, 16.)

LL.—Medb refuses help to her allies and brothers-in-law, says they do not require it "against that man."—22.

(Cairpre directs the Meath and Leinster clans to march to Rosnaree.—17.)

LL.—Conor reaches Accaill and Slige Brég (Cuain Glaisse of Sliabh Breg), encamps there, as he hears Rosnaree is held by Cairpre.—23, 24. *Sliab Brég is near Ardee.*

[1] In the later version, the herald, "Mac Róigh," is confounded with the royal warrior, Fergus Mac Róig; his name is Mac Roth in *LL.* 94 b, 95 b, 96 b, 97 b, &c.

(Cu Chulaind remains at Dundalk, getting men and provisions for the campaign.—18.)

(From Sliabh Brég Conchobor marches early towards Rosnaree; his vanguard reports to him that it is occupied.—19.)

Féic, sent by Conchobor to reconnoitre the enemy's position, crosses the Boyne, attacks them, (is wounded) and drowned.—25 (21). *In the later version Daig goes first, then Féic.*

Daig, sent as scout, attacks (!), is slain.—26 (20).

Iriel goes, sees, reports the numbers, &c., of the enemy.—27, 28, 29. *He is prudent in outpost duty, brave in battle, and fierce in pursuit; our tale points many a moral.*

(Iriel and his escort are attacked; he retires fighting; advises Conchobor to wait for reinforcements.—22.)

Conchobor is counselled by the Ulster captains to wait for reinforcements. This counsel is given in succession, as they bring their men to the Boyne, by Cathbad, Eogan, and Loegaire, &c.—30-33 (24, 25).

(Dáre arrives, is described, wants to fight at once, is stayed by Conchobor.—23.)

(Celtchair arrives, is described.—26.)

When the troops under Loegaire (or Celtchair) come, Conchobor crosses the Boyne, fights, is worsted, begins to retreat.—34-38 (27, 29, 30, 31).

(Description of Conchobor's battle-dress, &c.—27.)

(Description of Cairpre and his army, his speech.—28.)

Conall Cernach enters into the fight.—38, 39 (32, 33.)

(Dáire, Eogan, Cathfad, Iriel, Laegire vainly strive to withstand the Leinstermen.—34.)

Mes Dead, Anruth, Feithen Mór, Feithen Beg, and Aithirne arrive, but Leinster still prevails.—39, 43 (30).

Cú Chulaind appears on the scene, threatens to slay any Ulsterman who turns his back to the foe.—44 (35).

Conall Cernach kills 1000 men (!), is attacked by Cairpre, reluctantly kills three warrior-poets who come to Cairpre's help, and when he and Cairpre are separated by a charge of Leinstermen, he slays 1000 more (!)—45–47, (36, which only mentions that Conall slew *six*, whose names are given).

Cairpre kills 800 (!) Ulstermen, attacks Conchobor; 400 Ulstermen come to help their King; and Cairpre is brought safe away by the Leinstermen.—48–50, (31, which omits the numbers, and gives other details).

Cú Chulaind fights; seeks out Cairpre; after a hard contest kills him, cuts off his head, and shakes it at the Leinstermen.—51.

(Cú Chulaind routs the Leinstermen, challenges Cairbre to single combat, Cairbre accepts, war of words; they fight, their weapons are broken; Cú is reviled by Lóeg, kills Cairbre, cuts off his head and shakes it at the Leinstermen.—37–43.)

(Cú Chulaind, Conall, and Iriel press the Leinstermen.—43, 44.)

The Leinstermen are pursued by Iriel as far as the River Rye, near Leixlip, where Fidach stops their pursuit.—52, (45.)

(Cú Chulaind lays Cairpre's head before Conchobor.—46.)

LL.—Conchobor goes to Tara that night, at the end of a week is visited by Erc (his grandson) son of Cairpre, who "places his head on the breast" of Conchobor. From him Erc gets back his kingdom, a grandfather's blessing, and advice not to fight against Ulstermen, and particularly against Cú Chulaind; he also obtains Cú Chulaind's daughter in marriage. —53–55. (*See LL.'s description of Erc in MS. Materials*, 507.)

LL.—Conchobor takes Erc to visit the battle-field, says Cairpre prevailed up to Conall Cernach's arrival, and was beaten only by numbers.—55, 56.

On their return to Tara Conchobor again praises Erc's father and uncles.—57.

(When Cú Chulaind brings Cairpre's head, Conchobor praises Erc's father and uncles; Cairbre is buried, and the Ulstermen return home in triumph.—46.)

Such is the pleasant ending of our saga. But Cú Chulaind had cut off the head, not only of Cairpre, but of Calatín, and

Cúrúi, whom he basely murdered because Cúrúi had beaten him in fair fight, and bound him, and shorn off his hair. The sons of these three princes formed a league, ravaged Ulster, and cut off Cú Chulaind's head;[1] and so the beheading went on for years, because a Connacht gentleman did not hold his tongue, and an Ulster chieftain foolishly mislaid his temper.

VII.—The Early and the Later Versions.

From the foregoing analysis, and from what *is* and what is *not* in the later version, it is clear that it cannot be derived from the *LL.* story. The general plot is the same, of course; but the incidents, and the sequence even, are not. The later version is superior to the earlier in some respects; it introduces and describes Dáre, who was the cause of the war, and yet is not mentioned in the *LL.* saga as concerned in this battle. It says that Conchobor was resolved to fight if the auxiliaries did not come; that the Connacht herald went with those of Tara and Leinster; it gives the report of the envoys, descriptions of Celtchar, Conchobor, and Cairpre, the challenge of Cú Chulaind to Cairpre, and their war of words; it mentions that Cairpre's head was brought to Conchobor, and that he was buried; it contains six pieces of old poetry (§§ 27, 33, 35, 38, 39) which are not in *LL.* And most of these descriptions of appearance and dress are a faithful reflex of pictures found in other parts of *LU.* and *LL.*; for example, the description of Mac Róth, the herald, which is not in our *LL.* tale, but is found in another part of *LL.* and in *LU.* :—

Mac Roth techtaire Ailella agus Medba *is é timchellas Herind in óen ló.* Fethal líndu imbi; *lorg anfaid in a láim; calg dét* fó a ċoim; *léne culpatach* con *derg*-intliud imbi.—*LU.*, p. 68 a.

Mac Roth ind *echlach* . . . gilla dond drechlethan álaind; *bratt dond* derscaigthech immi; bruthgae umaidi na brut; *tarbsléni trebraid*

[1] *LL.* 45 a, 81, 121 b, 161 a, 169 b.

fri a chness; da bernbróic etar a da choiss is talam; mátad lorg findchuill issin dara láim; claideb lethféabair con eltaib dét isind láim anail dó. Aile, a gilla, ar C. *comartha n-echlaige* sin.—*LL.*, p. 70 b.

Is amlaid iomorro do bí Mac Róig.—*sirsiublac, lán-aisdreach; gon* éadac *eachlacha* uime .i. *léin throsall, treabnaide*[1] *re a cneas; brat leancorcra tairsib seachtair; mad lorg féitreannac ion a láim clí; cloidiom leadar-feabrac gon altaib déad ion a deas-láim; dá bearnbróig* breacdeanmaca *im a troigtib, a ccomarta ealadan re teactairioct* na h-Eirionn, go b-fios sgéal na ríog agus na ruireac leis do Meidb agus do Oilill go Cruacan Rata h-Aoi ré deirid *gach laoi.*—"Modern Version," § 16.

But if the modern version has sundry things not to be found in the earlier (?) account, the *LL.* saga contains alone the poetical pieces of §§ 4, 6, 19, 22, 29, 54, 56; describes the storm, the dispersion of the fleet, Conchobor's suspicions and Sencha's report, the dialogue with the princely yeoman, the loving reconciliation and happy marriage, thus ending as does the story of the Battle of Magh Lena and many a modern tale. If the recent redaction were derived from *LL.*, these interesting things would not have been omitted. It is less luxuriant in epithets than "the Battle of Magh Rath" and "the Battle of Magh Lena," is quite pagan in texture and complexion, contains many descriptions which are like those of other tales in *LL.* and *LU.*, and exhibits also many archaic inflexions, old vocables, and Middle-Irish survivals, which escaped the notice of the later compilers, or were purposely retained by them. All these things seem to show that it represents an old Irish version coeval with, but not very closely related to, the *LL.* saga, and claim for it special attention and substantive treatment.

The Stowe copy is well penned, on good paper, in well-spaced lines, by Brian mac doctuir leigis,[2] and is here printed

[1] *Treabnaide* is a mixture of "trebraid" of *LL.* 70b, and "srebnaide," which appear often in descriptions of the dress of warriors.

[2] Perhaps he was son of "Dr. Brian O'Loghlen, who departed this life 18th

as the best of the modern texts; when other copies yield other readings, such variants are given. The text of the Royal Irish Academy (on bad paper and in bad writing by John Mac Solly in 1715); and that of Egerton (by John Mac Solly and Richard Tipper in 1715), and of Maynooth (written in the 18th century), appear to be copies (or copies of copies) of one and the same manuscript; and the variations consist, for the most part, of insertions or inversions or omissions of epithets.

VIII.—The Printed Texts and Translations.

The first text is here printed from the "Book of Leinster" itself. The contractions are extended, and the extension represented by italics; proper names are spelt with initial capitals; the text is punctuated, and sometimes supplied with hyphens.

The translation is very close, and may appear very rugged;[1] yet will, I trust, be intelligible to the reader. An attempt has been made to translate[2] many vocables which are not found in dictionaries or glossaries; and even an honest endeavour has been made to render into English obscure passages the meaning of which is still somewhat doubtful to me. Such efforts are pointed out by a note of interrogation; they may have resulted in present failure, but they will attract the attention of scholars able to throw light on those obscurities. On this subject Dr. Atkinson says: "We do not know the import of many a word that occurs in our Irish texts, and we are not permitted the free licence of guessing indulged in by the past generation. At present there is scarcely the simplest piece of Middle-Irish prose of a few pages long but contains some word or phrase

---

Sept, 1773," as is written on p. 128. Under the compiler's name is written "Semuis O'Moran, master an leabhair so."

[1] "Above all things the translation should be *exact and literal.*"—Edm. Burke's Letter to Vallancy, O'Reilly's "Irish Writers," p. 181.

[2] "Don't hesitate to"—translate, holds good here, if fair warning be given. The Irish way has been not "to give notice"; at which the Germans, to borrow words of the late Laureate, give "Marvellous great shrieks and ghastly groans."

that must be passed over with a query or a blank space."[1] Hence we find Mr. Whitley Stokes writing thus: "Many of the words in this paragraph are obscure, and the renderings are mere guesses;"[2] hence also Dr. Windisch sometimes gives up any attempt at translating a difficult passage, as for instance in the "Táin Bó Regamon," p. 249;[3] and Dr. Thurneysen thus prefaces a version of twenty-eight lines: "The meaning of the following tale seems to be as follows, though many a particular word or phrase may be doubtful."—"Rev. Celt." vi. 92. The poetry is often omitted by editors either because it repeats what is in the prose parts or because of its obscurity; the pieces marked with *R.* in the margin of old manuscripts are bits of *Rosc* or *Retairic*, are hard to render into English as they are jerky, ejaculatory, allusive, or instances of aposiopesis or ellipsis. I have essayed a tentative and timid translation of them in the hope of helping others to do better; and I think that these difficult pieces could be successfully grappled with by any fair Irish scholar who would take the trouble to collate and index all of them that are found scattered here and there in our published books and manuscripts.

IX.—The Glossary of the Leinster Text.

This might be called an *Index Verborum*, as it gives only the briefest explanation and parsing of the words. My reason for giving a full Index may be set forth in the words of two scholars competent in such matters. Dr. Atkinson, in his Introduction to the Fac-simile of the "Book of Leinster," p. 3, says: "It is indispensable that individual poems and works

[1] "Lecture on Irish Lexicography," p, 33.

[2] Stokes on "Irish Ordeals," p. 222.

[3] And 254: "Auf die Ubersetzung des Ganzen verziehte ich." In preface to "T. Bó Darteda," he says: "Auch jetzt bleibt noch *mancher* dunkle Punkt." p. 186. See also pp. 29 and 31 in Stokes' "Translation of the Bodl. Cormac's Glossary." To these *roscs* may be applied Cormac's words (*ib.* 30): "Ní cech díalt tra rosegar inne," not every syllable attains a meaning.

should be carefully edited with careful glossaries honestly prepared, and not, as hitherto, with mere translations which never can be wholly satisfactory as long as the means of controlling the translator are not placed within the reach of scholars generally." Dr. Thurneysen writes in *Irische Miscellen*, "Revue Celtique," vol. vi.: "Unfortunately the exact meaning of new and unusual words can hardly be determined as they occur in obscure stanzas, and, with special frequency, in detached *flosculi.* The prose reading gives us very little assistance, as it, for the most part, passes over these particular forms. Even 'Stokes' Index' is not quite satisfying. In using it we find this difficulty, that frequently words which have been already established, as well as new words, are set down without their signification being added; any one who has not the whole collection of forms present to his mind is constantly obliged to search Stokes' earlier Glossaries, to discover whether a word has been already explained or is still to be explained. Furthermore, the passages of reference are not given in their entirety in the case of each word; so that the reader is not dispensed from the labour of compiling an Index for himself. What has induced the editor to depart from his earlier practice we do not know. We trust that the best-read of Celtic scholars will return to his former method in compiling these valuable Indexes; he will thereby render a great service to his colleagues."

These remarks are quoted merely to show that the time has not yet come for mere translations and a collection of rarer words, if we want to satisfy students of Irish, and to help towards the making of a dictionary of our language; yet I do not quite agree with Dr. Thurneysen as to the work of Mr. Stokes, whom I should be sorry to see turn to the drudgery of index-making from the close, exact, and crispy translations in which he has few or no equals.

The words of our text which are not found or are not explained in Windisch's "Woerterbuch" are marked with an asterisk in the Glossary. The numbers refer to the paragraphs of the text; the cases and genders are marked by their initials in italics, as *napm.* for nominative and accusative plural, masculine gender. "Dogebad sib," § 46, "dogena-sib," *LU.*, p. 99 b, show the early "analytic" use of the *3rd sing.* with pronouns of another number and person; the *pret. pass.* tucait, rucait, slaidit, rogaibit, rohindlit; rarmetair-ne, co ro churiur, fagaim-se, fagum (dependent forms), fagbaim, fagbam are noteworthy. So are the accusatives "uair," "in n-uair," § 13, *ap.* firu (than or as men), 13; the promiscuous use of "bar," "far," and "for," and of "do, ro, fo," "ra, ba." In "rábar" (for "la bar"), § 46, we see that "bar," the possessive pronoun, lengthens the vowel of "ra"; "ra" (with, in the opinion of), for "la," §§ 26, 27, shows that the confusion, which is now complete between "fri" and "la," had begun seven or eight centuries ago.

X.—The Versification.

I.

Ra airgestar Medb co mín
co dún Dáire 'n-ar ndeg-thír
  co dún Sescind ciped de
  co dún sír-glan Sobairge.

Syllables: 7777. Rhyme: 1 with 2, 3 with 4. Termination: 1213. But in the other stanzas, the Termination runs: 1112; 2312; 1223; 2312; 1211. The Internal Rhyme is not used. Alliteration irregular. Hence it may be assumed that the versification is not of the exact kinds.

II.

Ra-díglais chena co cruaid
a Chonchobuir claideb-ruaid
  brissiud catha—cuman lem—
  bar cethri choicid Herend.

Syllables: 7777. Rhyme: 1 and 2, 3 and 4. Termination: 1312. In other stanzas, the Termination is 1214; 1112;

122(?)2; 1223; 1212; 1113; 1112. No Internal Rhymes. Alliteration irregular. Therefore not of the exact kinds.

III.

Tancamar ó 'n Chruachain Chróda
nach bec blad
cucut-s' a Chonchobuir chóra
cruaid do gal.

Syllables 8383. Rhymes 1 and 3, 2 and 4. Termination 2121. Rhyme absent once; once replaced by Internal Rhyme in 4th verse. This is the measure known as *Sétrad nGairit*.

IV.

Da torset maicc Mágach
in sluag ḃrotla bágach
bud cró-derg al-lámach
i cath Ruiss na Ríg
Da tora rí Macha
saifiter a datha
claifiter a ratha
tairnfithir a bríg.

Syllables 66656665. Rhyme 1, 2, and 3; 5, 6, and 7; 4 and 8. Termination 22212221. In three out of five stanzas, verse No. 3 is absent. The 5th stanza wants the latter half. In each of the four complete stanzas, verse 8 rhymes *internally* with 5, 6, and 7. This is *Ochtḟoclach Mór*; *v.* Thurneysen's Versl. 94.

V.

Atát i ceilg ar do chind
issin ross imthéit Bóind
teora catha Clainne Deirg
lassait mar lassair dar leirg.

Syllables 7777. Rhyme 1 and 2, 3 and 4. Termination 1211. Termination in other stanzas, 1213; 1113. No Internal Rhyme. Not therefore a classic measure.

VI.

Beir mo bennact bí dom réir
na déna féin frithbeirt frind
da tuca dún tend fri tend
is derb lem dafaethais lind.

Syllables 7777. Rhyme 2 and 4. Termination 1111. Regular Internal Rhymes and Alliterations. This is the classic measure known as *Rannaigecht Mór*.

VII.

Ba escomol comrac fris
dichor Cairpri do chlar fiss
sochaide am rodoscloe
cossin laithe sin rosbae.

Syllables 7777. Rhyme 1 and 2, 3 and 4. Termination 1132 (1111 ?). Termination in other stanzas, 1222, 1111. Internal Rhyme and regular Alliteration absent. Not therefore a classic measure.

VIII.

Trí maicc Rosa Ruaid in ríg
gabsat in tír—buidnib sel—
Find i n-Alind Ailill i Cruaich
Carpre thuaid i Temair Breg.

Syllables 7787. Rhyme 2 and 4. Termination 1111. Internal Rhyme not regular, except in above stanza. Seemingly a variety of the classic measure *Rannaigecht Mór* (see VI.)

IX.

Dimbuaid fir
frithrosc madma
maidm ria ngnúsib
ócbad n-essairm
gillanrad diairm
dichra fedma
fuidb do anocht
follogod féile
rith fri geltaib
gair ri dogur
dál ri dimbuaid.

X.

Ni hi n-ám inrim errach
is fuar ga bél gaethach
garfit ili Elga
airderg in bith
bebsat buale Febra
fanna mila Marta
trena uile Aperóil
oenach morc maimthi
moaigsem ri céim nítha
connách i n-aim inrim errach.

These compositions are of the kind called "*Rosc.*" There are no stanzas, no regular number of syllables in the verse—if it may be termed verse—no rhyme, and, of course, no "termination." The only ascertainable characters seem to be (1) alliteration, (2) short, jerky sentences, and (3) a certain laconic and somewhat oracular diction. The *Luirech Pádraig*, the Formulæ of the Brehon Laws, Dubhthach's Judgment in the beginning of the *Senchus Mór*, the first poem in *Longes Macc n-Usnig*, are of this class.

XI.—Remains of the LL. Text in the Modern Version.

Par. 3. A mo ṗapa a Ċaṫfaiġ, ar sé, is mór ádḃar . . . agom-so, óir do ruaċtadar ceiṫre hollċóigiḃ Éirionn:
mo ḋeaġ-ḃailtiḃ : = mo deg-baleda.
,, 4. ní cat liomsa caṫ naċar ṫuit ríġ.
,, 5. ní ham . . . earraċ, &c.
,, 5. gurab cearcaill . . . gaċ fód féar-ġlas.
,, 7. cuir-si feasa ⁊ teaċta uait go.
,, 7. tar muinċinn mara ⁊ mór-ḟairgge.
(*some of the Norse, and other names*).
,, 7. ríġ (ar) an seaċtmaḋ rann do'n doṁuin Loċlannaiġ.
,, 17. tri caṫa Cloinne Deirg.
,, 21. ro cheil a ṁeanmain orro.
,, 22. miḋeas ⁊ móir-ḟéaċas.
,, 22. go ttig ḃur ttreoin.
,, 31. gur ġéis . . . an Ochaoin .i. sgiaṫ Ċonċuḃair.
,, 31. trí tonna . . . na hÉirionn . . . .i. tonn . . . Rudraiġe ⁊ tonn . . . Ċlíoḋna ⁊ tonn . . . Tuaiḋe.
,, 32. maḋma ⁊ móir-ṫeiṫṁe.
,, 32. Diombuaiḋ fear frioṫrosg maḋma maiḋm ré ngnúisiḃ . . . ógbaḋ asairm . . . díoċar feaḋma . . . riṫ frí gealtaċt. dáil go ndiogra. dul fá ḋiombuaiḋ.
,, 34. an caṫ ar do ċoimirce.
,, 43. gur ḃean a ċeann de. ⁊ croitios an ceann ris na sluaġaiḃ.
,, 46. maith aṁ intí . . . Trí mic Rossa Ruaiḋ in ríġ gaḃsat an tír . . . fine anallaḋ Oilill a cCruaiċ Cairbre an tua a tTeaṁraiġ Breaġ.
,, 46. A n-aoin-ḟeaċt . . . an triar . . . ann gaċ gleo . . . a mbeirdís a mbáiḋ.
,, 46. Bá trát n-a ttrí n-uaiṫne óir . . . ó . . . in treas . . .

XII.—Grammatical Remains of a Middle Irish Version different from the LL. Version.

Par. 5. réiḋe . . . séitriġ, sonairte . . . aḋṁara . . . ilḃreaġa . . . sleaṁna, slinn-ġéara.
" 5. caoṁa: *all the foregoing adjectives, being predicates, agree with the subject, contrary to modern usage.*
" 13. go aroile.
" 15. a ttoiġ (= i taig) R.
" 15. go traiġ n-Eochaille.
" 17. áit a mbí (= a mbaí).
" 17. go hionad a mbí.
" 18. do anasdar.
" 20. a ttorchair . . . go mbeart.
" 22. adchíḋ (for atchíu).
" 23. go n-aḋ ann isbeart (= asbert).
" 25. cairp(t)iḃ = *modern* cairbdiḃ.
" 27. a mbí do chlochaib (*mod.* a raiḃ).
" 28. don leith araill gonaḋ (ann) isbeart.
" 29. fiallaċ n-éadrom n-anḃfosaḋ.
" 34. anosa.
" 35. adbeart . . . am sliaḃ, &c.
" 35. aḋaiġ (*read* aḋaiḋ) a ġliaiḋ ngaisge as ⁊ a ḋearnoin ndearṁáir (*accusative of* gléo, dearna, dearṁár).
" 35. ionnus go mbí (= combaí, *mod.* go raiḃ).
" 36. aroile.
" 38. do ḃeart = tug.
" 38. ó ro ria chugam-sa.
" 39. ro adfiaḋ-sa soin (= rotbia-su sain) . . . isam triaṫ . . . am niaḋ, &c. . . . cairpteaċ (= *mod.* ċairbdeaċ).
" 40. tug gaċ aon dioḃ díograis ngon.
" 40. ar ḋromainn (= for drommaimm?)
" 40. tarraċtain.
" 41. torrachtadar.
" 42. sonairte soiṁeisniġ (*predicate in agreement*).
" 43. ní teárnóḋ.
" 45. torċradar, ruiġe, go ró so.
" 46. dia raiḃe = dá raiḃe.

XIII.—Contractions explained in Preface of the Stowe MS.

c = céad. l = caogat. m = muin. 2 = dá. ſ = ea. d. o = doirionn. ee = eile. ll = dáil. bb = Daiḃi. $\frac{a}{a}$ = ara. $\frac{e}{e}$ = Éire. $\frac{e}{o}$ = Eirionn. $\frac{á}{gd}$ = grád. $\frac{s}{f}$ = fear. $\frac{ss}{f}$ = fearr. $\frac{e}{n}$ = Eirinn. $\frac{n}{e}$ = é féin nó fáinne. $\frac{e}{g}$ = éirġe nó gré. $\frac{m}{f}$ = feiḋm. $\frac{ċ}{g}$ = gaċ. g = gaċ. $\frac{ḃ}{g}$ = garḃ. $\frac{l}{t}$ = fáilte. $\frac{m}{m}$ = imrim, nó muin ar muin. $\frac{r}{g}$ = fairrge. b∸ = buḋ. ch∸ = chuaiḋ. dh∸ = déag nó diaiḋ. b = -bann. b7 = bead. c7 = cean. de = duine. dc = dearc. dg = dearg. f = féin. g = gan, go. .i. = inġion. im = imurro. sg = sgeul. cp = corp. ct = ceart. cr = Críost. m = muḋ.

The Academy MS. has the following note at p. 42 :—

Finit. Ar n-a sgríoḃaḋ le Seon mac Eamuind ṁic Ḋonnċ(aḋa) ṁic Ṁuiris ṁic Solaiḋ an seaċtmaḋ lá do ṁí Abraoin, an ḃl[iaḋain] d' aois an Tiġearna 1716 ; 7 do ċuiṁniuġaḋ uaisle 7 aṫarḋa ċloinne Ruġr[aiḋe], 7c. Trócaire ó Ḋia go ḃfaġ(ḃaiḋ) an sgríḃneoir .i. Seon mac Solaiḋ.

On page 1 of Stowe E. iv. 3 :—

Ceaṫrar do ní díon dá
gaċ ealaḋain, ioḋón. .
Log, aimsior, taċad sgríḃinne, 7 pearsa.
Log don leaḃar-so, Maiġ Ġlas a cConntae an Ċláir,
a mbarúntaċt Uiḃ Breacáin, a ccóigiḋ Muṁan.
Aimsior fós don leaḃar-so .i. aimsior Seoirse
do ḃeiṫ n-a ríġ ar Ṡagsaiḃ, ar Albain, 7 ar Éirinn.
Taċad sgríḃinne an leaḃair-se .i. bliaḋain d'aois an
doṁain cúig ṁíle seaċt ccéad, 7. . . . ḃliaḋain déag,
7 d'aois Ċríosd, míle 7 seaċt ccéad, 7 seaċt mbliaḋna

fitċiot, an cúigiḋ lá do Mís Mái
Pearsa fós don leaḃar-so .i. Brian mac
doctúir leiġis.

[*And in a very bad hand*]

Semuis O Morán
Master an laḃair so.

Andrew Mac Curtin [Aindrias mac Cuirtín] also wrote in this book.

The contractions used in the collation of the modern texts are—A. M. S. for the copies of the Royal Irish Academy, of Maynooth College, and of the Stowe MSS., R.I.A., respectively. The other contractions are explained, as occasion requires, in other parts of this book, or are easily understood. The numbers refer to the pages of the books or manuscripts quoted, unless where the folio is mentioned; but in the Indices the sections are marked by the figures.

While urging in my Lectures the advantage of giving full indices of texts, I quoted the words of Dr. Thurneysen, but I did not concur in all he said; and I remarked that, in his most elaborate and learned Index of the words quoted in Zeuss' Grammatica, several hundred words were omitted, and, to use his own phrase, "the passages of reference are not given in their entirety in the case of each word." I added that I had made a list of such words, and would print them if it were thought useful. With the approval of the Academy I append this list of omitted words or word-forms as a supplement to the monumental work of Drs. Gütterbock and Thurneysen.

When writing a *Glossarium* to the Irish of the "Book of Armagh," and while compiling the Index to our *LL.* text, I felt that grammars and dictionaries did not give information enough with regard to the gender of nouns, and specially of the neuters. To begin with the latter I collected and classified materials which I trust go some way towards supplying a full treatise on the subject. The plan of the declensions I have taken from

Mr. Whitley Stokes' Treatises on "Celtic Declensions," and on "S-Stems in the Celtic Languages." I gratefully acknowledge that I got much of my materials from those treatises and from the prefaces of his books, in which he never fails to point out the neuters of his texts.

With regard to the whole of this volume I have had many helps and hints from Mr. John Mac Neill, B.A., who placed at my disposal the treasures of his knowledge of Old, Middle, and Modern Irish. To him, my former pupil and present learned friend, I beg to tender my cordial thanks.

EDMUND HOGAN.

December 3rd, 1892.

CATH RUIS NA RÍG.

THE BATTLE OF ROSS NA RÍG.

INCIPIT CATH RUIS NA RÍG.

1. Naim bái[a] *Conchobor* i *n*-Emai*n* mí*n*-et*r*ocht Macha ar[b] cur chatha na Tana lais. *Con*na bái bíad ra-tholathar dó, 7 *con*nar-chotail co sám, 7 conna ro-ataim do neoch d'Ultaib cid do-n-rat samlaid ri tremsi na teora coícthiges. Et atchuas d'Ultaib aní si*n* .i. *Conchobor*[c] do bith i sergg 7 i sír-gal*ar*, 7 conna bái biad ra-thol*athar* dó, 7 connar-chotail co sám, 7 conna ro-atai*m* do neoch d'Ul*taib* cid donrat sa*m*l*aid*.

2. Andsi*n* doringned tinól 7 tochostul ac Ultaib co h-Emain mi*n*-et*r*oct Macha. Et ra-comarliced accu-*som* da*no*, cia bad chóir do choibsegud na cnedi ra-cnedaig ríg[d] Ul*ad*, 7 in galair buirb ra-s-básaig 7 ro-s-bánaig ra tremsi na coicthiges, conna bái biad ra-thol*athar* do 7 conna ro-ataim do neoch d'Ul*taib* cid donrat sa*m*l*aid*. Iss-*ed* ro-raidsetar-*som* uili da*no*, corop é in nech ro-s-ail 7 ro-sn-irthócaib .i. Cathb*ad*[e] drúi deg-amra.

3. Ro-luid reme da*no* Cath*bad* drúi deg-a*m*ra co hairm i mbai *Conchobor*, 7 cíís déra folcmara f*or*-ruada fola cor bo fliuch blæ 7 brunni dó. Airchisis *Conchobor* do deór Chathb*aid*. "Maith ám and-si*n*, a mo phopa Chathb*aid*," ar *Conchobor*, "cid do-t-gní t*or*sech dobbrónach do-menmnach?" "Ro-fail ám a mor-abba dam-sa sai*n*,"

[a] *Or* La im-bái; in aim = when. [b] ár *in fac-simile*.
[c] Conchobor *in full*, fo. 174 b, 1; Conchobur, *LU*. 103 b, Conchubor, *LU*., p. 70; *g*. Conchobuir, *LU*. 34 b. In the translation the usual Conchobar is given; *d*. Conchobur, *LU*. 128.
[d] *Read* ríg n-.

---

[1] Navan Fort, near Armagh, on the road to Keady.
[2] Debated; "it is allowed" in Anglo-Irish = is agreed on.
[3] Cobsaighther, *confortetur*, *Atkinson's Glos.*, is from *cobsaid*; c. .i. sithugad no leasugad, *H*. 2. 15, p. 120, *lit. cognoscere* (cubus).

THE BATTLE OF ROSS NA RÍG BEGINS.

1. Once upon a time Conchobar was in smooth-bright Emain of Macha,[1] after the giving of the battle of the *Táin* by him, so that there was not food that pleased him, and that he slept not easily, and that he confessed not to any of the Ulaid what made him so, for the time of the three fortnights. And that thing was told to the Ulaid, that is, Conchobar to be in decline and in long-sickness, and that there was not food that pleased him, and that he slept not easily, and that he confessed not to anyone of the Ulaid what made him so.

2. Then was made a gathering and an assembling of the Ulaid to smooth-bright Emain of Macha. And it was allowed[2] by them then who would be proper to ascertain[3] the wound that wounded the king of the Ulaid, and the violent sickness that brought him to death,[4] and made him pale for the time of the three fortnights, so that there was not food that pleased him, and that he confessed not to anyone of the Ulaid what made him so. It is this that all these said then, that it was the person who reared him and brought him up, namely, Cathbad the famous druid.

3. So on went Cathbad, the right-wonderful druid, to the place in which Conchobar was, and he wept floodlike deep-red tears of blood,[5] so that his breast and bosom were wet. Conchobar took pity on the tear of Cathbad. "Good, indeed then, my master Cathbad," said Conchobar, "what makes thee sad, sorrowful, dispirited?"

[a] *The nom. and accus.* Cathbath in full, *LL.*, pp. 93, 106; *voc. is evidently* Cathbaid in § 5, last line, as the versification requires it. *n.* Cathbath, *LL.* 311, 3 col. He was a fénnid, or warrior, as well as a druid, *LL.*, p. 106. In the B. of Armagh the gen. is Cathboth, Cathbath, Cathbad, as if from *n.* Cathbu.

---

[4] i.e. was killing him; galar also means grief.

[5] Cú Chulaind's charger, The Grey of Macha, let fall big tears of blood, "cotarlaic a bolgdéra mora fola," *LL.* 119 b, l. 3.

ale *for* Cathb*ad*. "Na fetar ca cned ra-t-chnedaig 7 ca gal*ar* borb[a] ro-t-básaig 7 ro-t-bánaig ra tremsi na teora coic*thiges*." "Fail ám a mór-abba dam-sa," bar *Con*chob*or*. "Dáig da-*m*-riachtatar cethri oll-choícéda Hér*end*. Et tuctha leo-sum a n-aes cíuil 7 airfiti 7 admolta, combad leriti na hairgni, 7 combad moti na hurbada; 7 ra-loscit ar ṅdúnaid 7 ar ṅdeg-baleda *con*nach arddi íat 'nas[b] a n-airidni 7 a n-i*m*mell-*aige*. Et barroebris da*no* Aili*ll*[c] 7 M*edb* cath f*or*m-sa, 7 rucad láeg mo bo fadéi*n* a purt éicne uaim-se." Et iss-amlaid ro-bói 'ca rad 7 atb*ert* na bria*thra*-sa and:

4. "Ro-fail lim-sa do*m*na brói*n*[d]
dia festa-su, a Chathb*aid* chóir,—
Ulaid uile, aidble gal,
nir-bo cho*m*mairge d' oen-da*m*.

Ra-thinóil Medb aníar,
i*n*gen Ech*ach* ciarbanríad,
co ruc lé búar 7 brat
7 ór 7 arget.

Ra-airgestar Medb co mí*n*
co dún Dáire n-ar ṅd*eg*·thír
co dún Sesci*nd* cip ed de
co dún sir-glan Sobairge.

Ni ḟarggaib 'n-ar coiciud chain
múr *nó* bale can argain
na dún na máitís coscur
nó múr can a dían-loscud.

[a] *Read* galar m-borb, if it be not masc. here. [b] *For* indas, than.

---

[1] *borb* is said in Munster of a very heavy crop, and seems to mean here *excessive, intense: borrthorad.*

[2] Or strongholds; baile also signifies townland.

[3] A division of a house; i.e. half a house, *Petrie's Tara*, p. 202; isin airidin airthair (*LL.*), in the eastern half of the house; etir imdaid ocus airidin, *H.* 2. 16, p. 557; sin n-airidin, in the room (of the invalid), *LL.*, p. 52, l. 11; *T. Bó Reg.*

[4] The surrounding or outside premises. *Cf.* iomallaiche, "the outmost part,"

"I have indeed great-reason for that," replied Cathbad, "that I know not what wound has wounded thee, and what obstinate[1] sickness has deadened thee, and paled thee for the time of the three fortnights." "Great-reason indeed have I for it," said Conchobar, "for four great-provinces of Eriu have come to me, and with them were brought their men of music, and of amusement, and of eulogy, that the more conspicuous might be the ravages, and that the greater might be the devastations; and our fortresses and our fine-dwellings[2] were burned, so that no higher (were) they than their rooms,[3] and their outhouses.[4] And Ailill and Medb gained a battle too against me, and the calf of my own cow was taken from me out of a place of safety."[5] And it is thus he was saying it, and he uttered these words thereupon:[6]

4. "There is to my mind a cause of grief.
if thou wouldst know, just Cathbad,
the Ulaid all,—vastness of brave deeds,—
it was not a protection for one bull.

Medb assembled (them) from the west—
the daughter of Echu,—though it was a woman's raid[7]—
and carried off kine and raiment
and gold and silver.

Medb ravaged easily[8]
unto Dáire's fortress in our good land,
unto Dún Sescind, what there is of it,
unto the long-famous fort of Sobairge.[9]

She left not in our fair province
wall or stead without ravage,
nor fort in which they boasted not triumph,
nor wall without fiercely burning it.

[c] So in full, § 23, and *LL.* 170 b. [d] Two lines to one of the MS.

Scotch Bible, Numbers, xxii. 41. It seems to be compounded of *imm* and *ellach*, *junctio*.

[5] Lit., of force or violence.

[6] Or then.

[7] Or "Medb of dark-white chariots."

[8] Or "marched on," connected with *éirgim*.

[9] Dunseverick, Co. Antrim.

Mo dam-sa is dam dond Dáire,
'm-a láifeit óic ilgaire
nocho raba riam macc bó
'm-an mó donither d' anró
Ni lia esbaid daim na bó
acaind i coiced Emnó[a]
na esbaid laich dadluig[b]
ar n-a fothrucud 'n-a fuil." F. (*sic*)

5. "Maith am[c] a m' anam a Chathbaid," bar Conchobor, "cade do chomairli-siu dún?" 7 is amlaid ra-bái 'ca rád 7 atbert na briathra:

171 b "A Chathbaid, comairle dún;
do-n-ringni mertain mirun,
terna Medb assin chath gle
iss-ed am r-ar-metair-ne.
Nir bo chóir do Meidb don Maig
tinol ar cend mo daim[d]
cia-r-sa dam co nda mbeind óir,
beth acum nirb furóil.[e]
Ce mbad é a dam-si bad mó,
nirb furail di lǽg a bó;
lǽg ar mbó féin fath amne
nir-bo chóir a iarraid foirne.
Meir is forni im lǽg ar mbó
tuc ingen Echach anró
mithig dún dul d'a dígail
bar Meidb, bar-sin mór-rígain."

[a] *Sic*, for the rhyme. [b] A syllable wanting; *read* [óin]laich?

---

[1] Lit., "cow's son."

[2] Medb, his former wife, inflicted such loss on him at the battle of Gairech, that he could not follow up his victory.

[3] "My dear life" is an Anglo-Irish expression; it is to be found in the letters of some ladies of the kingdom of Kerry.—See *Life of Count Daniel O'Connell*, by Mrs. O'Connell Fitzsimon. *Cf.* "Your soul, how are you?" *Anglo-Irish*.

[4] Either the sickness (cesnaiden); or the cowardice of Medb and her echlach.

[5] = ro-*ar*-metair-*ni*, has cowed *us*; meata = cowardice, *O'R.*, *W.*; rar-mellais,

My bull and the brown bull of Dáire,
about which the warriors will give forth much shouting,
there was not ever a cow's bull calf[1]
about which more of misery is wrought.
Not more the want of bull or cow
to us in the province of Emain
than the loss of a hero that she cut down[2]
having bathed him in his blood." There is.

5. "Good now, my life[3] Cathbad," said Conchobar, "what is thy counsel to us?" and it is thus that he was saying it, and he said the words:

"O Cathbad, a counsel for us;
faintness[4] has wrought an evil design on us;
[that] Medb escaped from the famous battle,
it is this truly that has dismayed us.[5]
It was not right for Medb from the Plain
to muster [an army to come] for my bull:
though it were a bull with two horns of gold,
that I should have [it] was not too much.[6]
Though it were her bull that were the greater,
the calf of her cow was not too much for her;
the calf of our own cow, a cause of patience,[7]
it was not right to ask him from us.
Since [?] it is on us for our cow's calf
that Echu's[8] daughter has brought hardship,
time for us to go to avenge it
on Medb, on the great queen."

[c] ám *in fac-simile*. [d] Verse deficient; *read* tinol slóig (?).
[e] Syllable wanting; *read* a beth; *read* dambeind (ox-horn).

---

thou hast deceived us, *Fragm. of I. Ann.*, 14; nach-*ar*-léic = ne nos inducas, *Atk. Gloss.*, 545, col. 1; atar-fail, nachar-len, nachar-cobrai, *S. na Rann*, 55, 146.

[6] furóil, gl. *abundantia*, *Z.*

[7] Or "a reason or cause indeed." I divide this cheville thus: fath amne; aimne = patience, *O'R.*; or = *ita*, so, in *Z.* *Cf.* fáthairgne, "cause of plunders," *MS. Materials*, 492.

[8] Echu Fedlech, the father of Medb, and father-in-law of Conor. See *Irische Texte*, I. p. 266.

[*Cathbad.*] "Ra-díglais chena co cruaid,
a Chonch*obuir* chlaideb-ruaid,
brissiud catha—*cuman* le*m*—
bar cethri choicid Her*end*."

[*Conor.*] "Noco chath na tuitt rí redg
ar cruadbach ar co*m*ferg[a];
sluag do thérna*m* a cath chain
bothait rí mat ruanaid.
Suail nach ed[b] do-m-gni marb,
mo tharbga ac troit na da tarb,
meni thí mo throit-se de,
7 m*eic*c Matæ M*ur*isce.[c]
Meni thæth Ail*ill* is Medb
le*m*-sa 'ma*n* dail-se co derb
atb*er*im rib—aidblib tuir—
mebais mo chride, a Chathb*aid*."[d] A.

6. "Is hí mo chomairle-se duit," ale bar Cathb*ad*, "anad d' in chur-sa. Daig at garba na gǽtha, 7 at salcha na sligeda, 7 at móra na haibni 7 na huscida, 7 at gabalta lama lǽch ra dena*m* dunad 7 dindgna i crichaib echt*ra*nd. Et an dún i*n* tšin *con*-tuta[e] ṡamratta chucaind, corop cerchaill cach fót feránach, corop suntaich ar sen-eich, corop séitrig ar serraig, corop slána ar fir da fuilib 7 chnedaib a haithli chatha Thanad[f] Bó Cual*ngi*, coro gairdi na haidchi ri fot 7 ri f*or*aire 7 ri freccomas i *n*-iathaib bidbad 7 i críchaib echt*ra*nd." Is a*mlaid* ra-bói, ca rád 7 atb*er*t na bria*thra*:

[a] One syll. wanting; *supply* is *before second* ar.
[b] *Seems* na cured.
[c] *Read* Ocus . . . Muirsce, *or* Is . . . Murisce.
[d] *The rhyme requires voc.* Cathbaid; so it is an O-stem.

---

[1] ní cuman lem, gl. *nescio*, *Wb.* 8 a.
[2] *But cf.* bedg no redg, "start or fit," *Sench. Mór*, III. 180; redgach, "furious," "powerful," *B. of Magh Rath*, 278, 298; "fury or a mad cow," *O'Clery*. Redg was Ailill's jester or "cainte"; redgcaig, bedgaich, *LL.* 198 a.
[3] Or escaped; Medb had escaped from him, and he considers that it was not a victory for him.
[4] Or good *and* valiant.
[5] i.e. this has almost killed me.

[*Cathbad.*] "Thou hast already avenged it sternly,
O red-sworded Conchobar—
[by] the winning of a battle—I remember[1]—
over the four provinces of Eriu."

[*Conor.*] "It is no battle, in which a stout[2] king falls not
by hard-fighting, by fury;
an army to escape[3] from a goodly battle!
a king falls if they are valiant.[4]
It is almost this that[5] makes me dead:
my bull[6] at the fight of the two bulls,
unless shall come from it my contest
and [that] of the son of Mata of Muirisc.[7]
Unless Ailill should fall and Medb
by me in this encounter assuredly
I say to you, with prodigies of a host,[8]
my heart will break, O Cathbad."
O [Cathbad a counsel for us.]

6. "This is my counsel for thee," replied Cathbad, "to stay for the present. For the winds are rough, and the roads are dirty, and the rivers and the waters are great, and warriors' hands are occupied with making fortifications and strongholds in the territories of strangers. So wait for us until the summer weather comes to us, until every grassy sod is a pillow, till our old horses are spirited, till our colts are strong, till our men are whole of their wounds and hurts after the battle of the Táin Bó Cualṅge, till the nights [are] short to watch and to ward and to guard in the lands of enemies and in the territories of strangers." It is thus he was saying it, and he uttered the words:

[e] Tutta *in fac-simile*. *Read* contuta in t-ṡin ṡamratta chucaind (?); *it seems* contuda *in the MS.*

[f] Note *g.* tanad, and *g.* canad, § 7, *for* tana; Cualṅgi never in full, but it is so in *LL.* 56 b, *LU.* 65 b, 92 b; Cúailnge, *LU.* 55 a, *LL.* 93 a.

[6] tarbga = tarb, as Liathga (Cu Chulaind's horse) = Liath, *LL.* 103; *gen. sg.* or *pl.*, Mag Tarbga, *LL.* 166 b; *ac. sg.*, i Tarbga (some place in Meath), *MS. Mater.* 492; a tarbga na tuath, "who assaults the tribes" (*Man. & Cust.* III. 460, where it means bull or fight (?)), tlachtga of *LL.* 1156 = tlacht.

[7] i.e. Ailill.

[8] Or vastness of lords or multitude, *dp.*; it is a cheville; cf. aidble remend, *W.*, and *Adamnan*, p. 274; aidble bainn, vastness of deed, *S. na Rann*, p. 125.

R.[a] "Ni hi n-*am* *in*rim errach.[b]
is fuar gabél[c] gǽthach.
garfit ili Elga
airderg *in* bith
bebsat[d] buale feba[e] fǽbra.
fanna mila marta.
trena uile ap*er*óil
oenach morc mai*m*thi
mo aigse*m* ri céi*m* níthа
connach i n-aim inrim errach." N.

7. "Et an dún," ale bar Cathb*ad*, "dáig ní fuil tár dot' inchaibsiu and-si*n*. Dáig echlach ra-s-ruc *in* aithed ⁊ *in* élúd uait-siu *tri* lár catha fer ṅHer*end* síar sechtair. Et da ructha can digail bad chotamus doṅ chetamus fair si*n*. Acus[f] fáitti fessa ⁊ tecta uait-siu chena cot' chairdib écmaissi .i. co *Con*all crúaid coscorach co*m*maidmech cathbuadach claideb-derg co airm i fail ac tobuch a chisa ⁊ a chanad i crichaib Leódús, i *n*-i*n*sib Cadd, ⁊ i *n*-insib Or,[g] ⁊ i críchaib Scithia ⁊ Dacia ⁊ Gothia ⁊ Northman*nia*, ac tastel mara Ict ⁊ mara Torrían, ⁊
172*a*. ic slataigec*ht* sliged Saxan. Et fáitte fessa ⁊ tecta | uait no cot' chairdib écmaisse co iathaib Gallecda, co Gall-iathaib na nGall, .i. co Ámlaib (nó Ólaib)[h] hua I*n*scoa rig Loch*lainne*,[1] co Findmór *macc* Rof̄ir

[a] R. = Rann, or Rosc, or Roscada, maxims. *See O'Don. Suppl.*; rosc catha *is* a war-song. *Or* (as at p. 124 of *LL.*) R = in rethoric-se, a kind of rhapsody, retairic, *LU.* 91 a, 38 a. *Cf.* Cetamain cain ree, *Mac-Ghníomhara Fhind*, p. 44; *or* rithlerg, as in *Hyfiachrach*, p. 26. *Cf.* Amergin's *Ritairec* in Hardiman's "Minstrelsy," p. 350.

[b] *Cf.* ní hinbaid oenaig ind inbaid garb gemratta so, *LL.* 264 b.

[c] Gach bél? *ns.* Elga, *L. Hym. O. S. F.*, p. 38.

[d] *Cf.* beg briga bebsat bi bath midlách, "little energy forbodes the destruction of a coward" (!), *B. of Magh Rath*, 170.

---

[1] *Cf.* oenach n-uircc treith, the fair of the son of a king, *Stokes' Bodl. Cormac*, 26; in-óenach thuirc threith, *LL.* 187 b.

[2] *Cf.* "these tribes are freed from the hosting of Spring and Autumn"—sluaiged earraig ocus fogmair, *Tribes and C. of Hy-Maine*, p. 66.

[3] I have divided this R. into verses, conjecturally; and I have hazarded a timid and tentative translation; in aim = this time, in *Windisch.*

[4] *ale bar* occurs six times, and *ale ar*, *ale far* once; it seems to mean "continued." It begins sentences: Aile ar Mac Roig, Aile for Cu Chulaind, Ale leice as a Fherguis ar Medb; Aile a gilla, ar Cu Chulaind, *LL.* 55 a, 63 a, 61 a, 70 b.

R. "Spring is not the time for an invasion.
Every windy ford [or gap] is cold.
Many of Elga will shout,
famous the cause [world ?].
The good cow-droves of February have died [disappeared ?].
Weak are the animals of March.
Strong are all [cattle] of April.
A fair of hogs[1] . . .
. . . for a march of battle.
So that Spring[2] is not the time for an invasion."[3]

7. "So stay with us," now[4] said Cathbad, "for there is no disgrace to thy honour therein. For [it was] a horse-boy that carried it in flight, and in escape from thee through the middle of the battle of the men of Ériu away westward. And if it was carried off without vengeance, there shall be measure for measure[5] for that. And let there be sent tidings and messages from thee forthwith to thy friends in absence,[6] namely, to Conall the stern, the triumphant, the exultant, the victorious, the red-sworded, to the place where he is, raising his tax and his tribute in the territories of Léodús,[7] in the islands of Cadd, and in the islands of Orc,[7] and in the territories of Scythia and Dacia and Gothia and Northmannia, voyaging the Ictian Sea and the Tyrrhenian Sea, and plundering the roads of the Saxons. And let there be sent tidings and messages from thee too to thy friends in absence, to the Gallic lands, to the foreign lands of the foreigners, namely, to Amlaib or Olaib [*i.e.* Olaf] grandson of Inscoa,[8] King of Norway; to Findmór son of Rofher, the king of the seventh

[e] Febra fæbra, *in fac-simile*, seems *an erroneous repetition*.

[f] Acus *in full here* and § 11.

[g] *Recte* Orc *as infra*.

[h] no Ólaib *is a marginal note*.

[i] *Or* Lochland, *as in B. of Magh Rath*, 80, and *Cog. G.* 7 *G. passim*, it meant Norway and Denmark.

---

[5] Victory-attack (*cod-amus*), for the first attack (?). *cod* = victory, *O'Reilly*. Or *co-tomas* and *cet-tomus*; i tosuch cetumus, at the first attempt, *LL.* 114 b.

[6] Absent friends.

[7] Isle of Lewis, *Wars of the G. and G.*, Index, = *Ljódhús*, Stokes on the *Ling. Value of the Irish Annals*, p. 118. Inis Cat is "Shetland," Todd in *Wars of the G. and G.*; and Insi Orc are the Orkneys; but Crich Cat is "Cateness," Caithness, *Nennius*, p. 148; *written* Inis Gaid *in W.*

[8] i.e. "Big Shoes," a nickname, as Stokes surmises; *cf.* son of *Rofer*, "Big Man," *infra*; *cf.* fofer, "good man," *Tl.* 242.

co ríg sechtmad rainni de Lochl*ainn*, co Báre na Sciggire, co dunud na Piscarcarla, co Brodor Roth 7 co Brodor Fiúit, et co Siugraid Soga ríg Súdiam, co Sortadbud Sort co ríg *insi* Orc, co secht m*a*ccaib Rom-rach, co hIl, co Íle, co Mæl, co Muile, co Abram *macc* Romr*ach*, co Cet *macc* Rom*rach*, co Celg *macc* Romr*ach*, co Mod *macc* Herl*ing*, co *Con*chob*or* coscarach *macc* Art*uir* m*eicc* Bruide, m*eicc* Dungail, co *macc* ríg Alban, [7 Clothra *in*gen *Con*ch*obuir* a m*áthair*]."[a]

8. "Cia doragad risin tectairect s*in*?" bar *Con*chob*or*. "Cia doragad and," bar Cathb*ad*, "acht mad Findchad *macc Con*ch*obuir* and-sut, et Aed Caem *macc Con*aill C*er*naig, et Oengus macc Oenláma Gábae,[b] et Cano Gall do múnud eól*uis* dar munci*nd* mara 7 mór-fairge dóib." Is and-s*in* ra-lotar-s*in* rompu dar mu*n*cind mara 7 mór-fairgi co hairm i mbái *Con*all C*ernach* i crícha*i*b Leodús, et *con*dnoathatar da*no* na scela ro-batar accu do *Chon*all. Ferais da*no* fálte *fri* Fi*nd*chad *macc Con*ch*obuir*, 7 dobretha a láim dar a bragit 7 dobretha teora póc do. Is and da*no* barridnachtatar-s*om* dó-sum Táin Bó Cual*ngi* do breith a hUl*taib*. Scei*n*nis a chridi cruaid colo*m*da *Con*aill a mid-uact*ur* a chléib, i*m*mar thoir*m* tui*nn*e tr*e*than-glassi[c] ra tír. "Atdir-sa[d] brethir a*m*," bar *Con*all, "mad da mbei*nd*-se i crichaib Ul*ad* conna b*er*tha i*n* tái*n* si*n* can digail bad chotamus do'n chetamus fair." Iss a*mlaid* ro-bái Conall da*no* 7 fessa 7 furic ar n-a ndéna*m* dó and-s*in*,

[a] Parenthetical. [b] Oenláme gába, *LL.* 94.
[c] *Cf.* Do meadaigeadar ná tonna a ttrethan ocus a ttorman, *Ch. of Lir*, p. 132; trethan-tonn, *B. of Magh Lena*, 46. [d] *Read* atdiursa, *as in* §§ 28, 46.

---

1 i.e. Ey-Keggiar, the Færoe Islands, Stokes, *ubi supra*, pp. 58, 120.

2 Some town of the Færoe Islanders; the only word I find like this is *Dún na Trapcharla* in Munster, *F. Mast. an.* 1062.

3 Roth, Fiúit = Red and White, Norse loan words.—*Stokes.*

4 Sweden; or Suderoe, one of the Færoe islands.

5 i.e. Herlingr, *Stokes;* Romra, *g.* Romrach, is an Irish word in *S. na Rann*, l. 3982, and *LU.* 40 a. *Cf.* Tracht Romra = Solway Frith, *Adamnan* XLV.

6 Probably a Pictish name, *Stokes*, 117, *ubi supra;* but Cano also is Irish, and means a file of the 4th degree.

7 *Or* top; .i. uachtar mara, *L. Gabála*, p. 3, and *O'Cl.* O'Reilly renders it by headland or seacoast; *but* "tri muincinn mara Romuir," *S. na Rann*, l. 3987; for muncind mara, *Nennius*, 234.

8 "et condnoathatar"; batnoathar, § 21, should be, perhaps, batnoathatar. Is airi cotnoat-som (*Ml.* 112 b) seems to mean "wherefore they advertize or admonish him," though the Latin text, as given by Ascoli, omits some word like *commonere;*

part of Norway; to Báre of the Sciggér,[1] to the fortress of the Piscarcarla;[2] to Brodor Roth and to Brodor Fiúit,[3] and to Siugraid Soga, King of Súdiam;[4] to Sortadbud Sort, the King of the Orkney Islands; to the seven sons of Romra, to Il, to Íle, to Mael, to Muile, to Abram son of Romra,[5] to Cet son of Romra, to Celg son of Romra, to Mod son of Herling,[5] to Conchobar the victorious, son of Artur, son of Bruide, son of Dungal, to the son of the King of Scotland, and Clothra, daughter of Conchobar, [was] his mother."

8. "Who should go on that embassy?" said Conchobar. "Who should go upon it," said Cathbad, "but [if it were] Findchad, son of Conchobar yonder, and Aed the Handsome, son of Conall Cernach, and Oengus, son of Oenlám Gába, and Cano[6] the Foreigner, to teach the way over the surface[7] of the sea and of the ocean to them." It is then that those went forward over the surface[7] of the sea and of the ocean to the place in which Conall Cernach was in the territory of Leodús, and they manifested[8] then the tidings that they had to Conall. He made welcome to Findchad, son of Conchobar, and put his hands about his neck and gave[9] him three[10] kisses. It is then too that they conveyed to him that the *Táin Bó Cualnge* was taken from the Ulaid. The stern, steadfast[11] heart of Conall started from the mid-upper part of his chest like the noise of a sea-green wave against the earth. "I vow [I say a word] indeed," said Conall, "were it that I had been in the territory of the Ulaid, that that spoil would not have been taken without a vengeance which would be measure for measure for it!" It is thus, then, Conall was: feasts and festivities having been made by

---

noud, .i. urdarcagud, *O'Dav.*, p. 108, and *O'Clery*. I think *at*-noad (*W. Texte*, 142, l. 15) = let him declare; ro noad (*ib.* p. 79, l. 19) = was manifested. *W.* queries those words, but they are connected with words of our text.

[9] dobretha; *W.* gives three instances of this 3 *sg. pret.* in *ta;* here and § 53 are four more, including "robretha," *infra;* the form is that of the pret. 3 pl. pass.; this form is not in *Z.* or in *Atkinson's Glossary;* "confáitti," § 9, seems to be the same tense, if not an *historic pres.*

[10] teora póc; so "ra thairbir teora póc," *LL.* 58 ab, 59 ab; one would expect "teora póca," *apf.*; the *asf.* is póic, *Fled Bricr.* 50; (dorat, dobert, tug) póicc do, *Atkinson's Glossary. Cf.* di láim im Etain ocus póc di, *LU.* 131 b; thug sé tri póga do Ghrainne, *Diarm. and Grainne*, § 19. "Teora póc" seems a crystallized expression and a deflection from regular declension; *Joyce*, p. 98, says that teóra generally governs nouns in the *gen. plur.*, as "teóra ban."

[11] Or column-like? columnach = *columnaris*, *Ogygia*, 117; dove-like, or hide-like (di cholomnaib ferb, *LU. Táin Bó C.*), would not suit here.

7 ba gléire descad 7 ba aibbgetus a hóla and-sin. Et ro-bretha *Con*all *in* fleid *sin* do mathib Ul*ad*. Et faitte *dano* fessa 7 techta uad co a chairddib écmaisse fo iathaib Gallecda co Gall-*iathaib* na ṅGall. Is and doronad ti*n*ól 7 tochostul leo-sum *dano*. Et ro-hellamaigit al-lonti leo-sum *dano* 7 ra-gli*n*nigit al-loṅga 7 al-láideṅg. Et tancatar co hairm i *m*bái *Con*all.

9. Is and confáitti *Con*all fessa 7 techta uad co iathaib Ul*ad*, conna betis Ulaid i *n*-etarlén 'rithalma ar ci*n*d a *m*bidbad 7 a*n*-namat 7 a n-echt*ra*nd. Is and-si*n* ro-gniad co*m*airle la Ultaib d*ano*, 7 darónait fessa 7 fuireca leo-s*um* d*ano*. "Dogen-sa fled,"[a] ar *Cúchulaind*, "i n-accill 7 i n-airichill *Con*chob*uir*[c] ac dún drech-ṡolus Delgga." "Dogen-sa fled[a] mór-cháin mór-adbul aile," bar Celtchair m*acc*
172 *b* Uth*echair*,[b] "i *n*-accill | 7 i *n*-airichill *Conaill*[c] *Cernaig* m*eicc* Amairgi*n* ac carraic Murbuilg." "Dogen-sa no fled mór-chai*n* mór-adbul aile," f*or* Loegaire, "ac I*n*biur Ṡeimne thuaid."

10. Ra-ergitar t*ra* i*n* tro*m*-choblach mór muride am*al* atrubra*m*ar ba *Chon*all *Cernach* m*acc* *Amairgin*, et ma Fi*n*dchad m*acc* *Chon*cho*buir*, et ma Aed Cæm m*acc* *Conaill Cernaig*, et ma mathib Lochl*ainne*, et tancatar re*m*pu immach bar Sruthair na Maile Chind Tiri. Et at*ra*acht glass-anfud i*n* mara mór-adbuil dóib. Et at*ra*achtatar a rói*n* 7 rossail 7 a chorr-cind 7 a chenandai*n* 7 il-ríana in mara mór-adbuil dóib-siu*m* d*ano*. Is é tressi in n-anfaid ra-érig dóib co ro-rai*n*ned i*n*

[a] fleid *would be a better*.
[b] Uthidir, Uthichair in full, *LU*. 95, 103. [c] *Or* Chonċobuir, Chonaill.

---

[1] aibbgetus, ripeness, maturity (= aipcheacht, *O'Begley's Dictionary*); it seems synon. with "gléire" here, or with "aibnius," § 13. Gléire = abundance, purity, choice; and descad in *Z.* glosses *fæx*, *fermentum*; a hola = its drink, i. e. of the *fes*.

[2] So in *F. Masters*, III., p. 2272, and *C. Maige Lena*, 44.

[3] etarlen, mutual or deep sorrow; *g.* léin, sorrow, *B. of Fenagh*, 374. Cf. etargléod, decision, *LL*. 84; etar seems an intensitive, as etar-medón, lár-medón.

[4] "accill" and "airchill," thrice here and § 11, are synon.; for aicill do marbtha, in wait to slay thee, *Mac Gn. Finn*, § 32; do airichill, *twice*, *LL*. 106 b; ro hairichlit, they were expected, *LL*. 268 a, *bis*. *Cf.* i foichill, *F. Mast.*, p. 2124; oc airichill comraic, awaiting, preparing for battle, *LB*. 210 a.

[5] Dundalk; *d.* Delga, *LU*. 68 b., *shows that the nom. is not* Delg.

him there, and it was the abundance of leavings and the ripeness[1] of his drinking then. And Conall gave that feast to the nobles of the Ulaid. And there were sent then intelligencers and messengers from him to his absent friends, through the Gallic lands, to the foreign-lands of the foreigners. It is then that there was made a gathering and muster by them too; and their stores were prepared by them also, and their ships and their galleys were secured in order; and they came to the place in which Conall was.

9. It is then that Conall sent intelligencers[2] and messengers from him to the lands of the Ulaid, that the Ulaid might not be in much-concern[3] of preparation against [for] their foes and their enemies and their foreigners. It is then that counsel was held by the Ulaid, and feasts and festivities were held by them too. "I will make a banquet," said Cú Chulaind, "in wait and in preparation[4] for ConChobar at the bright-faced castle of Delgga."[5] "I will make another splendid vast banquet," said Celtchair, son of Uthechar,[6] "in wait and in preparation for Conall Cernach, son of Amairgen, at the rock of Murbolg."[7] "I too will make another splendid monster banquet," said Loegaire, "at Inber Seimne[8] in the north."

10. Now set out the great naval armament, as we have said, under Conall Cernach son of Amairgin, and under Findchad son of Conchobar, and under Aed the Handsome, son of Conall Cernach, and under the nobles of Norway. And they came forward out on the current of the Mull of Cantire. And a green-surge of the tremendous sea rose for them; and the[9] seals and walruses and crane-heads and 'cenandans' and 'ilrians'[10] of the tremendous sea rose for them too. Such was the strength of the storm that rose for them, that the

---

[6] Uthechair, in full, *LU.* 103 b; but Utidir, *LU.* 95 b. O'Curry, in *Man. and Cust.* III. 610, reads Uthichair, Uithidir, Uthair; Hennessy, in *Mesca Ulad*, reads "Uithidir."

[7] Murlough, Co. Antrim, *F. Masters*, I. p. 26. Dunseverick Castle was in Murbolg Dalriada, *ib.* *Cf.* Muirbolc, *Adamnan*, p. 40.

[8] Larne, Co. Antrim. Maghseimne was in Dalaraidhe, *F. Masters*, Index. Inis Seimhne = Island Magee.

[9] Lit., its.

[10] rossail *or* rosualt, walrus (?), *LL.* 118, *LU.* 11 a; corrcind, "crane- (or round-) heads," or sword fish (corr, sharp, *B. of Fenagh*, 400, 298). Cf. serrcend, serpent (?), *Tigern.* 1137; cenandan looks like ceinndán (little white head) of the *B. of Armagh*; il-ríana means the many water-ways; rossail = ross-hwæl, horse-whale (?).

cobl*ach* i *trí*. Tanic *trian* dib ma *Chon*all *Chernach* m*acc* A*mairgin* co carraic Murbuilg. Tanic *trian* aile ma m*a*ccaib Romra co hI*n*b*er* Semni. Dolluid *in* *trian* aile mo Álaib hua I*n*scoa ríg Lochl*ainne*, 7 ma Ḟindmór macc Raḟir ríg *in* sechtmad raind do Lochl*ainn*, et ma Báire na Sciggiri a dunud na Piscarcarla. Et dollotar sain co T*r*áig ṁBále m*eicc*[a] Búai*n*, co hI*n*ber Li*n*ni Luachai*n*ne.

11. Is *in* tan si*n* rol-luid *Con*chob*or* reme coicḟiur 7 *trí* fichit ar nói cetaib co hI*n*b*er* Li*n*ni Luach*ainne*. Et ra-hecrad tech n-óil 7 air-aibniusa leis i *n*dún drech-ṡolus Delga. Nir-bo chian do *Chon*chob*or* dia *m*bái and co facca na corr-gabla siúil, 7 na lo*n*ga lucht-lethna, 7 na pupla corcar-glana, 7 na merggida alle ill-dathacha, 7 na confi*n*gi catha, 7 na síblaṅga gorma glai*n*idi, 7 na hidna áig. "Maith and-si*n*, a deg-ǽs dána-sa thís. Tabraid curu 7 tenta 7 trebairi dam-sa." "Maith a thríath 7 a thig*er*na," bar Sencha m*acc* Ai*le*lla, "cid 'má 'tá lat-su sai*n*?" "Mét far ṅdolaid 7 far murir da*m*," far *Con*chob*or*; "febus mo cho*mm*ai*n* crichi 7 ferai*n*n 7 forbbaid *for*aib; febus mo cho*mm*ai*n* sét 7 máini 7 i*n*dmassa foraib. Na bad ḟuráil da*m* na ticfad d'ulc 7 do maith dam ó 'n chind bl*iadna* c'a chéile sib-si 'n-a ré*m*ur 7 'n-a airichill da*m*." "Maith a thríath 7 a thig*er*na," bar Sencha m*acc* Ail*el*la, "cid 'ma 'tá lat-su sai*n*?" "Nad-ḟetar-sa am," bar *Con*chob*or*, "act manip íat *in* Galían Lagen, *nó* *in* Mu*m*ni[b] mór-M*u*man, *nó* choiced Ólnec*macht* dariacht and; *acht* is mid-lán I*n*ber Li*n*ni Luach*ainne* 7 Tr*a*ig Báile m*eicc* Búai*n*." "Atiur-sa brethir ám," bar Sencha m*acc* Ai*l*ella, "nach tarmchillend Her*iu* óclách do neoch dobeir a lái*m* il-laim tig*er*na nach aichnid da*m*-sa. Et mad iat fir Her*end* bes and, iarfat-sa sossad catha *for*thu-s*um* no co cend cían cóicthigis f*or* mís. Acus mad iat do charait écmaisi bes and a iathaib

[a] *Or* maccu? [b] *Read* Mumnig.

---

[1] Larne. [2] The strand and river-mouth at Dundalk.

[3] corrgabla, round or beaked spears or forks.

[4] confingi (?).

[5] síblanga = sith-langa, long boats? *Cf.* sithlungi, of a long ship, *Togail Troi*, pp. 43, 109; sib-in (a bulrush) is a dimin. of sib; lang appears in Erc-lang, Dún-lang, etc.; sithlongaib, *LU.* 80 a.

[6] Supply "said Conchobor." [7] *Or*, why must thou have that?

fleet was parted in three. A third of them under Conall Cernach son of Amairgen came to the rock of Murbolg. Another third under the sons of Romra came to Inber Semni.[1] The other third went under Alaib, grandson of Inscoa, King of Norway, and under Findmór, son of Rafher, King of the seventh part of Norway, and under Báire of the Færoe Islands, from the fortress of the Piscarcarla; and these went to the Strand of Báile mac Buain, to the mouth of the water of Luachann.[2]

11. It is at that time that Conchobar came on [with] nine hundred and sixty-five men to the mouth of the water of Luachann. And a house of drinking and high merriment was prepared by him in the bright-faced castle of Delga. It was not long for Conchobar, when he was there, till he saw the bent spars[3] of a sail and the full-crewed ships, and the bright-scarlet pavilions, and the beautiful many-coloured flags, and the machines[4] of battle, and the blue bright lances [?],[5] and the weapons of war. "Good, then, ye good men of learning down here, give sureties and bonds and guarantees to me!"[6] "Well, O chief and lord," said Sencha son of Ailill, "why is it so with thee?"[7] "[For] the greatness of your charge and of your burden to me," said Conchobar; "[for] the excellence of my bestowal[8] of territory and land and property on you; for the excellence of my bestowal of jewels, treasure and wealth, that it may not be too much for me[9] that there should not come [of] evil or good to me from one end of the year to the other, [from] your [being engaged] in preparing and procuring it for me."[10] "Good, O chief and lord," said Sencha son of Ailill, "why is it so with thee?" "Because I know not indeed," said Conchobar, "if they be the Galían of Lagin, or the Munstermen of great Muma, or the province of Ólnecmacht, that have arrived there; but the estuary of the water of Luachann and the strand of Báile mac Búain are full."[11] "I give [my] word indeed," said Sencha son of Ailill, "that Ériu [Eire] surrounds not a soldier that puts his hand in the hand of a lord, who is not known to me. And if they be the men of Ériu that are there, I will ask a truce of battle from them till the

[8] commain *gs.* of comman; *but* commaine would be better, as the *n.* and *d.* are commáin, *Wb.* 6. 25. "Mét" and "febas" seem *dat.* of cause; "dolad," charge; imposts, *Stokes* on *Atk. Pass. & Hom.*, p. 37.

[9] i.e. it is due to me; it is the least I should expect in return.

[10] Preparing = rem(f)úr. He seems to reproach them with having brought the Leinster-men against him.

[11] midlán, half full, or quite full?

173 a Gallec*da* 7 Gall-*iathaib* na ṅGall, | ba ferr son let-su cam*main*."[a] "Da *m*bad iat," bar *Con*cho*bor*, "rapad lugaiti bar n-enecl*ann*-si."

12. Is and-si*n* ra-luid reme Sencha m*acc* Ail*el*la co airm i *m*bái i*n* tro*m*-choblach mór muridi si*n*; 7 ro-iarfach da*no* díb, "Cia dothæt and?" Is *sed* ro-ráidsetar-*sum* da*no* cor-bo iat carait écmaisi *Con*cho*buir* ro-batar and. Tanic remi Sencha co hairm i *m*bái *Con*cho*bor*. "Maith ám a m'an*am*, a *Chon*cho*buir*, iss-iat do charait écmaisi-siu failet and sút a iathaib Gall*ecda* 7 a Gall-iathaib na nGall. Cid *tra acht* nir chutulsa do Chonch*obor* i*n*[d] Heriu et*ir* ra mét leis a brotha 7 a bríge 7 a báige. Et ro-mebaid loim cráo 7 fola dar a bél sell sechtair. Et in chǽp chró 7 fola ro-bói *for* a chride issí rosceastar ra halt na huaire si*n*.[b]

13. "Maith a Ch*úchulaind*," bar *Con*cho*bor*, "gabtar latt gabra Maige Murthe*m*ni. Indlit*er* carp*ait* chethir-ríad *for*ro. Et tabar lett mathi Lochl*ainne* i carptib 7 i cethir-riadaib co Dún drech-ṡolus Delga. Corop fa dreich ríg Lochl*ainne* ecairther i*n* tech óil-seo 7 aíbniusa." Is and ro-gabait gab*ra* Maige Mur*themni* 7 ro-hindlit carp*ait* 7 cethir-*riad for*ro, 7 rucait i *n*-agid ríg Lochl*ainne*, 7 tucait iat co Dún ṅdrech-ṡolus ṅDelga. Et ra-falmaiged i*n* bruiden la *Con*chobor. Corop fa dreich ríg Lochl*ainne* ro-hecrad ass-a aithle hí.

Et ra-ergitar iartain rannair *fri* raind accu 7 dalema*in fri* dáil. Et ro-dáiled i*n*[d] fled sai*n for* mathib Lochl*ainne*, corbat mesca medar-

[a] *Or* cam*maib*, camai, *Z.*

[b] *Cf.* nírb uráil lim loim cró 7 fola issin ṁbél tacras sin, *LL.* 264 b; *and* nírb uráil lim lom cró 7 fola isain ṁ-bél tacras sin, *Mesca Ul.*, p. 20.

---

[1] camma*in*; *recte*, perhaps, "commaib," however, *Z.* 702.

[2] nir chutulsa; *but* nirbo chutulsa, § 15; it seems to mean "it did not satisfy," it was not a satisfaction. Isí nimdéni cutal (*Irische Texte*, I. 98) means (I think) "it [the advice] does not give me satisfaction"; *but* "codul do .i. iarraid do," *T. Bó Flidais.*

[3] cethir-riad, *gp.*, it was a four-wheeler, *petor-ritum*, *Auson.* Ep. viii.; *cf.* dé-riad, gl. *bigæ*, *Z.*; the *dp.* c.-riadaib, § 13, and *LL.*, p. 29. It seems

distant end of a fortnight in addition to a month. But if they be thy friends from abroad that are there, from the Gallic lands and the foreign-lands of the foreigners, that will please thee better however."[1] "If it be they," said Conchobar, "your honour-price shall be the less."

12. It is then that Sencha son of Ailill went forward to the place where that great naval armament was, and he asked them, "Who goes here?" It is this they said then, that they were the foreign friends of Conchobar that were there. Sencha came forward to the place in which Conchobar was. "Good now, my soul, Conchobar, they are thy foreign friends that are yonder, from the Gallic lands and the foreign-lands of the foreigners." However, the [whole of] Ireland did not please[2] Conchobar at all through the amount in him of his ardour and of his energy and of his fierceness. And a drop of gore and blood burst through his mouth a little out; and the clot of gore and blood that was on his heart, it is it that pained him at that juncture of time.

13. "Well, O Cú Chulaind," said Conchobar, "let the horses of the plain of Murthemni be caught by thee; let four-wheeled chariots[3] be harnessed to them. And bring with thee the nobles of Norway in chariots and in four-wheeled cars to the bright-faced castle of Delga. So that it may be for[4] the kings of Norway that this house of drinking and enjoyment is prepared." It is then that the horses of the plain of Murthemni were caught and the chariots and the four-wheeled cars were yoked to them, and they were brought to meet the kings of Norway, and they (*i.e.* the kings) were brought to the bright-faced castle of Delga, and the mansion was vacated[5] by Conchobar. So that it was for the kings of Norway it was prepared after that. And there arose thereupon carvers[6] to carve for them and butlers to deal out [drinks]. And that banquet was served to the nobles of Norway

---

neuter from *np.* ceithirriad, § 14: so in Latin. *Cf.* *rhēda;* but *p.-rĭtum* is short.

[4] fa dreich, under the face; *cf.* ar chiunn.

[5] Not in *W.*; in *Atkinson* it means "devastated"; folmúgad, to evacuate, *C. M. Lena*, 64.

[6] *Recte* rannairi, distributors to distribute; *np.* rannaire, *Mesca Ul.* 12. *Cf.* *LL.*, pp. 29, 30; *LU.* 101 a.

cháini. In n-uair ropo thressiu flaith firu, 7 ba comrád ca*ch* dessi 7 ca*ch* thrír díb, ra-curit i*n* an aitib 7 i*n* an imdádaib 7 i*n* a cotaltigib iat. Ro-canait ciúil 7 airfiti 7 admolta dóib; 7 tarrassatar-*som* and co solus-*tra*th éirge ar n-a barach.

14. Ro-érig im*morro* *Conchobor* moch-trath ar n-a barach. Et tucad *Cúchulaind* d'a saigid.

"Maith si*n*, a Ch*úchulaind*," bar *Conchobor*; "tabar i*n* deired fledi fail acut do mathib Lochl*ainne* corop bude-chaiti íat. Et faitti fessa 7 techta uait fó iathaib Ul*ad* cu hócaib Ul*ad*. Frithált*er* leo-*sum* no a carait Gall a Gall-iathaib na nGall, co ndigiur-sa co hInb*er* Li*nn*i Luach*ainne*; co ngabthar sossad 7 longphort lim and. Ráid dam da*no* risna *tri* coicait senorach[a] senlæch ro-failet i n-a ligi áisi fá Irgalach m*acc* M*acc*láig[b] m*eicc* Congaile m*eicc* Rud*rai*ge ár ndichur a ngascid 7 a n-arm; ráid dam-sa riu tiachtai*n* le*m* i*n* fect-sa 7 i*n* sluaged, co *m*bad d'a réir 7 d'a comairle donethea é." "Messi d'a rád riu!" bar *Cúchu*laind. "Ni ebber, 7 a ndul ní mesti lem da*no*."

15. Is and ralluid *Conchobor* reme issi*n* rigthech ro-mór ir-rabatar na senóraig 7 na senlaich. Is and-si*n* tuargabtar-*sum* a cind assa n-atib 7 assa n-imdadaib ra facsi*n* i*n*[c] ríg rosc-lethai*n* ro-*m*óir.
173 *b* Et nír-bo chutul-sa da*no* doib-siu*m* a me*n*ma. Suail na*ch* farroeblangatar in bruiden ir-rabatar díb. "Maith a thriath 7 a thig*er*na," bar

[a] *Insert* ocus *here, as about* 6 *lines infra:* na senóraig ocus na senlaich.

---

[1] *Or* when beer was stronger than men, when they were overcome by it; flaith = prince, § 22; reign § 54; here, "a kind of strong ale," as in *O'R.* and *W.* If so, this is the oldest instance of the word in that sense. In Mid. Irish the compar. governs an accusative, *firu*. Noteworthy are the "we won't go home till morning" habits of the Conchoborian Cycle.

[2] bude-chaiti, lit. thank-spent (?).

[3] no *for* dino, dano, 7, 9, 14, 25, 34, 41, 46, 51, *LL.* 79 b.

until they were drunk and right-merry. When a chief[1] was mightier than men, and it was a conversation of every pair and of every three of them, they were put in their apartments and in their couches, and in their sleeping-rooms. Tunes and amusing songs and eulogies were sung to them, and they tarried there till the clear time of rising on the morrow.

14. Now Conchobar rose early on the morrow, and Cú Chulaind was brought to him. "That is well, Cú Chulaind," said Conchobar. "Give the rest of the banquet that thou hast to the nobles of Norway, that they may be fully-satisfied.[2] And let intelligencers and messengers be sent from thee through the lands of the Ulaid to the warriors of the Ulaid. Let their foreign friends from the foreign-lands of the foreigners be ministered unto by them also,[3] while I go to the mouth of the water of Luachann, and a position and camp is taken by me there. Say for me too to the three fifties of elders [and] old champions that are in their repose of age under Irgalach son of Macclách son of Congal[4] son of Rudraige, having laid aside their exercise of arms and their weapons—say for me to them to come with me on this campaign and on the hosting, so that it may be by their will and by their counsel that it may go on."[5] "I to say it to them!" said Cú Chulaind, "I will not say [it]; and yet I think not the worse of their going."

15. It is then that Conchobar went on into the great royal-house in which were the veterans and the old champions. It is then that they raised their heads[6] out of their places and out of their couches to see the large-eyed majestic king. And their spirit was not indeed satisfactory to them.[7] They almost[8] leaped the mansion in which they were. "Good, O chief and lord," said they, "what has made thee

[b] *Or* Meicc Láig? [c] *For* ind ríg.

---

[4] Congal, *g.* Congaile—as Dunlang, *g.* Dunlinge (*B. of Armagh*)—*n.* Congal, *g.* Congaile, Congail; *n.* Fergal, *g.* Fergaile, Fergail, *Frag. Ir. Ann.*, 44, 40.

[5] do-n-ethea; do-n-ethe, § 15, see "donetha" and "atetha" in our vocabulary.

[6] *Nom. pl.* for *acc.*; it may also mean "their heads rose."

[7] The meaning appears to be that they could not contain themselves.

[8] "suail nach" = beg nach, almost; "bruden" should be brudin, *ast.* Some words are missing before *dib* (of them), or it is redundant as *de* often is.

iat-*sum*, "crǽt ro-t-ast*ra*ig 7 ro-t-imluaid chucai*n*ni i*n*diu?" "Nach cualabair-si," ar se, "in sluaged co*m*baga-sa tancatar cethri oll-choiceda Her*end* chucai*n*d? da tucsat a n-æs ciúil 7 airfitid 7 admol*ta* leo, co mbad leriti na hairgni 7 co *m*bad moti na hurbada; 7 ra-loscit ar ṅdúnaid 7 ar ṅdegbaleda connach airddi iat 'nas a n-airidni 7 a n-immellaigi. Et rop áil da*m*-sa da*no* sluage*d* co*m*bága chuccu-*sum*, 7 co *m*bad da bar reir-si 7 da bar comairle donethe i*n* fecht 7 i*n* sl*uaged*." "Gabtar ar sengabra latt 7 i*n*dlit*er* ar sencharp*ait* co ndechsum i*n* fect-sa 7 i*n* sl*uaged* latt." Iss-and ro gab*ait* a sengab*ra* leo-*sum* 7 ro hi*n*dlit a sencharp*ait*. Et tancatar rompu co hI*n*b*er* Li*n*ni Luach*ainne* i*n* n-aidchi si*n*.

16. Et ro-cuas do chethri oll-choic*edaib* Her*end* sai*n*. Et ro-chrithnaigsetar *tri* to*n*na Her*end* remi-si*n* i*n* n-aidchi si*n*, .i. Tond Chlidna 7 Tond Rud*ra*igi 7 T*ond* Tuage I*n*bir. Is and-si*n* folluid Eochu m*acc* Luc*hta* re*m*i co cla*n*naib dílsib do Recartachaib Dedad co Temraig Luachra aniartúaid. Is a*n*d-si*n*[a] Ail*ill* 7 Medb co Cruachan-ráith Connacht. Is and-si*n* falluid Fi*n*d m*acc* Ro*s*a rí Galía*n* co cla*n*naib Deirg i*m*me co Di*n*n Ríg ós B*er*ba banṡolais. Is and falluid Carp*re* Nia Fer co Luagnib Temrach i*m*me co Te*m*raig.

[a] *No verb and no lacuna in the MS.*; *but we must supply* folluid, *as 2 lines above, or* follotar.

---

1 From astrach, way-faring.

2 in fecht-sa ocus in sluaged; note the *particula augens* omitted after the second noun here, *and in* in tech óil-seo acus aíbniusa, § 13.

3 *Cf.* adcos uaim duit, *Chr. Scotor.*, p. 8; atchuaid, gl. *exposuit*, *Wb.* 21 d; atcós don ríg, was told to the King, *Atk. Gloss.*, p. 552; or, was sent.

4 *Or* trembled, shook at this.

5 Tonn Cleena, Glandore Harbour, Co. Cork (Index to *F. Masters*), in the Bay of Clonakilty (*C. M. Lena*, 95); T. Rudr. in Bay of Dundrum, Down; T. T. Inbir, at the mouth of the Bann, *ib.* Cf. *LL.* 168 b, *B. of Balymote*, 374 a, 395 b. The waves bounded for joy (sometimes, at least?), "Do ḟailtiġeadar tri tonna na Foḋla .i. T. Inbir ag freagra Thuinne R. acus T. Chioḋna ag freagra don dá thonn oile," *C. M. Lena*, 94: there was also a famous wave, "Tonn Luim," *B. of Fenagh*, 146.

travel,[1] and moved thee towards us to-day?" "Have you not heard," said he, "of this expedition of hostility [on which] came the four great provinces of Ireland to us, to which they brought their men of music and amusement and eulogy with them, that the ravages might be more manifest and that the depredations might be the greater? and our fortresses and our fine dwellings were burned, so that they are not higher than their apartments and their outhouses. And so I should like an expedition of hostility against them, and that it be by your direction [will] and by your counsel that the journey and the expedition may proceed." "Let our old steeds be caught by thee and let our old chariots be yoked by thee, till we go this journey and this[2] expedition with thee." Then their old chargers were caught by them and their old chariots were yoked; and they came on to the mouth of the Water of Luachann that night.

16. And this was told[3] to the four great provinces of Eriu. And the Three Waves of Ériu reverberated[4] before this that night, namely the Wave of Clidna, and the Wave of Rudraige, and the Wave of Tuag Inbir.[5] It is then that Eochu son of Luchta[6] went on with the native clans of the Recartaig Dedad to Temair Luachra[7] from the northwest. It is then that Ailill and Medb [went] to Cruachan Ráith of Connacht. It is then that Find son of Ros king of the Galían[8] went with the clans of Derg about him to Dinn Ríg[9] over the clear-bright Barrow. It is then that Cairpre Nia Fer went with the Luagni[10] of Temair about him to Temair.

---

[6] King of N. Munster, *Man. and Cust.* II. 21; Curói or his son was K. of the other part of Munster, *Cambren. Eversus*, I. 453.

[7] Near Abbeyfeale, *ib.* III. 132; Hennessy (*M. Ulad.* v.) thinks it was further north. Temair Erand was the burial-place of the Clanna Dedad who occupied a great part of Cos. of Cork and Kerry. As these came southwards to it, I think it was Mt. Eagle (near Castle Island), the highest summit of Sliabh Luachra.

[8] Galeóin, the Leinstermen, *Sench. M.* I. 70; *cf.* rige Coicid Galían, *LU.* (?). They possessed at one time the Orkneys, *Nennius*, 50.

[9] Burgage Moat, Co. Carlow; dind, .i. dún, *Stokes' Bodl. Cormac*, 16.

[10] A powerful race—slew Lugaid, K. of Ireland, A.D. 79, and Cathair Mór, A.D. 122 (*Tigernach*). They occupied the land from Glasnevin into Cavan, gave their name to (the baronies of) Lune and Morgalian in Meath, and to (the baronies of) Leyney in Sligo and Gallen in Mayo, *Cambrensis Eversus*, I. 471.

17. Is and-si*n* ra-co*m*arleiced co*m*airle ac Eochu m*acc* Luc*hta* 7 ac clannaib Dedad, .i. "Cach beó da aissec 7 cac*h* aissec da beó; imdenam a chríchi 7 a ḟerai*n*d do *Chon*chobu*r* m*acc* Ḟachtnai Ḟ*athaig*, .i. sond i*n* n-i*nad* ca*ch* suind, 7 gr*ían*an i*n* n-i*nad* ca*ch* gr*ían*a*in*; teg i*n* n-i*nad* ca*cha* tigi, bó i*n* n-i*nad* ca*cha* bó, dam i*n* n-i*nad* ca*ch* daim; et i*n* Dond Cual*ng*i fair anúas. Comleithet a aigthi do d*er*g-ór do Chonch*obur* don chur sai*n*, 7 can sluag*ed* combáge d'insaigid fer n̄Her*end*." Is and-si*n* da*no* ro-ḟessa[a] fessa 7 techta ó Eochu m*acc* Lucta, co Ail*ill* 7 co Meidb risi*n* comaid si*n*. Docuas do Ail*ill* 7 do M*eidb* aní si*n*. "Ro-gabtha gó-lá*m* dontí o tuctha na comairli si*n*. Uair i*n* n-airet bes ocai*nn*i nech ris ba heiti*r* erdorn claidib 7 sciathrach scéith do gab*áil* fó brágit, ní raga dó-sum i*n* cho*ma* sai*n*." "Nad orgena*m*ar-ni ḟort-su in chomairli si*n*, a merddrech út!" bar Ail*ill*. "Dáig ni*m*mó ar cuit-ni dá ícc sai*n* anda cuit ce*ch* ḟir do chethri oll-choice*daib* Her*end* do neoch ra-búi *for* sluagud Tana Bó Cual*ngi*." "Atfua limsa ón," bar M*edb*.

18. "Cia doragad risin techtairecht sai*n*?" bar Ail*ill*. "Cia?"
174 *a* ar Medb, "*acht* Dorn Ibair h*ua* Cipp Goba*n*d, | 7 Fadb Darach h*ua* O*m*na." Mebais a ḟáitbiud gáire f*or* Fergus. "Cid dob*e*[*i*]r th' orḟáiltius?"[b] bar Ail*ill*. "Fail a mor-abba da*m*-sa sai*n*," bar F*er*gus.

[a] *Perhaps we should read* fáitti fessa, fáitte fessa, *as* §§ 7, 8.

---

[1] Lit., "was allowed," = (Anglo-Irish) it was agreed on.

[2] They lived near Luachair Dedad, or Slieve Logher, near Castleisland, Kerry. Cf. *Joyce's Keating*, 166.

[3] Lit., doing up, border (?), gl. *limbus*.

[4] co cloidmib ocus sonnaib, cum gladiis et fustibus (*LB.* 72 bb) *Matt.* xxv. 55. .i. cuaille no tadbhán, a pole, *O'Clery*; sunn-chaistel, a bawned castle, *O'Cl.*; sondach, a palisade, *LU.* 236, *Siab. Ch. Con Chulaind*, p. 386, *Fled Bricr.*, p. 73.

[5] A summer house, .i. temair in tige, *Cormac*.

[6] Lit., on it from above; the Brown Bull of Cooley was dead at this time, but the South-Munstermen did not know it.

[7] Or falseness of hands; it seems to mean he made a false or unworthy retreat, cf. *W. v.* lám; gabail láma, to drive back.

17. It is then that a resolution was agreed[1] upon by Eochu son of Luchta and by the Clanna Dedad,[2] namely: "Every living [thing] for its payment and every payment for its living [thing], reparation[3] of his territory and of his land to Conchobar son of Fachtna Fathach, namely, a palisade[4] in the place of every palisade, and a grianán[5] in the place of every grianán, a house in the place of every house, a cow in the place of every cow, a bull in the place of every bull, and the Dond Cualnge over and above;[6] the equal-breadth of his face of red gold to Conchobar for that turn, and no expedition of hostility against the men of Eriu." It is then too that tidings, intelligencers, and messengers were sent from Eochu son of Luchta to Ailill and to Medb with that proposal. That thing was related to Ailill and to Medb. [Medb said] "A false hand was taken by him[7] from whom those counsels were brought. For so long as there shall be among us one to whom it will be possible to take the hilt of a sword and the shield-strap[8] of a shield about his neck, that proposal shall not go to him."[9] "We have not urged on[10] thee that counsel, thou bad woman,"[11] said Ailill. "For not greater is our share of that payment than the share of every man of the four great provinces of Hériu who was on the expedition of the Táin Bó Cualnge." "Thou art good as to that in my opinion,"[12] said Medb.

18. "Who should go on that embassy?" said Ailill. "Who," said Medb, "but Dorn Ibair, grandson of Cepp Goba, and Fadb Darach, grandson of Omna?" His chuckle of laughter broke out on Fergus. "What causes thy loud mirth"? said Ailill. "I have good reason for that," said Fergus, "the man that is the greatest enemy to

[b] = th-forfáiltius, *cf.* forfáilid, joyful, *in B. of Armagh*.

---

[8] sciath-rach is clearly here the thing by which the shield was held and carried "about the neck"; *cf.* cum-rech; s. = strap or trappings of a shield, *Man. and Cust.* III. 162. II. 331; it was sometimes mounted with (if not made of) silver, "s. argit," *LU.* 129; *dp.* (neuter?) sciathragaib, *LB.* 217 a.

[9] Medb calls Conor (her former husband) "him," "the man," § 22.

[10] Proposed, prepared, orgénamar here and § 33; "ni argensat," they did not prepare, *LU.* 58; "irgnam, urgnam," preparing, cooked, §§ 23, 24, from (urgníu); *cf.* forgea, forraig, forrgithir, press, hurt, *LU.* 71 a; *LL.* 205 b; 193 b (?).

[11] Lit., harlot; but Ailill would hardly say that to Medb in public, though her conduct was rather light; Chulaind called the ladies of Ulster "merdrecha," *LU.* 43.

[12] Or lit., I deem thee under him (fua) as to that, or I think thee good (fua) in that. She appears to agree with his view.

"Duni is mó is bídba d'Ultaib bar-sin bith[a] do Meidb d'a saigid. Uair cen co dernad d'ulc riam *nó* iara*m* friu, *acht* mad Mend *macc* Salcholgan do goi*n* bar renaib na Bói*n*ne, ropad lór d'ulc dó; 7 cid ed," bar Fergus, "ní hecal dó ní don chur-sa 7 teiged-*sum* and. Dáig nit feltaig airecta i*n* luct sai*n*." Is and-si*n* tancatar-sum ro*m*pu co Temraig.

19. Is and-si*n* falluid Find *macc* Rosa rí coicid lámdeirg Lagen co cla*n*naib Deirg i*m*mi-siu*m* co Temraig fathúaid co airm ir-rabi a brathair Carp*re* Nia Fer. Et atchúas dóib na comada sai*n*. Et racomarleiced accu cia doragad risi*n* tectairecht sai*n*. Iss-*ed* ro-raidsetar-*sum* co *m*bad é Fidach Ferggach Feda Gaible; dáig fer fathach fíamach fír-glicc é. Is and ra-lotar-*sum* rempu fathúaith co airm i *m*bái *Conchobor*, 7 ro-i*n*nisetar-*sum* dó na coma sai*n*, .i. "Cach beo d'a assec 7 ca*ch* assec d'a beó; i*m*dénam a chríchi 7 a ḟerai*n*d do *Chonchobur* *macc* F*achtnai*; 7 sond i*n* n-i*n*ad ca*ch* ṡui*n*d, 7 grianán i*n* n-i*n*ad ca*ch* grian*áin*, teg i*n* n-i*n*ad ca*ch* thigi, bó i*n* n-i*n*ad ca*cha* bó, da*m* i*n* n-i*n*ad ca*ch* dai*m*, 7 i*n* Dond Cual*ngi* ḟair anúas; co*m*leithet a aigthi do d*er*g-ór do *Chonchobur*; 7 can sl*uaged* co*m*báige d'i*n*saigid fer ṅHer*end* do'n chur-sa." Amlaid bái *Conchobor* cá n-acall*aim* 7 atb*ert* na bria*thra*:—

[Concobor.] "Canas tancatar na techta
sund do chéi*n*?
I*n* slai*n*nid da*m*-sa bar n-echtra,
in da*m*' réir?"
[Tecta.] "Tancamar ó'n Chruachai*n* chróda
na*ch* bec blad,
cucut-su a Chonch*obuir* chóra,
crúaid do gal.

[a] *Ellipsis of* da ḟaidiud, to be sent (?).

[1] *Cf.* Colcu g. Colgen, *Adamnan*; Mend m. Salchadæ, *LU.* 101 a.

[2] rén, gl. *torrens*, *Ml.* 134 b; rian muir réisi (sea, span), *O'Cl.*

[3] Lit., not fear to him is a thing on this turn, i.e. there is no danger. Note the inviolability of heralds.

the Ulaid in the world [to be sent] by Medb to go to them! For had he not done any wrong before or after to them, except to wound mortally Mend son of Salcholcu[1] on the waterways[2] of the Bóand, it would be enough of wrong for him. And though it be so," said Fergus, "he need not fear[3] for this time, and let him go thither. For the assemblies of that people are not treacherous." It is then that these proceeded to Temair.[4]

19. It is then that Find son of Ros, King of the redhanded province of Lagin, went with the clans of Derg about him to Temair northwards, to the place where his brother Cairpre Nia Fer was. And those offers were made known to them. And it was debated by them, who should go with that message.[5] It is this that they decided, that it was Fidach Ferggach of Fid Gaible;[6] for he was a wise, modest, truly prudent man. It is then that these proceeded northward to the place in which Conchobar was; and they told him those proposals, namely: "Every living [thing] for its payment, and every payment for its living [thing]. Reparation of his territory and of his land to Conchobor son of Fachtna; and a wall in the place of every wall, and a grianán in the place of every grianán, a house in the place of every house, a cow in the place of every cow, a bull in the place of every bull, and the Dond Cualnge over and above; the equal breadth of his face of red gold to Conchobar; and no expedition of hostility against the men of Eriu for this time." Thus was Conchobar addressing them, and he spoke the words:—

[*Conor.*] "Whence have come the envoys
hither from afar?
do you signify to me your adventures?
is it to do me homage?"
[*Envoys.*] "We have come from valorous Cruachu,
which is not little in fame,
to thee, just Conchobar,
stern thy valour;

---

[4] To join the Leinster envoys on their way to Ulster.

[5] On that embassy.

[6] Of Feeguile, parish of Clonsast, barony of *Coolestown*, King's Co., *L. na gCeart*, p. 214; *LL.* fol. 112 a. Gabal was the name of the river, and it is now called Fidh Gaible.

Tancamar ra himluad n-athisc
dait, a rí,
a Meidb is a Ailill amra,
calma a crí."
[Concobor.] "Slainnid dam bar n-athisc n-amra [*sic*],
nach bec blad,
a cheithern ro-gasta ra-glan,
cipé chan." C.

20. "Atbiur-sa brethir ám," bar *Conchobor*, "*con*nach geb-sa comaid dib-*side*, na[a] co raib *inad* mo phupla cacha cóicid i *n*-Herind feib ro-ṡaidset-*sum* a pupla, a *m*botha 7 a *m*bélscál*dna*." "Maith a Chonch*obuir*," bar iat-*sum*, "cáit i ṅgabai-siu sossad 7 mór-longphort *in*nocht?" "Ir-Ros na Ríg ás Bóind ban-ṡolus," bar *Conchobor*. Dáig nír-cheil *Conchobor* ria*m* bar a namait bail i ṅgebad sosad *nó* long*phort*; *con*na hap*r*aitís *con*bad[b] ecla *nó* uamun dob*er*ad fair can a rád.

21. Is and-si*n* ro-lotar-*sum* rempu co Temraig ḟades co hairm i mbái Carpr*e* Nia F*er* 7 Find m*acc* Ros*a*; et batnoathar dóib na scéla
174 *b* sai*n*. | "Maith and,"[c] bar Carpr*e* N*ia* F*er*, "mad cucai*n*ni dob*era* *Conchobor* 7 Ul*aid* a n-agid, ticed Ail*i*ll 7 Medb 'n-ar furtact-ni 7 'n-ar forithi*n*. Mad sechoi*n*d digset i coiced cend-ḟind *Con*nacht, ragmait-ni 'n-a ḟurtacht-*sum* 7 na forithin."

22. Is and-si*n* da*no* ra-lotar na techta si*n* rompo co airm i *m*bái Ailill 7 M*edb*. Et anuair rancatar, ro-gab Medb ac iarfaigid sél díb. Is aml*aid* ra-buí 'ca rád 7 atb*er*t na bria*thra*:—

["Can

[a] noco? *Cf.* atbert-sum na gebad coma for biṫ ón ríg aċt caṫ.—*C. M. Rath*, 42.

---

[1] athesc, a speech, words, *LB*. 206 b; *Tl.* 172, 244.

[2] crí; *cf.* hi colla crí, in carnal shapes, *F. Masters*, an. 926; i g-cri, in life (*Circuit of Ireland*, l. 244); body, *S. na Rann*, p. 132, 116, "i crí ria n-éc"; and *MS. Mater*. 512; *LL*. 307 a; *Félire*.

[3] *Cf.* "your distinguished orders" of tradesmen's circulars.

[4] Lit., of; *or* till all the provinces of Eirin have been a place for my tent.

[5] bélscálána, *np*. bélscaláin, §§ 23, 24: botha agus bélscalána, *F. Masters*, III.

We have come to move a proposal,[1]
to thee, O King!
from Medb and from noble Ailill,
brave their form."[2]
[*Conor.*] "Name to me your noble request[3]
whose fame is not small,
most sprightly handsome warrior-band,
whencesoever it be." Whence . . .

20. "I give my word, indeed," said Conchobar, "that I will not take terms from you, till there has been the place of my pavilion in[4] every province in Hériu, as they have set up their tents, their booths, and their huts."[5]

"Good, O Conchobar," said they, "where mayest thou take halt and encampment to-night?" "In Ros na Ríg above the clear-bright Bóind," said Conchobar. For Conchobar concealed not ever from his enemy the place in which he would take station or camp, that they might not say that it was fear or dread that caused him not to say it.[6]

21. It is then that these proceeded to Tara southward to the place where were Cairpre Nia Fer and Find son of Ros; and those tidings were announced[7] to them. "Good, then," said Cairpre Nia Fer, "if it is towards us that Conchobar and the Ulaid will turn their face, let Ailill and Medb come to our aid and to our help. If it is past us that they will go into the fair-headed province of Connacht, we will go to their aid and to their help."

22. So it is then that the envoys proceeded to the place where Ailill and Medb were. And when they arrived, Medb began to ask tidings[8] from them. It is thus she was saying it, and she spoke the words:—

["Whence

[b] *combad recte.* [c] maith ám, generally.

311; botha ocus bélscalána, *LL.* 57 a; sgáthláin, sheds, *C. M. Lena*, 76, 78; scálán, penthouse, scaffold, *O'Begley's Eng.-Ir. Dict.*

[6] A very foolish thing. He found the Leinstermen there before him, and was not able to attempt to dislodge them.

[7] A sing. verb with a plur. nominative; perhaps we should read "batnoathatar," they declared. *Cf.* condnoathatar, § 8.

[8] "sél" I take to be a scribal error for "scél."

"Can tecait na techta?
slai*n*nid da*m* far slecta
co Conchobor Cairn;[a]
i*n* n-ana*nd* in Emai*n*,
i*n* flaith cusna fledaib?
nó i*n* n-ed tic do debaid
i *n*degaid a tairb?"
"Nocho n-anat Ulaid
nocho chert na cubaid
damait dairecht Breg
ni ba crecha gairdi
na co roisset fairggi
na *co* *n*d*er*nat airgni
far Carpr*e* Nia Fer."
"Beit i *n*-a rith romai*n*d
ticfat a[b] cind da colai*n*d
mad da tí a thig
biat-sa sund i *m*balib
can locht is can anim
dáig is lór lim Lagin
i *n*-agid ind fir."
"Da torset m*eic*c Mag*ach*[c]
i*n* sluag brotla bágach,
bud crod*er*g al-lamach
i cath Ruiss na Ríg."

[a] i.e. of Armagh; cf. ó flaith Macha . . . ó iarlà in chairn, *B. of Fenagh*, 366. Cf. a Chongail Mullaig Macha, *B. of M. Rath*, 172.

[b] Line one syl. too long—omit this *a*.

[c] "Ni amlaid sin ba-sa, ar Ailill. . . . Tanac-sa dano. Gabsus ríg i sundi tunachus mo máthar; dáig ar bith *Máta Murisc ingen Magach* mo

---

[1] Or tell me (of) your tracks or journey; slecta = accounts (*C. M. Lena*, XXII.; *Hyfiachr.* 334) or facts (*Adamnan*, p. 268); *n.* slicht, *g.* slechta.

[2] (1°) Either "Cairn na foraire ar Sliab Fuaid" (*LU.* 78 a b), which was near Newtownhamilton, and guarded the pass to Conor's palace of Emain. Conor's son, Cormac, is called "nia an Chairn" (*H.* 3, 18, p. 594). Or (2°) it was the cairn of Armagh; *cf.* "A Chongail Mullaig Macha," *C. M. Rath*, 172.

[3] The banqueting prince; Medb, his divorced wife, seems to hint that he was fitter for the banquet-hall than for the battle-field.

[*Medb.*] "Whence come the envoys?
Tell me of your journey[1]
to Conchobor of Carn;[2]
waits he in Emain,
the chief of the banquets?[3]
or is it that he comes for strife
after their[4] bull?"

[*Envoy.*] "The Ulaid wait not:
it was not right or fitting,
they resolve[5] to watch the Bregians;
the plunders will not be slight,
until they reach the sea,
until they work ravages,
on Cairpre Nia Fer."

[*Medb.*] "They shall be running before us,
their heads shall come from their bodies[6]
if he come from home.
I shall be here in my homesteads,
without fault and without disgrace:
for I think the Lagin enough
against the man."

[*Envoy.*] "If the sons of Magach should come[7]
the bold, warlike band,
their shooting will be gory-red
in the battle of Ros na Ríg."

mathair."—*LL.* 54 a. "Urthatar techta aile co maccaib magach .i. Cet macc Ma*gach*, 7 Anlúan macc Ma*gach*, 7 Macc Corb macc Ma*gach*, 7 Bascell macc Ma*gach*, 7 En m̃acc Dóche maicc, (7) Scandal macc Ma*gach*" (Qu. read En m̃acc Magach, Dóche macc Magach?); Ailill, Anluan, Moccorb, Cet, En, Bascall, Dóche, *LU.* fo. 45.

---

[4] Perhaps we should read "a thairb," his bull.

[5] "damait," they suffer, yield, consent. Or "it is not justice (and it is not proper) that they concede to the assembly of the Bregians." *Cf.* daimh, .i. deoin, consent. I think it means here they "allow," resolve; *cf.* "comairleiced," comairliced, §§ 2, 17, 19, and my previous note on that word.

[6] Lit. body.

[7] These Connacht warriors were Cét, Anlúan, Mog-Corb, Bascell, En, Dóche, and Scandal (*see note to text*), Anfinn and Fergal, *Ogygia*, 269.

"Da tora rí Macha,
saifiter a datha,
claifiter a ratha,
tairnfithir a bríg."
"Da torset ar sluag-ni,
tinólfaider uanni,
bid condalb in cúani
i fir-catha can." C.

23. Imthúsa *Conchobuir*, tanic-*side* reme dírrám slóig móir co Accaill Breg 7 co sligid m̄Breg. And barrecaim *Ailill* flath-briugaid do-sum and. "Maith and a *Chonchobuir*," bar Ailill. "Cid in dirram slóig móir ro-fail i tegaid, 7 cid ass áil latt dol?" "Cor-Ross na Ríg ás Bóind ban-ṡolus and-so," bar *Conchobor*. "Noco glinnigthi duit-siu sain," ale bar Ailill, "*acht* is foen glinni. Daig ro-n-fuilet in Galían 7 Luaigne na Temrach and-sain bar do chind." "Geiss dam-sa dola dom' chonair," ale bar *Conchobor*, "et geiss dam dola i cath cach lín. Gabar sosad 7 longport acainn and-so fodectsa," bar *Conchobor*. "Sáitter ar sosta and-so 7 suidigter ar pupla. Gníter ar m̄botha 7 ar m̄bélscaláin. Dentar irgnam bíd 7 lenna. Dentar praind 7 tomaltus. Cantar ciúil 7 airfiti 7 admolta acaind and."

24. Is and ro-saittea a sosta 7 ro-suidigthea a pupla, ro-gnithea a mbotha 7 a m̄bélscáldin, ra-ataithé a tenti; dorin̄gned urgnam bíd 7 lenna. Doronait gretha glanḟothraicthi leo, 7 ro-slemun-chirtha a fuilt,

---

[1] "condalb"—*cf.* condalb sain, condelg n-ága; tanic ell condailbé im Ultaib do, *LL.* 57 b; or it is = condailbe, friendship, *O'R.* and *W.* "condalb" is not in the gloss. or dictionaries. With "cuani" *cf. ds.* "cuaine," breed (*Hyfiachr.* 93); cuana .i. buidne, *O'Cl.*; cuanene, .i. *pugil*, *Z.* (Cf. *éistid*, Stanza 20 of *Fair of Carman.*)

[2] "Can" is the first word of this poetry, which would go very well to the tune of "Go where glory waits thee," but it "sweeter far might be" to the envoys if Medb went with them. She brought the Leinstermen into this war, and then abandoned them and her brothers-in-law.

[3] I take Accall to be the highest point of Slieve Bree, about seven miles due north of Rosnaree, and Slige Breg to be the road there passing Sliab Breg. Conor was not at Accall (or Skreen), "near Tara," so called to distinguish it from other places of the same name. To get near Tara he had to fight a battle on the Boyne.

[*Medb.*] "If the king of Macha come,
his colours will be turned back,
his fortunes will be overcome,
his might will be lowered."
[*Envoy.*] "If our bands arrive,
a muster will be made by us,
there will be a rivalry of the fighting band[1]
for the real combats." Whence.[2]

23. To return to Conchobar—he came on [with] the multitude of a great army to Accall Breg and to Slige Breg.[3] There Ailill, a princely yeoman,[4] met him then. "Good then, Conchobar," said Ailill, "what is the vast number of a great army that is behind thee? and where is it your pleasure to go?" "To Ros na Ríg above the clear-bright[5] Bóand here," said Conchobar. "That [place] is not to be secured[6] for thee," replied Ailill, "but it is insecure.[7] For the Galían and the Luaigne[8] of Temair are there before thee." "It is an obligation to me to go my way," replied Conchobar. "And it is an obligation to me to go into the battle of every number.[9] Let a position and encampment be taken by us here for the present," said Conchobar. "Let our stations be pitched here, and let our tents be erected. Let our booths and our tents be constructed. Let preparation of food and drink be made. Let dinner and victuals be made. Let tunes and merry songs and eulogies be sung by us here."

24. Then were their positions fixed and their pavilions were pitched, their huts and their tents were made. Their fires were kindled, cooking of food and drink was made; baths of clean-bathing

---

[4] Large landholder; *nom. sg.* ríg briuga, *LL.* 160 b.

[5] "Os Bóind báin."—O'Hartigan's Poem in *LL.* "The clear, joyous river ran sparkling."—(*Smiles*, in account of the Battle of the Boyne). "Sons of the strong, stern race that forced the ford through Boyne's *dun* water."—(A poet, Mr. Austin, in a Sonnet to the Ulster Loyalists, *National Review* of August, 1892.)

[6] The past participle or *part. necessitatis* of "glinnigim"; glinn, stronghold, *O'Cl.*; glinni, securities, *Mesca Ul.* 4.

[7] A weak security; glinne, secure, *O'Don. Suppl.* Foenglinni is the name of a man in *Mesca Ul.* 40. *Cf.* the earth was void, *faon*, Gen. i. 2.

[8] The men of Leinster and Meath.

[9] However numerous the enemy; but he did not do so afterwards, he prudently waited and waited for all his troops to come into the field.

ra-min-glanta a cuirp, ro-caithed *praind* 7 to*m*altus leo. Et ro-canait ciúil 7 airfitid 7 admolta leo.[a]

25. "Maith and-si*n* a Ultu," bar *Conchobor*, "i*n* fagu*m* acaib nech dig do midem 7 do mór-descai*n* bar i*n* slúag?" "Ragat-sa," bar Féic ma*cc* Follomui*n* me*icc* Factna Fathaig. Is and-si*n* luid remi Féic ma*cc* Foll*omuin* me*icc* *Factna* F*athaig*; cor-ránic co Di*nn* na Bói*nn*e bán-ṡoilsi. Ar-sai*n* ro-gab ac midem 7 ac mór-descai*n* ar i*n* slúag. Et cessis a menma cu mór f*or*thu-*sum* no. "Ragat-sa fathu-áid i*n*nossa," bar Féic, "co hairm i failet Ul*aid*; 7 i*n*niasat dóib i*n* sluag do bith ico*m* fuatecht-sa. Ticfait Ul*aid* atúaid. Gébaid cach a lathir catha 7 co*m*lai*n*d 7 co*m*raic dib. Ni ba mó a nós na allud na erdarcus da*m*-sa i*n* chathaigthe ass-a aithle anda do ce*ch* oen ḟir d'Ultaib. Et cid da*m*-sa na curfi*n*d mo chomlund a chetóir ro*m*um?" Et ralluid-sium reme i*n*nu*n*d dar i*n*ber na Bói*nn*e. Et tuc bleith mulind tuathbil[b] f*or*thu. Tuc a n-airthiur f*or* a n-iarthur 7 a ndesciurt f*or* a tuasciurt; 7 ro-gairset i*n* slúag i *n*-oen-ḟecht i*m*mi-siu*m*. Et ni forulṅgither dó-su*m* beith i cind i*n* tslóig ro-móir; 7 tanic-sium ro*m*i d'i*nn*aigid i*nn* i*n*b*ir* dar a tanic i*n*nu*n*d. Et ní hed barroeblaṅgair do-*sum* it*ir* ón; *acht* ra-lingestar sæb-léi*m* i-si*n* ṁBoi*n*d ṁban-ṡol*uis*. Mar a bói i*n*ber bud do*m*ni a cheili ar a Bói*n*d[c] ro-li*n*gestar sǽb-léi*m* and co ro-thib tond tairis. Co ro-báded 'si*n* li*n*d si*n* can a*n*mai*n* et*ir*. Corop búan 7 corop marthanach d'a éis a i*n*nchomartha. Corop Li*n*d Féic[d] ai*n*m na li*nn*i ir-ro-báded.

[a] Cf. the *fulachta* before the battle of Moylena, *C.M. Lena*, 76.

[b] Is amlaid atad na catha go hanordaigithe 7 bleith muilinn tuaithfil orra, *Cog. G. 7 G.*, p. 198.

[c] Arabóind (*MS.*), *for* ar Boind *or* ar abaind. *Cf.* rostib tond, *LL.* 165 a.

[d] Perhaps it is the same as Linn Rois, on the Boyne. (See Index to *Four Masters*.)

---

[1] Commanding hill, either Knowth or New Grange; the former faces Rosnaree, and commands a fine view of it. *Cf.* tilach airechais ocus tigernais hErend .i. Temair, *Sick Bed of Cu*, 384.

[2] "cessis," §§ 25, 26, "nír cheiss," § 27; and "rosceastar," § 12; also "cessis a menna fair," *LL.* 70 a; "ac céssacht formsa," reproaching me, *Hogan's Irish Phrase-book*," p. 117; roba ceasachtach air, he grumbled at it, *C. M. Lena*, 64. The word means to suffer, *Z;* also to torment, afflict, Matt. viii. 29.

[3] fuadaigh, = put to flight, drive, force away, *Coney's Dict.*

[4] Lit., its.

[5] "inber," in §§ 25, 26, is *the river at Rosnaree*, which is not affected by the tides, and cannot be called a river-mouth or estuary at ten miles from the sea.

were made by them, and their hair was smooth-combed; their persons were minutely cleansed, supper and victuals were eaten by them; and tunes and merry songs and eulogies were sung by them.

25. "Good then, Ulaid," said Conchobar, "do we find among you one who will go to estimate and to reconnoitre the army?" "I will go," said Féic, son of Follomon, son of Fachtna Fathach. It is then that Féic, son of Follomon, son of Fachtna Fathach, went on till he reached the Fortress of the clear-bright Bóand.[1] Thereupon he began measuring and reconnoitring the army. And his spirit chafed[2] greatly about them. "I will go northward now," said Féic, "to the place in which the Ulaid are, and I will tell them that the army is driving me away?[3] The Ulaid will come from the north. Each of them will take up his station of battle and conflict and combat. The[4] glory and the honour and the distinction of the fighting will be no greater for me afterwards than for every single man of the Ulaid. And what is there for me that I should not engage my combat at once straight away?" And he went on over across the river[5] of the Bóand. And gave the grind of a left-handed mill on them.[6] Their van caught (or closed on) their rear, and their right wing (joined) their left,[7] and the army shouted at once around him. And it was not endured [dared] by him to be against the huge army, and he came on towards the river over which he had come across. And it is not that it was leaped by him at all, but he leapt a false leap into the clear-bright Bóand. Where was the water that was deeper than elsewhere, he leaped a false leap there, so that a wave laughed over him, and that he was drowned in that pool without life at all. And lasting and longlived after him was the memorial of it, for Féic's Pool[8] was the name of the pool in which he was drowned.

---

[6] i.e. he went around them in a wrong direction, lost his way, or, rather, ran amuck. Cf. "They are disorganized all round like the grindings of a mill turning the wrong way" (ocus bleith muilinn tuaithfil orra), *Cog. G.*, p. 198; "for tuaithbell," lefthand-wise, *L. na gCeart*, pp. 2, 12, *LL.* 114 b.

[7] *Or* "he bore (drove) their right wing in on their left, and their rear on their van" (!). An Irish soldier in the Peninsular War strayed from his quarters, and got drunk. To escape being shot by Wellington's orders, he brought French prisoners to the English camp, and, when asked how he managed to disarm them, he said—"I surrounded them." If the phrase be connected with what goes before, I fancy it means, "he took their east for their west, and their south for their north."

[8] Lind Féicc, *g.* Lind find Féic na fian, O'Hartigan's Poem in *LL.*

26. Rop i*m*gen ra *Con*chob*or* 7 ra Ult*u* ro-bói i*n* fer sai*n* 'n-a écmais. "Maith ém a Ultu," bar *Con*chob*or*, "i*n* fagai*m*-se acaib nech dig do midem 7 do mór-descai*n* da*m* bar i*n* slúag si*n*?" "Ragat-sa and," bar Daigi m*acc* Dega de Ul*taib*. Et ra-luid re*me* co*n*nici i*n* tulaig tig*er*nais cétna as ur na Boi*n*ne bán-ṡolsi. Ro-gab ac midem 7 ac mor-desci*n* i*n* tṡloig; 7 cessis a me*n*ma 7 a aicned 7 a i*n*nithim for thu fon cu*m*ma cetna. Ra-bái 'ca rád na cétna: "Ragat-sa fathuaíd ám," bar é-siu*m*, "7 i*n*niasat d'Ultaib na slúaig do bith ico*m* 'uáitecht út. Dorosset Ul*aid* atuáid. Gebaid cách a lathir catha 7 co*m*l*aind* 7 co*m*raic; 7 ni ba mó a nós na allud na irdarcus dam-sa i*n* chathaigthe anda do cech oen fir díb-siu*m*. Et ragat-sa d'i*n*naigid i*n* tṡlóig co ro-churiur mo cho*m*lond ro*m*om." Is and-si*n* dolluid-siu*m* dar i*n*ber na Boi*n*ne i*n*nund; 7 ro-mesc bar i*n* sluág é. Et ra-theigsetar na slúaig i*m*mi-siu*m* do dib lethib no; 7 bogníthа gui*n* gal[*ann*][a] de; co tor*chair* accu.

27. Ba i*m*gén ám ra *Con*chob*or* ro-batar sai*n*. "Maith ám a Irgalaig m*eicc* M*ac*claig m*eicc* *Con*gaile m*eicc* Rud*raig*e, i*n* n-abbrai cia as chóir do thechta do midem 7 do mor-desci*n* bar i*n* slúag?" "Cia doragad and," ale bar Irgal*ach*, "*acht* mad Iriel gascedach glunmar m*acc* *Con*aill *Chernaig*? Acht is *Con*all ar choscor é. Is *Cú Chulaind* ar chlessa*m*nacht. Is Cathb*ad* drúi deg-a*m*ra ar chéill 7 ar chomairle. Is Sencha m*acc* Ail*el*la ar síd 7 ar ṡo-b*er*la. Is Celtchair m*acc* Uth*echair* ar chalmacht. Is *Con*chob*or* m*acc* F*achtna* F*athaig* ar rígdacht 7 ar rosc-lethni, ar thinlucun sét 7 mái*n*i 7 i*n*mass. Cia doragad *acht* mad Iriel?" "Ragat-sa and," ale bar Iriel.

Is and luid Iriel reme co*n*nici i*n* taulaig tig*er*nais cétna ós ur na Bói*n*ne ban-ṡolsi. Gab ac mide*m* 7 ac mór-desci*n* i*n* tṡloig. Nir-cheiss

[a] gal- *in MS.* "Doronsat guin galann de," &c., *C. M. Lena*, 142; *LL.* 258 a.

---

[1] A great fact or wonder (?), imgen, § 26; imgén, § 27, for imchian.

[2] The meaning seems to be that he rushed blindly at them. Our native translators "get mixed" in attacking this phrase. It here means lit., "he plunged into the army." It is found in *LL.* 54 ab, "ro mesc in Badb forsin t-slóg; mescfid a ṡíl for Eirinn," "his seed shall *prevail* over E.," *C. M. Lena*, 152; mescthair ar cond, that confuses our senses, *Sick Bed of Cu*, 383; rasmescsat iat ar in t-ṡlúag, they mixed themselves through the host; ra cumasc for in sluag, he wrought confusion on the host, *Mescz Ulad*, 30, 32. It seems the idiom "cumaisg

26. It seemed very long[1] to Conchobar that that man was absent. "Good truly, Ulaid," said Conchobar, "do I find among you one who will go to estimate and to reconnoitre that army?" "I will go," said Daigi son of Daig of the Ulaid. And he went forward to the same hill of command, above the brink of the clear-bright Bóand. He began measuring and reconnoitring the army. And his spirit and his nature and his mind chafed about them in the same way, and he was saying the same [things]: "I will go northward indeed," said he, "and I will tell to the Ulaid that the armies are pursuing me yonder. The Ulaid will arrive from the north. Each of them will take up his station of battle and of conflict and of combat; and the glory and the honour and the distinction of the fighting will be no greater for me than for every single man of them. And I will go against the army, that I may put my combat before." It is then that he went over the river of the Bóand across, and he rushed rashly on the army.[2] And the hosts came around him on both sides also,[3] and a wound of lances[4] was made of him, so that he fell by them.

27. It seemed long indeed to Conchobar that these [two] were [absent]. "Good indeed, Irgalach, son of Macclach, son of Congal, son of Rudraige, sayest thou who is proper to go to estimate and to reconnoitre the army?" "Who should go there," replied Irgalach, "but Iriel, good at arms, great kneed, son of Conall Cernach. But he is a Conall for havoc, he is a Cú Chulaind for dexterity of feats. He is a Cathbad, the right-wonderful druid, for intelligence and for counsel, he is a Sencha son of Ailill for peace and for good speech, he is a Celtchair son of Uthechar for valour, he is a Conchobar son of Fachtna Fathach for kingliness and for wide-eyedness,[5] for giving of treasures and of wealth and of riches. Who should go except it be Iriel?" "I will go there," replied Iriel. It is then that Iriel went forward to the same dominating hill, over the brink of the clear-bright Bóand. He began measuring and reconnoitring the

---

ael air," mix lime with it, *Hogan's Irish Phrase-book*, p. 119. Lit. plunged: "mescaid in claideb and," he plunges, *Tl.* 70; "mescthus isin duiblinn fsin," *LU.* 95 a; "mescaís a chuaranu and," *LB.* 213 b; "romeasc cách ar dán a chéile," *MS. Mater.* 46; measgas iad féin air (*i.e.* muir or saogal), *Three Shafts*, 262.

[3] "No," too, indeed (seven times in our text), = dino, dono; not in *W.*

[4] guin gal[*ann*]. *Cf.* doronsat guin galann de, "they made a victim of lances nd spears of him," *C. M. Lena*, 142; *galan* appears in our modern texts.

[5] Breadth of view (?).

a m*en*ma na aicned na i*n*nithim *for*thu-*sum* it*ir*. Atetha a tuarascbáil leiss co hairm i *m*bái *Conchobor*.

28. "Cinnas, a m' an*am* a Iriel"? bar Conchobor. "Atdiur-sa brethir ám," bar Iriel, "dar lim-sa na fail áth *for* abai*n*d na lia *for* tilaig na chend-róit na sliged bar crig Breg *nó* Mide nach lán d'á ṅgr*a*igib 7 d'a ṅgill*aib*. Andar lim at lassar rígthigi di leirgg a tlachtga 7 a n-errid 7 a n-éttaid," bar Iriel.

Ro-ráid *Conchobor*:—

29. "In fir an atfiadat na fir,
a Iriel galaig glun-gil!
teora catha *for* clár chliu
ar ar ci*n*d i co*m*naidiu?"
"Atát i ceilg ar do chind
issin ross i*m*theit Boi*n*d;
teora catha Clai*n*ne Deirg,—
lassait mar lassair dar leirg.
"Na techta dachuatar úan
d'a ḟis ca lín atá i*n* sluág,
ni thicfat sund,—miad nar lac;
is e a ḟír a n-arfiadat." In.

30. "Maith a Ultu," bar *Conchobor*, "cade far co*m*airle dún in cath-sa lind?" "Is i ar co*m*airle," ar Ulaid, "anad co tisat ar treói*n* 7 ar tóisig 7 ar tig*er*nmais 7 ar fulṅgidi catha." Nir-bo ḟata i*n*n irnaide dóib 7 nir-bo chián[a] i*n* cho*m*naide, co faccatar t*r*i carptig d'á n-i*n*naigid. Buiden da cet déc i comair cecha carptig díb. Is iat ro-bái a*n*d-sai*n*, t*r*iar deg-æsa dána d'Ultaib, .i. Cathb*ad* drui deg-amra, et Aith*er*ni Algessach, 7 A*m*argi*n* i*n* fer dána.

[a] Or 57[2].

---

[1] sliged, *recte* slige, sligid, or sligeda; cendroit, head or end of a road (?).
[2] Hence I fancy he was at Knowth or towards Slane.
[3] A "ross" is a wooded promontory.
[4] Sons of Derg; from §§ 16, 19, 29, they were evidently the Leinstermen with their headquarters at Dinn Ríg on the Barrow. Derg was probably one of the two Dergs of Bruden da Derg or Bohernabreena, *S. Mor.* I. 46.

army. His spirit, or his mind, or his thoughts did not fret over them at all. He brings their description with him to the place in which Conchobar was.

28. "How, my life Iriel?" said Conchobar. "I give [my] word truly," said Iriel, "it seems to me that there is not ford on river, nor stone on hill, nor highways nor road[1] in the territory of Breg or Mide, that is not full of their horse-teams and of their servants. It seems to me that their apparel and their gear and their garments are the blaze of a royal house from the plain," said Iriel.

Conchobar said:

29. "Is it true, what the men declare,
O valorous white-kneed Iriel,
three battalions on the plain to the left,[2]
before us in waiting?"

[*Iriel.*] "They are in ambush before thee
in the wood that the Bóand goes round,[3]
three battalions of Clann Deirg;[4]
they blaze like fire across the plain.

"The messengers that went from us
to ascertain what strength the army is
shall not come [back] hither—an honour
that is not trivial—
it is the truth of it, what they declare."

30. "Good, O Ulaid," said Conchobar, "what is your advice to us [about] this battle of ours?" "Our advice is," said the Ulaid, "to wait till our strong men and our leaders and our commanders and our supporters of battle come." Not long was their waiting and not great was the stay, till they saw three chariot-warriors[5] approaching them, and a band of twelve hundred along with each rider of them. It is these that were there—three of the goodly men of science of the Ulaid, namely Cathbad the right-wonderful druid, and Aithemi the Importunate, and Amargin the learned doctor.[6]

---

[5] "cairptech" or "eirr" is a warrior who fights from a chariot, not an "ara" or *rhedarius*. In *LL.* 121 a. Cu Chulaind said when Lóeg was killed, "I am now charioteer as well as chariot-warrior"; culmaire, .i. cairpthech, *LU.* 109 a.

[6] "fer dána," man of science and art. Such men were also men of war, as appears from our text.

31. "Maith a ócu," bar *Conchobor*, "cade bar comairle dún?" "Is i ar c*o*mairle," ar iat-*sum*, "anad co tisat ar treoi*n* 7 ar tóisig 7 ar tig*er*nmais 7 ar fulṅgidi catha." Is and-si*n* ra-ansat. Nir-bo chián i*n* chomnaidi 7 nir' ḟata i*n*n ir*naide*, co faccatar t*r*i cairptig aile d'a n-insaigid, 7 buiden trí chet déc i comair ca*cha* carpt*ig*. Is iat tanic and-si*n*, Eogan m*acc* Dur*thacht*, et Gaine m*acc* Daurth*acht* 7 Carpr*e* m*acc* Daur*thacht*.

32. "Cade bar c*o*mairle dún, a ócu?" bar *Conchobor*. "Is í ar comairle," ar iat-su*m*, "anad co tisat ar treoi*n* 7 ar tóisig 7 ar tig*er*nmais 7 ar ful*ngidi* catha." Ro-ansat. Nir-bo chían i*n* cho*m*naidi 7 nir ḟata i*n*n ir*naide*, co fac*catar* t*r*i carp*tig* aile dá n-*in*saigid. Is iat tanic and-si*n*, tri m*eic*c Connaid Buide m*eic*c Iliach, .i. Loegaire Buadach 7 Cairell Coscarach 7 Aed Anglo*n*nach. Buiden cethri chét déc i co*m*air ca*ch* carp*tig* díb.

33. "Cade bar comairle dún a ócu?" "Is i ar c*o*mairle," ar iat-*sum*,[a] "anad co *tisat* ar treoi*n* 7 ar t[*óisig*][b] 7 ar t[*igernmais*][b] 7 ar fulngidi catha." "Nad-orgena*m*ar-ni ḟhoirb-si si*n* a ócu. Dáig atá t*r*ian slóig Ul*ad* sund, 7 ni ḟail *acht* t*r*ian slóig fer ṅHer*end* and-sút," bar *Conchobor*; "cid dun na tibri*m*mis i*n* cath?"

34. Is and-si*n* at*ra*acht *Conchobor* 7 ro-gab a chath-eirred[c] 7 comlai*n*n 7 co*m*raic i*m*me. At*ra*acht t*r*ian sloig Ul*ad* laisium no, et lotar dar inb*er* na Boi*n*ni i*n*nund. Et at*ra*ctatar na slóig aile dóib, ar ṅdul dar i*n*ber na Boi*n*ne i*n*nund. Et ro-gab cách díb ar slaide 7 ar slechtad araile, far foirtched 7 far foillged, co*n*na bái sa*m*ail Ulad ra halt na

[a] So here and 6 lines *infra;* read *cían.* [b] So 7 lines *supra.* [c] *Supply* catha.

[1] "doib," of similar phrase *supra*, is here omitted.

[2] Eogan, king of Farney, Co. of Monaghan, slew the children of Uisnech; he was father-in-law of Conall Cernach, *LU.*, p. 103 b.

[3] "nad orgenamarni," we have not served, obeyed (*cf.* fogniu, orgnam, and note at § 17); we did not suggest that to you (?).

31. "Good, O warriors," said Conchobar, "what is your advice to us?" "Our advice is," said they, "to wait till our strong men and our leaders and our lords and our supporters of battle come." It is then they waited. Not great was the[1] waiting and not long was the delay, till they saw three other riders approaching them, and a band of thirteen hundred along with each rider. It is they that came then, Eogan son of Durthacht,[2] and Gáine son of Daurthacht, and Carpre son of Daurthacht.

32. "What is your advice to us, O warriors?" said Conchobar. "Our advice is," said they, "to wait till our strong men and our leaders and our lords and our supporters of battle come." They waited. Not great was the waiting, and not long was the delay, till they saw three other chariot-fighters approaching them. It is they that came then, the three sons of Connad Buide [the Yellow], son of Iliach, namely Loegaire the Victorious, and Cairell the Havoc-worker, and Aed of the mighty deeds. A band of fourteen hundred along with each rider of them.

33. "What is your advice to us, O warriors?" "Our advice is," said they, "to wait till our strong men and our leaders and our lords and our supporters of battle come." "We have not prepared that for you,[3] O warriors. For there is a third of the army of the Ulaid here, and there is not but a third of the army of the men of Eriu yonder," said Conchobar. "What is there for us[4] that we should not give the battle?"

34. It is then that Conchobar rose and took his battle-gear [of battle] and of conflict and of combat about him. A third of the army of the Ulaid rose with him too. And they went over the river of the Bóand across. And the other armies arose to them on going over the water of the Bóand across. And each of them took to hacking and to cutting down the other, to destroying[5] and to wounding[5] till there was no similitude of the Ulaid at that juncture of time, except

---

[4] i.e. why.

[5] Conjectural renderings; foirtchead = destroying, *C. M. Rath*, 248; failgis = he cut, struck, *O'Clery*; they look also like *for-teched*, fleeing, and *foilged*, following, tracking (*cf.* fuilliucht); fortched, exciting, *C. M. Rath*, 170; see Glossary.

huaire *sin*. Acht na-beth rúad-daire ro-mór bar lár machaire 7 na-gabad mór-slúag na farrad, 7 ra-étlaithé a cháel 7 a mín *in* fheda ass, 7 ra-factha a railge rúada ro-móra da éis. Is a*m*laid-si*n* ra-slaidit a ṅgillai óca aitedcha-*sum* 7 a n-aes ócbad, *con*na raba *acht* a curaid 7 a cath-mil*id* 7 a ndeg-láith gaile d'a n-éis.[a] Cid *tra acht* nir-barulṅgither d'a ṅgillaib óca aitedcha-*sum*, na cor-me*m*aid rosc-béi*m* rígdaide díb *tr*ia-si*n* cath fothúaid.

35. Is and-si*n* ṙa-tuairced I*n*nóchái*n* scíath *Conchobuir* co ro-gésestar. Co ro-gésetar *tr*í to*n*na Her*end* .i. Tond Chlidna 7 T*ond* Rud*raigi* 7 T*ond* Tuage I*n*b*ir*. Co ro-gésetar scéith Ul*ad* uile *in* n-uair *sin*, cach óen ra-bói ar a ṅguallib díb 7 i *n*-a cairpdib.[b]

36. Is é *in* lá sain barrécai*m* d'Ultaib tidacht immach. Et barrecaim *Con*all ir-re*m*thús resna sluagaib. Acht cid airchind ra-bétis eich bad luaithiu ná eich *Con*aill and, ni ro-lam nech d'Ultaib aiged a ech na charpat do thabairt sech *Con*all. Iss-and-si*n* ra-*chon*catar glas-láth Ulad gnúis *Con*aill cucu ra halt na uaire si*n*. Et ra-ansatar, daig rap anad fa i*n*neoi*n* leo. Et rapo doss díten 7 rapo bui*n*ne bratha 7 ropo

[a] Compare the description of the battle of Clontarf: "Is amail sin amail robi caill Tomair ar loscad a minbaig 7 a hoccrund 7 na secht catha coictidis ar mis ic a gerrad 7 a railge romóra 7 a dairge diomóra in a sessam. Is amlaid sin atád na catha cechtarda ar ttuilim a fforba uile acht uathad da ttrénferaib 7 da ttrénmíleadaib na sessam."—*Cog. G.* 7 *G.*, p. 198.

---

[1] Lit. its; "(f)arrad, opposed to *secessio*, *Ml.* 42 a.

[2] ra etlaithe, 3 *sg. pres. pass.* of (es-tallaim) étlaim; 3 *pl.* ra étlaitis; *LL.* 268 b; or they flew away.

[3] "railge," *np.* of rail; *g.* ralach ro dírge, *LL.*, pp. 108, 109 a; darach na railgeadh, *L. Gabala*, p. 28; a railge ocus dairge, *Cogad G. ocus G.* 198; *ns.* rail, *infra.*

[4] "ócbad" seems *gen. pl.*, §§ 34, 38. The young, *juventus*; *cf.* findbad (*Ml.* 14), fidbad; *np.* ócbaid, warriors, *C. M. Lena*, 40.

[5] *Cf.* the description of the battle of Clontarf in *Wars of the Gaedel with the Gaill*, p. 199—"They appear to me the same as if Tomar's Wood was on fire, and the seven battalions had been cutting away its underwood and its young shoots for a month, leaving its stately trees and its immense oaks standing," etc. See note to our text, § 34; and *cf.* modern version.

[6] i.e. "and" *or* "so that."

[7] "roscbéim" = rush-stroke, or charge; *cf.* rusgadh, *O'R.*; frithrosc na conaire, *F. Masters*, v. 1862; rethait rithrosc, *S. na Rann*, 116.

[8] Innóchái*n*, § 35; Innochain, § 48; "indochoin Conchobuir," .i. scíath Conchobuir, *LL.* 107 a.

[9] They do the same in § 16; but "What are the wild waves saying"? And

it were a huge sturdy oakwood in the middle of a plain, and a great army were to go close to it; and the[1] slender and the small of the wood were cut off,[2] and its huge sturdy oaks[3] were left behind. It is thus that their young [and] youthful pages and their young folk[4] were cut off, so that there were none but their champions and their battle-warriors and their good heroes of valour behind them.[5] However, it was not borne by their young youthful pages, and[6] a kingly brilliant dash[7] of them burst through the battle northward.

35. It is then that Innócháin,[8] Conchobar's shield, was battered and it moaned; so that the Three Waves of Eriu moaned, namely, the Wave of Clidna and the Wave of Rudraige and the Wave of Tuag Inbir;[9] so that the shields of the Ulaid all moaned at that hour, every one of them that was on their shoulders and in their chariots.

36. It is that day that it happened to the Ulaid[10] to come out. And Conall happened to be in the forefront, before the armies. But though it is fleet[11] that the horses would be that would be swifter than Conall's horses there, none of the Ulaid ventured to bring the front of his horses or his chariots past Conall. It is then that the raw recruits of the Ulaid saw the face of Conall towards them at that juncture of time; and they halted, for they were fain[12] to halt. And a bush of shelter and a wreath of laurel[13] and a hand above was Conall to them. For

[b] *Cf.* ro-s-glannbeartaigit a sceith ar guaillib a n-gaisceadach, *B. of Magh Rath*, 140.

---

what have mythologists to say about this sonant sympathy between shield and shield and shields and waves?

[10] A fresh body of them came on the field under Conall Cernach, as the other Ulaid were retreating.

[11] Not found in dictionaries; it seems to mean *præcipites*, forward, headlong; airchinn (*principium*), *Z.* 868; is airchenn, *est certum* (*Z.* 343, not in the Index Verborum).

[12] *Cf.* dot' ain-déoin, against thy will, *C. M. Rath*, 160; but innéoin, support, *Hyfiachr.* 254. It is clear that the Ulstermen were running away, and that our version is so full of euphemisms that it must be an Ulster one. It was ever thus, from Rosnaree to Waterloo, that accounts of battles have been written. The "glasláth" (= recruits, *Man. Mater.* 102, and *O'Don. Suppl.*) were green or raw troops, with which *cf.* glas-gesceda, glas-darach, § 37, and glais-fiann (*Diarm. and Grainne*, 88).

[13] "buinne," a branch; *cf.* buinne-án, a branch (Job xiv. 7), buinne doat (*LU.* 134), branch, or ring of forearm. It also means a wave or torrent: buinne dilenn, *Cog. G.* 154. Bratha = of doom, or destruction (*O'Clery*); a wreath placed on the head of victors (*Cormac*).

lám i n-uachtur leo *Conall*. Dáig ba demin leo ni fil inad i faicfithé gnúis *Chon*aill ar a teichfithe and.

37. Is and-sin ra-lotar fón fid ba comnessam dóib, 7 ro-benatar dairbre glas-darach il-láim cech fir; et ro-redigsetar[a] inad d'a ndornaib intib; 7 tuargabtar ria n-aiss na glas-gesceda darach sain, 7 tancatar mar óen ra *Con*all i cend in chatha.

38. Is and-sin barrecaim á ríg Ulad *tri traigid* teohid do breith assin chath fathúaid. Dercais 7 fégais *Conchobor* dar a aiss 7 ra-*chon*naic gnúis *Con*aill d'a ṡaigid. "Maith a Chonaill," bar *Conchobor*, "in cath bar th' oesam 7 bar do chommairge." "Atiur-sa brethir ám," ar *Con*all, "*con*bad[b] assu lim-sa in cath do thabairt m'oenur a chianaib andá in maidm do fossugud innossa. Et dimbúaid do ríg cóicid far-sin ṁbith a fhaccíail[c] im-maidm no im-morthechiud." Et ss-amlaid ro-bói *Con*all [ca rád][d] 7 atbert na briathra-so and:

"Dimbúaid fir frith-rosc madma.
maidm ria ṅgnúsib.
ócbad n-ess-airm.
gillanrad di-airm.
dichra fedma fuidb do anocht.
follogod féile. rith fri geltaib.
gair ri dogur.
dál ri dimbúaid."[e] D.

39. Is and-sin selais Conall in claideb aith-ger iar-lebur ass a intig bodba, 7 dobert cocetul a chlaidib bar na sluagaib. Atchloss rucht

[a] *ro-redigestar* in *Fac-simile*. [b] combad? [c] *For* fácbáil.

---

[1] Lit., on which it would be fled there.

[2] Or it is = fri a n-ais, on their back; they must have thrown away their spears in their flight, since they had to get shillelaghs, when rallied by Conall.

[3] "essairm, diairm, ócbad, gillanrad," not in dictionaries, and the English is somewhat conjectural. These four lines are a rosc.

[4] "dichra" seems a noun here; but = fervent, *W.*, *Atkinson's Gl.*, and *Stokes' S. na Rann.*

[5] "fodb," arms, *W.*; fadb, weapon, *B. of Fenagh*; *as* fodb (= *spolia* ?), *LU.* 196; "fodbugud," to despoil, cut down, *C. M. Rath*, 216.

[6] "anocht," not in dictionaries, unless it is "fanachd," to stay, *O'R.*; or *inf.* of "aincaim," I protect.

[7] fullugim, follaigthe, gl. *abdo, neglecta.*

they were certain that there is no place in which Conall's face would be seen, in which there would be flight.[1]

37. It is then that they went through [into] the wood that was nearest them, and they cut oak-branches of green oak [and put them] in the hand of every man, and they smoothed a place for their fists in them, and they raised in front[2] of them those green branches of oak, and they came along with Conall towards the battle.

38. It is then it happened that by the King of the Ulaid were taken three steps of retreat out of the battle northward. Conchobar looked and scanned behind him and saw the face of Conall approaching him. "Good, O Conall," said Conchobar, "the battle on thy favour and on thy protection!" "I give [my] word truly," said Conall, "that I think it easier to give the battle by myself by far than to stay the rout now. And [it is] disaster for the king of [any] province in world, to leave him in a rout and in a stampede." And it is thus that Conall was [saying it], and he said these words then:—

"The countercharge of defeat is a man's discomfiture;[3]
a rout before [his] face:
youth unarmed:
followers disarmed:[3]
earnestness[4] of effort of weapon,[5] to succour:[6]
forgetfulness[7] of honour: running against madmen;
shouting in distress;[8]
meeting in disaster."

39. It is then that Conall drew[9] the sharp long sword out of its sheath of war,[10] and played the music of his sword[e] on the armies. The ring[11]

[d] Supply this as §§ 3, 5, 6. [e] *This, though not marked* R, *is* "Rethoric," *or* Rosc.

---

[8] "ri dog*ur*," against calamity; perhaps we should read dog*ru*.

[9] "selais," .i. lopped off, *W.*; "co-selastar," .i. dorat (*Z.*, 1093), .i. gave, brought.

[10] "intig," *ds. neuter* for (f)intig (?), *as.* fintech, *LL.* 111 a; but *d.* intiuch in *Ascoli's Glossary; cf.* ass a (f)intiuch, *LL.* 80 b; "Bodba" (here and §§ 40, 41, 43) = dangerous, *O'Don. Suppl.*; bealach bodba, *dangerous* pass, *C. M. Lena*, 26; *Mesca Ul.* 14, 26; *majestic* [phalanx], *C. M. Rath*, 216; beraib bodba, *fierce* darts, *Mesca Ul.* 22; bodba = of "steam, *fog*," and hence, "of danger" (*O'B. Crowe* in *Relig. Beliefs of the Ancient Irish*, p. 318); 6s an m-broinig blathbodba, over the *fine flowing* flood," *O'Dugan's Top. Poem*, p. 6, ruathar bodba, *LB.* 216 a. Bodb is a man's name in the *Ch. of Lir.*

[11] rucht, §§ 39, 48; groan, *O'Cl.*

claidib Co*n*aill dar na cathaib cechtarda ra halt na huaire si*n*. Cid *tra acht* feib ra-chualatar cocetul claidib *C*[*h*]*on*aill, ra-chuclaigetar a c*r*ideda, 7 ra-lua*m*naigsetar a ruisc, 7 ra-bansatar a ṅgnúsi, 7 ra-scuich cách dar a ais díb i *n*-a inad catha 7 co*m*lai*n*d 7 co*m*raic.

40. Cid *tra acht* is and-si*n* ra-dercastar Co*n*all dar a aiss. Et ra-*chon*nairc d'a i*n*naigid Mes Dead m*acc* A*m*airgi*n*. "Maith a m'an*am*," bar *Con*all, "a Meis Dead; i*n* cath ar th' oesa*m* 7 ar do cho*m*mairgi." "Is ucht ra mór-dili*n*d alt neich mar sei*n* it*rad*-sa," ale bar Mes D*ead*. Is a*n*d dercis 7 déchais Mes D*ead* m*eicc* A*mairgin* dar a ais; et ra-*chon*nairc d'a i*n*naigid Ánruth Mór m*acc* A*m*airgi*n*. "In cath bar th' oesu*m* 7 bar do cho*m*mairgi, a Ánraid Móir m*eicc* A*m*argi*n*," bar Mes D*ead*, "co ro-cherddai*n*d mo búraig f*er*ge 7 mo thigardail ṁbodba far na sluagaib." "Is saiget i coirthi alt neich mar sei*n* i t*ra*th-sa," ale bar Ánruth Mór m*acc* A*mairgin*.

41. Is and-sin fégais Anruth Mór m*acc* A*mairgin* dar a aiss, 7 at*con*nairc Feithen Mór m*acc* A*mairgin*. "Maith a Ḟeithin Móir m*eicc* A*mairgin*, i*n* cath f*or* th' oesu*m* 7 ar do cho*m*mairgi, co ro-cherd-dai*n*-se no mo búraig f*er*ge 7 mo thigardail ṁbodba f*or* na sl*uagaib*."

42. Is and-sin ro-dercastar i*n* Feithen Mór m*acc* A*mairgin* dar ais. At*con*nairc d'a i*n*naigid in Fethen Bec m*acc* A*mairgin*. "I*n* cath f*or* th' óesa*m* 7 ar do cho*m*mairgi, a Ḟethin Bic m*eicc* A*mairgin*," ar in Feithen Mór, "co ro-cherdai*n*-se mo bur*aig* f*er*ge 7 mo thigardail ṁbodba f*or* na sl*uagaib*." "Is essarcai*n* ci*n*d f*ri* hallib *ám* alt neich mar sain," ale ar i*n* Fethe*n* B*ec*.

43. Is and-si*n* fegais i*n* Fethe*n* Bec dar aiss. Atcho*n*nairc Athe*r*ni Alg*essach* d'a ṡaigid. "I*n* cath f*or* th' oesa*m* a Athe*r*ni Alg*essaig*," f*or* i*n* Fethe*n* B*ec*, "co ro-ch*er*dai*n*-se no mo bur*aig* f*erge* 7 mo th*igardail*

---

[1] i cuclaigi carpait, *LU.* 91 b; cucligid Temra, *S. na Rann*, 132.

[2] Lit., like that.

[3] búraig feirge (§§ 40, 41, 42, 43), charge of fury, or furious charge; .i. borr-ág, great exploit, *O'Clery;* .i. bellowing, *Mesca Ul.* 32; .i. vengeance, *C. M. Rath*,

of Conall's sword was heard throughout the battalions on both sides at that moment of time. However, as soon as they heard the music of Conall's sword, their hearts quaked[1] and their eyes fluttered, and their faces whitened, and each of them withdrew back into his place of battle and of conflict and of combat.

40. However, it is then that Conall glanced behind him, and he saw approaching him Mes Dead son of Amairgin. "Good my life," said Conall, "O Mes Dead, the battle on thy favour and on thy protection." "It is a breast against a great flood, the action of anyone under those circumstances[2] at this time," replied Mes Dead. It is then that Mes Dead son of Amairgin glanced and scanned behind him; and he saw approaching him Anruth the Tall, son of Amairgin. "The battle on thy favour and on thy protection, Anruth the Tall, son of Amairgin," said Mes Dead," till I cast my charge[3] of anger and my *tigardáil*[4] of war on the armies." "It is an arrow against a rock, the action of anyone under those circumstances this time," replied Anruth the Tall, son of Amairgin.

41. It is then that Anruth the Tall, son of Amairgin, looked behind him, and saw Feithen the Tall, son of Amairgin. "Good O Feithen the Tall, son of Amairgin, the battle on thy favour and on thy protection; that I too may deliver my furious charge and my *tigardáil* of war on the armies."

42. It is then that the tall Feithen, son of Amairgin, glanced behind him. He saw approaching him the small Feithen, son of Amairgin. "The battle on thy favour and on thy protection, O small Feithen, son of Amairgin," said the tall Feithen, "that I may cast my violence of anger and my *tigardáil* of fury on the armies." "It is the striking of a head against cliffs, indeed, the action of anyone under the circumstances," replied the small Feithen.

43. It is then that the small Feithen looked behind him. He saw Aitherni the Importunate approaching him. "The battle on thy favour, O Aitherni the Importunate," said the small Feithen, "till I

298; charge, *Cog. G.* 114; prowess, *Stokes' Siege of Howth*, 56, 54. *Cf.* gleó ferge, *LL.* 60 bb; anfot feirge, *Sench. M.* 336.

[4] tigardáil (§§ 40, 41, 42, 43, 46, 49), tiger-meeting (?) tig-fardail, supreme effort (fardail, the major part of a thing, *O'R.*; urdail, equivalent, *Atkinson's Gl.*); and *cf.* tig-lecht, the last bed or grave; or tig-ár-dail, final-slaughter-encounter. It means fight, § 46. *Cf.* with these proverbial sayings those of *LB.* 217 b.

[ṁ]bodba f[*or na sluagaib*]." "Ba chuta dom ṡeilb-se sain," ale [bar Atherne], "for seilb neich n-aill n-aile."

44. Cid *tra acht* iss-and-sin at*chon*dairc Ath*er*ne Alg*essach* Cú Chu*laind*[a] da ṡaigid. "In cath bar th' aesam, a *Chú Chulaind*," bar Aith*er*ni Alg*essach*. "Ba chuta da*m*-sa ón," ale bar Cú *Chulaind*. Inund són 7 daic dím. "Acht dob*er*im-se mo brethir ris," ar Cú *Chulaind*, "na*ch* fail do Ul*taib* nech dob*er*a a agid ḟorm-sa as-si*n* chath-sa, ar nad tressiu slaidfet-sa ca*ch* fer d'ḟeraib Her*end* na ca*ch* fer díbsium." Is and rab*ert* *Cú Chulaind* béim d'a lorgḟertais bar na sluagaib, corbdar comardda comchuibdi iat.

45. Imthusa *Con*aill sund *in*nossa. Tanic fo na sluagaib 7 dob*ert* cocetal a chlaidib forru, co torchratar deich cét fer n-armach leis. Ra-chuala sain Carp*re* N*ia* F*er* cocetal claidib *Con*aill C*ernaig*, 7 nirbruiṅgit*her* [do[b]] Chairp*riu* N*iaid* F*er* esi*de* it*ir*. Na co tanic reme co hairm[c] ir-raibe *Con*all. Et tucastar sciath *fri* sciath 7 dóit *fri* dóit 7 einech *fri* einech, 7 ro-gab ca(ch)[d] díb oc slaide 7 oc slechtad araile. Co[clos][d] gló-béim[e] scéith sceith[f] Cairp*re* N*iad* F*er* fá déis clai[dib][g] *Con*aill.

46. Et dariachtatar na t*rí* rigfil*id* robatar[h] oc ríg Themrach d'a ḟortacht 7 d'a ḟorithin[h] [.i.] Eochaid Eolach 7 Diarmait Duanach 7 F*er*g[al] Fianach; 7 ra-cho*m*moratar *in* tigardail i cend *Con*aill. Fegais *Con*all fo*rr*u. "Atdiur-sa brethir ám," bar *Con*all, "menbad ḟilid 7 ǽs dána sib dogebad sib[i] bás 7 aided lim-sa a chianaib; 7 úair

[a] *Sic, for* Coin Culaind.
[b] do, *indistinct*.
[c] airm, *indistinct*.
[d] cach *and* clos, *indistinct*.
[e] gló *appears an after-insertion*, as it is all outside the perpendicular line.

[1] I can only guess at Aitherne's meaning; *cf.* his words with those of Cuchulaind, § 44: "ba chuta dom ṡeilb-se sain," and "ba chuta damsa ón . . . inund són ocus daic dím." So "cuta" seems = "daic." Coda = right, equity, *O'R.*; cota na m-ban, an enclosure for women, *Man. & Cust.* iii. 564.

[2] daic = do aic, for a request (?); aic, aicc, to bind, *Laws*, II. 30.

[3] It is clear that the Ulaid were retreating.

[4] Or staff-spindle; "staff," *Mesca Ul.* 32.

[5] Level and harmonious, .i. the order of their ranks was restored (?).

spend my onset of anger and my dangerous tiger-fight on the armies." "That were a right of my possession," [replied Aitherni], "over the possession of any others whomsoever."[1]

44. However, it is then that Aitherni the Importunate saw Cuchulaind approaching him. "The battle on thy favour, O Cú Chulaind," said Aitherni the Importunate. "That were a part [?] for me," replied Cu Chulaind. That is the same as "to require of me."[2] "But I give my word for it," said Cu Chulaind, "that there is not of the Ulaid one that will turn his face to me out of this battle, but that not more strongly I will smite every man of the men of Eriu than every man of them."[3] It is then that Cu Chulaind gave a blow of his club-staff[4] on the armies, so that they were even and harmonious.[5]

45. The performances of Conall here now. He came among the armies and played the music of his sword on them, till ten hundred armed men fell by him. Carpre Nia Fer heard that, the music of Conall Cernach's sword, and that was not endured by Carpre Nia Fer by any means, and he advanced to the place in which Conall was, and brought shield against shield and hand against hand and face against face, and each of them began smiting and striking the other, till there was heard a strong stroke[6] of Carpre Nia Fer's shield under the blade of Conall's sword.

46. And the three royal poets, that the King of Temair had, arrived to aid him and to help him, namely Eochaid the Learned, and Diarmait the Songful, and Forgal the Just, and they kept up[7] the combat against Conall. Conall looked at them. "I give my word truly," said Conall, "were you not poets and doctors you should have received death and

[f] *Sic bis*, by scribal error. [g] dib, *indistinct.* [h] atar *and* in, *indistinct.*
[i] "Analytic" or impersonal construction; *cf.* cid dogena sib, what will you do? *LU.* 99 b.

[6] Straight blow (?). *Cf.* glo-snathe, gl. *norma*, *Z.* Perhaps we should read "gleó-béim," or "glond-béim."

[7] rachommortatar, 3 *pl. pret.*, § 46; commorais, 3 *sg. S.-pret.*, § 49, = ro mór, § 49. *Cf.* do commóradh aonach, a fair was convened, held, *C. M. Lena*, 40; "do commorad, fled"; ceann commortha, chief plotter, *C. M. Rath*, 200; ro morad aenach, *B. of Balymote*, p. 252; do morad irgaile, to excite battle, *Mesca Ul.* 30, 32. Perhaps the form "ro mór," used in the same sense as "commorais," forbids the equation with "con-fo-ferais," which has been suggested; racommortatar = do congbadar, *Stowe text*, § 41; cf. co folmaiset comeirgi, *LU.* 103 b.

is rá bar triath 7 ra bar tigerna berthai far mbáig cid dam-sa nach dígelaind foraib no?" Et dobert béim din lorg-fertais catha bói 'n-a láim dóib con topacht a tri cindu díb.

47. Is and-sin dariachtatar buden cóic cét déc do Luaigni na Temrach co tancatar eter Conall 7 Carpre Niaid Fer; co rucatar leo é ar lár medón a catha fodéin. Ro-gab Conall ac slaide in tslúaig co dremun 7 co barbarda, co uathmar 7 co dícheillid, co ro-s-cuir úad i n-a n-ágaib minta[a] 7 i n-a cethramthanaib fodalta. Co torchratar deich cét leis ar lar-medón in chatha.

48. Ro-chuala sain rí Temrach, 7 nir-borulngither dó beith oc éistecht ra rucht claidib Conaill; 7 tanic reime co lár-medón in chatha, co torchratar ocht cét læch lán-chalma leis; co rocht co airm ir-rabe Conchobor, 7 dobert scíath fri scíath 7 dóit fri dóit 7 einech fri einech do. Et ro-thuairgestar a sciath for Conchobor .i. Innochain sciath Conchobuir. Et feib ro-geisestar-side ro-geisetar scéith Ulad uile. "Maith ám a Ultu," [ale bar Conchobor], "nad-fetar-sa cosindiu ar bad chalmu in Galian Lagen na Lúagni na Temrach andathi-si."

49. Is and-sin tanic Loegaire Buadach macc Connaid Buide meicc Iliach budin[b] trí chét oclách; commorais a thigardail i cend Cairpri Niad Fer. Is and-sin luid Fintan macc Néill Niamglonnaig buiden[76] cét óclách co ro-mór a thigardail i cend Cairpri Niad Fer.

50. Is and-sin tancatar deich cét ar fichit cét din Galían 7 di Luagni na Temrach; et tuargabtar leo Cairpre Nia Fer il-lármedón a catha fadéin.

51. Is and-sin cunnis Cú Chulaind bar na sluagaib 7 bar Carpre Niaid

[a] *Cf.* Condaralsat é na ágib.—*LL.* 169 a.
[b] The acc. is used here, and the nom. in next line in like contexts.

---

[1] Aided = "bás" here; gl. *interitus* (*Wb.* 27); is not necessarily a violent or tragical death. In the *F. Masters*, Pref., p. 2; in *LL.* 66 a, 94 a; in *C. M. Rath*, 268; in *Fair of Carman*, p. 534, and in *Cog. Gaedel re Gall.* 68, "bás, éc, aided" are used as synon.; "aided," death from grief, *LL.* 127 a.

[met] your fate[1] by me long ago, and since it is with [for] your chief and with your lord that you bring your strife, what [reason is there] for me that I should not inflict punishment on you now?" And he gave a blow with the club-staff of battle that was in his hand at them, so that he cut their three heads off them.

47. It is then that a band of fifteen hundred of the Lúaigni of Temair came up, and came between Conall and Cairpre Nia Fer; and they carried him [Cairpre] with them in the very middle of their own battalion. Conall began smiting the army fiercely and furiously, fearfully and madly, so that he drove them from him in [their] broken bands,[2] and in [their] divided fractions.[3] So that ten hundred fell by him in the middle of the battle.

48. The King of Temair heard that, and he could not bear[4] to be listening to the sound of Conall's sword; and he advanced to the middle of the battle, and eight hundred full-brave heroes fell by him; and he reached the place in which Conchobar was, and he brought shield against shield and hand against hand and face against face to him. And he struck his shield on Conchobar,[5] *i.e.* The Ochain, the shield of Conchobar. And as it moaned, the shields of the Ulaid all moaned. "Good truly, Ulaid," [saith Conchobar], "I knew not till to-day whether the Galían of the Lagin or the Lúaigni of Temair were braver than you are."

49. It is then that Loegaire the Victorious, son of Connad the Yellow, son of Iliach, came [with] a band of three hundred warriors, so that he upheld his combat against Cairpre Nia Fer. It is then that Fintan, son of Niall Niamglonnach went [with] a band of a hundred warriors, so that he maintained his fight against Cairpre Nia Fer.

50. It is then that thirty hundred of the Galían and of the Lúaigni of Temair came, and by them was carried off Cairpre Nia Fer in the middle of their own battalion.

51. It is then that Cuchulaind sought for[6] the armies and for

---

[2] *Or* broken limbs; "ágaib," joints, limbs; *nap.* N. áge, áige, *LL.* 197 a; *T. Bó Froich*, 138; *S. Carp. Conch.* 382, 388. [3] Lit. quarters.

[4] Lit. was not borne by him.

[5] i.e. he struck Conor's shield.

[6] "cuinnis," *S.-pret.* of condaigim, = ro chunnig, *LL.* 114 b (na cuindig, ask not, *C. M. Rath*, 306); *cf.* selais = ro-selaig.

Fer. Et dolluid d'a *ins*áigid, 7 tuc sciath ra sciath dó, 7 tuc dóit fri dóit, 7 einech fri einech.[a]

Is and-si*n* ro-i*mm*ir Carpr*e* N*ia* F*er* a nert *for* *Co*[*i*]*n* Cul*aind* 7 ro-íad a da laim dar a ar*m*aib a*m*maig; 7 tarlaic rout n-urchair secha [ós][b] catha Gal*ian*. Is and-si*n* ro-luid C*ú* C*hulaind* tri-sna [ ] taib[c] immach can fuligud can fordergad [fair].[d] Is and barécaim Láeg m*acc* Rian-*gabra* do-sum 7 a airm sénta deg-mathi *Con* C*ulaind* i *n*-a láim .i. *in* Cruadín cotut-chend 7 in Duaibsech ecl*ach*.[e] Is and-si*n* ro-gab C*ú* C*hu-laind* *in* Duaibsech .i. a ṡleg[f] fadéi*n* i *n*-a lái*m*. Ra-boc 7 ra-b*er*taig hí, ra-Chroth 7 ra-chertaig, 7 tarlaic rout n-urchair uad di no, d' i*n*nsaigid Cairpr*i* N*iad* F*er*, cotarla 'n-a ucht 7 'n-a brunni, co ro-thregd a chride 'n-a chliab, co ro-rai*n*d a drui*m* dar dó. Ni ranic a chorp lár in n-uair dob*er*t C*ú* C*hulaind* side d'a ṡaigid 7 *con*topacht a chend de. Et crothais a chend[g] ri-sna slúag iartai*n*.

52. Is and at*ra*acht Sencha m*acc* Ail*e*lla 7 ra-chroth in craib sida, 7 ra-ansatar Ulaid.[h] Et dollotar i*n* Galian fa Ḟind m*acc* Rosa, 7 dob*er*-tatar sciath dar lorg dar a n-eis. Et ro-lenastar Iriel gascedach glunmar m*acc* *Con*aill C*hernaig* iat. Et ro-gab ac slaide 7 ic[i] slectad in tslúaig fades cach ṅdíriuch. Is a*n*d-si*n* ro-impá Fidach F*er*gach

[a] Cf. *LU.* 80 *b*, and *Windisch's Texte*, 280: dóit fri d. leóit fri l. gualaind fri g.
[b] ós *or* úas, *indistinct*.
[c] cathaib (?), cétaib (?): *cf.* cét, § 50.
[d] *Supply* fair? *From this on is blurred and indistinct.*
[e] eclach (?) cotut-chend = caladchend, *LL.* 194 a.
[f] [chruad]ṡleg, *or* ṡirṡleg, *or* chorrṡleg (as in *Cath. M. Rath*, p. 214). cruad-lann, *B. of Fenagh*, 220, *Hyfiachr.* 206, 210.

---

[1] Little steel (or hard) thing, the hard-head steelling. Cf. *LL.* 110 b, 254; arm cruaid catad, *LL.* 27 a b; *gs.* Caitt catotchind, *LL.* p. 29; cotut-lethar cruaid, *LU. Táin*; cadut comcruaid, *Cog. G. 7 G.*, p. 50; cruaid codut, *LB.* 217 b.
[2] *Cf.* naithraig n-duabais, *LL.* 223 a; "duaibsech," dangerous (of ships), *C. M. Lena*, 44; "is duaibsech romdúiscis, *C. M. Rath*, 170; duaibsib, gl. *nefastis*, *Z.*
[3] bogaim, I shake, *O'R.*; notbocctha, *te jactabas*, *Z.*; bócáil, ostentation, *O'Begley's Eng.-Ir. Dict.*
[4] A rush as of wind (?). Perhaps "bedg" was the word here: ro lá C. bedg, "C. dashed," *Mesca Ul.* 52.

Cairpre Nia Fer. And he went against him, and brought shield against shield to him, and brought hand against hand and face against face.

It is then that Cairpre Nia Fer plied his strength upon Cu Chulaind and clasped his two hands about his weapons outside, and launched the cast of a throw past him [over] the battalions of the Galían. It is then that Cu Chulaind went through the [battalions] out without bleeding, without wounding [on him]. It is then that Laeg son of Riangabair met him, with the charmed, right-good arms of Cu Chulaind in his hand, namely, the hard-headed *Cruadín*[1] and the terrifying *Duaibsech*.[2] It is then that Cu Chulaind took the *Duaibsech*, that is, his own spear, in his hand. He waved[3] and brandished it, he shook and adjusted it, and he launched a cast of a throw of it from him then towards Cairpre Nia Fer, so that it pitched in his breast and in his bosom, and pierced his heart in his chest, and cleft his back in two. His body had not reached ground, when Cu Chulaind made a spring[4] towards it and cut his head off him. And he shook his [Cairpre's] head[5] towards the armies[6] then.

52. It is then that Sencha son of Ailill rose and shook the branch of peace, and the Ulaid stood still.[7] And the Galían went under Find son of Ros, and put shield across track behind them.[8] And Iriel the good at arms, the great-kneed, son of Conall Cernach, pursued them. And he began smiting and cutting down the army southward in every direction.[9] It is then that Fidach the Wrathful of the Wood of Gaible

[g] This was a practice of Cuchulaind's: "ba foróil leu a ndorigni Cú . . . crothad in chinn frisin slóg," *LU*. 64 a.

[h] *Cf*. Atracht Senchai iartain 7 rochroth in cráeb sída ós na slúagaib combatar sídaig amal betis meicc oenathar 7 oenmáthar, *LL*. 111 a.

[i] ac *in fac-simile*.

---

[5] Carpre's head appears to have been sent to his brother Ailill, and was buried in Sid Nento or Mullaghshee, near Lanesborough, *LL*. 121 b.

[6] sluag, *recte* slúagu; or *ap. neuter*, slúag.

[7] *Cf*. Atracht Sencha ocus ro croith in craib, ocus contoiset Ulaid uili fris, *LU*. 103 b; "and they were peaceful as if they were sons of one father and one mother when Senchua shook the branch," *LL*. 111 a.

[8] i. e. covered the retreat.

[9] *Or* straight on.

Feda Gabli ris, et dorat comlund ar ath dó. "Fata *n* rigi doberat Ulaid foraind," ar coiced Lagen. *Con*id de atá *in* Rigi Lagen ar *in* n-abaind si*n*.

53. Is and-si*n* da*no* lotar Ulaid co Temraig rempu *in* n-aidchi sin. Et tarrasatar and co cend secht lathi[a] na sechtmai*ne*. Corop i ci*nd* sechtmai*ne* ra-chualatar-sum culgaire na carp*at*, 7 basc-be*m*nech na n-ech, 7 tetimnech na tét, 7 glond-béimnech na claideb, 7 muad-muirn *in* mór-slúaig dochum *in* baile. Is é ra-búi and, Erc m*acc* Carpr*i* 7 m*acc* Feidilmi Nói-chruthaige *ingi*n*i* *Con*chob*uir*. Et dobretha-*sum* a chend i *n*-ucht a ṡen-athar, 7 comnattacht[b] tír a athar fair. Et ba ċhota-*sum* aní-si*n* á *Chon*cho*bor*. "Maith a m*ei*cc," ar *Con*cho*bor*, "beir mo be*n*nachtain-se 7 bí do*m* réir." Is amlaid ra-bói ca rád 7 rab*er*t na bria*thra*-sa:

54. "Beir mo be*nn*act, bí dom réir,
na dena féi*n* frithbeirt frind;
da tuca dún tend f*ri* tend
is derb lem dafæthais lind.
Na cocthaig ra Coin na cless,
na cuir tress f*or* slicht do ṡen,
naratruibther i*m* rai*n*d crích
i*m*mar bíth Carpr*e* Nia Fer.

[a] lathi *in marg.*, ṁbl. *deleted in text.*

---

[1] "rige," reach (?), or "arm," *B. of Canticles*, viii. The Rye river joins the Liffey at Leixlip, *F. Masters*, *an.* 776; 6 Rige co Rig-Bóinn, *C. M. Lena*, 80; called Rige Lagen to distinguish it from other rivers named Rige: "rigid," reaches, *LU.* 111 a.

[2] chariot-rattle. Cf. cul-gaire, *LL.* 96 a; sceld-gaire, shield-clatter, *LL.* 98 a; cul, .i. carpat, *Cormac*, *LU.* fo. 76, 6 b; culgaire carpait, *LU.* 45 a.

[3] basc-béimnech. *Cf.* basgaim, I trample, *O'R.*, *not in W.*; bascad *in Atkinson's Gl.* = to hinder; basc = red, *Cormac*, *O'Clery*.

[4] tetimnech (= tét-béimnech ?), cord-striking; tétemnech, *LL.* 93 a, 96 a; breis-émnech, helmet-noise, *Man. & Cust.* iii. 426; possibly there is a neuter "ém" or "im" = twanging, creaking.

[5] glondbéimnech, straight-striking (?). *Cf.* gló-béim, § 45; gló-ṡnathiu, gl. *norma*, *Ml.* 35, = glonṡnathi, *Atkinson's Gl.*; gloinnbéimnech na ccloideṁ, *Fragm. of Irish Ann.* 122.

turned upon him, and gave battle and combat on a ford to him. "Long [is] the reach[1] that the Ulaid are making towards us," said the province of the Lagin. And it is from this that Rige[1] Lagen is the name of that river.

53. It is then that the Ulaid went on to Temair that night, and they tarried there till the end of the seven days of the week. And it was at the end of a week that they heard the roll[2] of the chariots, and the hoof-striking[3] of the horses, and the straining[4] of the traces, and the deed-striking[5] of the swords, and the trooping[6] of the vast army towards the place. It is he that was there—Erc son of Cairpre and son of Feidelm Noi-chruthach[7] daughter of Conchobar. And he placed his head on the breast[8] of his grandfather, and asked his father's land from him. And he obtained[9] that thing from Conchobar. "Good, O son," said Conchobar, "take my blessing and be obedient to me."[10] It is thus that he was saying it, and he said these words:—

54. "Take my blessing, be obedient to me,
do not thyself make opposition to us.
If thou givest us strong against strong[11]
I am certain that thou shalt fall by us.
War not with the Hound of the feats,
inflict not strife on the race of thy ancestors,
that thou mayest not be cut down[12] about division of territories,
as is Cairpre Nia Fer. . .

[b] So it seems written, but it is *conatacht*, *LL.* 20 b.

---

[6] muad-muirn, .i. mór-buidean, *O'C.*

[7] Conchobor's daughter. Nóichruthach (Nóicrothach, *W.*) = new-formed or ship-shaped or of nine beauties, as in *LL.*

[8] This and Conall Cernach's giving three kisses to his countryman present a charming picture of Irish customs. Compare "Luid dano in Liath Macha co tarat a chend for brunnib Conculaind," *LL.* 122 a.

[9] "ba hota" or "ba chota," § 53 (and "ba chuta," §§ 43, 44) seems = adchota. *Cf.* adcotat, gl. *acquirunt*, *Wb.* 26.

[10] Lit., (according) to my will.

[11] i. e. if thou contendest stiffly against us; tend = tight, stiff, bold, cutting, hacking.

[12] ratruibther = ra-t-ro-fuibther; *cf.* (fo-benim) fuibnim, fubæ *or* fobothaim.

Do gessaib ríg Temrach tair,[a]
a flaith Cermna can ni clé—
airdairc scél scáilter fa chách—
cocad ruind co bráth ce bé." B.

55. Doringned síd eter Erc macc Cairpri 7 Coinculaind. Et tucad Fínscoth ingen ConCulaind do mnái do-som. Et tancatar i cind sechtmaini do dechain in n-áir co hor na Boinne. "Bamar-ni lathi and-so," [ale ar Conchobor], "7 ba dulig cor ristí ro-bói and .i. ri Carpre Nia Fer, 7 ba esbach comrac ris, 7 menbad Chonall is forainne bad róen." Et ro-raid na briathra :—

56. "Bamar lathi—romda rind—
i tuaith Tem[rach] tess Boind:
bái fr[eccomas][b] ós ard feirt
ar ar sibthib bái ecrait.
Munbad Conall Cernach clóen,[c]
ropad forainne bad róen,
ar in leirg leith ifus[d]
is aire ro-gab-sum fos.
Ba escomol comrac fris,
dichor Cairpri do chlar fiss,
sochaide am ro-do-s-cloe
cossin laithe sin rosbae." B.

[a] *Cf.* Mad rígh díleas do Themair . . .
Co nach deárna cocadh coin
Ré slógh Choicidh Chonchobair,
Na falmaigthear Teamair de
Do chocadh chland Rudraige.—*L. na gCeart*, 238.

[b] fréccomas (?) *as* § 6. *Cf.* Conchobor's poem, *LL.* 331 :—
Rombói lathe rordu rind de thuait ċor des
boind. bái cendairech f̄ air birt. s̄ ar sithbe ba begairc
Batar cadaī f̄ clár clíu clan̄des gesi f̄ suidiu : ba
d̄g ar carpat uile ba lán cend ar netruide
Bafir ba Escmond firi scor aroeb issibor. ba hé
ar n̄gním glan gle. isindaithliu imbairne.

[1] Cermna of Dun Cermna, or Old Head of Kinsale, was brother of Sebuirge of Dunseverick. Cf. *LL.* 17 a: "Gabait Sobairche ocus Cermna Find ríge n-Erend."
[2] Whatever may happen.
[3] Sad turn for the person ("ristí" = frisinní).

[It is] of the prohibitions of the King of Temair in the East,
since the reign of Cermna[1] without partiality—
famous the tale which is spread through all—
to fight against us till doom, howsoever it be."[2] Take.

55. Peace was made between Erc, son of Cairpre, and Cu Chulaind; and Fínscoth, Cu Chulaind's daughter, was given to him for wife. And they came at the end of a week to behold the slaughter, to the bank of the Bóand. "We were here on a day," saith Conchobar, "and it was a sad affair for him[3] who was here, namely, for Cairpre Nia Fer, and it was a vain struggle against him, and if it had not been [for] Conall, it is we that should have been defeated." And he spoke the words:—

56. "We were on a day—it seems splendid to us—
in the country of Temair south of the Bóand:
there was [contention] above the high hill[4]
on our chiefs there was terror.
Were it not Conall Cernach the cross-eyed,[5]
we should have been defeated:
on the plain[6] on this side—
it is on it that he took position.
It was vain[7] to contend with him,
to repel Cairpre of wide knowledge[8];
[it was] numbers truly that defeated him;
until that day, that slew him."[9] We were.

[c] The next 8 lines indistinct.

[d] *Verse short by one syllable, because perhaps* leirg *was pronounced* leirig; *read* (cath *or* ár-)leirg (*cf.* ármag (battle plain), cath lathair (battle field), *C. M. Rath*, 218.

---

[4] Rosnaree, or Knowth, or New Grange, or the ridge embracing both opposite Rosnaree. fri[ ] = frithorcon, frithaire, frecomas = harassing, watching (?).

[5] "Conall the Cross-eyed was his name till then. For the Ulstermen had three blemishes, to wit, Cu Chulaind the Blind, and Cuscraid the Mute," &c., *Talland Etair*, *LL.* 117 a, ed. by Whitley Stokes, *Rev. Celt.* viii., p. 60.

[6] "leirg" (§§ 56, 28, 29), slope, plain *C. M. Lena*, 92, 146; *dp.* "fert illergaib," *LL.* 77 b, 76 a.

[7] "es-comol," difficult (a non-performance); *cf.* esbach, § 55, and comalnaim, gl. *impleo.*

[8] Level wisdom, experience (?); clár = board, flat surface, § 29.

[9] ro-s-bae; *cf.* ro-s-mbi, *gl.* ro-ben, *pret.* of benim. Perhaps these two lines = many truly, he overcame them till that day, he slew them; or, which was to him.

57. Tancatar rempu co Temraig aris. "Maith ám inti ro-bói and-so *co n*-a brathrib. Rapa leo-*sum* Heriu": 7 atb*ert* na briathra :—

> " Trí m*eicc* Rosa Ruaid i*n* rig[a]
> gabsat in tír buidnib sel :
> Find i *n*-Alind, Ai*l*ill i Cruaich,
> Carp*re* thuaid i Temair Breg.
> In n-oen-ḟecht comterbtis[b] a ngni*m*
> a t*r*iar brathar im ca*ch* gleó,
> i*n* oen-ḟecht dob*er*tis a *m*baig,
> ba crithail oen-mucci leo.[c]
> Batar 'n-a t*r*i n-uathnib oir
> i*m* a tilchaib, buan i*n* balc;
> is bern i *n*-a coṅgaib catha
> o fochera i*n* tres ma*cc*." T.

Ahain slúaged catha Findchorad, et i*n* trom-lo*n*ges timchell i Connachtaib, 7 Cath na Ma*cc*raide.

---

[a] Trí m*eicc* la Ross R*uad*, .i. Find File, Ailill ma*cc* Matae [*gl.* Mur(isce)], Corp*re* Nia Fer. Quidam addunt *aire filium* .i. Cathbath Drui ath*air* Concho*buir.* Ailill t*r*a ma*cc* Rosa 7 Mata Murisc a m*áth*air do ḟeraib Ólnecmacht : dib-side coṅ-gairther Connachta indiu. Rongabsat ir-rige ar a mathe .i. Dolluid Medb Chruacha*n* ingen Echa*ch* F*edl*ig co feraib Olnecmacht impi i Cr[uachain] combertatar Ail*il*l leo . . . rech do rígu Connacht, daig ba dib a m*áth*air . tu*r* (?) do denam oentad et*er*

---

[1] i.e. in their might ?

[2] comterptis (*perperam* comtentis *in Fac-simile*) from con-do-air-bnim (?). *Cf.* comthercomrac = con-do-air-c, "foirbthe," *perfectus*. Or it is formed from, or connected with, "taisbenim, taisfenim," or "tadbadim," *S.-fut.* 2 *sg.*, condárbais, gl. *ut demonstres ;* and so means " they would display " (?). Or con-do-érptis, they confided, committed ; terbaid, drive away, of *T. Bó Reg.*, would not suit here.

[3] crithail = grithail (the grunting of young pigs, *O'R.*), *figuratively for* litter (?) ; or "crithail" = crith-ḟail = ricketty stye (fail, st*y*e, *Coney's Dict.*), fail nir, *Bodl. Cormac*, p. 22 ; *cf.* mucc-ḟoil, gl. *hara, stabula porcorum.*

[4] *nef.* in chongab chruid, the seizure of cattle (?), *LL.* 296 a.

57. They came on to Temair again. "Goodly indeed [was] he that was here with his brethren. Ériu was theirs." And he said the words:—

"The three sons of Ros Ruad the king—
they held the land by battalions[1] awhile,
Find in Alend, Ailill in Cruach,
Cairpre in the north in Temair Breg.
Together they used to perform[2] their deed [of arms]
the three brothers, in every strife;
together they used to give their battle;
one pig's litter [?][3] was theirs.
They were three pillars of gold
about their hills, abiding the strength,
it is a gap in their grasp[4] of battle,
since the third son has fallen.[5]" The three.

Therefrom [originated] the expedition of the battle of Findchora[6] and the great sea voyage around among the Connachta,[7] and the Battle of the Youths.[8]

na dacoiᵣed 7 do chocad fri Conchobor 7 fri coiced n-Ulad. Corpre din i Temraig, Find File i n-Alind, Ailill i Cruachain. Unde Senchan cecinit:—Tri meicc Ruaid ruirig flaind, fiangal Find, Ailill acher, caem Car[pre . . .] Ailend chruind, Cruachu, Temair. *LL.* 311 b.

[b] comtenbtis, *Fac-simile.*

[c] Faded and indistinct, *cf.* mucce crai, muc cotri hal, *Laws*, ii. 368, 246.

---

[5] "fo-chera," falls (?), seems connected with docer, torchair, gl. *cecidit*, and erchre, gl. *interitus, eclipsis*; I cannot explain it satisfactorily: *historic pres. subj.* of "fochiur" (?). "Do" and "fo" are used promiscuously in *LL.*

[6] In *M. D'Arbois de Jubainville's Catalogue*, p. 66, Keating is the only authority for this tale. Add this from *LL.* and *Harl.* 5280, fo. 54 a, and our 2nd Version, 36.

[7] Not mentioned by M. D'Arbois.

[8] Not in *M. D'Arbois*; nor is "Dergruaba Conaill," which is cited in *C. M. Rath*, p. 176, though he gives "Dergruathar Conaill" from p. 222 of that book: add "Aided na Macraide," *LB*, 139; "macrad" = the sons of Calatin, Cairpre, and Cúrúi (?).

CAṪ ROIS NA RÍOĠ FOR ḂÓINN AND SO SÍOS.

1. Trách fá raiḃe Conċuḃar mac Faċtna Faṫaiġ áird-ríġ Ulaḋ[a] a meirtne ⁊ a móir-chear ré rae ċían ⁊ ré haimsir ḟada; ⁊ níor ċodail ⁊ níor ṫoṁuil bíaḋ ris an rae sin, ⁊ níor luiḋ toil iona inntinn leis, ⁊ ní ḋearrna gen[b] ġáire iona forḃfaoilte ré mnaoi ná ré fear d'ḟearaiḃ Ulaḋ ré huċt[c] na haimsire sin. Agas baḋ himḟníoṁ mór le hUlltaiḃ uile an ní sin.

2. Agas do ráḋrad ré Caṫfaḋ[d] caoṁ-ḋraoi[e] a ráḋ ré Conċuḃar gan ḃeiṫ[f] is an meirtne iona san míolaoċas roim inna raiḃe, ⁊ do ċan Caṫfaḋ[g] sin ris.

3. Freagras Conċuḃar ḋó, ⁊ is eaḋ[h] aduḃairt: "A mo ḟosa a Ċaṫfaiḋ,"[i] ar sé, "is mór aḋḃar ⁊ daṁna agam-sa, óir do ruaċtadar ceiṫre hollċóigiḋ 'Eirionn, ⁊ do ṁúrsad mo ḋaingin ⁊ mo ḋúntaiḃ, ⁊ mo ḋrom-ṫulċaiḃ, a n-írliḃ, ⁊ a ngleantaiḃ, ⁊ do loisgriod mo ċoṁdaiġe[j] ⁊ mo ċaṫraċaiḃ, ⁊ mo ḋeaġ-ḃailtiḃ,[k] ⁊ do rugsad uaim mo ṁic, ⁊ mo ṁnáiḃ, ⁊ mo ṁacaoiṁ, ⁊ rugsad uaim fós mo ḃú, ⁊ mo ḃó-ṫáintiḃ buan-ḃleaċta, ⁊ mo eaċraċaiḃ áille allṁurḋa, ⁊ mo ṫuirc ṫroma ṫaoiḃ-leaṫna, ⁊ mo ṫairḃ ṫrodáin ṫoġaiḋe gan ḟaċain uaim." Agas is cuma do ḃí ag a ráḋ, ⁊ do sgeiṫ brúċt aḋḃal-ṁór do ċrú a ċroiḋe tar a ḃéal amaċ.

4. "Ní ráḋ aṁra ḋuit-si sin, a áird-ríġ," ar Caṫfaḋ, "óir is maiṫ do ḋíoġail Ulaiḋ sin ar ḟearaiḃ 'Eirionn, d'ar ḃrisiodar[l] caṫ Gáiriḋe ⁊ lolġáiriḋe orro." "Ni caṫ liom-sa caṫ naċ ar ṫuit ríġ, a Ċaṫfaiḋ," ar Conċuḃar; "aċt ċeana dearḃaim-si na móide ḋearḃaid Ulaiḋ, go ttuitfid ríġe ⁊ ruiriġ[m] riom-sa dom ṙeaċt, nó go ḃfaġ(ḃ)ar éag ⁊ oiḋeaḋ."

1–4] [a] idir Conċuḃar Rí Ulaḋ ⁊ Cairbre Niaḋfer Rí Teaṁrach, M. [b] gean, A.S. [c] heḋ, M. [d] do ráiḋ siad le Caṫf(aḋ), M.A.; Caṫfaiḋ, S. [e] caomḋraoi, A.S. [f] gan a ḃeiṫ, M.A.

THE BATTLE OF ROSNAREE HERE BELOW.

1. Once upon a time, Conchubhar son of Fachtna Fathach, high king of Ulster, was in depression and in a severe sickness[1] for a long time and for a lengthy period; and he slept not and ate not food during that time, and he had neither will nor intelligence, and he made not a smile of laughter or of gladness to woman or to man of the men of Ulster within that period. And that was a great trouble among all the Ulstermen.

2. And they said to Cathfadh the noble druid to tell Conchubhar not to be in that depression or unwarriorlike state in which he was; and Cathfadh spoke thus to him.

3. Conchubhar answered him, and this is what he said: "My master Cathfadh," said he, "I have great cause and reason *to be so;* for the four great provinces of Ireland have come and have destroyed my strongholds and my forts, and my ridge-hills in lowlands and in valleys, and they have burnt my fastnesses and my walled towns and my good home-steads, and they have taken from me my lads and my women and my youths, and they have taken from me too my cows and my herds of constant milk and my beautiful foreign steeds, my heavy side-broad hogs, and my choice fighting bulls, without provocation from me." And just as he was speaking a wonderful great vomit of his heart's blood burst out[2] through his mouth.

4. "That is not a strange saying of thine, O high-king," said Cathfadh, "for well have the Ulstermen avenged that on the men of Ireland, when they gained the battle of Gaireach and Iolghaireach over them." "I deem it no battle in which a king has not fallen, O Cathfadh," said Conchubhar; "however I swear the oaths that the Ulstermen swear that kings and chieftains shall fall by my hand for my right [?], or that I shall meet death and a tragical fate."

---

[g] Caċfaċ, A. [h] ar é, A. [i] Ċaċfaiġ, S. [j] dúntaiḃ repeated, S.
[k] beag-ḃailtiḃ, A.M. [l] ḃririoḃan, A.M. [m] ruire, S.

---

[1] móirċeas, falling sickness, *O'R.* [2] *Or* he threw up.

5. “Is í mo ċomairle-si ḋuit,” ar Caṫfaḋ, “anṁain go saṁraḋ; óir is fliuċ fuar gáiḃṫioċ gaoṫ-ḃuaḋarṫa geiṁre(aḋ), ⁊ ní ham eirġe[a] earraċ, óir is frasaċ fraoċḋa Faḃra, ⁊ is moċ an Marta, ⁊ ní huille Abraon ré haonaiġe,[b] ⁊ is mairg a mí Mái do(ġ)ní mór-ċuairt. Gonaḋ aire sin is cóir an sluaġ do ṫoirmeasg go saṁra(ḋ), go maḋ réiḋ raṫṁar na ródaiḃ, go maḋ éasgaḋ éadoṁuin na háṫa, gursaḋ aoiḃinn[c] árd na tulċa, go maḋ séitriġ sonairte ar sluaiġ, gursaḋ suanaiġ soiċearda ar ríoġa, gursaḋ cróḋa céim-neiṁneaċ ar ccuraḋaiḃ, gursaḋ éasgaḋ aḋṁara ar n-óig, gursaḋ aitheolaċ ilḃéarlaċ ar n-ollaṁuin, gursaḋ lúṫṁar láin-ġlic ar laoiċ, gursaḋ gléasta gaḃalta ar ngroiḋe, gursaḋ léiḋṁeaċ lúṫṁar ar láṁsgor[d] gursaḋ ilḃreaġa iongantaċ ar n-éadaiġe, gursaḋ cruaḋ-ḟaoḃraċ cros-órḋa ar ccloiḋṁṫe, gursaḋ sliorṫa sleaṁna slinn-ġéara ar sleaġa, gursaḋ cóiriġṫe clár-ḋaingean ar ccarbaid, gursaḋ caoṁa coṁġlas(a) na coillṫiḃ, gursaḋ dídiona na dosa dlúṫ-ḋuilleaċa, gur baḋ fairtriona gaċ fionn-ċarnn, ⁊ gurab cearcaill codalta gaċ fód féar-ġlas.

6. “Gonaḋ aire sin is cóir an sluaġ do ṫoirmiosg,” ar Caṫfaḋ, “go ttaguid Ulaiḋ uile d'éin-deóin ⁊ d'aon-láiṁ do ḋíoġail Tána Bó Cuailgne ar ḟearaiḃ 'Eirionn.

7. “Aċt atá ní[e] ċeana, cuir-si feara ⁊ teaċta uait go luċt do ṫuarasdail féin tar ṁuinċinn mara ⁊ mór-ḟairgge .i. go Muille ⁊ go Ruan, go Siogra rí Arcadía, go Mál, go Maolán, go hIomsgoa[f] ríġ[g] an seaċtṁaḋ rann do'n doṁuin Loċlannaċ, go Canaḋ na nGall, ⁊ go Maolán míliḋ, go rí hInse hOrc, go Conċuḃar mac Dúire meic Dunġaile, go h'Artúr Ruaḋ.”

8. Is ann sin do ċuir Conċuḃar Fionnċaḋ[h] mac Conċuḃair ⁊ Fionnċaoṁ mac Conuill Ċearrnuiġ do ṁóir-ṫionól na nGall soin tar ċeann maiṫiosa ⁊ mór-ṫuarasdail dáiḃ, ⁊ a n-oircill go ndíoġaldaois a nuilc ⁊ a n-éagcóra ar ḟearaiḃ 'Eirionn. “A Ċaṫfa(iḋ),” ar Conċuḃar, “anfad-sa fris na roċaiḋiḃ úd[i] ⁊ doḃeirim-si mo ḃriathar,” ar sé, “dá ttigid gin go ttigid

5-8] [a] ní ham aon-roda, S. [b] haonaiġiḃ, A.M. [c] éattrom, A. [d] laom-sgor, A.M. [e] aon ní, A. [f] Maoilin, Imsgo, S.A. [g] ríġ, A.M. [h] Fionnċaoṁ, A.S.M., see note, p. 6. [i] úd, go ttoirsead ċugam go raḋad-sa, &c., A.: ⁊ doḃeirimsi mo ḃriaṫar tar ċeana, ar sé, da ttigid mó gin.go dtíosaiḋ sin ċugam, go raḋadsa, M.

5. "This is my advice to thee," said Cathfadh, "to wait until Summer; for Winter is wet, cold, dangerous, storm-troubled, and Spring is no time for setting out; for February is rainy and tempestuous, and March is early, and April is not fitter[1] for assemblies, and woe to him who in the month of May makes a long circuit. Wherefore it is meet to stay the army until Summer, till the roads are smooth and safe, till the fords are rapid and shallow, till the hills[2] are pleasant and high; till our army corps are vigorous and strong, till our kings are valiant and dexterous, till our champions are valorous and stout-stepping,[3] till our youths are nimble and in good form,[4] till our sages are sharp-witted and eloquent, till our heroes are active and full-cunning, till our horses are trained and broken in [?]; till our hand-teams are strong and spirited, till our garments are of varied beauty and rare aspect, till our swords are hard-edged and hilt-golden, till our spears are sharp-pointed, smooth, and blade-keen, till our chariots are put in order and board-firm, till the woods are fair and all green, till the thick-leaved bushes are shelters, till every fair carn is conspicuous, and till every grass-green sod is a pillow of sleep.

6. "Wherefore it is meet to stay the army," said Cathfadh, "till all the Ulstermen come with one will and with one hand to avenge the Foray of the Kine of Cooley on the men of Ireland.

7. "Meanwhile send thou messengers and envoys forth to thy own mercenaries past the surface of sea and ocean, to wit, to Muille and to Ruan, to Siogra King of Arcadia, to Mál, to Máolan, to Iomsgo, King over the seventh part of the Scandinavian world, to Canadh of the Foreigners, and Máolan the warrior, to the King of the Island of Orc, to Conchubhar son of Dúire son of Dunghal, to Artúr the Red."

8. Then Conchubhar sent Fionnchadh son of Conchubhar and Fionnchaomh son of Conall Cearnach to muster largely those Foreigners for bounty and great pay to them, and to prepare them that they might avenge their wrongs and their injuries on the men of Ireland. "Cathfadh," said Conchubhar, "I shall wait for yonder hosts; and I give my word," said he, "whether they come or come not to

---

[1] uille, *compar.* of oll, greater, better; perhaps we should read huisse, fit, proper.

[2] *Or* meeting places, "rate-hills."

[3] *Cf.* sceim-neimnig in *Atkinson's Gloss.*

[4] adhmar = lucky, fortunate, in *O'R.*

ċugam[a] go raċad-sa go Teaṁraiġ go Cairbre Niaḋ Fear ⁊ go Fionn mac Rosa an ríġ-ḟéine, ⁊ go Luġaiḋ mac Con-Raoi, go hEochaiḋ mac Luċta, go Meiḋḃ ⁊ go hOilill go n-ionnsar ceiṫre ollċóigiḋ 'Eirionn, ⁊ go ḃfáġḃar leaċta ⁊ liaga ⁊ feartaiḃ fear a ḃfaonluiġe seaċnóin 'Eirionn, mur do ḟágḃadar-san mo ċóigeḋ-si."

9. Ciḋ tra aċt ódċlos[b] do Ṁeiḋḃ an ḃriaṫar[c] tug Conċuḃar, gonaḋ aire sin adubairt; "Is cóir ḋúinn teaċta do ċur uain(n) go Conċuḃar ⁊ a ráḋ ris cáċ do ṫoirmiosg ciort[d] a ċogaiḋ féin frí rae na bliaḋna-so, ⁊ géill do ḃeiṫ ó ḟearaiḃ 'Eirionn iona láiṁ-sion, ⁊ géill uaḋ-san dóiḃ-sion ré tairise na bliaḋna so." "Cia baḋ cuḃa(i)ḋ[e] ré hiomráḋ na n-aiṫiosg soin?" ar Oilill. "Cia do raċaḋ ann," ar Meaḋḃ, "aċt Mac Róiġ an ríġ-ṁíle?" Do laḃair Mac Róiġ ⁊ do rá(i)ḋ: "Ní raċar-sa ann soin eidir, óir ní ḃfuil móin ná maiġ, daingean, ná deaġ-ḃaile, na leaċt luiġe[f] laoċ a n-Ultaiḃ uile dár milleaḋ lé fearaiḃ Connaċt naċ mise is cionntaċ ris." "A Ḟearġair, na habair sin," ar Meaḋḃ, "óir ní béar[g] d'Ulltaiḃ aċmusán[h] do ṫaḃairt do ṫeaċtaiḃ do ġréas. 'Oir dá marḃaḋ neaċ aṫair nó bráṫair gaċ aoin díoḃ, ní baḋ oṁan[i] dó iad iar ndul na cceann."[j] D'aontuiġ Mac Róiġ an ní sin, ⁊ adubairt Meaḋḃ ris dul go Fionn mac Rosa ríġ Laiġean, ⁊ go Cairbre Niaḋ Fear ríġ Teaṁraċ, d'innisin na ccoṁaḋ soin dóiḃ.

10. Ráinig an ríġ-ṁíleḋ[k] go Fionn mac Rosa ⁊ ráiḋios[l] Fionn ré Doirn-iuḃra ua Ḟir-ġabann ⁊ lé Fioḋaċ Folt-ġarḃ dol leis go Teaṁraiġ[m] go Cairbre Niaḋ Fear ⁊ ró innseadar a ttosga et a ttoiċim dó.

11. Cuirios iomorro Cairbre Faḋḃ ua hIomnaḋa leo go Conċuḃar mac Neasa, .i. ríġ neartaṁail[n] nUlaḋ; ⁊ ro ċansad a n-aithiosga ris. "Is briaṫar ḋaṁ-sa,"[o] ar Conċuḃar, "naċ geaḃad-sa coṁaiḋ[p] ar bioṫ go roiċear[q] Cruaċan-Ráṫ[q] hAoi, ⁊

8-11] [a] ċugad, S. [b] atċlos, S.; adċlos, M. [c] an ḃriaṫar . . . do ṫug, A. [d] ar ċeart, A. [e] cuḃaḋ, S.; cuiḃe, A.M. [f] leaċt nó luiġe, M. [g] beóċt, M. [h] acusan, A. [i] uaṁan, A. [j] cceaḋ, A. [k] ríġṁíliḋ, A. [l] abrar, M.A. [m] Teaṁraiġ na ríoġ, A.M. [n] neart-ṁar, A.M. [o] daṁsa, M. [p] cuṁaiḋ, S. [q] roiċar . . . Ráṫa, S.

me, that I will go to Tara to Cairbre Nia Fear and to Fionn son of Ros, the king-warrior, and to Lughaidh son of Cû-Raoi, to Eocha son of Luchta, to Meadhbh and to Oilill, till I ravage the four great provinces of Ireland, and till I leave the monuments and tombstones and graves of men lying prostrate throughout Ireland, as they have left my province."

9. Now the vow that Conchubhar took was heard of by Meadhbh, who thereupon said: "It is meet for us to send envoys to Conchubhar and say to him [that] everyone [should] stay the right of his own war[1] during the space of this year, and that he hold in hand hostages from the men of Ireland and give hostages to them during the armistice[2] of this year." "Who would be suitable to announce those terms?" said Oilill. "Who should go thither," said Meadhbh, "but Mac Róigh, the king-warrior?" Mac Róigh spake and said: "I will not go thither at all, for there is not a moor or a plain, a stronghold or a goodly homestead, or a heroes' monument in all Ulster that has been ravaged by the men of Connacht, but that I am to blame for it." "Fearghus,[3] say not so," quoth Meadhbh, "for it is not ever a custom of the Ulstermen to offer reproach to envoys. For if one should kill the father or brother of every one of them, he should not have to fear them, having gone to meet them."[4] Mac Róigh conceded this, and Meadhbh told him to go to Fionn son of Ros, King of Leinster, and to Cairbre Nia Fear, King of Tara, to inform them of those conditions.

10. The king-warrior came to Fionn son of Ros, and Fionn said to Doirniubhra [Fist of yew] grandson of Ceap-ghabha [Fetter-smith], and to Fíodhach Coarse-hair, to go with him [Mac Róigh] to Tara of the Kings, to Cairbre Nia Fear; and they told their business and their mission[5] to him.

11. Cairbre likewise sends Fadhbh grandson of Iomnadh with them to Conchubhar son of Neas, the mighty King of Ulster; and they announced to him their proposals. "It is my vow," said Conchubhar son of Neas, "that I will accept no terms till I reach

---

[1] Maintain an armed truce (?).

[2] tairise = tairisem, cessation, stay; *or* "friendship," *O'R.*

[3] Mac Róig, the herald, is confounded here with Fergus Mac Róig; or something is omitted. The herald is always called "Mac-Roth" in *LU.* and *LL.*

[4] i.e. as an envoy; so Daire did not molest the messengers of Medb; *see* Preface.

[5] *Lit.* journey, i.e. its cause. Cf. *cid is toisc do Patraicc*, what is P.'s desire? *Trip. Life*, 128; it also means "business."

go n-ionnsar ceiṫre hollċóigiḋ 'Éirionn,[a] go ndíoġlar mo ṫarḃ[b] ⁊ mo ṫána orro.”

12. Ní cian do ḃádar ar na hiomráitiḃ sin, an tan tangadar teaċta na loingsi aḋḃal-ṁóire allṁurḃa ró cuireaḋ ré Conċuḃar,[c] iar ngaḃáil cuain[d] a ttráiġ áluinn inḃir ⁊ ag Tráiġ Ḃaile Ḃuain ⁊ ag Sruiṁ Innse hOiliolla: ⁊ táinig Conċuḃar iar sin 'n-a ccoinne go Dún Dealgan, ⁊ tángadar[e] maithe na loingsi allṁurḃa sin 'n-a ċoinne[f] ann go teaċ Con gCulainn ṁeic Suḃaltaiṁ.[g]

13. Agas fearas an Cú fáilte go mioċáir muinntearḃa riu, go ndubairt, “Mo ċean ḃur n-aiṫne ⁊ ḃur neaṁ-aiṫne, ḃur maiṫ ⁊ ḃur saiṫ,[h] bur n-óig ⁊ bur sean,” ar sé. Do ḃádar mar sin ó'n taoi seaċtṁaine[i] go aroile ag ól ⁊ aoiḃneas. Is ann soin do ṫiomáin Conċuḃar ceiliobraḋ do Ċo(i)n gCulainn, ⁊ d'Éiṁeir ingin Ḟorgaill Monaḋ, go ndubairt: “Fleaḋ ċoitċionn do ḟleaḋ, a Ċoin gColuinn; mioḋ ar ṫruaġuiḃ ⁊ ar ṫréanuiḃ do ṁioḋ.”

14. Is ann sin adubairt Mac Róiġ: “'O nach anaiḋ[k] ar ċoṁaiḋ, a Ċonċuḃair, ca conair a raċair ar so?” “Raċad-sa,” ar Conċuḃar, “go Cuan Ġlaise Sléiḃe Ḃreaġ,[l] ⁊ ar soin go Ros na Ríoġ for Ḃóinn, go Cairbre Niaiḋ Ḟear, ⁊ go maiṫiḃ líonṁara Laiġean, go ndíoġólar[m] orra a ndearnrad ar an ttáin[n] don ċor so.”

15. Iomṫusa Ṁic Róiġ ⁊ na teaċta,[o] tángadar reampo go Teaṁraiġ go Cairbre, ⁊ innsid dó, “Conċuḃar d'obaḋ na ccoṁaḋ[p] réaṁ-ráite, ⁊ é féin go n-a loingeas do ḃeiṫ a ttiġ[q] Ċon cColuinn fria ré seaċtṁoine ag ól ⁊ ag aoiḃneas, ⁊ Fionnċaḋ[r] mac Conċuḃuir, ⁊ Fionnċaoṁ mac Conaill Ċernaiġ do ṫeaċt ris na heaṫruiḃ allṁurḃa sin go Tráiġ n-Eochaille,[s] ⁊ go Tráiġ Inġine Fleiḋir, ⁊ Conċubar do ṫeaċt go Cuan Ġlaise Ḃréaġ[t] ⁊ ar soin go Ros na Ríoġ for Ḃóinn do ċur caṫa riḃ-si.” Is eaḋ[u]

11-15] [a] riom, S. [b] ṫairḃ, S. [c] an tan do ċoncadar na teaċta loingis aḋḃal-ṁóra éigciallaiḋe allṁurḃa róḃár ró cuireaḋ ó Ċonċuḃar, A.M. [d] ⁊ calaiḋ, A.M. [e] táinig, S. [f] ċuige, A. [g] Suḃaltaiġ, A. [h] saiġ, S. [i] o 'n tseaċtṁuin, A.M. [j] do ráiḋ, A. [k] read ana = later anair, thou stayest (?) or ccoṁaiḋ = (our) terms (?). [l] Cuan Ġlaise breaġ, A.M. [m] díoġalar, M. [n] for a ttáinig, S.M.

Cruachan-Rátha [Rathcroghan] of Magh Aoi, and till I ravage the four great provinces of Ireland, till I avenge my bull and my herds upon them."

12. Not long were they upon that parley, when arrived the messengers of the vast foreign fleet that had been invited by Conchubhar, having taken haven on the beautiful strand of an estuary, [and] at the strand of Baile Buain, and at the stream of Inis Oiliolla; and Conchubhar came thereupon to meet them to Dundalk, and the chiefs of that foreign fleet came to meet him there, to the house of Cû-Chulainn son of Subhaltamh.

13. And the Hound bade them welcome affectionately and kindly, and said, "Welcome to your known and your unknown, your good and your bad, your young and your old," said he. They were thus from one end[1] of a week to the other drinking and merrymaking. Then Conchubhar bade farewell to Cû-Chulainn, and to Eimhear daughter of Forgall Monadh, saying: "A common[2] feast is thy feast, Cû-Chulainn; an honour for the weak, and for the strong thy honour."

14. Then said Mac Róigh, "Since our terms stand not,[3] O Conchubhar, *by* what way wilt thou go hence?" "I shall go," said Conchubhar, "to Cuan-Ghlaise of Sliabh Breagh, and thence to Rosnaree on the Boyne, to Cairbre Nia Fear and to the numerous chiefs of Leinster, until I avenge on them what they have done on the Foray this time."

15. As for Mac Róigh and the envoys, they went forward to Tara to Cairbre, and told him that Conchubhar refused the aforesaid terms, and that he himself with his foreign auxiliaries were in Cû-Chulainn's house for a week's time, drinking and merrymaking, and that Fionnchadh son of Conchubhar and Fionnchaomh son of Conall Cearnach had come with those foreign ships to the Strand of Eochaill and to the Strand of the Daughter of Fleidheas, and that Conchubhar was coming to Cuan-Ghlaise Breagh and thence to Rosnaree on *the*

---

[o] na ttteaċta, A. [p] ccoṁaḋ, S.A. [q] ttoiġ, A. [r] Fionnċaoṁ, A.M.
[s] n-Eoċaille, A.M. [t] C. Ġ. ſléiḃe bṗéaġ, M. [u] ar é, A.M.

---

[1] taoi = turn, *O'R.*

[2] *Or* public.

[3] *Or* since thou stayest not for the terms; anad ar = to abide by.

aduḃairt Cairbre go ḃfriṫeolaḋ féin é, ⁊ go ttioḃraḋ caṫ dó; ⁊ téiḋ iomurro Mac Róiġ go Cruaċain-Ráṫa[a] hAoi, ⁊ innisios na sgéala soin ann.

16. Is aṁlaiḋ iomorro do ḃí Mac Róiġ, fear tailc tarḃḋa treatalta[b] é, ⁊ é siorṫaċ slait-réiḋ[c] sír-ṡiuḃlaċ, léiḋmeaċ lúṫ-ṁar lán-airḋreaċ, feaḋmṁar fír-ġlic fuireaċair ré heidir-ġleoḋ ceard ⁊ caingean a leagaiḃ ⁊ a leaḃraiḃ taiġleoireaċta ⁊ teaċ-tairioċta; go n-éadaċ eaċl(aġ)a[d] uime .i. léine ṫrosall ṫreaḃ-naiḋe ré a ċnear, brat-lomann lean-ċorcra táirsiḃ seaċtair, maḋ-lorg féiṫreannaċ iona láiṁ ċlí, cloiḋioṁ líoṁṫa leadar-ḟaoḃraċ, go n-altaiḃ déad iona ḋear-láiṁ, dá ḃearn-ḃróig ḃreac-ḋéanṁaċa im a ṫroiġṫiḃ, cuaċ-ḟnaiḋm coṁḋaingean curaḋ dá ḟolt im a ċúl, bearraḋ leaṫan liaṫ lais ar fad a ċeann-ṁullaiġ a ccoṁarṫa ealaḋan[e] re taiġleoirioċt ⁊ ré toirim-ṫeaċt ⁊ re teaċtairioċt na h'Eirionn, go ḃrios sgéal na ríoġ ⁊ na suireaċ leis do Ṁeiḋḃ ⁊ do Oilill go Cruaċan-Ráṫa h-Aoi ré deireaḋ[f] gaċ laoi ⁊ innisios a sgéala dóiḃ, aṁail buḋ ġnáṫ leis.[g]

17. Iomṫúsa Ċairbre Niaiḋ Fear, cearṁaiġṫear sonn seal oile: do ċuir teaċt uaiḋ ċum a ḃráiṫre ⁊ ċum a ċáirde féin, dá ccruinniuġaḋ ⁊ dá ccoiṁṫionól ré ffearḋal caṫa do Ċonċuḃar ⁊ d'Ulltaiḃ ar ċeana. Do riaċtadar na teaċta soin go tréan-ḟearaiḃ troiġ-éarġaḋa ċóigiḋ[h] Laiġean, ⁊ go Collaṁnaiḃ Ċríċe Ḃreaġ ⁊ Míḋe. Tángadar ann fós trí caṫa Ċloinne Deirg ⁊ caṫ Tuaiṫe Ḃreaġ[i] ⁊ Míḋe go Teaṁraiġ,[j] áit a mbí Cairbre Niaiḋ Fear, ⁊ do rinneaḋ[k] coṁairle leo ann .i. ionnsaiġe a ccoinne[l] Ċonċuḃair go hionad a mbí a ḋáil ag Ros na Ríoġ ros Ḃóinn; óir[m] níor ṁiaḋ ⁊ níor ṁaise sir na hoireaċtaiḃ aḋḃal-ṁóra sin neaċ ar biṫ dá n-ionnsaiġe ar ttús gan iad féin do

15-17] [a] Cruaċan, A. [b] treitealda, M. [c] slait-réiḋ, A. [d] eaċlanna, M.; echlaige, *LL.* 70 b. [e] a n-iomċoṁarṫa ealaḋna, A.M. [f] deiriḋ, S. [g] ḋó, A. [h] ċóigiḋ leaṫan-ṁóir Laiġean ⁊ go Collaṁnaiġ coṁḋaingne, &c., A. [i] Tuaiṫ mḃreaġ, A. [j] T. na ríoġ, A. [k] do cuireaḋ, A. [l] a n-aircís, A. [m] do ċuadar ann ssir, óir, &c., A.M.

[1] *Or* "harassing," *O'R.* *Cf.* sluag sirechtach, *S. na Rann*, l. 8133.
[2] treaḃnaide for léne ṫrebnaid srebnaide, streaked shirt, *Man. & Cust.*

Boyne to give them [*lit.* you] battle. This is what Cairbre said: that he himself would attend to him and that he would give him battle; and Mac Róigh went to Cruachan-Rátha of [Magh] Aoi, and told those tidings there.

16. Now of this description was Mac Róigh: a stout, bull-like, stalwart man was he, and he was searchful,[1] rod-smooth, long-striding, robust, active, full-travelled, deedful, cunning, watchful for contention of questions and disputes in the stones [?] and books of embassage and diplomacy; with a herald's raiment about him, to wit, a girded shirt of hide[2] next his skin, a corded purple [or scarlet] cloak over it [*lit.* them] outside, a woodbine[3] [?] hand-staff in his left hand, a polished keen-edged sword with hilt[4] of ivory in his right hand, two variegated gapped-shoes[5] on his feet, a champion's firm curl-knot of his hair on his head; a wide grey tonsure[6] he had all over his crown, in token of proficiency in the diplomacy and ambassadorship and embassage of Ireland, bringing a report of the tidings of the kings and chieftains with him to Meadhbh and Oilill, to Cruachan-Rátha of [Magh] Aoi at the close of every day:—and he told them his tidings *on this occasion*, as it was customary with him.

17. Concerning Cairbre Nia Fear there is question here for another while—he sent off an envoy to his brothers and to his own friends, to gather them and to assemble them to offer battle to Conchubhar, and to the Ulstermen in general. Those envoys reached [to] the swift-footed brave men of the province of Leinster and the Collamhna[7] of the territory of Bregia and Meath. Thither also came three battalions of Clann Deirg and a battalion of the people of Bregia and Meath to Tara, where Cairbre Nia Fear was; and a resolve was taken by them there, to wit, to advance against Conchubhar to the place where his tryst was, at Rosnaree on the Boyne; for those mighty clans[8] deemed it not honourable or seemly that anyone should attack them first,

---

III. 95, 97; srebnaide, gl. *membranaceus;* ṫrosall for rosall, = walrus hide shirt. Cf. *Siab. Ch. Con C.*, 425.

[3] Seems a compound of feiċ and reannach, pointed; fech = smooth.

[4] *Cf.* cloidheamh co n-altaib, *L. na gCeart;* co n-eltaib déc, *Man. & Cust.* III. 94.

[5] Leggings, or "a divided skirt." O'Curry renders it "firm shoes," *Man. & Cust.* II. 297; but it seems the garment from waist to feet. *Cf. Zimmer's Kelt. Stud.* III., pp. 82 to 84.

[6] Closely cut, but not shaved. [7] Columns. [8] Assemblies.

ḋol go calma na ccoṁḋáil. Do rinneaḋ leo an ċoṁairle sin, ⁊ éirġid na ceiṫre caṫa coṁṁóra sin fa toirn-ċriṫ airm ⁊ iolḟaoḃair, go rángodar Ros na Ríoġ do ḟreasdal caṫa do Ċonċuḃar. Do ċuireadar a ndiormaḋa gléasta glain-reaṁra ⁊ a n-eaċraḋa áille allṁurḋa ann soin ar ṡraiṫiḃ ⁊ ar ṡíṫ-ġleanntaiḃ Innḃir na Bóinne bruaċ-áirde, ⁊ do ṡuiġiodar a ccuraḋa ⁊ a ccaiṫ-ṁíleaḋa[a] ⁊ a laoiċ goile ⁊ gairgiḋ[b] ar ṫulċaiḃ ṫaiḋḃreaċa[c] an ṁaiġe, ⁊ ar ḟorg-ċnocaiḃ fonn-ġlasa[d] féarṁara ⁊ ar ródaiḃ réiḋe ró-ṡoillse ós an mḃóinn mbruaċ-ġloin[e] mbraiscíġniġ[f] go subaċ soirḃeaṁuil.[g]

18. Dála Ċonċuḃair iomorro: ar tteaċt ó Ḋún Dealgan dó, d'ḟeiseaḋ an oiḋċe sin ag Cuain Glaise Sléiḃe Breaġ, ⁊ do anasdar Cú Ċulainn a nDún Dealgan d'éis Ulaḋ ré ḟreasdal ⁊ ré friṫeolaṁ a lóin ⁊ ré teagar ⁊ ré tionól a ṁuinntire ⁊ ré háirioṁ ⁊ ré hordugaḋ gaċa[h] neiṫe oile buḋ cuḃaiḋ[i] ċum turair.

19. Iomṫúsa Ċonċuḃair, ro éiriġ amoċ do ló ar n-a ṁáraċ ré heagar a ḋeaġ-ṡluaiġ, ⁊ do ċuir eaċlaċa airdir[j] ⁊ a luaiṫ-leoṁain ⁊ a lonn-óglaoiċ roiṁe do ġaḃáil foraḋ ⁊ longṗoirt ag Ros na Ríoġ for Bóinn; go ḃfacadar uaṫa na haiseaċta móra múirneaċa ⁊ na groiḋe leaṫan-ṁóra láin-ġléasda ⁊ na buail-tiḃ bir-ġéara boḋḃa, ⁊ taiġle[k] na sleaġ slinn-ġéar[l] sleaṁain-ċruaiḋ, ⁊ forgaḋ[m] ⁊ fír-ḋeallraḋ na sgiaṫ n-ilḃreac n-éag-saṁail,[n] ⁊ na n-earraḋ n-daingean n-iongantaċ n-allṁurḋa, ⁊ na luirioċ ndlúiṫ[o] ndriṫleannaċ[p] ndeaġ-ṡolais, seasdán ⁊ séiseilḃ na sluaġ, gáir-ġlór ⁊ grod-luaṁain na ngruagaċ rompa[q] ann. Ciḋ trá aċt ró iompuiġeadar an ġiollanraḋ iar soin san ċonair ċeadna tar a n-ais,[r] ⁊ ró inniriodar do Ċon-ċuḃar, go ḃfacadar trí caṫa Ċloinne Deaġaḋ et mór-ċaṫ na cCollaṁnaċ ⁊ Fear mBreaġ ar a cceann ag Ros na Ríoġ.[s] "Ní fear[t] dúinn aṁ naċ fíor sin," ar Conċuḃar, "aċt cuirfiom féinneaḋ forasda fír-ġlic d'féaċain orro sain."

17-19] [a] miliḋ, M.; mileaḋaiḃ, A.S. [b] gairge, S. [c] taiḋḃreana, A. [d] fionn-ġlasa, A. [e] mb. glain, M. [f] mbraiséigniġ, M. [g] subaċ sianṡanaċ soirḃneaṁail, A.M. [h] gaċa tionnċuire eile baḋ ċuiḋe ċum feasta fleaḋa, A. [i] ċuṁaḋ, S. [j] airdir, ⁊ astar-ċoin turusa, A.; note the a omitted before eaċlaċa. [k] taiḋleaḋ, M. [l] slinn-ġéara, A.S. [m] forcaḋ, M. [n] eaxaṁail, A. [o] ndlúiṫe, S.

while they themselves went not boldly to encounter them. That resolve was taken by them, and those four so great battalions set out with resonance of weapon and of many a blade, until they arrived at Rosnaree to offer battle to Conchubhar. They set their ordered fair sturdy troops and their comely foreign cavalry there on the flats and on the peaceful [or fairy] glens of the Inver [estuary or river] of the high-banked Boyne, and they placed their champions and their battle-warriors, and their heroes of valour and chivalry on the showy [or haunted] hillocks of the plain, and on the pleasant-green grassy shelter-knolls, and on the level shining roads above the bank-bright, quick-bounding [?] Boyne, merrily, happily.

18. About Conchubhar further: having come from Dundalk, he was resting that night at Cuan Glaise of Sliabh Breagh; and Cú-Chulainn stayed in Dundalk behind the Ulstermen to provide for and attend to his stores, and to gather and assemble his people, and to list and arrange everything else that would be proper for a march.

19. To return to Conchubhar: he rose early of the day on the morrow, to array his good army, and he sent his pioneers and his swift lions, and his bold warriors before him, to take position and camp at Rosnaree on the Boyne; and they saw at a distance the great marshalled [?][1] clans, and the broad-large perfectly-ordered horse, and the sharp-shafted squares [?][2] of war, and the sheen of the keen-bladed smooth-hard spears, and the covering and great splendour of the many-hued variegated shields, and of the stout, wonderful foreign armour and of the dense, sparkling, fair-bright hauberks, [and they heard] the cry and murmur[3] of the host, the shouting voice[s] and rapid movements of the goblins[4] before them there. However, the soldiery turned back in the same path, and informed Conchubhar that they had seen three battalions of Clann Deagha and a great battalion of the Collamhnachs and the men of Bregia before them at Rosnaree. "We know not but that that is true," said Conchubhar, "but we shall send a skilled prudent soldier to reconnoitre them."

---

[p] ndriċleannaḋa, A.S. [q] reampa, A. [r] ceadna dia n-air, A.
[s] dionn, A. [t] fior, A.

[1] *Or* clamorous, *C. M. Lena*, 104.

[2] Pens, folds. [3] *Man. & Cust.* III. 426; *LL.* 57 b, 54 a.

[4] Also means "chieftains"; but *cf.* ro gairsetar imme boccanaig ocus bánanaig ocus geniti glinni ocus demna aeoir, *LL.* 82 b, fo. 59 ba.

20. Is ann sin d'éiriġ aon-ḟear úḋṁall úiréarsaḋ úrspraic-ṫeaċ d'Ulltaiḃ .i. Dáiġ mac Deáġaḋ, et aduḃairt, "Raċad-sa d'ḟios ⁊ d' úir-ḟéaċain[a] an tsluaiġ úd"; et do ġaḃ a ċaṫ-arm uime iar soin ⁊ ráinig an ionad radhairc ar na ruaḋ-ḃuiḋniḃ sin. "Is fíor," ar sé, "is líonṁar an sluaġ úd; aċt aṁáin ní mó ná díol mo ġaisgiḋ-se im' aonar atá ionntaiḃ[b];" et leis sin ró ionnsaiḋ go haindréanda[c] ainiarmurtaċ aṫġarb iad, ⁊ tug ruabairt ḟaol-ċon fúṫaiḃ,[d] gur ċuir mórán a n-úir-ċréaċtaiḃ ⁊ a n-oṫair-linntiḃ éaga ⁊ aḋarṫa díoḃ; giḋeaḋ do rinneaḋ buaile boḋḃa uime-sion iar soin, go ndearnaḋ goin ġalann[e] de; et Duṁaḋ Dáiġ ainm in inid ar marḃaḋ[f] é, ⁊ is ann ro haḋnacaḋ.

21. Buḋ fada le Conċuḃar do ḃí Dáiġ, ⁊ ro ċuir fear oile d'ḟios an tsluaiġ .i. Féiġ mac Fallaṁuin[g]; ⁊ an tan ro ċon(n)-airc soin an sluaġ ar ḃrú na Bóinne, ro ċeil a ṁeanmain[h] orro, go ṅduḃairt:[i] "Ní raċad-sa d' iarra(i)ḋ soċaiḋe oile ċucca súd aċt mé féin;" ⁊ téid fúṫaiḃ[j] aṁail faol-ċu fó ċaor-ċuiḃ, nó aṁail leoṁan fó lár-ġroiḋiḃ, nó aṁail seaḃaic fó ṁin-éanaiḃ, gur ġaḃ ag a cciorrḃaḋ ⁊ ag a ccíoraḋ, ag a ttuinnṁeaḋ, ⁊ ag a ttearsaḋ, go ttug leoḋ ⁊ leadraḋ[k] mór orro, ⁊ do ċuir ára éidríoṁta ar na sluaġaiḃ, nó gur ḃrúġrad croinn a ṡleaġ fá a ḋornaiḃ, gur lúbaḋ ⁊ gur láin-tearsaḋ a ċloiḋioṁ iona ċroḃ; ⁊ iar[l] ndíobaḋ á airm ann soin, do[m] linngriod na sluaġaiḃ air, gur ṫuairsgriod ⁊ gur ṫrom-ġoinsead[n] é. Ró ḟaiḋ-siom rompa[o] iar soin is an mBóinn gur báitheaḋ innte é; gonaḋ uaiḋ ainmniġṫear Linn Féiġ ar Bóinn ó ṡoin ale.

22. Is ann sin ro éiriġ Irial Glúnṁar gairgeaṁuil mac Conuill[p] Ċearnaiġ dá ḃféaċain; et miḋear ⁊ móir-ḟéaċar iad. "Is fíor," ar sé, "gurab iomḋa álainn allṁurḋa na hoir-eaċta úd adċíu,[q] ⁊ is neiṁneaċ naṫarḋa a n-arm, ⁊ is fuileaċ

20-22] [a] úrḟaicsin, A. [b] ionnta: aċt atá aon ní ċeana, d'ionnsoiġ, &c., A.M. [c] Unassailable: see note *infra*. [d] Fúṫa, A. [e] gal, A.S.; galan, M. [f] ionaid a ttorċair, A. [g] Follaṁain, A. [h] meanma, A.; read, ro cheir a ṁeanma (?). [i] go mbeart, A. [j] féiṫ, A. [k] leadraḋ ⁊ aṫċomaḋ orra, gur ċuir, &c., A. [l] gur

20. Then arose a stirring, active, energetic man of the Ulstermen, to wit, Dâigh son of Deagha, and said: "I will go to know about and examine yonder army"; and he took his battle-armour about him thereupon, and arrived at the place of outlook upon those strong bands. "It is true," quoth he, "yonder army is numerous, but yet it is no more than the price of my valour alone that is in them [they are no more than equivalent to my valour alone];" and therewith he attacked them roughly, recklessly, rudely, and made a wolf's onset at them, until he laid many of them in deep wounds, and in sick pools of death and prostration;[1] yet there was made a ring [penfold] of slaughter [?] round him thereupon, so that a mortal hostile[2] wound was made of him; and *Dumhadh Dâigh* is the name of the place where he was slain, and there he was buried.[3]

21. It seemed to Conchubhar that Dâigh was long *absent*, and he sent another man to inspect the army, to wit, Fêigh son of Fallamhan. And when he saw the army on the bank of the Boyne, he concealed his mind about [from ?] them, and said: "I will not go to seek other numbers but myself against those yonder [*i.e.* the enemy, or the Ulstermen]:" and he goes at them like a wolf at sheep, or like a lion at herds of mares, or like a hawk at small birds, and began to hack and to tear them, to crush and to cut them, till he wrought great carnage and havoc, and put countless destructions on the troops, until the shafts of his spears broke under his hands, till his sword was bent and deep-hacked in his grasp; and then, having destroyed his arms, the hosts leapt upon him, and crushed and sore-wounded him. He retired before them into the Boyne, and he was drowned therein; and from him is named Linn Fêigh [Fêigh's Pool] on the Boyne thenceforward.

22. Then went forth Irial Glûnmhar [the great-kneed, or the high-descended], the valorous, son of Conall Cearnach, to inspect them; and he measured and reconnoitred them. "It is true," said he, "that many, comely, splendid [*lit.* foreign], are yonder clans I see [?], and venomous, serpent-like their arms, and bloody and keen

---

ḋioḃaḋ, A. [m] ġuṗ, A. [n] ċṗom-ġoineaḋ, S., *perp.* [o] ṗeampa. [p] Conaill ċalma Ċaeṗnaiġ ḋá ḃṗéaḋain a ccéaḋóiṗ, A.M. [q] aḋóíḋ, S.; [r] ḋóíḋ, A.

---

[1] Lit., "of pillow," i.e. he laid them low. [2] ġalann = ġaiṗceḋ naṁaḋ, *O'Cl.*
[3] Ḋuṁaḋ Ḋaiġ is Dowth (?); Ḋubaḋ in the *Annalists* and *Mesca Ulad.*

faoḃraḋ a ḃforġona; ⁊ ní ṫioḃar-sa mo ċosgar féin ná cos-gar mo ṁuinntire dóiḃ. Aċt áit a ttioḃraid Ulaiḋ uile a ccuid caṫa dóiḃ, doḃéar-sa mo ċongnaṁ go ndíċioll leo;" ⁊ fillios a ḃfriṫing[a] na conaire céadna. 'Odċoncadar na Gaileoin sin, do leansad dronga dísgire deaġ-ṡluaiġ é, ⁊ do léig-siod graifne data donn-luaṫa iona ḋiaiḋ,[b] go rugsad air; ⁊ tug Irial sgiaṫ tar lorg tar éis a ṁuinntire, go rug iomlán leis iad go háit a raiḃ Conċuḃar, iar marḃaḋ móráin don druing do lean é; ⁊ d'innis mar do ċonnairc na sluaġ(a). "Et is eaḋ is cóir ḋaoiḃ," ar sé, "gan buain riu go ttig ḃur ttreoin ⁊ ḃur ttreitill ⁊ ḃur laoiċ goile ⁊ gaisgiḋ ċugaiḃ; ⁊ taḃraiḋ caṫ d' aon-taoiḃ ḋóiḃ."

23. Ar mbeith dóiḃ ar na hiomrátiḃ sin, do ċoncadar buiḋean ríoġ(ḋ)a ró-ṁór dá n-ionnsaiġe go ccosṁailios céad-laoċ; ⁊ fear fraoċda fearḋa forḋonn a n-úrṫosaċ na buiḋne sin, ⁊ é bruas-ṁór[c] brioċt-náiṁdiġe bruiṫion-ġarḃ, ⁊ é srón-ṁór seang-ġruaiḋioċ sáir-ġeanaṁail, áluinn olṁar[d] uḃall-rosgaċ; folt trom teiṁiol-ġarḃ[e] air, úrlaḃra úrfraicṫeaċ aṫġarḃ aindréanda[f] lais: ⁊ sgiaṫ ċoṁraiġṫeaċ[g] ċalaḋ[h]-ḃuailteaċ for a ċlé-ġualainn, go n-a dí ḃile[i] iarrnaiḋe na húirṫimċioll; cloiḋioṁ catat cruaiḋ-ġéar clar-lonnraċ for a ċlí; manaois mór-ṁúirneaċ áisgidiḋe ré hais a ġualann; brat gorm gaḃaltaċ uime, ⁊ eo airgid éin-ġil ann; léine leaḃair-líoġa ṡróill ré a ċneis,[j] carbad mór miḋleaṫan for ḋá eaċ donna daṫ-áille faoi;—baḋ dian deimneaḋaċ[k] ró ċing an carbad gus an marc-ṡluaġ[l] ḃí uime. Baḋ saṁalta go ḃfrais-diu-ḃraicdís[m] mór-ḟóḋaiḃ ⁊ mion-ċloċa na maiġe, go ccaiṫdís ceaṫa tiuġa-dlúiṫe duḃ-ġorma uaḋa, do loim-ġriana luaiṫreaḋa na luiġe. Agas is é do ḃí ann: .i. Dáire Donn Duḃ-Ċuailgne, do ḃíoġail a tán ⁊ a ṫarḃ ar ḟearaiḃ 'Eirionn; gonaḋ ann isbeart

---

22, 23] [a] iarsin aḃfriting, A.M. [b] ḋiaiġ, S. [c] bruaḋt-ṁór, A. [d] Perhaps oll-ṁór, very great. [e] tiṁiol-ġarḃ, S. [f] aindréanta, A.M.; *pl.*, "unassailable," *C. M. Lena*, 82. [g] coṁraicṫeaḋ, M. [h] ċalad, Ab.; caṫlod, S.; cf. cruaid, calad, *LL.* 78 b. [i] ḃile aite iarnaiḋe, A. [j] ċnear, S. [k] deimneaċ, M. [l] -ṡluaiġ, S. [m] ḃfraisdiuḋraictis.

their woundings; and I will not give my own slaughter or the slaughter of my people to them. But where the Ulstermen all will give [their share of] battle to them, I will give them my assistance with endeavour;" and he returned in the backward direction[1] of the same path. When the Gȧleoin saw this, fierce bands of a goodly army followed, and they dispatched comely, brown-swift troops of horse [chasers] after him, until they overtook him: and Irial put a shield across track behind his people [*i. e.* covered their retreat], till he brought them safe with him to the place where Conchubhar was, having slain many of those who pursued him; and he related how he saw the armies: "And this is what is proper for you," said he, "not to meddle with them till your mighty ones and your horsemen and your warriors of valour and chivalry come to you; and give ye battle together to them."

23. While they were in this parley, they saw a kingly numerous band approaching them, with the semblance of a hundred champions; and a fierce, manly, dark-brown man in the fore-front of that band; stately, spell-hostile, skirmish-rude was he; and great-nosed, hollow-cheeked, exceeding comely, handsome, drinksome, apple-eyed was he. He wore heavy murky-rugged hair. His speech was energetic, rough, and precipitate. He bore a fighting,[2] hard-smiting shield on his left shoulder, with its two iron rims all around it, a hard, steel keen,[3] bright-hilted [?][4] sword on his left, a heavy-weighted silvered lance behind his shoulder, a blue clasped [?] cloak about him, and a brooch of bird-white [or uniformly white] silver therein, a long fine shirt of satin next his skin. A great middle-broad chariot on two brown beautiful-coloured steeds was beneath him. Fleetly, steadily leapt the chariot towards [with ?] the cavalry host that was around it. They seemed as though they were shower-spraying the great clods and the pebbles of the plains, as though they were casting thick, dense, black-blue showers from them of the bare soil of dust lying [there].[5] And this it was who was there, Dâire the Brown, of Black Cooley, to avenge his herds and his bulls on the men of Ireland: and thereupon

---

[1] *Cf.* táinig a ḃfriṫing na conaire ceudna, *Diar. & Graine*, 184.

[2] *Or* bossy, coḃraḋaċ (?).

[3] *Or* hard, keen.

[4] clas, clais, pit, *O'R.*; *perhaps* cleas-lonnraċt, feat-bright (?).

[5] *Or* as it lay.

sé Conċuḃar, "Créad doḃeir ort beiṫ ann so?" ar sé. "Atá ádḃar fuiriġ agom," ar Conċuḃar; "óir atá ceiṫre caṫa cróḋa Ċloinne Deaġa ag fuirioċ caṫa ḋúin(n) ag Ros na Ríoġ for Ḃóinn, ⁊ ni ḃfuilmíd-ne líon caṫa do ċur siu ar a ccoṁḋaingne; ⁊ do sinniomar coṁairle uiṁe, ⁊ ní hobaḋ caṫa ḋúin(n), anaḋ sé ar soċaḋaiḃ ann so." "Dar ar mbréiṫir," ar Dáire, "gion[a] naċ tugair-se caṫ ḋóiḃ, doḃéar-sa féin ḋóiḃ é." "Na habair sin, a Ḋáire," ar Conċuḃar, "óir ní hionḋula uathaḋ[b] sluaiġ a ccaṫ; ⁊ ansom sé ar n-oireaċtaiḃ." Oirisior Dáire iar soin ar ċoṁairle Ċonċuḃair.

24. Mar do ḃádar ann, do ċoncadar[c] díorma daingean deaġ-ṡluaiġ dá n-ionnsaiġe; drong díoḃ ⁊ brait ḃuiḋe iompa, drong go mbrataiḃ uaiṫne, ⁊ drong oile go mbrataiḃ dearga: fear fionn-ċas forarḋa fíor-áluinn, fear donn dreaċ-ṡolais daṫ-ċorcra, ⁊ fear seang seata[d] solas-ġlan, ⁊ fear suiṫionda sói-ḋearg[e] go ccraoḃaiḃ suaiṫniḋe síodaṁla iona láṁaiḃ,—⁊ gaċ fear ar leiṫ[f] a n-áirneaḋ gaċa buiḋne díoḃ. Agas is iad aos dána Ulaḋ do ḃí ann sin, im Ṡeancha mac Oiliolla, ⁊ im Ḟaċtna mac Ṡeancha ⁊ im Aiṁirgín file ⁊ im Ċatḟaḋ caoṁḋraoi; ⁊ do ṡuiġeadar[g] a n-iomḟogas do Ċonċubar, ⁊ d'iarr Conċuḃar coṁairle orro.[h] "Is í a(r) ccoṁairle ḋuit," ar siad, "gan an caṫ do ċor go mbeidís Ulaiḋ uile líon a n-iomairge ar aon-láṫair." "Níor ċomairce ḋaṁ-sa Ulaiḋ," ar sé, "fá'n ttáin do ḃreiṫ uaim, ⁊ ní anam siú anois." "Ná habair sin," ar siad, "ár do ḃíoġlais do ṫáin ar ḟearaiḃ 'Eirionn a ccaṫ Gáiriḋe ⁊ Iolġáiriḋe; ⁊ is iomḋa laoċ loinnċréaċtaċ do fuair a oiḋeaḋ ionnta."

25. A haiṫle na hiomagallṁa sin, do ċoncadar fraoċ-ḋrong sora(i)ḋ sóirleaṫan, go ccairriḃ clár-ḋaingne cuṁdaiġṫe, go n-eaċaiḃ ána[i] allṁurḋa, go laoċraiḋ ṁir ṁór-laḃarṫaiġ, go

23–25] [a] da ttugair-se caṫ ḋóiḃ, go ttiuḃar-sa caṫ ḋóiḃ; ⁊ fór gion go ttugair, doḃéar-sa fein caṫ ḋóiḃ, A. [b] lé uaṫaḋ, A. [c] iḋċoncadar, A. [d] seada, A.; séḋa, M. [e] so-ḋearg suaiḋeanta, A. [f] sa leiṫ, A. [g] do ionnsuiġeadar, S. [h] orra um an ccaṫ do ċur. [i] anaḋ, S.

he said to Conchubhar, "What causes thee to be here?" quoth he. "I have reason for tarrying," said Conchubhar, "for there are four brave battalions of Clann Deagha awaiting battle with us at Rosnaree on the Boyne; and we are not *sufficient in* number to give them battle, on account of their stalwartness. And we have adopted a resolve about it, and it is not a refusal of battle on our part, to wait for our numbers here." "By our word," said Dâire, "if thou give not battle to them, I will give it to them myself." "Say not that, Dâire," said Conchubhar, "for scantiness of an army ought not to go into battle. So we will wait for our clans." After that, Dâire stayed, on the advice of Conchubhar.

24. As they were there, they saw a stout squadron of a good army approaching them; part of them wearing yellow cloaks, part of them with green cloaks, and another part with red cloaks; a fair-curled intelligent truly handsome man, and a brown face bright hue-ruddy man, and a slender tall bright-clear [-complexioned] man, and a fiery [-haired?][1] deep-red [-complexioned] man with evergreen[2] silky (!) branches[3] in his hands; and each man [of these four] separately in charge[4] of each band of them; and those who were there were the doctors of the Ulstermen, around Seancha son of Oilill and around Fachtna son of Seancha and around Aimhirgin the poet and around Cathfadh the noble druid; and they drew nigh[5] to Conchubhar, and Conchubhar asked counsel of them. "This is our counsel to thee," said they, "not to give battle till all the Ulstermen may be [of sufficient] numbers to engage them [the enemy] altogether."[6] "The Ulstermen were no protection to me," said he, "in the case of the carrying off of the Foray from me, and we do not wait for them now." "Say not that," said they, "for thou hast avenged thy Foray on the men of Ireland in the battle of Gâireach and Iolghâireach, and many a fierce-wounding hero met his fate therein."

25. After that debate, they saw a steady wide extending furious-multitude, with floor-firm covered chariots, with splendid foreign steeds, with active great-spoken champions, with beautiful green

---

[1] *Or* radiant, resplendent. [2] Variegated, *O'R.*

[3] *i.e.* Sencha, with his branch of peace, Craeb sída (sídaṁla).

[4] *Or* in front, i n-airenuċ.

[5] ionnsuiġeadar. *Or* they sat near, suiġeadar.

[6] On one field.

n-éadaiġib áille uaiṫne, go ṙéadaṫaib gorma gloiníḋe, go ccloiḋṁṫib troma tort-ḃuilleaċa, ⁊ go ṙleaġaib crann-ḃuiḋe coirr-ġéara; ⁊ triar laoċ mór-uallaċ mear-ġlonnaċ a meoḋan na ríġ-ḋíorma roin: gonaḋ iad do ḃí ann .i. trí ríġ Ḟear-maiġe[a] i. Eoġan, Conċuḃar, ⁊ Crioṁṫann; go ndubairt Eoġan: "Créad doḃeir an coṁnaiḋe[b] corrac cóimeata ro oraiḃ?" "Atá," ar Conċuḃar, "Cairbre Niaiḋ Ḟear go n-a ḃráiṫriḃ ⁊ go móir-ṫionól ḃḞear mḃreaġ, Miḋe, ⁊ cóigiḋ Ġailian 'n-a mbruiġean ḃoḋḃa ag rúr caṫa dúin(n) ag Ror na Ríoġ ḟor ḃóinn." "Ní anḟamuid-ne,"[c] ar Eoġan, "go ḃḟaicḟiom na buiḋniḃ rin."

26. Ar mbeiṫ dóiḃ ar na hiompáitiḃ rin, adċoncadar[d] dirim mór múirneaċ meir-léimneaċ ċucca, ⁊ ḟear gáireaċtaċ gruaḋ-ċorcra a ttoraċ na buiḋne rin, ⁊ ḟolt[e] car cíorr-ḋuḃ air; brat lán-ṁór leaṫan-ċorcra lair, ⁊ rgiaṫ ṁór ṁíleata ar a ċlí, ⁊ cloiḋioṁ trom toir-ċlearaċ tairir; manaoir ṁór, ṁear-ġlonnaċ' ṁuiriorṫrom, uilleannaċ, imġéar,[f] ċóirr-leaṫan, ċeann-ruaḋ' ċrann-raṁar ré air.[g] Agar baḋ raṁail[h] ré reol-ċrann rríoṁ-loinge an rearga rnáiḋte rleaṁan-ċruaiḋ do ḃí a n-ionnrma na craoiriġe crann-raiṁre[i] ceáṫar-uillionnuiḋe do ḃí ar a láiṁ an laoiċ-ṁíleaḋ, go cceiṫre reamonnaiḃ ag a ċoṁḟo-raḋ ḟor an ccrann ccoṁḋaingean roin. Baḋ hiongnaḋ tráṫ airġeana[j] na rleiġe rin; óir do ṁuiġidír rraonanna teineaḋ treaṫan-ṁóire tre n-a rlearaiḃ[k] amaċ, ⁊ ceaṫrar aṁar[l] roiṁe ⁊ ḟionn-ċoire uṁaiḋe eattorro, go n-a lán ḟola ann; gonaḋ ann ró toṁṫaoi[m] an trleaġ neiṁneaċ roin gaċ uair do ḃáthaḋ a neiṁe. Agar ir é táinig an rin .i. Ceallcaċair mac Uiteaċ-air;[n] ⁊ d'ḟiaḟraiġ do Ċonċuḃar: "Créad um a ḃḟuirioċair ann ro?" ar ré. Ró innir Conċuḃar áḋḃar a ḟuiriġ dó. "Agur cáide do ċoṁa(i)rle-ri, a Ċeallcaċair?" "Adeirim-

25, 26] [a] *Recte* Ḟearnṁuiġe.
[b] ċoṁnaiḋe ċorraċ ċroiṁeata, A.
[c] anḟuim-ri, S.: ḟanḟamid-ne, A.
[d] do ċoncadar dirim ṁor ṁuirneaċ, A.
[e] ḟolt ċar ċiorr-ḋuḃ a(i)r, brat leann-ṁór lán-ċorcraleir, A.
[f] ait-uilleannaċ, A. [g] re air, S. [h] raṁalta, A.
[i] crainn-reiṁre, A. [j] airgeana, A. [k] gionġaiḃ, A.
[l] aṫaċ, A. [m] toṁṫaiġ, S. [n] Uiteaċair, A.

garments, with blue crystal gems [?], with heavy stout[1]-striking swords, and with shaft-yellow beak-sharp[2] spears; and three haughty brisk mighty heroes in the midst of that royal squadron. And it is these that were there, namely, the three kings of Farney, to wit, Eoghan, Conchubhar, and Criomhthann; and Eoghan said: "What causes this wavering cowardly tarrying in you?" "Cairbre Nia Fear," said Conchubhar, "with his brothers and with a great muster of the men of Bregia, Meath, and the province of the Galian, are in their war-fort [?] seeking battle with us at Rosnaree on the Boyne." "We *for our part* will not wait," said Eoghan, "till we see those bands."

26. While they were upon this parley, they saw a great heavy brisk-bounding squadron *coming* towards them, and a loud-voiced cheek-ruddy man in the lead of that band, wearing curling deep-yellow[3] hair. He wore an ample wide scarlet mantle; and *he carried* a great warrior-like shield on his left side, and a heavy dexterous sword over it, a great nimble-featful burden-heavy angular, keen, bill-broad,[4] head-red, shaft-stout lance behind him: and like to the sail-mast of a large ship was the carved smooth-hard ꞅeaꞃꞅa that was in the setting of the shaft-stout four-cornered spear that was in the hero-warrior's hand, with four rivets fastening it to that firm tree.[5] Wonderful indeed were the attributes[6] of that spear; for flood-great streams of fire used to burst out through its sides, and there were four hired soldiers before him, with a brazen bright cauldron between them, filled with blood, in which that venomous spear was dipped every hour, to quench its venom. And he it was who came there, namely, Cealltachair son of Uiteachar, and he asked of Conchubhar: "Wherefore waitest thou here?" said he. Conchubhar told him the reason of his tarrying. "And what is thy counsel, Cealltachair?" "I say,"

---

[1] coiꞃcaṁail, stout, *O'R.*; coiꞃc, quantity, 'gross,' *O'Begly*.

[2] *Or* smooth, sharp.

[3] *Or* beetle-black; cioꞃꞃ, short; ciaꞃ, dark-brown, *O'R.*; cíꞃoub, darkish yellow or dark grey, as Zimmer shows in *Kelt. Studien*, III. pp. 33, 35.

[4] *Or* smooth, broad.

[5] *Or* shaft, handle.

[6] *Cf.* aiꞃᵹeanna báiꞅ, symptoms of death, *Diarmait agus Grainne*, p. 184; *cf.* a like description of this spear in *LL.* 267 a.

si," ar Ceallcaḋar, "caṫ do ṫaḃairt dóiḃ, gion go ḃfuilmíd leaṫ nó trian riú; óir ní tré iomad sluaġ ċuirid Ulaiḋ caṫ do ġréas."

27. "Gaḃaiḋ iomaiḃ ḃúr ttreallṁa caṫa," ar Conċuḃar. Is ann sin do ġaḃ Conċuḃar féin a iorraḋ iomairg[a] uime .i. léine ċaoiṁ-ġeal ċúplaiḋeaċ fó n-a ċnear,[b] ⁊ ionar sróill solarda tairis sin a n-uaċtar, ⁊ cliaiḃ-ionar cóṁḟuaiḋte caoiṁ-ċuṁdaiġte[c] do ḟormna n-oċt n-aiṁḟearga ndartaḋa tairis sin, ⁊ caiṫ-ċrios cóṁlán do ṫaoḃaiḃ teora tairḃ-searga ó árd a leise go mullaċ á oċta,[d] ⁊ luireaċ ṫreaḃraiḋe tréan-dualaċ dá ḋídion ar ṡleaġaiḃ, ⁊ ḟoiġiodaiḃ, ⁊ ar ḟiṫ-ḃearaiḃ; a caṫ-ḃarr cíoraċ cláraċ ceaṫair-ċiuṁraċ[e] um a ċeann ⁊ sgiaṫ ċaoiṁ ċoṁpagaċ[f] iolḃuaḋaċ ilḃreaċtaċ uime. Do ġaḃ iomorro cloiḋioṁ cruaiḋ-ġéar curata, go n-a altaiḃ do ċnáiṁ áluinn eileaphaint, go niaṁ n-órḋa n-ilḃreaċtnaiḋe, go ttruaill ḟitte[g] ḟionn-druinne for a ṫaoiḃ clí. Do ġaḃ a ḋá ṡleiġ ċaoṁa ċrann-ṡeaṁra 'n-a láiṁ leaḃair léidṁiġ,[h] ⁊ do ġaḃrad laoċraḋ goile ⁊ gairgiḋ Ulaḋ uile umpa ar ċeana; gonaḋ ann isbeart[i] Conċuḃar in sitleasg:

"Cinnioṁ cáin coṁairle,
a ċlannaiḃ 'Ir iorgalaiġ,
frí haireaċ na himrearna,
is frí ḟian-sgor sras-ḟaoḃar:
saiġeam go soiṁeanmnaċ
go ró clann[j] Ruaḋ-Rosa,
frí ċarbaḋ caoiṁ-ionad
coingeonam cian-ċlú."

'Eirġid Ulaiḋ uile iar-soin ar ġalaiḃ aoin-ḟir im Ċonċuḃar

26, 27] [a] iomairge, A. [b] ċulpaiḋeaċ fa n-a ċneis, A.M. [c] cóṁḟuaite caoṁċuṁdaiġ, S. [d] oċta ḋó, A.M. [e] c. ċiumaċ, A. [f] . . . .i. Oċaoin, M. [g] fite, A.; read figte. [h] léidṁiḋe, A.; all from do ġaḃ to léidṁiḋe omitted from S. [i] aduḃairt, A. [j] ro-ċlann, S.

[1] cúplaḋaċ; or culpaḋaċ, hooded; lene gel chulpatach, co culpataib, *LU.* 122 a, 27 a.

[2] Read n(d)aṁ-uirge, and cf. dam dilend, water ox, do formna sech ndam-seched ndartada, *Siab. Ch. Con C.* 424, 425; formna means body, great part, .i. umad, *O'Dav.* 83, *LL.* 60 b; *LU.* 101 a, 107 a, 108 a, 112 b.

[3] Perhaps sreaḃnaiḋe, leathern; *cf.* note 2, p. 68.

said Cealltachair, "to give them battle, though we are not half or third of their numbers; for not through multitude of armies do the Ulstermen usually do battle."

27. "Put ye on your gear of battle," said Conchubhar. Then put Conchubhar himself his attire of conflict on, to wit, a comely-white folded[1] shirt on his skin and a vest of shining satin over that without, and a well-sewn finely worked body-vest made of hide of the body [?] of eight yearling water-oxen (?)[2] over that; and a complete battle-belt of the sides of three strippers [?] from the high part of their thighs to the peak of their breasts; and a skilfully made[3] [?] stout-linked coat of mail to defend him from spears and arrows and enchanted darts; his crested flat four-bordered helmet on his head, and a comely warlike many-victoried many-hued shield about him, that is the Ochaoin. He took also a hard-keen heroic sword, with its hilt[4] of beautiful ivory with golden variegated sheen, with interlaced scabbard of white-bronze, on his left side. He took his two handsome shaft-stout spears in his long, strong hand. And the heroes of valour and chivalry of the Ulstermen all put *their war attire* on likewise; whereupon Conchubhar spake the *following* impromptu[5] :—

"Noble adoption of a resolve,
O descendants of valorous Ir,
towards the rousing[6] [?] of strife
and towards the heroic loosing[7] of showers of blades.
Let us advance spiritedly
unto the Children[8] of Ros the Red,
towards the wasting [?][9] of noble places,
we will succour[10] *our* ancient fame."

All the Ulstermen go thereupon to fight[11] around Conchubhar,

---

[4] Lit. joints; for eltaib déc, hilt of (ivory) teeth, *LL.* 70 b, 55 b.

[5] Cf. rith, running; leirg, motive, *O'R.*

[6] Or read airecht, meeting; airec, finding (?).

[7] *Or* cutting; cf. scor, a notch by a sword, *O'R.*

[8] go ró = corrice (?); cf. doró, it will, may reach. *M'Solly* has ró-chlann, great clan: cf. ró from róichim: co ró F. for nem, *MS. Mater.* 523.

[9] I read corbaḋ; carbad = roof, palate, in *M'Curtin.*

[10] *Fut.* of con-gníu; or read congeoḃam, we will uphold.

[11] Cf. etha Cú C. ar galaib óenfir, C. goes to single combat, *LU.* 77 b.; robítha leirium ar galaib oenfir, they were slain through the brave deeds of one man, *LU.* 70 b; *LL.* 79 a b.

⁊ tógḃaid doireaḃa doinn-ġéara dá sleaġaiḃ loinnearḃa ⁊ buaile daingean díoṫoġlaiḋe dá staraḃaiḃ[a] na n-úirṫimċioll. Ciḋ tra aċt dorónsad caṫ cadat coṁ-ḋaingean díoḃ, ⁊ é dlúṫ díoġlaċ díoġain deilgneaċ daor-uaṫṁar dian-ċosgraċ, dána, díoċra, dúr-ċroiḋioċ. Agas baḋ saṁalta ré tuile ruaḋ-ṫuinne ag brúċtaḋ[b] tré ṁullaċ gairḃ-ṡléiḃe, go mbrúġaiḋ ⁊ go mbrisiḋ a mbí do ċloċaiḃ ⁊ do ċrannaiḃ ar a ċionn,—is mar sin d'ionnsuiġiodar Ulaiḋ go Ros na Ríoġ for Ḃóinn, airm a raḃadar Laiġin.

28. Dála iomorro Cairbre Niaiḋ Fear go n-a ṡoċraide bráṫar ⁊ ċloinne dreaċ-áille Deirg ar ċeana,—ó 'dċoncadar Ulaiḋ ċucca, do ġaḃadar a n-earraḋa caṫa umpa, ⁊ a n-iongnaċa áiġ ⁊ iorġaile iona láṁaiḃ lonna léiḋṁeaċa; ⁊ do sinniodar buaile bioraċ brioċt-deilgneaċ[c] dá n-armaiḃ aiṫġéara úrnoċta ós a gcionn, ⁊ sgeiṁiol dá sgiaṫa(iḃ) iona n-úirṫimċioll; ⁊ d'éirġiodar 'n-a ndruing ndíoġain ndíoċonair-ċleaṫaċ 'n-a n-aghaiḋ do'n leiṫ araill. Gonaḋ ann sin isbeart Cairbre: "Is mór-ġarḃ mór-ḋálaċ meir-ṁeanmnaċ, ⁊ is gruama gráineaṁail an ġarraḋ[d] ṫig in ḃur n-aġaiḋ. 'Oir is cróḋa calma cosnaṁaċ a ccura(i)ḋ, ⁊ is rúin-ṁear róineartṁar rian-aṁnuraċ[e] a ríoġa, ⁊ is maṫġaṁna mearḃa mór-ġlonnaċa a míleaḋa; is loinnioċ lúṫṁar a laoiċ goile, ⁊ is leoṁain loinn-ċréaċtaċa a sonn-ċaṫa, ⁊ is foraiḋe[f] féiġe[g] fíor-ġarga a ḃflaiṫ-ríoġa, um Ċonċuḃar ċróḋa mac neart-ġalaċ[h] Neasa. Agas ní baḋ furáil ḋaoiḃ-si drong díoċra deaġ-laoċ do ṫoġa ré tuarsgain a sgéiṫe ar Ċonċuḃar féin."

29. Is ann sin do ġaḃsad seaċt ḃfir ḋéag do laoiċ goile na nGailianaċ do láiṁ-ḟriṫeolaḋ Ċonċuḃair im ṫuarsgain a sgéiṫe air is an ccaṫ .i. Eochaiḋ mac Rosa, ⁊ na trí Ruaiḋċinn a Raiṫin,[i] ⁊ na trí Rotha Muiġe Ḃreaġ, ⁊ Faḋḃ ua hIomna,

27–29] [a] starraḋuiḃ, S. [b] ruaḋ ró-ṫuinne ag bruċtaiġ, A. [c] buaile mbiora mboḋḃ mbrioċtdeilgneaċ, A. [d] garraiġ, S.; garraiḋe, A. [e] aṁnuraċ, A.; aṁuraċ, S. [f] foraiġ, S.A. [g] féiġ, A. [h] neart-ġoileaċ, A. [i] Raiṫeann, A.

[1] So from the context; but in *O'R.* and *O'Don.* sgeiṁiolta = scouts; in *F. Mast.* an. 1542, sgeiṁleaḋ = a detachment.

[2] díoċonaire, unpassable, *O'R.*

[3] Cf. cáit a ḃfuil an ṁórḋáil, where is boasting? Rom. iii. 27.

and they raise the brown-sharp forests of their shining spears and a strong impregnable enclosure of their bucklers all around them. Howbeit, they made a hard very firm battalion of themselves, thick, vengeful, dense, bristling, stern-terrible, fierce-destructive, bold, vehement, hard-hearted; and like the tide of a strong torrent belching through the top of a rugged mountain, so that it bruises and breaks what there is of stones and of trees before it, thus advanced the Ulstermen to Rosnaree on the Boyne, where the Leinstermen were.

28. Now concerning Cairbre Nia Fear with his host of brothers and of the comely-featured Clann Deirg in general,—when they saw the Ulstermen *coming* towards them, they donned their attire of battle and took their weapons of slaughter and strife in their bold stalwart hands, and they formed a bristling spell-thorny rampart of their keen naked weapons above their heads, and a pent-house[1] of their shields all around them, and they advanced, a dense impregnably[2]-wattled host, against them (the Ulstermen) on the opposite side. And Cairbre spake: "Very fierce, very boastful,[3] quick-spirited, and sullen, horrible, are the troops that come against you; for valiant, brave, defenceful are their champions, and resolute, most mighty, sharp-minded[4] are their kings, and nimble great-deedful bears[5] are their warriors, and mighty and vehement are their heroes of valour, and fiercely-wounding lions are their props[6] of battle, and fierce truly-cruel supports are their chieftain-kings around valiant Conchubhar, the strongly-brave son of Neas; and ye must[7] choose an eager band of goodly heroes to smite his shield for Conchubhar."[8]

29. Then they selected seventeen men of the heroes of valour of the Gailianachs to deal with[9] Conchubhar by battering his shield in the battle,—to wit, Eochaidh son of Ros, and the three Redheads from Raithin, and the three Roths of Magh Breagh, and Fadhbh grandson

---

[4] rian, a way, mood; aṁnus, sharp, *O'R.*; *M'Solly* has aṁusaċ, passionate, *Coney's Dict.*

[5] Said of warriors; *n.* beṫir; *g.* beṫrach, *LL.* 274 a, *B. of Lec.* 635–6; *voc.* a beṫir, *LU.* 100 b.

[6] Read suinn ċaṫa; cf. am sonn caṫa, I am a bulwark of battle, *C. M. Rath*, 202; sonn, stake, pole.

[7] Lit., "it would not be too much for you."

[8] *Idiomatic for* to smite Conor's shield.

[9] To attend on.

⁊ Doirn-iubra ua Cir-ġabann, ⁊ Cairbre Niaḋ Fear féin, go n-a ṁóir-ḟeirear cúl-ċoiṁéaduiġe. Cid tra acht do ċóiṁéir-ġiodar na caṫa comóra consaḋaċa sin a ccomairc[a] a ċéile, ⁊ ró ḃúirsiod na daṁra diain-dearṁáir[b] sin aṁail daṁaiḃ ag daṁ-ġaire do'n dá leiṫ ceaċtarḋa. Ró sgiobsad[c] na buiḋne bailc-ḃríoġṁara go díċéilliḋe díomsaċ danarḋa doiḟḟearḋail, do ḟrioċólaṁ[d] na hiomġona sin, gur ċrioṫnaiġ an talaṁ trom-ḟódaċ[e] fá ċosaiḃ na ccuraḋ ccoṁraṁaċ soin; go raḃadar a ḃfreagarṫa ⁊ a ḃfuarmanna a ḃfrais-néallaiḃ fanna fuaċt-naiḋe an aiḋeoir ⁊ a ḃfoċuaraiḃ fras-ġarḃa na firmaimeint; gur líonsad iomorro baḋḃa ⁊ brain-eoin ⁊ fiasta gineaċa goib-ġéara an ċóigiḋ fá'n doire dlúiṫ-ġéar doinn-ḟleaġ, ⁊ fá na feaḋaiḃ fuileaċa faoḃraċa do ḃí ór cionn gaċ leiṫe[f] díoḃ; gur ḃaḋ lór d'furáileaṁ time ⁊ teiṫṁe ar aos óg ⁊ fiallaċ n-éadrom n-anḃfora(i)ḋ,[g] ⁊ ar ḃaoiṫ-ḟearaiḃ meara míoġair-giḋ,[h] na gárṫa[i] ⁊ an ġolfúrtaċ ⁊ an guirt-ġréaċaḋ dorónsad na haireaċta sin um ċeannaiḃ ⁊ um ċaol-rannaiḃ a n-arm ⁊ a n-iolḟaoḃar ór ccionn. Ró ḋiuḃracsad na caṫa ceaċtarḋa cóṁḋlúṫa frasa díoċra deilgneaċa do ḟaiġdiḃ séda[j] síoṫ-ġorma, ⁊ do ċolsaḋaiḃ[k] cruaiḋe ceann-ċruinne a ccrom-stuag[l] ccrann-raṁar na mboġa mbeannaċ[m] mbir-ġéar, ⁊ do ḟoġaiḃ fuileaċa foluamna, ⁊ do[n] craoisioċa(iḃ) crann-raṁra cró-ḟairsinge, ⁊ do ṫrom-ċloċaiḃ tulamair na talṁan, ⁊ do leaġaiḃ[o] díoġla díḃfeirge; ionnus gur tollaḋ taoiḃ ⁊ gur treaġdaḋ cuirp áille aoin-ġeala uaṫa, ⁊ gur ruaiṁniġeaḋ ruirg, ⁊ gur clóḋaḋ céad-raḋa curaḋ ⁊ caiṫ-ṁíleaḋ; gur bánaḋ beoil ⁊ gur crioṫnuiġeaḋ cosa ⁊ cáirne do'n trear sin. Ṙó luiġsiod trom-luiḋe na ttréin-ḟear ttreaḃar-ċalma ro ḃádar a ccaṫ na nGailianaċ

29] [a] ccoṁairceir, A. [b] an daṁra dian dearṁáir, A. [c] sgrioḃsad, A. [d] do ḟrioċólaṁ omitted by S. [e] ḟóideaċ, A. [f] ór gaċ leiṫ, A. [g] n-anḃfiorsaċ, A. [h] míoġaire, S. [i] an ġarrṫa, A. [j] Or seata. [k] ċolsuiḃ, A. [l] gcrom-stuiġ, A. [m] mboġaiḃ mbeannaċa, S. [n] do chraoiseoċaiḃ creannraṁra, M. [o] leaganuiḃ, A.

1 consaḋaċ, roaring, *Coney's Dict.* 2 *Or* in crying at each other.

3 daṁra for daṁ-raḋ (?); daṁra, people, wild beasts, *O'R.*

4 sgiob, sweep away, *Coney's Dict.*; sciobeaḋ, course of a thing, *O'R.*; sciobiuḋ, to move, *Stokes' Voy. of Mael Duin*, p. 470.

of Iomna, and Doirn-iubhra grandson of Ceap Gabha, and Cairbre Nia Fear himself with his seven rear-guards. Howbeit, those huge, roaring[1] battalions rushed together in mutual conflict,[2] and those fierce-enormous herds[3] roared like bulls in a bull-challenge, from the two sides on either part. The strong mighty bands swept on[4] madly, proudly, cruelly, to attend and ply that mutual wounding, until the heavy-clodded earth trembled beneath the feet of those powerful champions; until their answers and their tumults[5] were in [*i.e.* reached] the faint chilly shower-clouds of the air and the shower-wild vaults of the firmament; until they [the combatants] gorged moreover the vultures[6] and ravens and the beaked keen-mouthed reptiles of the province, beneath the thick-keen forest of brown spears and beneath the bloody thickets of blades that were above each party of them; till sufficient to cause[7] fear and flight in the youths and the light unsteady folk,[8] and the nimble unvaliant vain men were the shouts and the lamentations and the bitter-shrieking that those clans made around the heads and slender-points of their weapons and various blades overhead. The dense battalions on either side hurled eager thorny showers of long deep-blue[9] arrows, and of hard head-round bolts[10] from the tree-stout curved arch of the horned spit-sharp bows, and of bloody fluttering javelins and shaft-stout ring[11]-wide spears, and of the quick-hitting[12] heavy-stones of the earth, and of stones[13] of vengeance *and* wrath—so that sides were pierced and comely all-white bodies were transfixed by them, and that eyes were anger-flushed[14], and the senses of champions and battle-warriors oppressed, and lips were whitened and feet and bodies[15] were shaken by that strife. A heavy pressure of the prudently valiant brave-men who were in the battalion of the Gailianachs bore on the battalions of the Ulstermen, until

---

[5] fuasmanna for fuasanna. Cf. cáthair ḟuasnaiḋċeac, Isaiah xxii.; or, fuasma, blow, *O'R.*

[6] baḋḃ, vulture, Levit. xi.

[7] *Recte* d'furáil, impose, enjoin.

[8] fiallaċ = fianlaċ, *W.*, knight-errants, wild people, *Coney's Dict.*

[9] fíoċ, an intensitive, *W.* [10] colba, post, stalk, *Coney's Dict.*

[11] cró, bar, *Coney's Dict.*, = metal hoop (of a spear), *W.*

[12] tul, quick; amus, attack, *W.*; *or* torrent-hurled.

[13] leagantuiḋ, *A.*, small stones.

[14] ruaim, flush of anger, *Coney's Dict.*

[15] carna, flesh, *W.*

for ċaṫaiḃ Ulaḋ, gur róttaiḋ[a] raḃarṫa na ruiroiċ ⁊ na ríġ-ṁíleaḋ, ⁊ sian-sgolba na sochaiḋe, ⁊ tortromaḋ[b] na ttaoisioċ, ⁊ foirḋinge na ḃfear-óglaċ, ag ionnsaiġe an ṁór-ṡluaiġ; gur ṫuitriod greaḋa ⁊ giollannraḋ, aos óga, fannaiġ ⁊ fann-óglaoiċ, gur ba samalta uaiṫneaḋa iorġaile ⁊ fuinn díḃfeirge ⁊ collaṁuin congṁála ⁊ laoiċ goile ⁊ gairgiḋ[c] na nUlltaċ, ar na ruineaḋ na n-ionadaiḃ caṫa d'éis a muinntire, ré doire doir-leaṫan deaġ-ḋlúiṫ ar na leagaḋ ar maiġ réiḋ ró-ḟairsing ar leiṫeaḋ[d] ⁊ ar léir-ṫionól, ag dlúṫ-ṫuitim ar; go naċ ar ḟágsad aċt na hiomnaḋa úrárda antroma is na reilgiḃ réiḋe róiḋeasga na sguṫ-ḃuinníḋiḃ sgéirdiġṫe sgoiṫ-ṫeasgaiġṫe ar láir-ṁeaḋón an ṁaiġe; gur folṁaḋ flaiṫ-láiṫreaċa[e] fair-sionga foluaimneaċa rompa do'n ruaṫar soin.

30. Iomṫúsa Ċonċuḃair ró ċongaiḃ féin a sgiaṫ is an láṫair 'n-a raiḃe, ⁊ Cealltaċar mac Uiteaċair ar a láiṁ ḋeis, ⁊ Aiṁirgín an fear dána ar a ḋeis sin, ⁊ 'Irial Glúnṁar mac Conuill Ċearrnaiġ ar láiṁ an ḟir ḋána, ⁊ Aoḋ 'Eigios mac Aiṁirgín ar láiṁ Iriail, ⁊ Mirdeaġaḋ mac Aiṁirgín ar a láiṁ sin; Eoġan mac Dúṫraċta ar ċlí Ċonċuḃair; Dáire Donn Duḃ-Ċuailgne a n-iomḟogas dó-san; ⁊ ró ċongaiḃ siad, an luċt soin, sgéiṫe sgeiṁealta ⁊ cloiḋṁe clóḋ-ḃuilleaċa ⁊ sleaġa sioṫ-árda ⁊ craoisioċa crann-ṁóra, go foirṫréan fearḋa féiḋm-láidir, ⁊ go bailc bríoġṁar[f] borrḟaḋaċ, a n-aġaiḋ na nGailianaċ; gur taosgaḋ trom-aiḋle teaċt-fola a cneasaiḃ curaḋ ⁊ a láṁaiḃ laoċ ngoile na Laiġneaċ uaṫa.

31. Aċt atá ní ċeana, ó 'ḋċoncadar an luċt do ġaḃ do láiṁ Ċonċuḃair do ḋiongoḃáil sin, ró ionnsuiġiodar go hairm a ḃfacadar é .i. Cairbre Niaiḋ Fear ⁊ an drong do ġaḃ leis, mar aduḃramar ṫuas, ⁊ céad laoċ mar aon riu; ⁊ ro ṡaiṫriod sleaġ gaċa fir ac Conċuḃar, ⁊ ró ṫuairgriod iar soin a sgiaṫ

29–31] [a] go ro ttáid, A. [b] tortṫromaḋ, A. [c] gairge, S. [d] leaṫ-ḟad, A. [e] flaṫ-laireaḋa, S. [f] bríoġṁara, S.

[1] rodaḋ, to lance, *O'R.*; rod, a throw, *O'Cl.*; see rout, *LL.* version, *perhaps* until fell (róttait being a form of tuitim or teit?).

[2] Raḃarta = over-running (flood), *Nahum* i. 8; *springtide* in spoken Irish.

[3] sian, noise; sgolbánaċ, stripling, *Coney's Dict.*

[4] tortromaḋ, heavy weight or pressure, *W.*, *Atkinson's Gloss.*

[5] fordingim, *opprimo*; or for-dinge, great wedges (?).

it penetrated[1] the masses of the chiefs[2] and royal warriors, and the noisy-striplings[3] of the multitude, and the heavy-forces[4] of the generals, and the compactness[5] of the young warriors attacking the great army; so that horses and pages, youths, weaklings, and faint-warriors fell; so that the pillars of strife and the foundations of wrath and the columns of support and the heroes of valour and chivalry of the Ulstermen, sundered[6] in their stations of battle behind their people, were like a bush-wide goodly-dense grove, laid low on a smooth extensive plain at stretch and gathered together as they fall thickly down, until they have not left but the towering ponderous oaks,[7] and the smooth ruddy oak-trees in tight[8] lightly-cut[9] rows here and there on the middle of the plain; so that wide moving princely positions were swept bare before them in that onset.

30. As for Conchubhar, he himself upheld his shield on the spot where he was, and Cealltachar son of Uiteachar on his right hand, and Aimhirgîn the poet on the right of the latter, and Irial Glûnmhar son of Conall Cearnach at the poet's hand, and Aodh Éigios [the Bard] son of Aimhirgîn at Irial's hand, and Misdeagha son of Aimhirgîn at his hand; Eoghan son of Duthracht on Conchubhar's left, Dâire the Brown of Black Cooley near to him; and these, that lot, upheld locked[10] shields and victory-smiting swords, and lofty spears, and shaft-great lances, bravely, manlily, effort-strongly, and stoutly, mightily, haughtily, against the Gailianachs, until a heavy-remnant[11] of coagulated[12] blood was drained from the bodies of the champions and from the hands of the heroes of valour of the Leinstermen by them.

31. Howbeit, when those who took in hand to ward off Conchubhar saw that, they advanced to the place in which they saw him, that is, Cairbre Nia Fear and those that he took with him, as we have said above, and a hundred warriors together with them; and they thrust the spear of each man at Conchubhar, and they battered his shield

---

[6] Read roinn; or ruinneaḋ, consumed, *O'R.*

[7] iomnaḋa, phonet. for omnaḋá; cf. *LL.* text, § 34.

[8] Cf. sciortaiḋe, tidy, *Coney's Dict.*

[9] Cf. sgaṫḃuail, beat lightly, *Coney's Dict.*; sguṫ .i. céimniuġaḋ, *O'Cl.*; buiniḋe, thick border, or set off (in basket-making), *Coney's Dict.*; *or* bush-rings (?); or scuṫ = sgaṫ, a bundle; or sgoṫ alight, as in note 4.

[10] Skirmishing, *O'R.*; scouts, *O'D. Suppl.*

[11] aiḋle for aiṫle (?).

[12] Cf. teuctaḋ, coagulation.

air do ḃraċ-ḃuillib[a] móra míleaṫa, gur ġéir ⁊ gur ġló-ḃúirrioḋ[b] an Oċaoin .i. sgiaṫ Ċonċuḃair, aṁail baḋ béas di, ré truime an tréan-ċoṁloinn ⁊ ré ḟóir-neart na feaḋma ⁊ ré hiomurca an anḟorlainn do ḃí ar Ċonċuḃar is an ccoṁrac. Aċt éin-ní ċeana, do ṫuitriod sgéiṫe Ulaḋ uile dá ngualliḃ, ⁊ dá nglacaiḃ ⁊ do ríġṫiḃ ríġ-ṁíleaḋ, ⁊ d'ḟaiġleannaiḃ[c] iomċoiméada ar ċeana ré héin-ġéim na hOċaoine an tráṫ sin. Ró ġáirrioḋ iomorro ⁊ ró ġlonn-ḃúirrioḋ trí tonna tul-ġorma treaṫan-ġarḃa na h'Eirionn ré heagcaoine an éagcoṁlainn do ḃí ar Ċonċuḃar, .i. tonn ḃruṫṁar ḃarc-longaċ ruaḋ Ruḋraiġe, ⁊ tonn luċt-ṁar long-ḃáiḋteaċ ċuḃar-anḟaḋaċ Ċlíoḋna, ⁊ tonn tul-árd taoḃ-raṁar Tuaiḋe. Adconnarcar iomorro d'Ulltaiḃ,[d] ann gaċ dú a raḃadar, an móir-iṁsníoṁ 'n-a raiḃ Conċuḃar tré ṫuitim a sgiaṫ dá n-arġleannaiḃ.[e] Is ann sin iomorro do ḃolgsaḋ Ulaiḋ ar a ndúntaiḃ ⁊ ar a ndiongnaḋaiḃ a ndiaiġ Ċonċuḃair.

32. Iomṫuso Ċonaill Ċearrnaiġ, táiniġ roiṁe a ccomaiḋ[f] ċáiċ, ⁊ tarla dronga diana dísgire dian-luaṫa do luċt an ṁaḋma ḋó, san ċonair a ttáiniġ. Agas d'aiṫin Conall gur ḃa[g] luċt maḋma ⁊ móir-ṫeiṫṁe iad; ⁊ do ṫuig gur ba teiṫeaḋ gan[h] riaċtain a leas é; óir ní ḟaca fuiliuġaḋ ná fuirḋeargaḋ orra. Gonaḋ ann aduḃairt Conall:

"Diombuaiḋ fear,[i]
frioċrosg maḋma,
maiḋm ré[j] ngnuisiḃ,
gáir éin-sgeoil,
ógḃaḋ asairm,[k]
easbaiḋ ngaisgiḋ,
díoċar feaḋma,
aṫċar éaċta,

31, 32] [a] bracbuillib, M. [b] ġlonn-ḃuirreaḋ, A.; plural, by mistake, for singular. [c] aiṫġleannuiḃ, A. [d] adċoncadar Ulaiḋ iomorro, A. [e] nasgaiḃ ⁊ dá n-aṅġleannaiḃ, A. [f] ccoinn, A. [g] gurḃ, A.; gurab, S. [h] go, A. [i] ḟear, A. [j] ria, A. [k] ararm, A.

[1] braṫ, .i. milleaḋ, *O'Cl.*

[2] forlonn, pain, Psalm cxvi.; or anforlann, violence; *or* the disadvantage which was felt by C.

[3] *Or* grasps.

thereupon with great warlike murder[1]-strokes, until the Ochaoin, *i.e.* Conchubhar's shield, shrieked and roared, as it was wont, from the weight of the strong conflict and from the over-might of the effort and from the excess of the great distress that Conchubhar laboured under[2] in the fight. Howbeit, all the shields of the Ulstermen fell from their shoulders and from their palms[3] and from the arms of the king-warriors, and from the armoury racks[4] in general, at the single cry of Ochaoin at that hour. Then the three flood-blue[5] surge-rough Waves of Ireland cried out and mightily bellowed in lament for the unequal fight that Conchubhar bore,—to wit, the furious[6] barque-sailed red Wave of Rudhraighe, and the freight-bearing ship-sinking foam-stormy Wave of Cliodhna, and the flood-high side-swollen Wave of Tuadh.[7] There was seen moreover by the Ulstermen in every place where they were the great distress in which Conchubhar was, through the falling of their shields from their shelves[8]. Then, indeed, the Ulstermen broke out[9] after Conchubhar from their fortresses and strongholds.

32. As regards Conall Cearnach, he came on with[10] all; and violent moblike headlong crowds of the fugitives[11] met him on the way by which he came; and Conall knew that they were routed forces and fugitives, and he understood that it was a flight without necessity,[12] as he did not see [any marks of] bleeding or wounding upon them; whereupon Conall said:

"Disaster of men,
counter[13] stroke of rout,
rout before faces,
shout of one-tidings,
youth disarmed,
defect of chivalry,
abandonment of effort,
cessation of achievement,

---

[4] Guarding shelves or racks (throughout Ireland?), *recte* aidlenaib, *see* Zimme in *Zeitsch.* of Kuhn, Band xxx., pp. 101–112.

[5] *Or* face-blue. [6] Glowing. [7] *Read* Tuagh.

[8] *Or* racks; read aidleannaiḃ.

[9] Bubbled out; bolgán uisge, a bubble; bolg, a pimple, a swelling.

[10] a ccomaiḋ, in company with, *W.*; MS. A has a ccionn, towards, against.

[11] Lit., folk of rout.

[12] Lit., any use.

[13] Cf. rusgaḋ, striking, *Coney's Dict.*

céad-lúṫ clóḋ,
collaḋ cróḋaċta,
anuair do ríoġnuro,[a]
riṫ frí ġealtaċt,
dáil go ndioġra,
dul fá ḋiombuaiḋ."

Do ġluais Conoll roiṁe iar-soin, ⁊ do ṁeas bás d'imirt ar gaċ neaċ do riṫfeaḋ uaḋa, go ttoirrioḋ gur an ccaṫ. Is ann sin tráṫ ró baḋar ag sraonaḋ Ulaḋ ar a n-ionadaiḃ caṫa, tré anḟorlann, ⁊ tré iomursa sluaiġ ⁊ soċaiḋe.

33. Dearcus Conċubar seaċa, go ḃfaca Conoll ċuige, go nduḃairt:

"A Ċonuill coṁramaiġ,
a ċroiḋe ċóṁċoḃraiḋ,
á ḃá(i)r for ḃíoḋḃaḋaiḃ,
a ḃeiṫir ḃruṫ-ġoile,
a ṁionn for ḃan-ċuire,[b]
an caṫ ar do ċoimirce,
ar do neart niaḋaċais,[c]
ar do ḃáiḋ ḃráiṫreara
ré ríoġ-ċloinn Rúḋraiġe,
a neiṁ ór naṫraċaiḃ:
corain an laṫair-si,
a ċonfaḋ ċosgar-ċon.

An caṫ ar do ċoimirce, a Ċonuill," ar Conċuḃar. "Is snáṁ a n-aġaiḋ sroṫa sin," ar Conoll, "⁊ ní ḟaoṁaim-si é."

34. "An caṫ ar do ċoimirce, a Ḋáire ṁic Ḟiaċraiġ," ar Conċuḃar. "Is roṫ fri learga soin," ar Dáire, "⁊ ní ḟaoṁaim-si é." "An caṫ ar do ċoimirce a Eoġain," ar Conċuḃar. "Is urċar ó ṫéiḋ ó láiṁ[d] anosa," ar Eoġan, "⁊ ní ḟaoṁaim-si[e] é." "An caṫ ar ḃur ccoimirce a aos dána Ulaḋ," ar Conċuḃar.

33, 34] [a] uair do ríoġnura, A. [b] bánchuire, S. [c] do nerniaḋċus, M. [d] urċar ṫéiḋ a laiṁ, S. [e] ḟaoḃaim-si, S.

[1] lúd, luṫ, motion, velocity, force, *W.*; cétlúd sine sampaid, *Cormac.*

first throb[1] of defeats,
sleep of valour,
when I acted [?],[2]
running through panic,
concourse with eagerness,
going through disaster."

Conall proceeded forwards thereupon, and he thought to inflict death on everyone that would run away, until they reached the battle. Now it was at that time that the Ulstermen were being routed from their places of battle through violence and excess of army and numbers.

33. Conchubhar glanced aside and saw Conall *coming* towards him, and said:

"O warlike Conall,
O steadfast heart,
O death to enemies,
O bear of glowing valour,
O diadem on woman-kind,[3]
take the battle under[4] thy protection,
under thy strength of heroism,
under thy friendship of brotherhood
with the king-race of Rudhraighe,
O venom surpassing serpents,
defend this position,
O fury of slaughter-hounds.

Take the battle under thy protection, O Conall!" said Conchubhar. "That is swimming against a stream," said Conall, "and I accept[5] it not."

34. "*Take* the battle under thy protection, Dâire son of Fiachrach," said Conchubhar. "That is a wheel against rising-grounds," said Dâire, "and I accept it not." "Take the battle under thy protection, Eoghan," said Conchubhar. "It is the cast of a cord from a hand now," said Eoghan, "and I receive it not." "Take the battle under

---

[2] dorigniur-sa (?), *or* in the hour of perversity, dorionṫachta (?).
[3] banċuire, woman-group, *B. of Armagh*; bánċuire, fair-band in *M'Solly*.
[4] Lit., on.
[5] Cf. ciar femṫa-so, gl. *si accepisti*, *Wb.* 8 d; here it means "I grant."

"Is ailleacán a láiṁ leinḃ sin anosa," ar Aiṁirgín, ⁊ ar Caṫḟaḋ, "⁊ ní ḟaoṁam-ne é." "An caṫ ar do ċoimirce, a Iriail," ar Conċuḃar. "Is dlaoi frí ḋian-ġaoith[a] sin anosa," ar Irial, "⁊ ní ḟaoṁaim-si é." "An caṫ ar do ċoimirce, a Laoġaire Ḃuaḋaiġ," ar Conċuḃar. "Is easarġain darac do ḋoirniḃ sin anois," ar Laoġaire, "⁊ ní ḟaoṁaim-si é."

35. Is ann sin táinig an míleḋ mór-uallaċ meir-ṁeanmnaċ .i. ceann gaile ⁊ gaisgiḋ na nGaoiḋiol ⁊ uaine iorġaile na h'Eirionn .i. Cú Chulainn mac Suḃaltaiṁ, fá na hiomráitiḃ sin ċucca; ⁊ dearcus Conċuḃar air ⁊ aduḃairt an rosg so:[b]

"Ráil coṁloinn Culann-Ċú:
clisiḋ[c] caṫa cruaiḋ-ċleasa:
cinniḋ ar a ċóṁaosaiḃ:[d]
congḃaiḋ caṫa ó Rúḋraiġe:
earr eangnaiṁ 'Eirionnaċ:
laoċ ruaṁnus ráil.

"An caṫ ar do ċoimirce a Ċú Ċulainn," ar Conċuḃar. "Faoṁaim-si sin," ar Cú Ċulainn; ⁊ adbeart[e] na briaṫra-so:

"Am[f] sliaḃ frí ṫonna,
am[f] tairṫe[g] frí hear,
am[f] fuilingiḋ[h] frí gloine,
am[f] árraḋ frí hiorġaile,
am[f] leoṁan fri long(aḋ?),
am[f] cur frí ḋóiṁneart."

Ciḋ trá aċt, ró gríosaḋ iomorro Cú Ċulainn, ar ḃraitrin Ċonċuḃair ⁊ Ulaḋ a néaccoṁlann, ⁊ aḋnaiḋ[i] a ġliaiḋ ngairge as, ⁊ a ḋearnoin nḋearṁáir. Agus tugsad Ulaiḋ uile aiṫniḋ air, ar na ċlos, ⁊ ró éiriġ a mbruḋ[j] ⁊ a mbríġ ⁊ a mborrfaḋ, ⁊ ró ċosnadar go danarḋa diċéillḋe dúr-ċroiḋeaċ an láṫair ar a

35] [a] ḋaoinġaoiṫ, S.; ḋian-ġaoiṫe, A. [b] aduḃairt sé ann, A. [c] clisiḋ, M. [d] ċoṁaosaḋ, S. [e] aduḃairt, A. [f] aṁail, A. [g] tairṫa, M. [h] fuilngiḋ, M. [i] aḋaiġ, S. [j] bruḋ, A.; bruiṫ, S.

[1] Cf. do ġlac mise ar ḋlaoiġ dom ġruaig, he took me by a lock of mine hair, Ezech. viii. 3.

your protection, ye poets of Ulster," said Conchubhar. "That is a toy in a child's hand now," said Aimhirgín and Cathfadh, "and we accept it not." "Take the battle under thy protection, Îrial," said Conchubhar. "That is a lock[1] of hair against a strong wind now," said Irial, "and I accept it not." "Take the battle under thy protection, Laoghaire the Triumphant," said Conchubhar. "That is striking an oak with fists now," said Laoghaire, "and I grant it not."

35. Just then the haughty quick-spirited warrior, to wit, the head of the valour and chivalry of the Gaoidheals, and the pillar of the bravery of Ireland, even Cû-Chulainn son of Subhaltamh, came during that parley towards them; and Conchubhar glanced at him, and uttered this *rosg:*

"An oak of conflict is Culann's Hound:
he achieves battles of hard-feat:
he excels his fellows:
he wards off battles from Rudhraighe:
hero of Chivalry [2] of the Irish:
sternest warrior, oak.

"Take the battle under thy protection, Cû-Chulainn," said Conchubhar. "I accept that," said Cû-Chulainn, and he spake these words:

"I am a mountain against waves:
I am a rock [?] [3] against a cataract:
I am a prop against glass: [4]
I am a pillar [5] against bravery:
I am a lion against [for ?] voracity:
I am a champion against great strength."

Howbeit, Cû-Chulainn was stirred to see Conchubhar and the Ulstermen in straits of battle,[6] and he kindled his combat of valour thereby, and (stimulated) his mighty hand. And the Ulstermen all recognized[7] him, when they heard him, and their glow and force and fury[8] arose, and they maintained fiercely, insensately, stern-heartedly

---

[2] Weapon-skill (?); "bravery," *Man. & Cust.* III. 515. [3] Read coirċe.
[4] *Sic!* [5] Read ursa (?); or arsaiḋ, veteran.
[6] Lit. in unequal combat, at a disadvantage in.
[7] Idiom.; cf. *Hogan's Irish Phrase-book*, p. 17.
[8] Cf. a bruċ 7 a bríg 7 a borrḟad, *Fled Bricr.* §§ 46, 79.

los; gur ṫoirn-ċrioṫnaiġ an talaṁ trom-ḟóḋaċ[a] fó ċosaiḃ na ccuraḋ ccoṁramaċ ag coṁṫuargain a ċéile; gur bá hiomḋa a n-ionsaṁlaḋ lé luċt a n-éirtioċta an tan sin. 'Oir baḋ samalta ré forgaḋ garḃ-ġaoiṫe geiṁriota ré fíoḋḃaḋ fáin-ḟeaḋa, fogar ⁊ foṫrom ⁊ faiḋreanna[b] ḃfoġa, dá ḃfrais-diuḃ-racaḋ idir na caṫaiḃ ceaċtarḋa. Dá samalta fós ré fíoḋḃaḋ moṫar-ḋlúiṫ, gá hiomsgoltaḋ ⁊ gá hantuargain a nglacaiḃ ⁊ a mbacaiḃ a ċéile re hiomraobaḋ na gaoiṫe gairḃe glóraiḋe, brosgar na sleaġ sleann-ġorma slaḃraḋaċ, gá ráthaḋ a ccorpaiḃ caoṁ-ċuraḋ san ccoṁruaṫar soin. Ionnus go mbí seiseilḃe móra is an ccaṫ in tan sin .i. iaċtaċ na n-ógḃaḋ, ⁊ osnaḋaċ na n-anraḋ, uċḃaḋaċ na n-earr,[c] siain-ġréaċaḋ na seanóireaḋ, ⁊ brosgár na mbaḋḃ ⁊ na mbrain-éan ré hiomarca an anḟorloinn. Iomḋa ann fós fir 'n-a ḃfaon-luiḋe aḃḟuair-linntiḃ, ⁊ méiḋe maoil-dearga ar n-a min-leadraḋ, ⁊ buinn[d] ḃána ag bíogarnaiġ, ⁊ beoil ḃriaṫair-ḃinne ag bán-ġlasaḋ[e] ⁊ gnúise geala ar [n-a] n-aḋraḋ,[f] ⁊ suisg ró-ġlasa ag a ro-ḋor-chaḋ, ⁊ céadfaḋa connla gá ccómmbuaiḋriḋ.

36. Cid trá acht, ró ionnsaiḋ Conoll an láṫair caṫa ann a raiḃe Conċuḃar ag a ċoṁ ṫuargain is an ccaṫ, gur ṫuit leis Fíoḋaċ Folt-garḃ Feaḋa Gailḃe, ⁊ Faḋḃ ua hIomna,—aċt gé adeirid araile gurab a ccath Fionnċoraḋ do ṫuit Faḋḃ. Dála Ċonuill iomorro, do roċtadar na trí Ruaiḋ-ċinn a Reaṫain[g] ċuige, ⁊ é ar ḃéalaiḃ Ċonċuḃair; ⁊ ró ḟáiṫriod sleaġ gaċa fir aca ann; ⁊ ró ḟaiṫ-siom sleaġ ann gaċ aon díoḃ-san; ⁊ ró sgarrad ré ċéile iar sin, go ttarla Eochaiḋ mac Rosa ar ḃéalaiḃ ċáiċ ċum Conaill, gur ḟearrad coṁlann niata náiṁ-diḋe naṫarḋa: ⁊ tug Eochaiḋ trí gona ar Ċonoll; giḋeaḋ tug Conoll goin[h] díoġlaiġ dian-ḃáis dó-san, gur ċorgair a ċeann dá ċoluinn.

37. Acht atá ní ċeano,—sgúċar Cú Ċulainn fó ċaiṫ na nGailianaċ, ⁊ tug fobairt bíoḋḃaḋ for ḃíoḋḃaḋaiḃ orro, gur

---

35–37] [a] ḟoideaċ, M. [b] faiḋreann a ḃ. (?). [c] earraḋ, M. [d] buinneaḋ, M. [e] builceḋ(aḋ), A. [f] gnúise geala ag garḃ-ġlasa(ḋ), A.; for aḋraḋ read aṫruġaḋ, *alteration*. [g] Réaṫán, A. [h] béim, A.

[1] Cf. gan foḋord gan forcionaċ, without murmur, *O'Cl.*; forgaḋ, approach, *O'R.*, might suit here; perhaps it is connected with forechim, gl. *tribulo*.

the position by reason thereof: so that the heavy-clodded earth loudly shook under the feet of the powerful champions, as they smote one another; so that manifold was their semblance to *the minds of* those who listened to them at that time. For like the sough [?][1] of a rough winter wind against a forest of sloping wood was the sound and noise and whirring [?][2] of darts as they were hurled in showers between the battalions on either side. Like also to a cluster-dense forest *whose trees are* a-rending and a-smiting into the forks and crooks of one another by the riving of the rough roaring wind was the crashing of the slate-blue chained spears a-thrusting into the bodies of comely champions in that mutual charge; so that there were great uproars in the battle at that time, to wit, the shouting of the youth, and the moaning of the warriors, the groaning of the chariot-fighters, the scream-shrieking of the old men, and the crying of the vultures and ravens, through the excess of the strife.[3] Many there, too, were the men lying prostrate in cold pools, and the headless[4] gory [?] trunks torn to bits, and the white soles close together [?], and the word-sweet lips turning pale-grey, and the bright faces very blanched[5], and the deep-grey eyes deep-darkening, and the intelligent senses confused.

36. Howbeit, Conall approached the place of battle where Conchubhar was a-smiting, when fell by his hand[6] Fiodhach the Hair-rugged of Fiodh Gaibhle[7] and Fadhbh, grandson of Iomna (though others say that it is in the battle of Fionnchoradh that Fadhbh fell). Concerning Conall, however—the three Redheads from Reathain came up to him while he was in front of Conchubhar, and thrust a spear of each man of them at him, and he thrust his spear at each one of them; and they parted from each other thereupon; and Eochaidh son of Ros chanced *to come* in front of all towards Conall, and they plied a heroic hostile serpentlike combat, and Eochaidh inflicted three wounds on Conall; yet Conall inflicted a vengeful wound of violent death on him, and smote his head from his body.

37. Howbeit, Cû-Chulainn advanced among the battalions of the Gailianachs, and made an assault of foes against foes on them, wound-

---

[2] ꞃenꝺ, point, *W.*

[3] Struggle, *violentia.*

[4] ṁaol means hairless, hornless, *and, here,* headless (?).

[5] So *MS. A;* aḋꞃaḋ, seems phonetic for aṫꞃuġaḋ, altered, changed; *g.* aḋaꞃ-ꞇha, 20; aḋꞃaꝺ, adhering, *C. M. Rath,* xv.

[6] Lit., by him.

[7] *Now* Feeguile.

ċréaċtnaiġ ⁊ gur ċiorrḃaiġ sochaiḋe iomḋa ḋíoḃ a ḃfuiliḃ ⁊ a ḃforgonaiḃ. O 'ḋconcadar garraḋ Gailian sin, ró ḃúirsioḋ ⁊ ró ḃrioċt-ġáirsioḋ im Ċo(i)n gCulainn ar gaċ árd do'n ċaṫ, go ró ḟás 7 ró ḟorbair[a] fiuċaḋ fíoċṁar feirge ac Coin cCulainn[b] ḋe sin; óir ro ḋásaċtaḋ[c] uime aṁail tarḃ troḋáin dia ttaḃarṫar droċ-ḃualaḋ, gur dian-sgaoileaḋ dlúṫ-ḃuiḋne leis; ⁊ gur ċuir trom-árṁaċ[d] ar na tuingiḃ[e] do'n treas-gleo sin; gur ġaḃadar aos gairgiḋ gráin ⁊ oṁan,[f] ógḃaḋ ⁊ anḟlaṫa sgannraḋ, fear-óglaoiċ ⁊ sean-laoiċ ⁊ saor-ċuraiḋ na nGailian tréanruaṫar ⁊ torann-ċriṫ[g] ón ngleo soin; gur ḃainreaḋ[h] buinn frí ṁeiḋiḃ[i] ⁊ meiḋiḃ frí ḃonnaiḃ uaṫa seaċnóin an ċaṫa; ⁊ níor an tráṫ do na hanraḋa sin, gur ionnsaiḋ an cró caṫa 'n-a ḃfaċa an mionn ríoġḋa, ⁊ an t-áird-ríġ .i. Cairbre Niaiḋ Fear féin.

38. Ba fraoċḋa forġranna fraoċ-ġruama ainṁín aindréanta easccáirdeaṁail an feaġaḋ féiġ feoċair fursuaṁanta dobeart cáċ ar a ċéile díoḃ, deannaiḃ[j] na rosg rúin-ṁillte fá ṁall-ḃruaċaiḃ na moṫar-ṁala ngrangaċ ngrágánaċ.[k] 'O 'dċonnairc Cairbre Niaiḋ[l] Fear an ionnsaiġe sin, gaḃar eagla ⁊ uroṁan é; ⁊ tángadar trom-laoiċ a ṫeaġlaiġ ⁊ a ṫréan-ċuir[m] ⁊ díoġluim a ḋeaġ-laoiċ 'n-a ḟiaḋnaise, ⁊ tug Cairbre aiṫeasg toiḃéime ar Ċoin gCulainn[n] ar an láṫair sin. Imḋeargṫar im Ċo(i)n gCulainn tríd sin; ⁊ cuingeas coṁrac aoin-fir ar Ċairbre, go ndubairt:

"Ceart coṁloinn[o] áillim-si
fri hiomaireaċ iomgona:
aiḃliúḃa clú codroma:
roġa arm aon-ḃuille:

37, 38] [a] ḟorbair, A. [b] Congculainn, S. [c] ro ḃásactaiġ, A. [d] trom-árḃaċ, A. [e] tuinniġṫiḃ, A. [f] ur-uaṁain, A. [g] toirn-ḃrioċ, A. [h] ḃain, S.; ḃainraḋ, A. [i] bonna fri méde, *F. Mast.* i. 330. [j] tteannaiḃ, A. [k] ngrangcaḋ ngrugánaċ. [l] Read Nia. [m] ṫreantuir, A. [n] Ċongolann, S. [o] coṁlann, A.

---

1 Lit., it was raged (?).
2 árṁaċ, slaughter, Isaiah xxxiv. 2; árḃaċ, havoc, *O'R.*
3 tuingib for tuinniġṫiḃ, *A.*; tuinniġib of *O'R.* (?).
4 bonn fri méde, indiscriminate slaughter, *F. Masters*, i. 330; co torcratar bonn fri bonn 7 méde fri méde; bond fri méde, *LU.*, p. 80 b; i.e. heads and points, in a heap.

ing and hewing down great numbers of them in bloodshed and deep wounds. When the soldiery of the Galian saw this, they roared and weirdly shouted around Cû-Chulainn from every quarter of the battle; whereat grew and swelled Cû-Chulainn's fierce boiling of wrath, for he was raging[1] around him like a fighting bull to which an evil stroke is given; and dense bands were violently scattered by him; and he inflicted heavy slaughter[2] on the strong men[3] in that stout affray, till the men of arms took horror and dread, the youths and chieftains panic, the young warriors and old warriors and free-champions of the Galian stampede and quaking from that strife, till their soles touched necks and their necks [touched] soles[4] along the *field of* battle; and he desisted not a moment from those champions till he approached the ring of battle in which he saw the royal diadem and the high-king, even Cairbre Nia Fear himself.

38. Wrathful, horrid, wrath-gloomy, ungentle, very angry,[5] unfriendly, was the keen, angry, very fiery[6] look that each of them cast on the other from the flashings[7] [?] of the intent-ruinous eyes under the soft [?] brinks of the frowning,[8] wrinkled[9] cluster-brows. When Cairbre Nia Fear saw that approach, fear and terror seized him, and the heavy warriors of his household and his strong lords[10] and the select[11] of his goodly-champions came before him; and Cairbre uttered an insulting proposal[12] to Cû-Chulainn on that spot. Cû-Chulainn is provoked thereby, and demands single combat of Cairbre, saying:

"Right of combat I demand,
unto strife of mutual wounding;
the greater[13] shall be our equal fame;
choice of arms of one stroke;

---

[5] drenn, quarrel, rough, *W.*

[6] Cf. ruaimniġṫe, fixed, *O'R.*; ruaim, flush of anger, *Coney's Dict.*

[7] Read de deannaiḃ, d'innib, *ex acie* (?), colours; or de ṫeannaib, from the fires (?). Cf. teann .i. losgaḋ, *ODavoren;* teann .i. teine, *O'Cl.*

[8] granc-fúileaċ, sour-eyed, *M'Curtin's Dict.*, p. 257.

[9] grug, wrinkle, austere, *O'R.*; grucánac, wrinkled, *Fled Brier.*, p. 271.

[10] The gentlemen of his body-guard; tor .i. tiġearna, *O'Cl.*

[11] díoġlum, a gleaning, Micah vii.; *M'Curtin*, pp. 173, 261.

[12] *Or* speech of Alexander, *LB.* 206 b; words, "Bodl. Cormac," 12; *Tl.* 244.

[13] For aiḋbliu de; or aiḋbliuġaḋ, increasing, *O'R.*

saoḃaḋ súl[a] soċaiḋe:
iolar arm eagcoṁlann[b]:
baidhead broin[c] bíoḋḃaḋaiḃ:
briseaḋ neart niaḋaċar:
is mise ro ṫúr riangon-sa:
do na clesaiḃ cóṁḋaingne
taoċraḋ dom neart[d] Niaḋ-Ċairbre,
ó ro ria ċugam-sa
a ccró an ċoṁloinn ċeartaiġ so."
Ceart.

39. "Ró adfiaḋ-sa[e] soin, a Ċu Ċulainn," ar Cairbre:

"Dóiġ isam[f] ṫriaṫ fria ṫreiṫ-ruire,[g]
am[h] niaḋ frí huair iorgaile,
am[h] laoċ frí luaṫ-láṁaċ,
am[h] ċur frí ċruaiḋ-ġrearaiḃ,
am[i] ṫiġearna fri ṫioḋnaic[ṫ]iḃ;
am[i] ríġ frí ríġ-ḃéargna,[j]
am[i] ráil frí ró-ġonaiḃ,
am[i] ḋaingean díoċoġlaiḋ."
Dóiġ.

Is ann sin aduḃairt Cú Ċulainn na briaṫra beaga for-ṁolta so[k] air féin:

"Am sonn[l] sláinte soċaiḋe,
am[i] uaiṫne a n-am[m] iorgaile,
am[i] leoman lonn lasamail,
am[i] ċur ċiorrḃar curaḋa,
am[i] ḋáiġ ḋioġlas díleanna,
am[i] earr neart-niaḋaċais,
am[i] ṁíliḋ ṁór ṁíleata,
am[i] cairpṫeaċ céim-ionnsaiġṫeaċ,
am[i] niaḋ náṁaḋ neart-áiṫir,[n]

38, 39] [a] sál, S. [b] eagcoṁlainn, A. [c] bróin, A. [d] daṁ-neart, A. [e] Read roṫḃia-sa (?). [f] is um, A. [g] ṫre ruire, A. [h] im, A. [i] um, A. [j] ríġṁeargna in MSS. [k] beaga so forṁolta, A. [l] sonnaḋ, A.M. [m] ám, A. [n] neartuiġeas, A., instead of neart áiṫir.

[1] *Or* of unequal combats.

[2] For báiġeaḋ (?); let sorrows drown enemies, *A.*; *cf.* ra tógaiḃ

deluding of the eyes of many;
multitude of weapons disabled[1];
let ravens contend with[2] enemies;
let might break heroism;
it is I that have sought this field-wounding
by the powerful feats;
Niadh-Chairbre's might may fall by my hand,[3]
when he shall have reached me
in the ring of this rightful combat."
Right *of combat I demand.*

39. "Thou shalt have that, Cû-Chulainn," said Cairbre:

"For I am a lord for a noble chief;
I am a hero for the hour of strife;
I am a warrior for swift shooting;
I am a champion for hard attacks[4];
I am a noble for gifts;
I am a king for royal way of life;
I am an oak for (against) deep-woundings;
I am a stronghold impregnable."
For *I am a lord.*

Then spoke Cû-Chulainn these little words of high praise of himself:—

"I am a prop[5] of the weal of many;
I am a pillar in time[6] of strife;
I am a fierce flaming lion;
I am a champion who maims champions;
I am a fire that avenges floods[7];
I am a [chariot-]warrior of mighty heroism;
I am a great *and* soldierly soldier;
I am a stride-assaulting chariot-rider;
I am a hero of enemies of mighty sharpness[8];

ḃaḋḃ cenn ecuppa, 7 baoı mapḃaḋ móp ecuppa pán can, "Frag. of Ir. Ann." 190.

[3] Lit., by me. [4] *Or* provocations.

[5] ponnaċ or ponnaḋ, *MA.*, a rampart.

[6] *Or* a band of strife; for such laudations *cf.* "Ir. Texte," i. 291, etc.

[7] Takes vengeance on floods; and so, wards off; or ḋíġbaṗ, takes off.

[8] áıċeṗ, *g.* áıċhıṗ from áıċ, sharp (?); or *dat. sg.* aċhıṗ, with strong insult or outrage.

am[a] ċur calma ac cruaḋ-ġonaiḃ,
am[a] ṫriaṫ tréan frí ṫroim-ġreasaiḃ,[b]
am[a] ṫuir tornn trom-ainsgleaċ,[c]
am ríġ-niaḋ frí ró-ḃuiḋniḃ,
am[a] ḟearg sáiteaċ[d] sluaġ suire,
am ḟearḋa frí ḟearḟoġlaiḋ."

40. Do ṫuairgriod an dias soin a ċéile, ⁊ tug gaċ aon díoḃ díograis ngon dá ċéile coṁruic, gur ḟearsad gleo fraoċḋa furánaċ fíor-ġruama[e] feiḋm-láidir ré ċéile, gur luaiṫiġeadar láṁa ré lonn-ḃualaḋ, ⁊ coraiḃ ré cóṁḟorúġaḋ ré tarann ain áiġ[f] ⁊ iomġona ar a ċéile. Aċt ċeana bá bailc na béimionna, ⁊ bá borb na beo-ġona,[g] baḋ daingean na deaġ-ḟáite, baḋ díorġ(aḋ)[h] an dúr-ċaṫuġaḋ, ⁊ baḋ crua(i)ḋ na croiḋeaḋa; gur bá tuargain dá ṫréan-ċuraḋ, baḋ leadraḋ dá leoġan, baḋ mire dá ṁaṫġaṁna; baḋ dá ṫarḃ ar tulaiġ ⁊ baḋ dá ḋaṁ ar ḋromainn iad fá'n ionḃaiḋ[i] sin.

41. Ciḋ trá aċt, do ḃí do ḋíocra(ċt) an ċoṁraic dorónsat, gur ḃriṡ Cairbre arm is an ccoṁṫuargain; go ttángodar naonṁar dá ṁuinntir ar a ḃéalaiḃ san iomḃualaḋ, ⁊ do ċong-ḃadar an coṁlann a n-aghaiḋ Ċon gCulainn go ttugaḋ airm do Ċairbre; ⁊ do ṫuitiodar an naonṁar curaḋ re Cú Ċulainn faoi sin. Ró ḟearsad an coṁlann go calma iar sin, gur briseaḋ airm Ċon cCulainn[j] do ḃraṫ-ḃuilleaḃaiḃ Ċairbre; ⁊ tángadar naonṁar deaġ-laoċ ar ḃéalaiḃ Con gCulainn is an iorġail, do ċongḃáil a sgíaṫ ré Cairbre; ⁊ ro ṫuitiodar uile lais. Aċt atá ní ċeana, do ḃí do ḋíocraċt[k] an iomairge, gur briseaḋ airm gaċ aoin díoḃ fó ṫrí, ⁊ gur ṫuitiodar trí naon-ṁair sir gaċ n-aon díoḃ ar ḃéalaiḃ a ċéile fris an rae sin.

42. Do ḃí fós do ḋaoire[l] an deaḃaiḋ, nár ḟulingiodar airm do Ċo(i)n Ċulainn, go ttángodar[m] á airm dísle féin ċuige lé Laoġ mac Rianġaḃra .i. an Duaiḃseaċ sleaġ Ċon cCulainn[n] ⁊

39–42] [a] um, A. [b] faoi ṫrom-ṫreasaiḃ, A. [c] ḋorn-trom ainscleaċ, A. [d] saiṫeaċ, A. [e] furasaċ fíor-ġranna, A. [f] re tarraċtain áiġ, A.M. [g] bioċ-ġona, A. [h] Read díoċra (?). [i] ionnbaiḋ, A. [j] Ċuċulainn, S. [k] ba hé dioċraċt, A. [l] ḋaoirse, A. [m] ttorraċ-tadar, A. [n] Cúċulainn, S., *perp.*

[1] *Or* combats, treasaiḃ, *A.*

[2] Leader of thunder; heavy; great boasting; tornn, thunder; sgleo, boasting.

I am a champion valiant at hard woundings;
I am a strong lord for heavy provocations[1];
I am a leader[2] of chiefs of heavy affrays [?];
I am a royal-hero for strong bands;
I am a thrustful reed of hosts of chieftains;
I am manly against a plunderer."

40. Those two smote each other, and each of them inflicted abundance of wounds on his opponent,[3] and they plied furious, angry,[4] truly grim, effort-strong strife against each other, and they quickened hands to smite fiercely and feet to hold firm against the oncome of[5] the fight and of mutual wounding. Howbeit, stout were the strokes and fierce the live-wounds, strong were the good thrusts, earnest[6] was the hard fighting, and stern were the hearts, for[7] it was a smiting of two brave champions, it was a lacerating of two lions, it was a madness of two bears; two bulls on a mound and two steers on a ridge were they at that time.

41. Now, such was the vehemence[8] of the fight they made, that Cairbre broke his weapons in the mutual smiting; when nine of his household came before him in the conflict, and maintained the fray against Cû-Chulainn till arms were brought to Cairbre; and the nine champions fell by *the hand of* Cû-Chulainn within that *time*. After that, they plied the fight bravely, until Cû-Chulainn's weapons were broken by the search-strokes[9] of Cairbre; and nine good warriors came before Cû-Chulainn in the strife to uphold their shields against Cairbre; and they all fell by his [Cairbre's] hand. Howbeit, such was the vehemence of the conflict that the arms of each one of them was broken thrice over, and that three nines fell by *the hand of* each one of them during that time.

42. Such too was the rigour of the quarrel that they suffered not arms *to be brought* to Cû-Chulainn, till his own proper arms came to him with Laogh son of Rianghabhair, to wit, the Duaibhseach,[10]

---

[3] Lit., fellow of fight. [4] ꞅuꞃanaċ, cautious; ꞅoꞃꞃánach, destructive, *O'R.*

[5] So in *AM.* ꞇaꞃaċꞇain for ꞇoꞃaċꞇain; M'Solly has a corrupt reading, which may be = "against the thunder of fight and great mutual wounding."

[6] *Or* straight. [7] Lit., so that.

[8] Lit., there was of fervour; ꝺíochꞃaċꞇ in full, 9 lines *infra*.

[9] bꞃaċ, spying, Gen. xlii.; *or* treacherous blows: see § 31.

[10] The Grim One.

an Cruaiḋín cadat-ċeann a ċloiḋioṁ, ⁊ a ilċleasa lúiṫ ar ċeana .i. uḃaill-ċleas, ⁊ cleitín-ċleas, ⁊ fóid-ċleas,[a] ⁊ bir-ċleas,[b] ⁊ béim go ccumas, ⁊ a ṫrealṁa gaisgiḋ[c] ó sin amaċ. Ġaḃas Cú Ċulainn a armaiḃ dísle[d] féin; ⁊ sonairte soiṁeirniġ leis á il-ċleasa[e] 'n-a n-aeḋiḃ urġranna aḋuaṫṁara do ḃeiṫ 'n-a úirṫimċioll an tan sin; gur baḋ loinne ⁊ lúṫġáir ⁊ láin-ṁeanma leis gaċ áiġ ⁊ gaċ iorġail ⁊ gaċ neart-ġáḃaḋ dá ḃfaġ(ḃ)aḋ ionnta. 'Oir baḋ fear foránaċ fíoċḋa fraoċ-anfaḋaċ, anam caṫa ⁊ coṁraic, an fear soin. Do ġaḃ mar in ccéaḋna Cairbre a airm dísle dionġḃála féin ċuige; ⁊ do ġaḃadar iar soin ag tuarġain[f] a ċéile do ḃraṫ-ḃuilleaḋaiḃ bíoḋḃaḋ buan-raobṫa; ⁊ baḋ fraoċḋa fuaṫṁar fíor-ġranna an féiḋm-ṫrear,[g] ⁊ baḋ aindreanda[h] anaiṫniḋ ainṁeararḋa an arairg. Do ḃádar ar in láṫair sin, gur baḋ suaill naċar léigrioḋ foirḃḟir ⁊ feall-óglaoiċ, luċt maoiṫe ⁊ míoġairge, a ngreamannaiḃ caṫa díoḃ ag feiṫim[i] na míleaḋ mear-ċalma[j] soin.

43. Agas do ḃí d'ḟeaḃus na himḋeaġla dorónsat, naċ raiḃe gona ná doṁain-ċréaċta ar ċeaċtar díoḃ san ccoṁlann sis in rae sin; gur éiriġ Laoġ mac Rianġaḃra, do ġríosaḋ Ċon cCulainn, go mbioḋ ag á aiṫiriúġaḋ tré ḟaill imiorṫa á airm ⁊ ag aḋṁolaḋ feaċt oile tré imirt a ċleas go calma; gur éiriġ ḃruiṫ ⁊ bríġe ⁊ borrfaḋ,[k] corgar ⁊ calmaċt ⁊ cruaḋ-ċonfaḋ ag Coin cCulainn ḋe sin; gur aṫraiġ an tsleaġ ḋuaiḃreaċ ḋoiḋionġḃála[l] san láiṁ álainn aiṁḋeis, ⁊ gur aḋnaiġ áiġ iomġona dá leiṫ clí seaċ bile na sgéiṫe go Cairbre. Do luiġ Cairbre an sgiaṫ síos d' imḋíoion a ċuirp ar in tsleaġ .i. an Duaiḃrioċ; óir ní ṫéarnóḋ neaċ uaiṫe dá ngointear[m] lé. Leisin cuireas Cú Ċulainn an cleitín-ċleas iona ḋeasláiṁ gur[n] léiġ tar bile na sgéiṫe go Cairbre é, d'ionnsaiġe á aiġṫe, go ttarla a ḃfóċlár a éadain, go rug a inċinn 'n-a caobaiḃ cró-ḋearga

---

42, 43] [a] soid-ċleas, A.S. [b] birr-ċleas, S. [c] gaisge, S.; trealaṁa gascid, A. [d] dile, S. [e] ill-ċleasa, S. [f] mar an ccéadna ní luġa ro ġaḃ Cairbre a earraḋ caṫa féin uime ⁊ a a(i)rm dioġruise dionġḃála, gur ġaḃ các ag tuarġain, &c., A. [g] feaḋ-ṫrear, S. [h] aindreanta, A. [i] Read feiṫeaṁ or feiḋm (?). [j] mór-ċalma, A. [k] borrb(aḋ), S. [l] ḋoionġaḃála, S.; nduaḃreaċ nḋóiḋionġṁala, A. [m] ngontar, S. [n] dar, A.

[1] The Little Hard One. [2] lúd, *velocitas*, *Z.*

[3] Those feats are mentioned in *LU.* 103 b, and in *LL.*

Cû-Chulainn's spear, and the hard-headed Cruaidín,[1] his sword, and *the apparatus of* his various feats of dexterity[2] in general, namely, apple-feat, and dart-feat, and turn-feat, and spit-feat,[3] and stroke with power, and the rest of his apparatus of martial skill. Cû-Chulainn took his own special arms, and he deemed it strengthening and encouraging that his various feats were around him as terrible fires [?] at that time; for fury[4] and joy and fullness of spirit to him was every battle and every strife and every mighty danger that he found in them; for a fierce, impetuous, fury-swelling man, in time of[5] battle and of conflict, was that man. Cairbre likewise took to himself his own proper arms. And thereupon they fell to smiting one another with hostile, long-rending, danger-strokes, and furious, dreadful, truly-horrific, was the effort-combat[6]; and ferocious,[7] unknown-of unrestrained was the smiting.[8] They remained in that position until aged[9] men and recruits,[10] and unwarlike folk, almost let go their grips of battle from them while watching the quick-valiant warriors.

43. And such was the excellence of the defence they made, that no wounds or deep gashes were *inflicted* on either of them in the fray during that time; until Laogh son of Rianghabhair arose to incite Cû-Chulainn, and was reviling him for neglecting to wield his weapon and at another time praising him for plying his feats bravely; so that glow and force and fury, slaughter and valour and stern-tempest arose in Cû-Chulainn therefrom, and he changed the Grim Spear of good-defence into the comely left hand,[11] and gave a shot[12] of wounding from his left side past the rim of the shield to Cairbre. Cairbre lowered the shield to guard his body from the spear,[13] that is, the Duaibhseach; for of those who are wounded with it not one ever escaped from it *alive.* Thereupon[14] Cû-Chulainn put the dartlet-feat in his right hand, and let it go over the rim of the shield at Cairbre, against his face, so that it took effect in his forehead,[15] and carried his brain

---

[4] Wild excitement. [5] *Or* a life and soul of battle.

[6] féid-ṫreas, long fight, *S.*; for féiġ, sharp (?). [7] drend, rough fight.

[8] *Or* tumult; for easargain, tumult, Amos ii.; esairchnea, gl. *flagella.*

[9] foirb for foirfe, old, perfect; or for mearb fir, false men.

[10] Lit., of softness; with fellóglaoich *cf.* felmac, a student.

[11] *Or* and rises the Grim Spear . . . in his comely fair hand (aib, cf. aoibinn).

[12] atnaig, put, *LL.* 72 b; atnaiġ, proceeds, *LB.* 214 a; áig, lit. battle attack.

[13] Ferdiad did the same: rabert béim din sciaṫ, sír d'anacul iachtair a chuirp, *LL.* 60 a.

[14] With that, *in Anglo-Irish* = then. [15] clár a éadain *means* forehead.

tré n-a ċuil-ṁéiḋe siar seaċtair, gur ṫuit Cairbre ar in láṫair sin do asargain an urċair, ⁊ á airm faon fóṫrarrna faoi.[a] Agas easargar Cú Ċulainn é do ḃráṫ-ḃuilliḃiḃ bíoḋḃaḋ, gur ḃean a ċeann de; ⁊ croiṫios an ceann sir na sluaġaiḃ, ⁊ maoiḋiḋ a ṫeaġlaċ an trom-ċorgar. Iompuiḋios Cú Ċulainn fó ċaṫ na nGailian, gur bá samalta ré sruiṫ-léim sanntaċ siuḃlaċ sár-loinge ré siorga na sian-ġaoiṫe, in síḋe sanntaċ soluaiṁneaċ rug fúṫaiḃ seaċnóin an ċaṫa. Agas ro ḟearsad Ulaiḋ an caṫ go cróḋa, an g(c)éin do ḃí Cú Ċulainn san ccoṁrac séaṁráite.

44. Dála Ċonuill iomorro, téid fó 'n ccaṫ, ⁊ dorad a amarrán orro, go ttug á aġaiḋ lé hásaiḃ, ⁊ a ċlí lé corgaraiḃ, ⁊ a ḋeis lé daor-ḃualaḋ, ⁊ a ṫroiġ lé trom-ḟoruġaḋ, gur réiḋiġ bearrna ċéad, ⁊ sliġe ruaiṫniḋ roċaiḋe roiṁ annsaḋaiḃ Ulaḋ is an ccaṫ. Agas dorad Conall a ḃoirb-ṫrear díḃreirge orra, ⁊ Ulaiḋ uile fá'n ccuma céadno, gur ḟearsad an caṫ go cróḋa conraḋaċ,[b] ⁊ go díoċra dúr danarḃa, ⁊ do ḋíoġladar a n-anċroiḋe, ⁊ a n-anḟorlann orro, go raḃadar tiug-ára móra ar na Gailianaiḃ ⁊ ar in sluaġ ar ċeana.

45. Gurḃ é Irial mac Conuill Ċearrnaiġ baḋ láṁ ladrann ag díoċuġaḋ[c] laoċraiḋ Laiġean seaċnóin an ċaṫa. Cid trá aċt ó ró ṫuit Cairbre,—ní gnáṫ caṫuġaḋ ar ndíoṫ tiġearna,—⁊ ró ḟaoṁrad Laiġniḃ ar a láiṫrib caṫa, ⁊ ro ṁaiḋ[d] in coṁlann orro. Agas ró leanadar Ulaiḋ iad go Ríġe Laiġean, gurḃ ann-soin ró anrad díoḃ; gonaḋ ann aduḃradar, "Is lór linn a leanṁuin go ró so": gonaḋ ḋe sin ró lean an t-ainm do'n aḃuinn an(d)iu .i. Ríġe; roċaiḋe trat a ttorċradar díoḃ go ruiġe[e] so.

46. Ro ḟoiċriod Ulaiḋ iar sin go hairm a raiḃe Conċuḃar

44–46] [a] frioṫnoċt fiar-ṫarrna, A.M. [b] corgar-ċonraċ, A.M. [c] díoċaḋ, A. [d] ṁuiġ, S.; ṁaoiṫ, A. [e] ruige, A.

[1] *Or* in presence of.
[2] Cf. síġe or síḋe, blast; *or* pressure, as siasgánta, tight, *O'Don. Suppl.*
[3] Noisy wind (?).
[4] Cf. síḋe gaoithe, rush of wind.
[5] Brought woe to them.
[6] Lit., heavy.
[7] Lit., easily recognized.

out backwards through the nape of his neck in gore-red lumps, so that Cairbre fell on that spot, his weapon lying crosswise beneath him. And Cû-Chulainn smote him with hostile search-strokes, and he cut his head off; and he shook the head towards[1] the hosts, and his household boasted the great triumph. Cû-Chulainn turned through the battalion of the Gailian, and like the eager striding tide-leap of a great ship before a blast [?][2] of the storm-wind[3] was the eager nimble rush[4] that he made among them throughout the battalion; and the Ulstermen plied the battle bravely, as long as Cû-Chulainn was *engaged* in the aforesaid duel.

44. Concerning Conall, now, he went through the battle and inflicted his distress upon[5] them, and turned his face to slaughters and his left to havocs and his right to cruel-smiting and his foot to firm[6] staying, and cleared a gap for a hundred and a clear[7] road for a multitude before the chiefs of the Ulstermen in the battle. And Conall inflicted his fierce strife of wrath on them [the enemy], and all the Ulstermen in the same fashion, and they plied the battle bravely, ragefully, earnestly, sternly, cruelly; and they avenged their *former* wrong[8] and violence on them [the enemy], so that great final-slaughters were *inflicted* on the Gailians and on the army in general.

45. And it was Irial son of Conall Cearnach that was a brigand's hand in destroying the championry of the Leinstermen throughout the battle. However, when Cairbre had fallen—it is not usual to fight after losing[9] a commander—and the Leinstermen betook themselves from their positions of battle, and lost the fight.[10] And the Ulstermen pursued them to the Rye of Leinster, where they left off from them; and here they said: "We are satisfied to have followed them up to this."[11] Whence the name has stuck to the river *till* to-day, namely the Rye [*i.e.* the "reach"]: many indeed *were* those of them who fell till they[12] reached this.

46. After that the Ulstermen arrived[13] at the place in which

---

[8] Better aincriḋe = Old-Irish ancride.

[9] Yielded; the word usually means to take.

[10] Lit., the conflict burst on them.

[11] Lit., till it may or shall reach this, *s-fut.* of rochim; cf. corrice so, go ruiġe so.

[12] Lit., it reached; there is *a jeu de mots* in Ruiġe and Riġe.

[13] soiċ, .i. ránic no tanic, *O'Clery;* doroiċ, rosoiċ, he reaches; *W.*, under dorochim, rochim.

go mbuaiḋ ccorgair ⁊ ccoṁmaoiḋṁe; ⁊ do ġabadar ag aḋnacaḋ a ccaoṁ ⁊ a ccarad; go ndubairt Conċubar: "Is olc liom an caradraḋ so ó Ċairbre .i. tionól sluaiġ am aġaiḋ-si do ṫabairt caṫa daṁ." Agas do ḃí ag caoineaḋ go mór ós cionn Ċairbre, go ttáinig Cú Ċulainn do láṫair, ⁊ ceann Ċairbre leis; ⁊ do léig a bfiaḋnaise Ċonċubair é. Agas adubairt Conċubar. "Maiṫ aṁ intí ar a raiḃ an ceann so," ar sé; "óir baḋ mór raiṫ na cloinne dia raiḃe;" ⁊ adubairt an laoiḋ-si síos ann:

"Trí mic Rosa Ruaiḋ in ríġ,
gaḃraḋ an tír rúnaḋ feaḋ:
Fine a n-All(aḋ),[a] Oilill a cCruaiċ,
Cairbre an tua[b] a tTeaṁraiġ ḃreaġ.

A n-aoinḟeaċt do ċlaoiḋís caṫ,
an triar fá gnáṫ ann gaċ gleo:
teann láiṁ a mbeirdís a mbáiġ[c]:
baḋ glan a líon[d] máiġe leo.

Bá tráṫ n-a ttrí n-uaiṫne óir,
na trí honċoin,[e] fá tóir bailc;
is béarna a ccuimne na ccleas,
ó do ṫuit linne in treas tailc."

Ró haḋnacaḋ Cairbre iar soin, ⁊ tángodar Ulaiḋ dá ttiġiḃ go mbuaiḋ ccorgair ⁊ cóṁmaoiḋṁe. Finit 9° die Julij. 1727.

46] [a] rinne anall[aḋ], A. [b] tuaiḋ, A. [c] mbáiḋ, S.; mbuiḋe, A. [d] ḃun, A. [e] ogċoin, A.

---

[1] Lit. their dear ones. [2] Lit. and.

[3] Read ráṫ. *Cf.* Ass annsin tangattar dream a n-aiġiḋ Flainn acus cenn Cormaic an Riġ acca. As eo ro ráidsiod re Flann: "Betha acus sláinte a Rí chuṁachtaiġ! acus cenn Cormaic againn duit; acus amal as bés dona ríoġaiḃ, tógaiḃ do ṡliasad acus cuir in cenn so foithe acus fordíng é doo'

Conchubhar was, with triumph of victory and exultation; and they took to burying their relatives[1] and friends. And Conchubhar said: "Ill I deem this friendship from Cairbre, to wit, assembling an army against me to give battle to me." And he was lamenting much over Cairbre until Cû-Chulainn came in presence, *bringing*[2] Cairbre's head with him, and laid it down before Conchubhar. And Conchubhar said: "Good indeed was he on whom this head was," said he, "for great was the grace[3] of the family of which he was," and he spoke the following lay thereupon:

"The three sons of Ros Ruadh the king
held the land, quiet the division,[4]—
Fine in Alladh,[5] Oilill in Cruach,
Cairbre in the north at Teamhair Breagh.

Together they gained battle;
it was customary *for* the three in every strife;
steadfast *the* hand with which they waged their conflict;
bright was the filling of a plain[6] by them.

They were once three pillars of gold:
the three wolf-dogs[7] of strong chase;
there is[8] a void in respect of[9] feats,
since by us the third strong one has fallen."

After that Cairbre was buried, and the Ulstermen came to their homes with triumph of victory and exultation. *Finit nono die Julii*, 1727.

ḟliasaiḋ" . . Ragab Flann an cenn 'na láiṁ, acus ro póg é, acus dorád 'na ṫimchioll fo thri . . . Rugaḋ uaḋ iartainn an cenn go honórach d'ionnsaiġiḋ an chuirp . . . acus ro hadnaiceaḋ go honórach é.—"Fragm. of Ir. Ann." p. 212.

[4] Cf. runnaḋ and seḋ in *O'R.*

[5] Read Find a n-Ailinn.

[6] With soldiers or with slain.

[7] Leopards, *Coney's Dict.*; but they were not known to the Irish.

[8] Lit., it is.

[9] Lit., the.

ON IRISH NEUTER SUBSTANTIVES:

BEING A CONTRIBUTION TO

IRISH GRAMMAR AND LEXICOGRAPHY.

In the year 1853 Zeuss established the existence, in Old Irish, of a neuter article, neuter substantives, adjectives, and pronouns, and, in Welsh and Breton, of a neuter demonstrative pronoun.[1] In 1871 Ebel referred about twelve neuters to the S declension; to these Dr. Thurneysen added ríd and tír; and Dr. Whitley Stokes contributed nine or ten more in 1888, and drew attention to thirty-five neuters in -ách, which conform to the O declension in all the singular, and in the genitive plural, while they follow the S declension in the other cases.[2]

But Zeuss, Ebel, and others have erroneously stated that there remains no trace of the neuter in Modern Irish.[3] O'Donovan knew nothing of the neuter in Irish[4]; and when he or Dr. Joyce sang—

> "On Lough Neagh's banks as the fisherman strays,
> When the clear cold eve's declining,
> He sees the round towers of other days
> In the wave beneath him shining"—

they little suspected that they saw before them shining a petrified Irish neuter in the word Lough *N*-eagh. I should have said, perhaps, a living one; for it and many Irish neuters still survive, and assert their presence

---

1 "Grammatica Celtica," pp. 228–280, 332–374, 398.

2 Stokes' "Celtic Declension," and his "S-stems in the Celtic Languages."

3 Zeuss' "Grammar," 1st ed., p. 228. Ebel's "Celtic Studies," p. 57 of Sullivan's translation.

4 "Grammar," p. 72.

and power by acting on the vocal organs of Irish-speaking men, and by producing an "eclipse" on our lakes, rivers, plains, mountains, hill forts, and tribe-names. And this power will be felt as long as shall live on the names of Lough Neagh, Lough Gall, the Nanny Water, the Delvin River, Moynalvy, Moynalty, Maynoe, Moygene, Magunnihy, Mount Grud, Slieve Golry, Slieve Gallen, Slieve Gullion, Slieve Gooa, Dun Golman, Dunglady, and the Barony of Kinelmeaky;[1] while the neuter demonstrative pronoun will live and breathe as long as Irishmen shall be able to say "yes" or "no" (ꞅeaꝺh, ní heaꝺh) in their native language.

The "transported ɴ" of the nominative of certain substantives puzzled our native grammarians, and was looked on by them as an intruder, "a mere grammatical accident," "a case of redundant eclipsis without any grammatical reason whatsoever."[2] It is really the neuter ending of the nominative, as is the N or M of the Greeks and Latins; and it appears extensively in Irish place-names after cenél, ꝺál, ꞅíl, ꞇellach, ꞇíꞃ, ꞅliab, maᵹ, ꝺꞃuim, ꞃinn, loch, enach, ꞇochaꞃ, ꝺún, etc. Here are a few instances from modern, or comparatively modern, books. In Keating[3]:—Loch (mbꞃennainn, n-Ailinn, nᵹlaꞅan), Ꝺún, (ᵹCꞃoꞇ, ᵹCláiꞃe), Maᵹh (n-Aᵹhaiꞃ, mbꞃeaꞃa, n-Ealꞇa, ᵹCéiꝺne), Ꝺꞃuim n-Aꞃail, Rinn mbeꞃa. In O'Duggan's and O'Heerin's "Topographical Poems"[4]:—Cenél (mbéci, mbinꝺiᵹh, mbaich), Ꞇíꞃ (n-Enꝺa, n-Oilella), Síol mbꞃain, Ꞇellach mbꞃeaᵹꝺa mbꞃaonáin. In the "Four Masters"[5]:—Loch (n-Uaiꞃ, n-laiꞃn, n-Aillenꝺ, nꝹaiꞃbꞃeach, n-Ainninꝺ, n-En, ᵹCall), Maᵹh (n-Oenꞅᵹiach, n-Eo, n-Oꞃbꞃaiᵹe, n-Ebha, mbꞃenꞅa, n-Ailbhe, n-Aiꝺhne, ᵹCéꞇne, ᵹCoinchinne, n-Ealꞇa), Ꞇíꞃ n-Amalᵹaiꝺh, Ꝺal ᵹCaiꞃ, Cenel mbéce, Cenél n-Eoᵹain, Síol ᵹCuin. In the "Four Masters,"

[1] The "transported" or "transvected" ɴ of the neuter nominative singular is found in:—Loch n-Echach, Loch ᵹ-Call, Inbheꞃ n-Ainᵹe (Nanny), Inbheꞃ n-Ailbhine (Nelvin, Delvin), Maᵹh n-Ailbhe, Maᵹh n-Ealꞇa, Maᵹh n-eo, Maᵹh ᵹ-Coinchinne, Maᵹh ᵹ-Ceꞇne, Sliabh ᵹ-Cꞃoꞇ, Sliabh ᵹ-Calꞃaiᵹhe, Sliabh ᵹ-Cua, Sliabh ᵹ-Callain, Sliabh ᵹ-Cuillin, Ꝺún ᵹ-Calmain, Ꝺún ᵹ-Cloiꞇiᵹhe, Cenel m-bécce.

[2] O'Donovan's "Grammar," pp. xiv, 71, 372. Dr. Joyce's "Names of Places," I. 171, 5th ed.

[3] Joyce's ed., pp. 82, 30, 106, 84, 88, 74. Haliday's "Keating," 322, 326.

[4] Pp. 24, 28, 102, 124, 54, 90.

[5] Vol. I. 8, 10, 38, 50, 316, 140, 144, 178, *anno* 1113; III. 220, 474; II. 920.

also, we find Sliab (Callain, Cuillin, Cailraighe, Cua), Dún (Cloitighe, Calman) uneclipsed; but the pronunciation of the people near those places shows that they should be eclipsed. In O'Flaherty's "Ogygia"[1]:—Mag (n-Aire, n-Ailbhe), Dún mBress, Dal gCair, Síol mBloid, Cenel (nGabhráin, n-Aongusa, n-Echach). In the "Tribes of Hy Maine"[2]:—Cenél (nDomangain, nGeigill), Dal nDruthni. In "Hyfiachrach."[3]:—Cinel (n-Aongusa, n-Eunda, nGuaire, mBeccon), Enach nDubain. In the "Annals of Loch Cé"[4]:—Sliabh Crot (Mount Grud), Tír (n-Enna, n-Oilella), Dál n-Araidh, Síl (mBriain, gCearbhaill, gCeallaigh).[5] In the "Book of Fenagh"[6]:—Dún (mBaile, nGaire). In Mac Firbis' Tract "De Episcopis"[7]:—Dún mBaile. In "Mac Gniomhartha Find"[8]:—Ath nGlonda, Tochar nGlonda. In "Diarmait ⁊ Grainne"[9]:—Sliabh gCua. In O'Connell's "Dirge of Ireland"[10]:—Síl gConchobuir (the O'Conors).

Some Marks by which a Neuter Noun may be identified.

A substantive is neuter—

1. If preceded by the article a n-; which becomes a, al, am, ar often before mutes, l, m, r. The proleptic possessive pronoun a (his, their, etc.) is the same in form as the article, and might sometimes be mistaken for it; but if the noun be followed by isin, sin, cétne, se, isiu, the preceding a n- is the article.
2. If eclipsed by dá n-, two.
3. If aspirated by trí, ceithir, three, four.
4. If preceded by the nom. plural article, inna, na, when the noun is not feminine.
5. If referred to by neuter pronouns, ed,[11] ced, alaill, araill; Cf. "Zeuss," 356, 920.

[1] Pp. 261, 267, 322, 387, 470. [2] Pp. 13, 72, 84. [3] Pp. 6, 14, 32, 54, 282. [4] Vol. II. 677, 222, 236, 418, 641; I. 578, 102. [5] *I.e.* the O'Briens, O'Carrolls, O'Kellys. [6] Pp. 112, 124, 252. [7] P. 108. [8] P. 38, 2nd ed. [9] P. 158, 1st ed. [10] Stanza, 86.

[11] "iss-ed sétche Samsóin," this is Sampson's wife (*Turin* Gl. 2 c.), is abnormal, perhaps erroneous, or issed is for edón, idón.

6. If qualified by a neuter pronominal adjective, as aill.
7. If its nominative or vocative singular eclipses the following word.[1]
8. If the adjective of its nominative or vocative, though not showing eclipsis, on account of its initial letter, eclipses the word following.
9. If its nom. and accus. sing. and plural are the same in form.
10. If its dative sing. is formed by adding imm, im, or its nom. or acc. plural by adding an, and.
11. If its nom., gen., and accus. plural are formed by suffixing e.
12. If it is not feminine, and its nom. plural or that of its adjective is formed by suffixing a (except a few masculine u stems).
13. If in termination and derivation it bears a family likeness to well-known neuter nouns.

When I have found one or more of these marks on a word I have put it down in my list and given references. I know that some of those vocables are also masculine in the "B. of Leinster" and the "L. na Huidre," and even in old glosses; but they are treated as neuters even in the Middle or Modern texts which I quote, and specially in topographical names, which are very conservative, and in those peculiarly Irish petrified, stereotyped chevilles, handed down from bard to bard from the preglossarial, and (speaking linguistically) prehistoric times. If I have sometimes erred, and I fear I have often been mistaken, I crave the kind indulgence of Celtic scholars, who know the difficulty of the subject, as well as its importance to the grammarian, the lexicographer, and the linguist.[2]

---

[1] In the "Annalists" and "Leabhar na gCeart," the genitives, dáil, síl, ceniúil, etc., often cause eclipsis; this is not in accordance with Old-Irish usage, but it witnesses to the nazalising power of such words, and so to their gender; we even find sometimes in those books the neuter pronoun ed referring to old neuters: is*eadh* a ainm, as*eadh* in dligeadh, "L. na gCeart," pp. 28, 56.

[2] The Irish name for neuter is neutor, neutar in the Old Glosses, but also deme, traaeth in "Cormac": cech neutur lasin Laitneoir is deme lasin filid ngaedelach, traaeth cech neotur, "Cormac," 17, 42.

Declensions of Neuter Nouns.

These nouns are here distributed under six declensions, and in each declension they are grouped according to their final syllables, or their formation.

Let c stand for any final consonant or consonant group; v for any final vowel or diphthong. The following paradigms exhibit in general outlines the inflexion of neuter nouns:—

Stems in—	Man, Men	S	I	U	O	IO
Nom. Accus. Voc.,	m	vc	ıc n-	vc n-	vc n-	v n-
Dative, . .	m + ım	ıc[1]	ıc	vc	uc	u, ın
Genitive, .	m + e	ıc + e	vc[2] + o *or* a	vc[2] + o *or* a	ıc	ı
Dual Nom. Acc., .	m + ann	vc	ıc	vc	vc	v
Dative, . .	m + annaıb	ıc + ıb	ıc + ıb	vc + aıb	vc + aıb	ıb, aıb
Genitive, . / *Plur. Nom. Acc.,* . / *Genitive,* .	m + ann	ıc + e	vc[2] + a / vc + e	vc[2] + a / vc[2] + e	vc[3]	v
Dative, . .	m + annaıb	ıc + ıb	ıc + ıb	vc + aıb	vc + aıb	ıb, aıb

I have omitted the eclipsing N of the *accus. sg.* and *gen. pl.* as it is common to all genders and declensions.

O'Donovan's 1st declension corresponds to the O-stems; his 2nd to *Men*- and S-stems; his 3rd to I-, U-, and *Men*-stems; his 4th to IO-stems.

Ebel says that in spite of much obscurity in details, the I- and U-stems by no means so fully coincide in their origin as would appear from Zeuss' statement (Sullivan's ed. of Ebel's "Celtic Studies," p. 76). Yet it is often difficult to distinguish them, from lack of data or other reasons. For instance, if we had not got the *genitive singular* of Ꝺuıblınn (Dublin), we could not tell whether it is an I-, U-, or S-stem, or whether it means "Black Pool" or "Black Ale," *i.e.* porter, as both names would seem appropriate. In the Scandinavian sagas it is called Dyflin, and in Burns' poems Divelin—"As sure 's the Deil is in Hell or Divelin city." "Dyflin," and Maurice Regan's "Diviline," written *circ.* 1170, show that the b was aspirated seven or eight centuries ago; and the *genitive* Ꝺuıblınne (not Ꝺuıblenna) shows an S-stem.

[1] In these paradigms ı stands for itself, and also for attenuation; thus the datives and genitives of teᵹ, ꞅlıab are tıᵹ, ꞅléıb, tıᵹe, ꞅléıbe.

[2] The v here may be a, e, o, u, according to the various words.

[3] Also, and oftener, and later, vc + a in the *nom.* and *acc. plural;* like *Lat.* a.

The I-stems preserve the I even in modern times; the U-stems have no I in the nominative, or in modern times "infect" it, thus ending in a broad vowel. Hence, muir, guin, tráigh, buaidh, druim, *g.* dromma (pronounced drím in Munster), etc., are I-stems; linn (now lionn, in Munster liún), fid (fiodh), *d.* fiuch in the "Tripart. Life"; id (iodh), mid (miod), rich (rioch), lín (líon), minn (mionn), gin (gion), bir (bior), smir (smior), firt (fiort), fir (fior), gním (gníomh), are U-stems, and so are recht (reacht), deirmirecht (deirmireacht), etc. The presence of u, a, or o in the *nom.* or *dat. singular* points to a U-stem, and so does affinity with U-stems in the Indo-European languages, as fid with Gaulish "fidu," Saxon "widu."

Recht is given as a *neuter* in "Windisch's Grammar"; but it is *masc.* in all the old glosses; na trí recte, *Wb.* 29 a, which led Zeuss to say it was also *neuter*, is, I think, the *gen. pl.* governed by *testibus* of the text, or by teirt (*testimonio*) of the thought of the Glossarist, so that *tribus testibus* = teirt na tri recte.

SOURCES.

1. All the Glosses and Glossaries hitherto published.
2. Zeuss' "Grammatica Celtica," Windisch's "Irish Grammar," and Stokes' "Celtic Declension" and "Treatise on S-Stems."
3. The "Bk. of Leinster" and "Bk. of Balymote," "L. na Huidre," "Bk. of Armagh."[4]
4. The four volumes of "Laws," and the many books edited by Drs. Whitley Stokes and Windisch, O'Donovan, O'Curry, and others.

I omit such neuters as a n-óen ar ḟichit, the twenty-one, *Ml.* 2 d, dá n-ocht, dá ndeich, *LL.* 128 a, 129 b, a '*prudentia*,' a '*sapere*'; the Welsh a '*muin*' a m-'*braut*,' to which the neuter article is prefixed, after the manner of the Greek article τὸ before Latin words.

The cases, numbers, and genders are marked by their initials, thus: *gsf.*, *npm.* = *genitive singular feminine*, *nominative plural masculine.* *S.*, *Z.*, *W.*, *Bk. of Armagh*, *Tl.*, refer respectively to "Stokes' Works," "Zeuss' Grammar," "Windisch's Dictionary," my Glossary of the "Book of Armagh," and Stokes' "Tripartite Life." The other marks of abbreviation are easily understood. When I doubt about the gender of a word, I append a note of interrogation, thus (?).

[4] When I quote the "Book of Armagh" I refer to my "Index et Glossarium," which, I believe, contains all the Irish vocables of that venerable Codex.

I.—MEN- OR MAN-STEMS.

All stems in **Men** *and* **Man** *are neuter. Compare the Latin "teg-men," "no-men."*

beim (béim), béimm, blow, stroke; *d.* óenbémim, *LU.* 58 b; bemmim, "Man. & Cust." iii. 507; *np.* bemen, *Wb.* 17 d; *ap.* benaim bémend ágmara, *LU.* 76 a; *ds.* béimium, "Laws," i. 230, 240; béim n-, *LU.* 111 b.

aithbeim, athbéim (*LU.* 109, *Ml.* 56 b), return to, falling back on; gl. *recapitulatio;* aithbéim forais, *recapitulatio, Ml.* 94 c, 131 c; athbéim, *LU.* 109 a.

balcbeim, bailcbéim, mighty blow; balc .i. trén, "O'Dav." 58.

bloodbeim, onset, "Cog. G." 180.

blosgbéim, sounding stroke, Meyer's "C. Finntraga," p. 100.

braithbéim, braithbéimm, a mighty blow; braisbéim, a quick stroke; *np.* braithbemend, *LU.* 127 a; bras .i. mór.

croisbeim, cross-stroke, "C. M. Lena," 128.

cúlbéim, back stroke, "Rawl. B." 512, fo. 118.

feoilbéim, flesh-cut, "C. M. Lena," 84, 130.

fódbéim, sod-cut, "Man. & Cust.," ii. 372.

forbéimm, *percussio.*

glóbéim, a straight stroke or dash (?), *LL.* 177 a.

il-béim, gl. *offensio, as., lapidem offensionis, Wb.* 4 d; *for* ailbéim?

oilbéim, ailbéim, albéim, stumbling-block, *offensa* (a stumble, Isaiah xxviii.)

óinbéim, one stroke.

cnocbéim, a blow that causes a lump, "Laws," iii. 352.

plágbéim, plágbéim, a stripe, punishment, *Ag.*

rosc-béim, *LL.* 176 a, a rushing dash? *cf.* rusg in "O'Reilly," and rethait rithrosc, "S. na Rann," Index v., rith.

sesbéim, sessbeim, seisbeimm, sesbeimm, distance which a boat goes at one stroke of the oar, a stroke, *LU.* 26 a; *np.* ses-bémend, *LU.* 26 b, *Tl.* 88.

beım—*continued.*

ṗúılbéım, fascinating with the eye.

cachbéım, cáıchbeım, caıchbéım, "return stroke," one of Cuchullain's feats; *as.* caıchbéım, "vertical stroke," "Sick Bed of Cu," 372; *repercussio: cf.* "Ch. of Uisnech," *ap.* cáıchbeımenꝺ, "Toch. Emere", horizontal blows; caꝺbéım, *LU.* 106 a.

coıbéım, cobéım, "Cog. G." 60, reproach, insult, outrage; cabéım, reproach: "Hyfiachrach," 186; cobéımm, W.

capcbéım = caıchbeım (?).

cporcbéım (staff-stroke ?), "Cog. G." 196, resounding blow ?

banbéım, white blow, which does not draw blood, or cause a lump, or discolouration, "Laws," iii. 352.

beım ṗopaıp, coming back on a thing, *recapitulatio*, *Sg.* 138 a, *Ml.* 94 c, 131 c; béım ṗopıp, *Wb.* 9 c, 11 c, 26 c, 28 a.

ceımm (céımm), céım, step, *gradus*; *d.* ceımmím, *Ml.* 41 d, c; *ap.* ceımmen, céımmen, cemmen, cemmenꝺ, *Ml.* 133 b, "Bk. of Armagh"; *gp.* cemenꝺ, "Nennius," p. 26; *n.* ceım n-ápꝺ, *LU.* 102 b; *gp.* cemenn, *Tl.* 124.

ápꝺcheım, áıpꝺchéım, high degree, high position.

ballcéım (balc céım ?), ꝺallcéım, "O'Dav." 98.

ceıccheım, first step.

coṗcéım, coıṗcéım, coıṗcém, step, spring, ascent; ıṗ é coṗceım, "Cog. G." 186; *pl.* coṗṗcheımmenꝺ, footsteps, "Mer. Uilix, 61.

cochoıṗcım, a following, *Ml.* 37 a.

cpuaıꝺcéım, "Pass. and Hom.," quick step.

ꝺeṗceım, a step to the right (?); *cf.* ꝺeṗlemenꝺ, *W.*

ṗcéım, a leap; but ṗcéım, gl. scemate is fem. *Ml.* 31 c.

ṗochéım, succession, series, step, gait, *LB.* 219 a.

ṗoıṗchéım: *cf.* ṗoıṗcımem, gl. *optimum.*

ımmchım, ruin: *cf.* "Cog. G." 68; ımchım ꝺo bṗéıchpıṗıu, "Bec Fola," 180; violation, "Four Masters," ii. 602; ımcım .ı. eınceımnıᵹuꝺ, "Laws," ii. 352, "O'Dav." 98; ımmchımm, *W.*

cochéım, slow step or pace.

ceımm—*continued.*

τόchımm, τochımm, τochım, τochαım, going, journey, march, advance; *d.* τochαım, from ᴅochıŋʒım, céım; *but* in τochım, *LU.* 100 a.; τochım n-, *LU.* 102 a; τochım = ımτhechτ, *LL.* 395, *LB.* 215 b; τóchım, oenτochımm, *LB.* 208 b.

τoꞃchım ꞅuαın (?), fit of sleep, "Fragm. of Irish Ann.," 24.

τꞃıchem, rushing (?) advance; .ı. τꞃénchemmnıʒuᴅ, "O'Dav." 78.

ꞅechım (?), *as.* to follow, *Sg.* 30 *a.*

ʟeım (léım), léımm, leap, jump; *g.* ınᴅ lémme; *d.* lémαım, *LU.* 111 b; *g.* lémmı, "Táin Bó Cuailnge"; *cf.* léımnech; Léımı, *g.* Loop head, "L. na gCeart," 74; *ns.* léım n-, O'Conor's "Scriptores," ɪ. Pars. 2, xxxiv.; *n.* αl léım, *LU.* 111 b.

αıτhléım, ατhléım, resilience; gl. *resultando*, *Cr.* 10, 11 c.

eταꞃléım, *g.* eταꞃléıme, "Bk. of Balymote," 325; "L. na gCeart," 2; *ap.* αꞃᴅlémmenᴅ, high jumps, *LU.* 50 a.

báeτhléımm, a wild leap; *ap.* ᴅeꞃlémenᴅ, jumps to the right, *LU.* 50 a.

cατhlαem, army on march, "C. M. Rath," 180.

ꝑoléım, a leap, subsilience; ımléım, "C. Findtragha," 76.

luʒléım, a small leap; ꝑꞃıτhléım, "O'Reilly."

ꞃuıᴅléım, a leap.

ꞅαebléımm, a false leap or step.

ꞅcíτhlım, "Rev. Celt.," v. 197; ꞅꞃuıτ̇léım, "C.R. na Ríg," § 43.

ꞅτuαᴅléım, a wave-leap, "C. Findtragha," 108.

τuꞃlαım, ταıꞃꞃlım, ταıꞃlımm, an alighting ("L. na gCeart," 10, 2, *Tl.* 88), from ταıꞃlenʒαıτ, they alight; τuıꞃleım, *g.* τuıꞃléıme, alighting, "C. M. Lena," p. 98.

αıꞃlım n-, eıꞃlım n-, eꞃlım, *gs.* αıꞃlıme, *np.* eıꞃlımennα, trespass by *leaping* a fence, "Laws," i. 90, 92, 94, 104, 108; lınʒeꞃ eıꞃlım, *ib.* 110; ταıꞃlım ταꞃblαınʒ, "Thurn. Versl." 34; αıꞃlem, *g.* αıꞃlıme, *np.* αıꞃlemαnnα, "O'Dav." 78.

ʀeım (ꞃéım), ꞃéımm, ꞃém, *cursus* (*Z.* 268), αꞃ-ꞃéım, *LU.* 105 b, "Félire," Oct. 16, course; *g.* ꞃémme; *d.* ꞃéımım, expedition, "Nennius," p. 140; ꞃαıτh αꞃ-ꞃem-ꞅın, he ran that course; ꞃeım n-oll, a great course; *ngp.* ꞃemmenᴅ, ꞃemenᴅ, "Amra Ch. C." ch. 4; "Adamnan," 274; *ns.* ın ꞃéım, "Amra Ch. C." p. 12; ꞃéım n-, "Fragm. of Ir. Ann." 224; also means "genitive," "Bodl. Cormac," "Cormac," 24.

ReIm—*continued.*

baıchpéım, foolish course, = baochpéım, "Four Masters," A.D. 1587, *LL.* 344 a; popım, *d.* popımım, bird-hunting, *LU.* 69 b.

buaᵭpéım, victorious course; *np.* buaᵭpemmenᵭ, *LL.* 78 a.

cachpéım, caıchpéım, battle course, triumph; *g.* cachpéıme, "Four Masters," iii. 628; ᵭıpéım .ı. péım nᵭeᵭa, "Cormac," 24.

pím, pímm (?), counting, number; *g.* rimæ, *Z.* and Index to "Félire"; cupım, reckoning, "Ir. Texte," i. 29.

ᵭípımm, number, multitude; *nap.* ᵭıpmanᵭ, "Félire," Oct. 11, *Epil.* 143; *d.* ᵭípmmaım, *Tl.* 70.

ımbpımm, ımmpım, ımpımm, ımpım, going about; ımpım and poımpım eıch, "Laws," i. 168, 280; *cursus, circuitio; fem., LB.* 267; *gen. sing.* ımpımme, "Man. & Cust." iii. 484, riding; *d.* ımpımım, *LL.* 115 a; ech ımpíme, "Laws," ii. 160.

epım, epımm, eppıpam, riding out, journey; *g.* epma, *LU.* 105 b; "Laws," iii. 258, ii. 154, 160; *d.* epmaım, "Toch. Emere"; épım n-, "S. na Rann," 21, 80; "C. M. Rath," 82; épaım n-, "S. na Rann," ll. 1071, 1468, a faring.

cáıbpeım, caoıbpeım, genitive (case); punnpaᵭ caoıbhpéıme.

cuıbpéım, the dative case.

cınᵭpem, an expedition, "Nennius," 146; .ı. cınpcecul, "O'Dav." 124.

péım, a genitive; *dp.* pémenᵭaıb, "Stokes' Bodl. Cormac," 44.

eSCRImm, trappings, form; *ds.* eıpcpımmımm, "Do Ch. in da Muccaid," l. 110; i. e. ecopc, "T. B. Dartada."

PORSCamON (?), *np.* terraces or steps.

ᵹReIm (ᵹpéım), ᵹpeımm, bit, hold, power, force, advantage over, effect; *np.* ᵹpemmen; *ap.* ᵹpémmann, "S. na Rann," p. 141; *ap.* ᵹpemman, *pacta*; *ds.* ᵹpemmaım, *vigore*; *g.* ᵹpemmae, *sceptri*, *Ml.* 128 d, 31 c, 110; *d.* caċᵹpeımım "Cormac," 10.

maıchᵹpéım, good hold; ᵹleᵹpaım, "S. na Rann," 22; *LB.* 111.

ᵹapbᵹpeım, rough hold, "S. na Rann," p. 140.

ınᵹpeım, ınᵹpeımm, ınᵹpaım, ınᵹpaımm, persecution; *g.* ınᵹpaımme, ınᵹpımme; *d.* ınᵹpaımmım, ınᵹpımmım (*Ml.* 74 b, 56 c, 87 c, 75 a), "Stowe Missal," 63; *np. gp.* ınᵹpemmen, ınᵹpaımmen, ınᵹpamman, *Wb.* 25 d, 30 c; *d.* oc ınᵹpımm, "Fiac."; *dp.* ınᵹpaımmannaıb, *Ml.* 756.

conᵹpaımm, "cunning," *com-plexio* (?), apparel, appearance, "Echtra Nerai"; *d.* conᵹpaımmım, *LU.* 102 b; *LU.* 105 b.

bReim (?), bpoımm, *LL.* 28 a, 85 a, hence bpoımnıg, *LB.* 217 b, *crepitus ventris.*

ᴅReim N- (ᴅpéım n-), "S. na Rann," p. 71, ᴅpéımm, effort, attempt, endeavour, ascent; *dp.* ᴅpeımennaıb, "Laws," iii. 182.

Nem, *Sg.* 113 b; *gp.* nemanᴅ, pearls, *LL.* 55 b; *d.* nemannaıb, "Windisch."

ᵹeim (ᵹéım), "C. M. Lena," 4, shout, noise, bellow; *ap.* ᵹemenᴅa, ᵹeımınno, "Echtra Nerai"; *g.* ᵹéme; éᵹem (?), outcry.

foRᵹemeN, *nap.*, skins, "Man. & Cust." iii. 424, *LL.* 82 b.

Seim (péım), rivet; *ap.* pemmanᴅ, "Cormac"; *gp.* pemmanᴅ, studs, "Táin Bó Fróich"; ıl-pemman, *LL.* 99 a; *dp.* pemannaıb, "Man. & Cust." iii. 158; *gp. ap.* pemmenᴅ, "Bodl. Cormac," 4, 22; "Cormac," 32.

Sleim (pléım), snow-flake.

ém: an ém; *g.* éme; *d.* éım, haft, "Bodl. Cormac," 18.

ᴛoem (ᴛóem) (?), ᴛóem n-ᵹlé.

(**aim** ?), *manus*, hand, handful; *d.* ammaım, *Ml.* 36 d.

maim (?), handful; *dual*, ᴅa maım, "Laws," iv. 98.

boim, boımm, buım; bit, morsel; *np.* bommann eᵹaı, hailstones, *LB.* 106 a; *dp.* bomonnaıb, fragments, "C. M. Lena," 136; buım, a spark, "Four Masters," i. 242, *Tl.* 242.

loim, loımm, loımb, sip, sup, drop, drink, *Pr. Cr.* 96, "Felire" Index; "Laws," iii. 84, wave, milk; but ın loım, *LB.* 65; *dp.* lommanaıb, *LU.* 111 a; *ds.* lomom, milk, "Fragm. of Irish Ann." 74; *g.* loma, "L. na gCeart," 168; *ap.* lomann, "Four Masters," i. 506; *as.* a loım, *LU.* 129 a.

ᵹloimm, ᵹláımm, a growl, baying of a hound; *g.* ᵹlaıme, *as.* ᵹlam, *W.* 285 a.

uaimm, seam, *W.*; uaım, .ı. ᴛobéım, "Ir. Metr. Glosses," 31.

uaim, cave; *g.* uama; *d.* uamannaıb, "Fragm. of Irish Ann." 152; loċ uama, *lacus specûs*, AA. SS. 373.

fuaimm, fuaım, fuam, sound, noise: fuaım n-ampa, a wonderful noise (cf. "S. na Rann," p. 139); *g.* fuama; *np.* fuámanᴅ, *W.*, "Ir. Metr. Glosses"; ᴛellḟuaım, "Bodl. Cormac"; "Cormac," 42.

comuaım n-, harmony, "Laws," iii. 32, i. 16; uaım, ımuaım, harmony, *ibid.* i. 298.

tuaim, a hill, fort; ba Tuaim n-aba a ainm, "Lives from Bk. of Lismore," p. 63; Tuaim n-(Eatain, Eidin), "L. na gCeart," 88, 92; *gp.* Tuamand, "L. na gCeart," 14; *gs.* tuama, "Four Masters," i. 44, iii. 26; *collis*, "Tigernach," an. 719.

sruaim, sróim, srúam, stream, *Z.* 24, *W.* (but *np.* sruama, "Fis Adamn."); *dp.* sruamannaib, "O'Dav." 117; *voc.* a ṡruaim, "Four Masters," i. 470; *np.* sruamandai, *LB.* 207 a; sruaim .i. sruth, "O'Dav." 115.

slam-sruaim, slimy stream (?).

osailcim (?), to open, *Ml.* 98 a.

sechim (?), to follow, *Ml.* 128 d.

foglaimm, fóglaimm, learning; *g.* foglaimme, *Ml.* 42 c, *fem* (?).

diglaim n-, distinction, "Laws," i. 212, 214, 238, description (?).

fordiuclaim, a swallowing up, *voratio*, *Ml.* 104 b; *ds.* fordiuclaimmim, *Ml.* 19 d, 102 a, 34 d; Ascoli does not give the gender.

eclaim, *discussio*, *Ml.* 114 b: an eclaim.

digluim (?), .i. tinól, "O'Dav." 73.

teclimm, gl. *acceptio*, *Wb.* 1 d; a teclimm, *ib.*

dauteclaimm, *exceptio*, *Ml.* 35 a; *p.* comteclamand, "O'Dav." 65.

targla(i)m, to collect, "C. M. Rath," 60.

dithim n-, delay, issed d.; *g.* dithma; *nap.* dithmand (forfeitures), "Laws," i. 160, 196, 198, 210, 212, 262, 264, 280, 284, 288; ii. 104; *ap.* dithmanda, *ib.* 262.

tothimm, tothim, totaim, dothaim, a fall; *ap.* totman, *casus*, *Wb.* 5 b, 131 b, 61 b, 42 d; *Ml.* 131 b, 19 d.

etarthothimm, etharthotaim, *interitus*, *Ml.* 40 d.

cuitim, collapse, fall, ruin (*for* co-thotaim); cutuim, cutimm, *ruina*, *dissolutio*, *Ml.* 91 c; .i. cuitim, "O'Dav."

comthuitim, a falling together.

tuirthim (?), dearth, "O'Dav." 168.

condem, entertainment; *g.* condme, "Laws," i. 270; condmim, = coyney or billeting ("Stokes' Ling. Value of the Irish Annals," p. 61, 2nd ed.), is *neuter* if the 2nd and 3rd forms are *genitive* and *dative*.

torruim n-, a reckoning, "Laws," i. 288.

breisim, shout, uproar; but *np.* bresma, "S. na Rann," p. 129.

ꝺRUIM, ꝺꞃuımm (*Ml.* 44 a), ridge, back; ꝺꞃuım n-aꞃꝺ, "C. M. Lena," 164; ꝺ. n-Ꭺꞃaıl, *LL.* 202 a; *g.* ꝺa ꝺꞃumanꝺ, "Cog. G."; *np.* ꝺꞃomanꝺ; *gp.* ꝺꞃumman, "Bk. of Armagh"; *dp.* ꝺꞃuımnıb, "Four Masters," i. 28; "L. na gCeart," 10; *ap.* ꝺꞃommanꝺ, backs (of men), *LU.* 19 b; but *g.* ꝺꞃommo, *d.* ꝺꞃuım, in "Bk. of Armagh"; *cf.* ꝺꞃuımnech, Ꝺꞃuım n-Ꭺꞃaıl, Ꝺꞃuım n-Ꝺaıꞃbꞃech, *LL.* 192 a, 202 a; also *np.* ꝺꞃomanna, "Nennius," 72.

Caonꝺꞃuım = Uıꞃnech; Caınꝺꞃuım at Durrow, "Adamnan," 270.

cınꝺꞃuım, cınꝺꞃuımm, *alveus fluminis*, or *alveus* = *lebes*; *ds.* cınꝺꞃuım, cınꝺꞃummaım, *Ml.* 74 b, 78 b, 126 c.

Ꝺeꝺꞃuım ṅ-, *LL.* p. 170 a.

Echꝺꞃuımm, horseridge.

ꝼıꝺꝺꞃuım, woodridge, *LU.* 48 b.

Ꝼaelꝺꞃuım.

Ꝼoꞃꝺꞃuım ("Bk. of Armagh"), Fardrum, in Westmeath.

ᵹlé-ꝺꞃuımm, "S. na Rann," 140.

Nóınꝺꞃuımm; *g.* Noınꝺꞃommo, *Sg.* 226.

Sıꝺhꝺꞃuım, Cashel, "L. na gCeart," 28.

ꞅíꞃꝺꞃuımm.

ꝺRONNANN (?), *ap.*, "Bk. of Fenagh," 114.

ꞇOEM N- (ꞇóem n-), a jet, "S. na Rann," p. 153; of this declension (?).

MAIꝹM, bursting, burst, break, rout, defeat; a break or pass in a mountain; maıꝺm, maıꝺım, "Cog. G." 32, 82; maıꝺm caꞇha, *ib.* 32; *d.* maꝺmaımm, "Fragm. of Irish Ann." 182; *g.* luchꞇ maꝺma, a defeated party; *g.* maꝺmae, *Ml.* 84 c; *ap.* maꝺmanꝺ, maꝺman, *ib.* 24, 82, 66; *n.* am maıꝺm.

bánmaıꝺm, bloodless victory, "Four Masters," *an.* 1094.

caꞇhmaıꝺm, battle-breach, "Bk. of Fenagh," 162.

ꞃomaıꝺm, great burst, breach, "S. na Rann," p. 148; *LB.* 206 b.

commaıꝺm, *g.* commaıꝺme, "exultation," outburst, "Fragm. of Irish Ann." 40; *g.* ᵹáıꞃ commaıꝺmı, *LU.* "Fled Bricr."

ꝺıumaıꝺm, *ds. inruptione*, *Ml.* 85 c.

maidm—*continued.*

foṙmaidm, *irruptio*, a burst into; bresmaidm, "Four Masters," iv. 674.

tomaidm, *np.* tomadmann, "S. na Rann," p. 118, a bursting up, *eruptio*, outburst (of water); tomaidm n-esce, a bursting up of fish, "Amergin's Poem," *LL.* 12 b.

cathtomaidmmaim, *ds.* battle-break, victory, "Man. & Cust." iii. 505.

lochtomaidm, lake eruption, "Four Masters," p. 6.

Naidm, *nexus*, *obligatio*, bond, compact, covenant, *i.e.* nascar, "O'Clery"; *nap.* nadmand; *d.* nadmundaib, covenants, "guarantees," "Laws," i. 266 and iv. 54, where also is *np.* nadm; *g.* nadma, "Laws," i. 214.

ernaidm, urnaidm, irnaidm, *connexio*, *Ml.* 2 d, contract; *np.* urnamand, bonds, "Mesca Ul." 8; *np.* ernadman, *Ml.* 2d; *g.* urnadma, "Laws," ii. 380, 408, 94.

fonaidm, covenant, "Siab Ch. C."; *d.* fonaidmaim, binding, "Laws," i. 280, 226; "Toch. Emere," *LU.*

fornaidm, condiment, "Laws," ii. 20, 32.

forṅaidm, *as.*, *nexus*, *necessitas*, *Ml.* 27 d, bargain, "Laws," ii. 98; *ds.* forṅaidmaim, "Táin Bó Cualngi."

comnaidm, *g.* comnadma, right, covenant, "Laws," iv. 8, 34.

dondnadman, *np.*, covenants, "Laws," iv. 60.

nenadman, *pl.*, letter joinings, *Ml.* 2d; .i. caolfathe, "O'Dav." 108.

snáidm, snaidm, a knot, *nodus*; *d.* snaidmaimm, "Tóg. Troi," l. 1460; *gp.* snadmann, *LB.* 387.

úrsnaidm, pin to fasten cords of a harp, knot.

fo-ṡnaidm, fonaidm, covenant; cuachnaidm, "O'Dav." 64.

Taidm (?), *contentio*; cf. taidmneach, contentious.

Aidm (?), ox.

Adm (?), knowledge.

Feidm, féidm, effort, service, *Z.*; an n-deanann tú feidhm do ṡhlighe eile, do you make use of any other means? "Dunlevy"; *ns.* feidm, "C. M. Rath," 204; *g.* fedma catha, "Cog. G." 70; *d.* fedmum, "Laws," iii. 266; *ns.* in feidm, *LL.* 57 a, *pl.* fedman, "Ann. of Ulster," 821.

bithféidm, "S. na Rann," p. 128.

peidm—*continued.*

compeidm, joint performance, "S. na Rann," p. 131.

crith-ḟeidm, "S. na Rann," p. 132.

in-ḟéidm, service due to a chief.

scíth-feidm, fatiguing effort, "L. na gCeart," 38.

trénféidm, strong effort.

sleidm (sléidm), sleidm, *saniem*, *Sg.* 218 b, *Z.* 776; *dp.* sleidmenaib, *sputaminibus.*

isleidm, *sputamen*, "Tur." 2 b: onaisleidmenaib or onai(b) s. (?).

tedm, téidm, teidm, *tabes*, pest, disease, "a fit"; *d.* tedmaim, tedmaimm, *Ml.* 58 a, 15 b, 123 b, 149 a; "Fragm. of Irish Ann." 198; *np.* tedmand, *LL.* 188 c; teidm n-, "O'Dav." 97. *masc.* *LL.* 57 a; *ap.* tedmann, "Bk. of Hymns," ii. 124; *Z.* 270; *gs.* tedma, "Brocan's Hymn," "Félire" 194.

beidm (béidm), blow, *see* béim.

greidm, bit, *see* gréim. buidm (?) .i. mun, "O'Dav." 57.

deilm, delm; a n-deilm, noise, *LL.* 59 aa, 192 a; .i. torann, trost, erith, "O'Clery"; "Amra Ch. C." ch. 1; delm n-, "S. na Rann," p. 133; *g.* delmae, *LU.* 111 b; *n.* in deilm, *LL.* 189 b; "Ch. of Uisnech"; *ds.* delmaim, "Félire," Prol. 154, *LB.* 104, "O'Dav." 75.

crithdeilm, "S. na Rann," p. 132.

mórdeilm, great noise, "Amra Ch. C." ch. 1.

ainm, *nomen*, name; *d.* anmaim, anmimm; *g.* anme, *Wb.* 27 c, 21 a; *np.* anmand, "Bk. of Balymote," 255 a; *ap.* anmand, *Sg.* 61 b; *a. dual*, da n-ainm, *Wb.* 30 c, 21 d, 34 d; *png.* anman, *Ml.* 86 c, *Wb.* 16 a; a n-ainmm n-, *Sg.* 31 a, 209 b.

mac-ainm, "Amra Ch. C." ch. 19.

ilanmmanaib, *dp.*, *Sg.* 30 a, *np.* ilanmann, many names, "Bodl. Cormac," 36.

comainm, *cognomen*, *LL.* 57; senainm, old name, *LL.* 395.

forainm, nickname, "Tribes of Ireland," 38, *Tl.* 126.

lesainm, nickname, *LU.* 100 b, "Laws," i. 176; *g.* lesanma, "Laws," i. 184, 236; *d.* lesanmannaib, "Ir. Texte," i. 102; gnathainm, "Gen. Corca. Laide," 28.

remainm, gl. *prænomen*, "Med. Tract on Celt. Declension."

tírainm, country name, "Táin Bó Fróich," 156.

LENOMNAIB (?), *lituris*, *Sg.* 3.

SENM, seinm, senim, sound, blast (of a horn); *d.* senmaim, (playing the harp) ("Táin Bo Fróich," 142); *d.* senmim, sound of trumpet, *Wb.* 13 d.

ilsenim, *np.* ilsenman, many sounds, *Z.* 858, 367, *Wb.* 12 c.

comsinm, *ds.* accompaniment, *LU.* 5 aa, "Amra Ch. C." ch. 1.

eirṡinm, playing (the tympan), "Fragm. of Irish Ann." 220.

LEINM, *saltus; see* léim.

SCEINM, *pl.* scenmanna, slipping, "Laws," iii. 184, 284; *ds.* sgeinm, "Four Masters," ii. 1012.

dirsceinm, *lapsus*; cf. dirsceinmnecha, *lapsi*, "Bk. of Hymns," ii. 207, 230; aithsceinm, "Cormac," 16.

TEINM, .i. goirt nó cnamh; *cf.* teinm ⁊ tomailt, *LL.* 200 a.

teinm, stream; teinm laeda, "a stream of poetry"; teinm laega, "Mac Gn. Find," 44; a tenm láida, "Stokes' Bodl. Cormac," 4, 8, 20, "Thurn. Versl." 102; *g.* tenma, "O'Dav." 118.

CUIRM, coirm, ale, beer; *g.* corma, *d.* cormaim ("Cod. S. Pauli"), cormuimb; *g.* coirme, "Ir. Texte," 203, "O'Dav." 122.

FUIRMIM, *ds.* march, "L. na gCeart," 38; forom n-, "S. na Rann," 139; foraim, *LU.* 104 a.

GAIRM N-, a cry, call, *LL.* 27 b; *g.* garma, "Fiac's Hymn"; *d.* garmmaim, "Man. & Cust." iii. 511.

tagraim, demand, "Bk. of Fenagh," 368.

athgairm, revocation.

togairm, a torgairm ("Southampton Gl." 34 a), call, *appellatio*, *compellatio*, invocation, vocation, *LB.* 187 b; *d.* togarmaim, *Wb.* 27 c; *gp.* togarmand, titles, "Man. & Cust." iii. 513; *gp.* cis lir toggarmanda (?), what is the number of titles, appellations? *ap.* togarmanna, "Bk. of Hymns," i. 74.

nóebtogairm, holy invocation or call; holy calling, "Sanctan's Hymn"; comtogairm, *convocatio*, "O'Dav." 47.

trénthogairm, strong invocation or title; a torgairm, gl. *compellatio*, "Ps. Hampton," 34 a.

TOIRM, tairm, torm-, tormm-n, torum-n, "S. na Rann," 153; toirm n-glan, tairm n-, torum n-dil, "Bk. of Balymote," 391 a; toirm, .i. molad, "O'Dav." 122.

tairm (?), trampling, "Nennius," p. 142; "Man. & Cust." iii. 532, "Bk. of Lismore," 148 a.

am (ám), ámm, agmen, company; *d.* ammaim; *ap.* ámna.

am (ám), amm, hand; *dat.* am, ámmaim, *Ml.* 34 c, 36 c, 36 d, "Ascoli," *Z.* 268–9.

commaim (?), *ds.* wife, "Bk. of Fenagh," 310.

im, imm, imb, butter; *g.* imbe, "Man. & Cust." iii. 104; *d.* imim, "Laws," ii. 254; *ds.* imbim, immim, immum, *LB.* 63, "Man. & Cust." iii. 482, 485, 487; Ascoli makes it *masc.*

arbe, "corn-meal"; *d.* arbaimm, "Man. & Cust." iii. 483; *ap.* arbhanna; *gp.* arbann, (kinds of) corn, corn-meal, "Laws," iii. 264; "Man. & Cust." 481, 482; *n.* (arb ?); *g.* arba, *d.* arbim, "Laws," ii. 41, 39, 392, 366.

linn, liquid; *np.*, *ap.*, lennand, *LU.* 97, 211.

mir (mír), part, portion, bit; am-mír, *Ml.* 76 a; *ap.* mirenn; *pl.* mirenna, *LL.* 303 b; *ac. pl.* min-mirend, *LU.* 111 a; *ap.* minmirenda, "Egerton"; *np.* mírenna, "Laws," iii. 204.

coinmir, con-mír, gl. *offa*, *Z.* 21, *Sg.* 103 b.

mímir, a charmed morsel, "Laws," i. 176, 180; *Z.* 265; *LU.* 110 a, 101 a.

curathmír, hero's portion; curathmír n-ucut, yon warrior's portion; *g.* curatmiri, *LU.* 109, 99; a c., *LU.* 104, 105, 107; *but* in c., *LU.* 110 a, 107 b, 100 a, 101 b.

drantmír, greedy bit, or snarling bit, about which heroes contend as hounds (?); *cf.* drantaim, I snarl, "Laws," i. 176, 80.

dantmír, morsel, "Stokes' Bodl. Cormac," 30; "Laws," i. 176; dant, mouth, "O'Dav." 76; cétmír, first morsel, *LB.* 214 b.

liacht N- (?), *lectio*, "Stowe Missal," 63; but *acc.* in liácht, *ibid.* p. 64; liachtu is *fem.*

cretem N- (?), faith; *g.* creitme, "Man. & Cust." iii. 536.

mell (?), a lump; *np.* maellann airgit, bands (lumps ?) of silver.

II.—S-Stems (*All S-Stems are Neuter*).

Neb, nem, heaven; *gs.*, *ngp.*, nime, *d.* nim, *Z.*, "Ebel," "Stokes," *Ml.* 45 b, 145 d; *g.* rindnime, "Ninine's Poem," *Tl.* 140.

nóemneb, holy heaven; *d.* noemnib, "Stokes."

rindnem, starry heaven, "Mar. O'Gorman," Aug. 1; *g.* rind-nime, "S. na Rann," 8; clochnime, *gs.* "Thurn. Versl." 56.

Nem, poison; *gs.*, *np.*, neime, nimi, *Sg.* 33, 112, 139; *ap.* nime, "Four Masters," ii. 578.

Nem (?), ceiling; gl. *laquear*, *Sg.* 97 a; *cf.* French, *ciel de lit;* German, *Bett-himmel*, a tester.

Ub, egg, *Incant. Sg.*, "Stokes"; see ug; ob, "Bodl. Cormac," 26.

Toeb, tóib, side; *g.* tóibe deirr (*LB.* 251 a, in MacCarthy's "Stowe Missal," 264); *d.* tóib, táib (*Wb.* 20 d, and "Stokes' Siege of Howth"); *as.* and *n. dual.* tóib, *Ml.* 131 c, 67 d.

Sliab, mountain, *Z.*, *ns.* sliab n-Orra, *Sg.* 63 a; *ds.* sleib, *Ml.* 39 d and "Bk. of Armagh"; *nap.* slebe, *Ml.* 81 c. a; *n.* Sliab n-Echtga, *LL.*, where, however, it is *masc.* in sliab, 265 b; *dp.* slebib, "Siab. Ch. C." 380.

mórsliab, *Z.*, big mountain; *n.* moirrleb (!), *Ml.* 55 d.

magsliab: sliab is made synonymous with móin or muin; it means a heathy, hill-shaped ground, "O'Brien's Irish Dict.," Preface.

Corrsliab, the Curlew Hills in Roscommon and Sligo, translated *praeceps mons* in "O'Sullivan's Hist. Cath. Compendium," p. 164.

airsliab, arsliab, *g.* airslebe, airslébe, *LL.* 156, 243 b, *LB.* 218 b, "Brocán's H."; a hill-slope, mountain side (Crowe, in "Guardsman's Cry of St. Patrick," 293); face or front of a mountain (?); *cf.* airchind, front (of house, etc.).

Treb (?), house; *g.* rígtreibe, "Laws," iii. 272, "Nennius," 38; *gp.* cethartrebe, "Fiac's Hymn."

Ag (ág), ox, calf, deer; *n.* ág, *g.* aige, "Laws," i. 238, 254; ii. 252, 254, 258; iv. 102, "Nennius," 182; *nap.* aige, *W.* "Táin Bo Fróich," 138; "T. B. Flid." l. 86; "B. of Lecan," 763; *gp.* aigi, "S. Celt. Decl.," aidi, "L. na gCeart"; *na. dual*, da n-ág n-, "Reeves' Adamnan," 270; "Mac Gn. Find," p. 32.

aʒ, joint ("Stokes"); *dual*, ᴅa n-aʒ, "Do Chopur in dá Muc." 242; *nagp.* áıʒe, áʒe, aıʒı, "Laws," i. 48, *LL.* 197 a; "T. B. Fróich," 138; "Siab. Ch. C." 382, 388; *dp.* aʒıb, "C. R. na Ríg"; *pl.* aʒe, "Bodl. Cormac," 30.

oʒ, egg, *Sg.* 8 b; *n.* uʒ, *g.* uıʒe, *d.* uıʒ, *dp.* uıʒıb, "C. M. Rath," 30, 129, 130; *ds.* uıʒ, "Laws," i. 28; *gs.* uıʒe, uıʒı, *np.* uʒaı, "Cog. G." 100; but *gp.* uʒ, "L. na gCeart," 154, 158.

loʒ n- (lóʒ n-), ("Laws," i. 92, 124), lóʒ, lúaʒ, luaċ, *Z.*[2]; louʒ ("Egerton," 1782, fo. 71), price, value, reward; *g.* lóıʒe, lóʒe, *Wb.* 3 c, 10 d, "Laws," ii. 252, 258, 330, 338; *d.* luaıʒ (*bis*), "Third Charter of Bk. of Kells"; *np.* lóıʒı, "Laws," ii. 160; *dual*, ᴅá luaʒ, "Laws," i. 290; lóoʒ, *Tl.* 196.

ꝼoplóʒ, price; *ds.* "Bk. of Armagh"; for ꝼoplúa(ı)ʒ, as the "Bk. of Kells" shows, above; ꞅáplóʒ, *LU.* 129.

ᴅaʒlóʒ, good price, "S. na Rann," p. 132; lánlóʒ, "Cormac," 19.

lethlóʒ; *dp.* lethlóʒıb, half-values, "Thurn. Versl." 49.

ᴅelʒ n-, thorn, brooch, *LU.* 65 b, 96 b; a n-ᴅelʒ, "Sg. Incant."; *nap.* ᴅelce, ᴅelʒae, ᴅeılʒe, *LU.* 64 b, 64 a, 93, "Laws," iii. 290; ii. 146; ᴅelʒ n-, "O'Dav." 56, "Cormac," 7.

. lıa-ᴅelʒ, "Stokes' Irish Ordeals"; clochᴅelʒʒ n-, "Man. & Cust." iii. 496.

ᴅronʒ n-ınʒen, ᴅponʒ nʒılla, "S. na Rann," *l.* 6279; *g.* ᴅpuınʒe (?), a throng, group.

maʒ ("Ebel"), *campus*; *gs.* and *np.* maıʒe; *d.* maıʒ, "Bk. of Armagh," where the gender is reflected in *hoc est campum*; am-maʒ, *Wb.* 12 a; *g. dual*, maıʒe, *LL.* 300 a; maʒ m-bpéʒ, "Cog. G." 12, *LL.* 203, "Bk. of Balymote," 406 b; *as.* tappa maʒ, "Táin Bo Reg."; maʒ cCéıtne, "Keating," p. 88; maʒ n-Aıᴅnı, "Bk. of Balymote," 382 b, ıꞅ aılᴅıu am-maʒ; maʒ n-Ealta; *nap.* maıʒe, "Amra Ch. C."; *gs.* and *pl.* maıʒe, "Bk. of Armagh: see my prefatory remarks; *gp.* maʒ, "Hyfiachrach," 234; *voc. sg.* muıʒ, "Four Masters," ii. 596; áʒmaʒ, battlefield, "AA. SS." 603, or oxfield (?), Aılmaıʒe, *gs.*, "Bk. of Armagh"; ápmaʒ, field of slaughter, battlefield; *ds.* apmuıʒ, "C. M. Rath," 84; *d.* apmuıʒ; *g.* apmaıʒe, "Laws," i. 174, 176; Aᴅhapmaʒ, "Fragm. of Irish Ann." 216; Athmaʒ, "Nennius," 142; ᴅpechmaʒ, ᴅpeʒmaʒ; *g.* ᴅpechmaıʒe, "Hyfiachrach," 244; ᴅpeʒmaıʒe, maꝺ—*continued.*

"Four Masters," i. 360; "Cog. G." 32; *d.* ḃpechmıꝺ, "Bk. of Armagh"; *ns.* a maꝺ, am maꝺ, *LU.* 105 b, 106 a, 129.

clapmaꝺ, "S. na Rann," l. 508; Capnmaꝺ, "Mescą Ul." 38.

cloċhmaꝺ, famous field, plain, "S. na Rann," l. 7031.

Cpuachanmaꝺ, the Croghan Plain.

cluıchımaꝺ, cluchemaꝺ, game-place, arena, *LU.* 122 a; *d.* cluchımaıꝺ, *LU.* 112 a, "Toch. Emere."

Ꝺepmaꝺ, Ꝺepmach, Ꝺupmaꝺ, Ꝺaıpmaꝺ, Ꝺaupmaꝺ ("Adamnan"), Durrow; *g.* Ꝺepmaıꝺe, "Four Masters," i. 360; *d.* Ꝺaupmaıꝺ, *Roboreti campus*, "Adamnan"; Deruach, "Gir. Camb." 387; *g.* Ꝺepmaıꝺe, *Tl.* 82.

ꝺopmaꝺ, bushy plain; elıċmaꝺ, "AA. SS." 603; "Bk. of Lecan," 251 a; ꝼépmaꝺ, "Miscel. of Celt. Soc." 358.

Ꝼalmaꝺ, Ꝼemenmaꝺ, "Fragm. of Irish Ann." 216; "Ir. Texte," i. 98; ebepmaꝺ, "Thurn. Versl." 57.

ꝼeoılmaꝺ, (?) quarter of venison or mutton, etc.

Ꝼepnmaꝺ, Farney.

ꝼeapċmhaꝺ, .ı. ꝼeapanmaꝺ, "O'Clery."

Ꝼınꝺmaꝺ, *Albus Campus*; *g.* Ꝼınꝺmaıꝺe, "Bk. of Armagh."

ꝼopoꝺmaꝺ na hemna, theatre, place for spectators; *d.* ꝼopoꝺmaıꝺ, *LL.* 109 a.

ꝺlapmaꝺ, .ı. ꝺlapmuıp, the sea.

Laıꝺenmaꝺ, "Four Masters," ii. 740; Leinster.

lepmaꝺ, the sea plain; lıanmaꝺ, "S. na Rann," p. 144.

ıaċhmaıꝺe, *gp.* ("Fiac's Hymn."), land plains; *ap.* "Nínine."

Luaċhmaꝺ, *LL.* 305; Lachċmaꝺ, "Stowe MS. 992," fol. 50 a.

lıanmaꝺ, "S. na Rann," p. 144; leċhanmaꝺ, *LB.* 218.

Luachmaıꝺe, Lochmaıꝺe, *gs.* "Four Masters," i. 162, 40; vi. 2082, Loughmoe.

Luꝺmaꝺ, Louth (= *Agelluli*, "Adamnan," p. 7 ?), "Four Masters," iii. 23; *Tl.* 226, 248.

Lupmaꝺ, now Lusmagh, King's Co., "Hymaine," 5.

mallmaꝺ, soft plain, "C. M. Lena," 46.

mupmaꝺ, "L. na gCeart"; *g.* mupmaıꝺe, sea marsh, "Laws," i. 166; ppímmaıꝺıb, *LU.* 129.

póemaꝺ, poenmaꝺ, "S. na Rann," pp. 8, 148, battle plain.

Moenmaꝺ, "Bk. of Balymote," 382 b.

maᵹ—*continued.*

Senmaıᵹ elᴛa eᴅaıꞃ, *LL.* p. 5; ꞅaeꞃmaᵹ, "Man. & Cust." iii. 534; *gp.* Sechᴛmaıᵹe, near Arra in Tipperary, "L. na gCeart," 49.

Ᏽenmaᵹ, Ᏽaılᴛenmaᵹ, "Fragm. of Irish Ann." 218.

ᴛuaᴛhmaᵹ, north plain, or plain-land, "MS. Mat." 492.

ᴛulmaᵹ, *LL.* 161 b.

INᵹ (is of this declension (?), "Stokes").

ᏆeCh, ᴛeᵹ (ᴛeᵹn-, *Wb.* 4 a); a ᴛech n-, *LU.* 99, 112 a; ᴛech nᴅaꞃach, *LL.* 280; *g.* -ᴛıᵹe, *d.* ᴛıᵹ, ᴛıch, "Bk. of Armagh"; *cf.* *Z.*, *W.*; *g.* ᴛaıᵹe, *d.* ᴛaıch; *n. dual*, ın ᴅa ᴛech, "Mesca Ul." 40, 44; ᴛıcce, *gp.*, "Bk. of Armagh."

auꞃᴛech, *g.* auꞃᴛıᵹe, oratory, *W.*

baıꞃᴛech, cowshed, "L. na gCeart," 64.

bóᴛech, cowhouse; *d.* bóᴛıᵹıb, "Laws," iv. 102.

ceolᴛech, music house; *g.* ceolᴛıᵹı, *Tl.* 34.

clocᴄᴛhech, cloıcᴛhech, cloıᵹᴛech, bell-house, "Cog. G." 138: "Man. & Cust." iii. 541; "Ann. of Loch Cé," 20.

clochᴛhıᵹe, *gs.*, stone-house, *LL.* 308 a.

coᴛalᴛech, sleeping-house, *LL.* 263 a; *d.* coᴛalᴛıᵹıb, "C. R. na Ríg."; *dormitorium*, "Med. Tract on Celtic Declension."

cuchᴛaꞃᴛhech, *np.* cuchᴛaꞃᴛhıᵹe, ("Mesca. Ul." 12), cooking houses, *LL.* 263 a.

cuıꞃmᴛhech, *g.* cuıꞃmᴛhıᵹe, "Man. & Cust." iii. 511, 567; "Laws," i. 230; ale-house.

culᴛech n-, kitchen ("Ebel"), "Ml. Poems."

ᴅálᴛech ("Ebel"), *forum*, "Bk. of Armagh," fo. 215 bb; *dp.* ᴅalᴛıᵹıb, "Harl. Gl." 1802.

Ꭰaıꞃᴛech, *g.* Ꭰaıꞃᴛhıᵹe.

Ꭰeaꞃᴛhaıᵹe; *d.* ᴅeꞃᴛoıᵹ ("Four Masters," an. 717, 804); ᴅauꞃᴛech, ᴅuꞃᴛhech, ᴅeꞃᴛech, ᴅeꞃᴛhach; *ap.* ᴅıꞃᴛıᵹe, "Fragm. of Irish Ann." 116, oratory, chapel; *d.* ᴅeꞃᴛaıᵹ, *oratorio*, "Adamnan," p. 386; "Ann. Ult." 508; but ᴅuıꞃᴛhech, ᴅoıꞃᴛech, had 300 tables in it, "Bk. of Fenagh," 206, 212.

ꝼalᴛech, ꝼoılᴛech, pen, shed, "Mesca Ul." 57; *dp.* ꝼalᴛaıᵹıb, *ib.*; ꞅeıꞃᴛech, *g.* ꞅeıꞃᴛıᵹı, "O'Dav." 116.

tech—*continued.*

fartech, empty house, "Stokes' Bodl. Cormac," 28.

fertige, *gs.*, feast house, "Laws," ii. 212.

feoiltech, shambles; fertige, *gs.*, banquet-house, "Laws," ii. 212.

fialtech, water-closet, privy, "Fragm. of Irish Ann." p. 12; same as *g.* in tige coitchinn, "Mar. Scotus," 67 a.

fintech, intech, sheath, scabbard, *LL.* 111 a; *d.* intig ("C. R. na Ríg), but intiuch, "Ascoli"; arr a(ḟ)intiuch, *LL.* p. 80 b.

fledtech, banqueting house; *dp.* fledtigib, *Ml.* 80 b; fleteg, *Wb.* 11 d.

idultech, idulteg ("Ebel"), house of idols; gl. *fanum*, *gs.*, idaltaigae, gl. *fani*, *Sg.* 66 a.

iltech, illtech, group of houses.

ith-tech, ítech, corn-house; *np.* or *gs.* ithtige, ítige; gl. *horrea*, *Ml.* 98 a.

longthech, gl. *telonium*, "Harl. Glos." 1802; *g.* longthig, *ibid.*

martartech, *domus martyrum*; *d.* martarthaig, *Tl.* 192, 468, 194, 250; *g.* martortige, "Bk. of Armagh."

nemthech, heavenly mansion, *Tl.* 36; "S. na Rann," p. 146.

oigtech, guest house; ogthech, "Bodl. Cormac," 26.

óltech, óiltheach, drinking house.

psalmthech, house of psalmody, "Four Masters," ii. 720.

praintech, prointech, refectory, "Bk. of Armagh"; *g.* proin-tige, *LB.* 37; *d.* prointig, "Bk. of Hymns," ii. 204.

rígteg, rígthech ("Ebel"); gl. *prætorium*; *n.* ar rígthech, *LU.* 102 a, 103 a, 107 a, 110 b, *Wb.* 23 b.

rígdáltech, royal court.

rathtig, *ds.*, *macello*, market house; *Wb.* 11 b.

slintech, gl. *tectorium*, shingle-roofed house, from slind, gl. *imbrex*.

sluagthech, sluaigtech, barracks, "C. M. Lena," 160; *LL.* 263 a, *LB.* 215 b.

uairthech, cold house or grave, "Fragm. of Irish Ann." p. 240; "Four Masters," ii. 576.

sotech, gl. *lupanar* ("Stokes"), *Sg.* 64 a.

Nech, something; *nap.* nechı, neıche, *gp.* neıche, "Laws," iv. 36; *np.* neche, "O'Dav." 112; *d.* neuch, *Ml.* 17 c.

INtech (?), a way, journey; *d.* ıntech ("Maelduin's Cur." 484); it seems an O-stem.

fıdbach (?), *g.* fıdbaıge, wood, "Laws," iv. 102; for fıdbaıde.

Id: da n-ıd, two gads or chains; *np.* ıdı, *LL.* 72 b, 60 aa; may be an S-stem as síd and led; *ap*, a ıdı, *Tl.* 234.

SId (síd), sıd n-, *LL.* 246 a, 10 ba; elfmound, "Ogygia," 220; *gp.*, sıde, "Bk. of Armagh"; ıssed síd n-, *gp.* sıde, "De Chop. in da M." 243; *gs.* sıdui, "Echtra Nerai"; *gs.* síthe, "Four Masters," vi. 2028; *g.* sıde, ıssed síd, *LL.* 246 a.

SIId (síıd), síd, peace, *Wb.* 24 b, 27 c; *g.* síde, *Wb.* 24 b, shows S-stem, or a *fem.*; síd n-, "S. na Rann," 110, *W. Ag.* make it *masc.*, but their texts do not do so; essíd, .ı. ní sıd, "Cormac," 18; O-stem: laıthe ın sıth, "Fiac."

Leth, led, side, part; *g.* leıthe; *d.* leıth, leıd, "Ascoli's Glossary," *Ml.* 66 d, *Wb.* 4 b, "Cog. G." 118, 120, 66; *g.* leıthe, leıthı, "Four Masters," ii. 664.

Loth (?); *g.* loıthe; *d.* loıth, *cœnum*, Lerna, *neut.* or *fem.*; *Sg.* 34 a, 127 a, *Ml.* 60 a, "Ascoli's Gl." does not give gender.

Met (mét), size, extent; *g.* metı, "Arma Ch. C." 18; in ısfhed a mét (*Z.* 707 *seven times*), the a may be a pronoun "its," as méıt is distinctly *fem.* twice; yet met n-, med n-, "C. M. Rath," 52. "Cog. G." 94.

GRUAD (gruad), a ngrúad, the cheek, *Sg.* 14 a; da ngruad, *Z.* 228; *g.* grúadı (*W.*); gruada, "Cog. G." 118, 120, 66; *d.* gruaıd, *ib.*; "C. M. Rath," 146; *ngap.* grúade, grúaıde, *Ml.* 96 c, 39 d, "Laws," iv. 14; *LL.* 108 a; *LB.* 219 a; cf. *S.*

All N-, rock, cliff, chief, "Félire," Jan. 6; "Fragm. of Irish Ann." 222; "Four Masters," ii. 574; *g.* aılle, "Maeld. Curach," 468; "Siege of Howth," 64; *np.* aılle, aıllı, "Bk. of Lismore," 122; *ap.* alla (*recte* aılle, as metre shows), "Fragm. of Irish Ann." 84; *ap.* alle, *LU.* 26 a; *LL.* 279 a; *gs.* aılle, "Bk. of Lismore," 20 a; *d.* aıll, *LL.* 115 b; dá n-all, *ap.* alle, *S.*

All, rein; dá n-all, "Bec Fola;" "Man. & Cust." iii. 160; "Fled. Bricr."; "Siab. Ch. C." 376; *LU.* 105 b, 106 b; may be an O-stem; *as.* all, "Laws," i. 124.

SAL (ṛál); *g.* ṛáile, sea, "Stokes' S-Stems."

TIIR (tír), tír, land; *ager, terra*; a tír, a tír n-, "Four Masters," ii. 654, 596; *g.* tíre, *Z.*, *W.*, *Wb.* 29 d; *Sg.* 33 a; *as.* tír, "Bk. of Armagh"; *ap.* tíre, *Ml.* 66 c, "Bk. of Armagh"; *masc.* already in *LU.* 37.

ailethír, foreign land, "Siab. Ch. C." 382, *Tl.* 174; Dubthíri, *gs.*, *LL.* 203 a; *p.* mintíre, "Laws," ii. 12.

ḟoirthír, foreign land; Mumaintír, Munster, *LB.* 219 b.

GEIN, birth, child; gein n-; *g.* gene, *W.*; *np.* prímgene, "Laws," 32, 38; a ngein, *Tl.* 160, *LU.* 129; *np.* geine, *Tl.* 86. But Foidbgen is *masc. n. viri*, "Four Masters," i. 14.

aithgen, regeneration, restitution; *Ag.* marks it *neuter*.

ECEN (?), *g.* écne, force, *violentia*, is *fem.* (Ascoli, Windisch, and Atkinson); but I find no sure sign of that except *ac.* ecin, *W.*; ar écin may be dative.

TEN, fire; *d.* tein, "Stokes."

RUITHEN, ray, "Stokes"; *nap.* ruithni, "Táin Bó Fróich"; *W.* does not give the gender; *ns.* in ruthen, "S. Bodl. Chalcidius" of 12th cent.; ind ruithen, *Tl.* 6.

ONN, ond; *g.* uinde, a stone, "Stokes," *W.*; issed hond, *g.* uinde, "Cormac," 5; *g.* uinne, *d.* uinn, "O'Dav." 109.

borr-onn, big stone; *g.* uathuinne, *LL.* 187 b.

clothonn, famous stone, "Amra Ch. C." 77, "O'Dav." 109.

DUN (dún), *arx*, *Sg.* 51 b, "Bk. of Armagh"; *d.* dúin, "Bk. of Armagh"; *gs. ap.* dúine, "C. M. Rath," 68; *LU.* 26 a, "Four Masters," pp. 26, 1116, i. 308, vi. 2014, "Laws," i. 140, 154; *LU.* 129, *LB.* 213 a; *dp.* dúinib, "L. na gCeart," 222; *ns.* a ndún, *LU.* 18 b, 103 a, "Mesca Ul." 52.

prímdún chief fort, *dual*, *W.*, "S. na Rann," 147.

rígdún, royal fort, *Tl.* 192; *np.* rígdúine, Stokes' "Bodl. Cormac," 18; dún n-, "L. na gCeart," 86, 90.

GLUN (glún), knee; *gs. ap.* glúne, glunae, *Ml.* 36, 47; *Sg.* 172 a.

RUN (rún), secret; *d.* rúin; *gs. nap.* rúine, *Z.*, *W.*, *Ag.*, *Tl.* 2, *LB.* 228 a, 230 b; *ap.* rúne, *LU.* 9 a; *af.* rúna, *Wb.* 12 c.

GLENN, glend, valley; *gs. ap.* glinne, "Four Masters," i. 538; *LU.* 77 b; *ds.* glinn, glind, *Z.*, i nglinn da linn, "Brocan"; *ap.* midglinni, *LU.* 106 a; but in glend already in *LU.* 29 b.

ᵹLENN—*continued.*

comᵹlenn ; *ap.* comᵹlinne, *convalles* ; *Ml.* 81 c.

Lechᵹlenn ; *gs.* Lechᵹlinne = Leighlin, "Four Masters," i. 372 ; "Fragm. of Irish Ann." 148.

Arᵹatᵹlend, "Four Masters," i. 84.

ᵹlenn (?), *caus* ; *Sg.* 138 a.

LINN, lind, pool of water ; is not in "Ascoli's Gloss." or the Index to *Z.* ; *ndN.* linn ; *as.* a mor(lind), *W.* ; *g.* lindi, "Táin Bó Fróich," 146 ; linne, linde, "Four Masters," i. 300, 374, "Laws," i. 110 ; M'Firbis' "DeEpiscopis," 118 ; *ap.* linni, *LU.* 37 a.

Cairlinn, Carlingford, *g.* Cairlinne, "Four Masters," v. 1452.

Duiblinn, *g.* Duiblinne, "Four Masters," i. 122, Dublin, "L. na gCeart," 4 ; "Thurn. Versl." 44.

erlind, salmon pool, "Cod. S. Pauli" ; perhaps cataract pool.

éiclind, death-pool, "Sanctan's Hymn."

ᵹlairlinn, "Ann. of Loch Cé," i. 366 ; *ap.* ᵹlasrlinne, green pools, *LL.* 388 a.

íachlind, salmon pool, *Ag.*

crólinn, blood-pool.

mórlind, great pool, "Irische Texte," i. p. 81.

lochlind, *mare cœnosum* (?), "Ascoli."

muirlinn, sea-pool, "S. na Rann," p. 146 ; rcribinn, "Fragm. Irish Ann." 216.

duiblinn, black pool, *LU.* 95 a.

sruthlind, stream-pool, *ib.* p. 151 ; "S. na Rann," 151.

raithlinn, *g.* Raithlinne, "Four Masters," ii. 568.

rind, rinn, 1°, a point (of land) ; Rinn mbera (point of a spit ?), "Joyce's Keat." 106 ; it seems an I-stem from *gs.* Renna Dúin, *dp.* rennaib, "Ann. Loch Cé," i. 296 ; 4, 2°, point (of a spear), a rind, "Siab. Ch. C. ;" *nap.* rinne, rinde, rindi, *LL.* 4 a, *H.* 2. 16, 919, "Félire," xlv. Ascoli is uncertain of gender and declension ; *W.* makes it *masc.* ; but I think I have shown it is *neuter*, though rinnd, gl. *cacumen* in *Z.*, is not ; *np.* rind, promontories, "Laws," i. 160.

airrinde, *ap.* (?), signs *or* fore-points, "Tog. Trói."

AIRCIND, front (as opposed to taeb) ; da n-aircind, "Laws," i. 274.

ess (érr) (?); *gp.* érre, reins, "Siab. Ch. C."

am, time; *d.* aim, "Windisch," but (?).

dia, day; *as.* de, "Ebel"; *ns.* die, "Cormac," 15.

be (bé), bée, woman, wife, *LL.* 160 a; bee n-, "Echtra Nerai," l. 167; "Cormac," 5; "Thurn. Versl." 36; and twice in *W.*; a mbé in "Stokes' Celt. Decl." 36; and "S. na Rann," 87; *voc.* a bé, *LL.* 260 a.

gne (gné), species; *ns.* gné n-aill ("Bk. of Balymote," 307 b, 326 a, "Thurneysen's Mittelir. Verslehren," pp. 56, 57; "Pass. & Hom." 7001); a ngné, *Sg.* 108 a, "Beda Cr." 33 c; *gs.* gnée, "Bk. of Hymns," ii. 207; *np.* gnee, gnée, gnéchi, "Laws," ii. 96, "Amra Ch. C." p. 16, "Mesca Ul." 26; *dp.* gnéib; *n. dual*, gne, "Laws," ii. 96, i. 194; *g.* gnée, *LB.* 208 b.

raingné, special form, *Wb.* 5 a; raimgné, summer *or* blooming form, "Man. & Cust." iii. 532

ilgné, *np.*, many kinds, *Ml.* 97 a.

lee; irnal-lee, *Tl.* 160 (?).

re (ré), moon; ré n-, *Ml.* 32 b; *gs.* rehe, *Wb.* 4 c.

ree, *gp.*, spaces, *Cr.* 18 c; *dp.* réib, *Wb.* 22 a; *n.* ind ré, *Ml.* 54.

rei, *np. sidera*, *Cr.* 2 d; ré, space of time, seems *fem.*

o (ó), au; *g.* aue, ear, "Metric. Glosses," "Cormac," 4; *np.* óe, *ib.* 15; *dp.* óib, *H.* 2. 16, col. 777; *dual*, dá n-(óe, ó, áo), "Cormac," 15, 36, 40; *ds.* aui; *as.* ou, ó; *n. dual*, dá n-o, *ds.* óe, *LU.* 48 a.

gleo (gléo), battle; *ns.* mellgléo n-, *LL.* 92 a, 92 b; *np.* gleóichi, "Bk. of Fenagh," 218; bángléo, bloodless fight, "S. na Rann," 127; *d.* cath-gleo, "C. M. Rath," 162; but *g.* gliad.

oa (?) *jecur*, *Sg.* 656.

go (gó), gáo, gáu, falsehood, *Ml.* 21 c, 28 c; *g.* gue, *Wb.* 14 c, 31 b; *gp.* góa, "Amra Ch. C." *ap.* góa, *Wb.* 31 b; *W. Ag.* make it *fem.*; perhaps it is.

immargó, falsehood, "Circ. of Ireland," 38; "Félire," cxvii.

uccu, election; *ngs.* *Wb.* 30 d, 32 b; dígu, non-election, *rejectio*, *Wb.* 4 d.

uccu, forgu, rogu, togu, terchogu, forgglu seem stems in S. ("Stokes' Celt. Decl." 34); they are neuter: roga n-, toga n-, *LL.* 58 a, 58 b; "S. na Rann," p. 153; *gd.* togu, *Wb.* 20 d, 4 c, "Carm. Paul," *Tl.* 164.

CLU (clú), fame, *Sg.* 46 b; perhaps *neuter*, "Stokes"; clú n-, "S. na Rann"; *g.* clú, "Hyfiachrach," 182.

CRU (crú), cró, gore; "perhaps an S-stem," Stokes; *n.* crúu, *W.*

CUA (?), *gs.*, of food, "Laws," ii. 358.

RO (ró) (?), happiness, "C. M. Rath," 40.

LI (lí), colour, "Stokes' Celt. Decl." 24; *n.* líi; *d.* lí, *Wb.* 12 b, 37 c.

CRI (crí) (?), body, "Four Masters," ii. 616, 582, 898, "C. R. na Rig"; *as.* *LL.* 307 a.

BRI N- (brí n-) (?), right, "Man. & Cust." iii. 540.

III.—O-Stems, *called* A-Stems *by Windisch.*

They are masc. and neuter; the marks of the neuters have been already given.

RAD N- (rád n-), rách, grace, *gratia*; issed ar rath, *Wb.* 14 c; a már-rách, *LB.* 260; rad n-glé, "Poem of Ollamh Fodla"; *g.* ráich, *Wb.* 14 c; *np.* racha, "Bk. of Hymns," ii. 205; *gs.* racha, "Pass. & Hom."; rach n-aill, "Thurn. Versl." 52.

GRAD N- (grád n-), a ngrad, *Tl.* 158, *Wb.* 4 b, 29 a, holy orders; *g.* gráid, *Wb.* 31; *np.* grád, gráda, *W.*; *LU.* 276; *Tl.* 3; comgrád, *g.* comgraid, prímgraíd, "Man. & Cust." iii. 502, 504, 487; fograd, subgrade, "S. na Rann," p. 138; *dp.* fogradaib, "M'Carthy's St. Missal," 257; ilgrád. ollgrad, great dignity, "Four Masters," i. 250.

GRAD (grád), love; a n-grád, *W.*; but *g.* gráda, "Pass. & Hom."

RAD n-gó, a false saying, "Fair of Carman," p. 538.

RATh (?), stock; *g.* raich, "Laws," i. 216, also *g.* racha, *qv.*

MRATh (?), am-mrach; gl. *factio*, *Ml.* 33 a.

TRATh (?), conical hour; trí thrach, *W.*, p. 847, col. 2; *ap.* trach, tracha, *W.* and *Ag.*; *gen. sg.* tracha (*W.*) shows U-stem.

GNATh (gnách), custom, seems an adjective used as a substantive; a n-ingnad ro, a ingnach, wonder, *Sg.* 167 a, "Echtra Nerai," p. 222.

LATh N-, *LL.* 41. issed dach, "Cormac," 8.

SCATh, *ap.* (?), *figuras*, *Sg.* 108 a.

LITh N-GAILE, *LL.* 153 a; "Bk. of Balymote," 363 a; lich n-, "S. na Rann," pp. 41, 144.

luch N-, "S. na Rann," p. 144; see U-stems.

crodh N-, assembly, assembling, "L. na gCeart," 20.

mod N-, "Bk. of Balymote," 39 a; "S. na Rann," p. 145; "O'Dav." 107; *g.* muid, *Sg.* 148 a; *d.* mud, work, means, *ap.* moda, "Bk. of Balymote," 298 a.

cloch (?), *ap.* clocha, rumours, *Ml.* 129 a.

bruud N-, *LL.* p. 187, col. 1, a U-stem (?); cf. bruch.

rout n-aurchora, a shot's throw *or* way, "Táin Bó Fróich," 146; *d.* rouch, *stadio*, *Wb.* 11 a; *ap.* rotta, "Four Masters," ii. 572.

ed N-, small space, distance (*Tl.* 64, 138, 144); a n-ed, *LU.* 101 b, and *W*; *d.* arrind ed, *LU.* 110 a.

bet (bét) (?), a stroke (of murder) *or* a deed in general, *LU.* 60 a, 86 b; in bet, "Cormac, 13.

cet N- (cét n-), a hundred; cet mbó; *pl.* tri chét, cethir chet, *W.*; gall-chét, gallant hundred; *g.* céit, *Z.*

tret (trét), flock; *nap.* treta; *d.* treot, *W.*; *g.* treoit, "Pass. & Hom."; *np.* tréot, *LU.* 100 b.

cáirechthrét, sheep-flock, "S. na Rann," p. 129.

led, lech; *g.* leith; *d.* leuch, half, *Sg.* 5 a; *Cr.* 3 b; *ns.* al-lech n-aill, "Bk. of Hymns," ii. 144; *Tl.* 58; "Laws," iii. 6; "Bodl. Cormac," 4; tercert-lech, southern half, *LB.* 214 b.

blad-N, "O'Conor's Scriptores," i. pars 2, xxxv., blossom (?).

mech N-, decay, *LL.* 247; "Táin Bó Fróich," 142, 144; "Táin Bó Flidais"; "Laws," ii. 276; *W.*, p. 831, col. 1; *g.* mecha, of "O'Donovan's Suppl.," points to a U-stem; *np.* meacha, "Laws," ii. 276.

biad N- (bíad n-), food; *g.* biich, *Wb.* 9 b; bíad n-aill, "Bodl. Cormac," 12; *LU.* 110 b; *ap.* biada, *Wb.* 6 c; *d.* biud, *W.*; *g.* bíid, *Tl.* 236; *nap.* *biada*, "Pass. & Hom."; *ns.* in biad, *LL.* 304 b; fobíad, inferior food, "Laws," ii. 224; *np.* fobiada; bánbíd, *gs.*, white meats, *LB.* 218 b.

priam-mbíad, chief food, "Laws," ii. 224.

gaimbíad, winter food, "Man. & Cust." iii. 484.

dagbíad, "S. na Rann," 132; goirtbíad, salt food, "Lismore Lives," 393.

sáim-mbiad, condiment, summer food, "Man. & Cust." iii. 484.

MIAD (míad), *fastus*, honour, glory, *Ml.* 826; *Sg.* 106 b; *Wb.* 13 b; miad n-, "Bk. of Fenagh," 314, 338, 350; "Bk. of Balymote," 42 b; "Four Masters," 336; "C. M. Rath," 146, 132; *LL.* 128 b, am míad, *LU.* 129; a U-stem: dímíada, "C. M. Rath," 268.

remmíad, *ds. prærogativa*, *Ml.* 83; *ap.* remiada, "Bk. of Hymns," ii. 206.

dímíad, disrespect, "Bk. of Fenagh," 220.

glanmíad, "S. na Rann," 140.

romíad, glory, *LU.* 33 a.

RIAD (?), journey, "Nennius," 232.

cethir-riad, a four-wheeler, *np.* and *gp.*, "C. R. na Ríg," § 13; *cf. petor-ritum, rheda;* dériad, *bigae*, *Sg.* 54 a.

FIAD N-, fiad n-oiged, guest's welcome (?), *LL.* 63 b.

IATH N- (íath n-), land, "Thurn. Versl." 38, "Amergin's Poem"; *Sg.* 78; *voc.* a íaṫ! "O'Hartegan's Poem," *LL.*; *pl.* iatha.

all-iath, rockland, "Amra. Ch. C." § 21; corriath.

nem-íath, nimíath, heaven, *Sg.* and "Bodl. Cormac," 22.

rígiath, kingsland, *i.e.* heaven, *W.*, *Sg.*; iath, *ap.*, "O'Dav." 109.

BUAD N-, palm (thrice in "Bk of Fenagh," 142), the same as buaid, *qv.*

FUAD, FUATH N- (fúad, fúath n-), *figura, forma*, *Sg.* 137 b, *Wb.* 32 c, *Z.*; but *apm.* fuathu, "Siab. Ch. C." 376; *ds.* fúath, *Ml.* 38 c; fuath n-, "Cormac," 2, 21.

UATH, uathad n-, úathath, uathed n-, óthad, uadath, uaithed, *g.* odid; *d.* uathuth, óthud, *Z.* 801, &c.; *Sg.* 71 d, 41 a; fewness, few, first decade of the moon, the singular number; *n.* uathad n-, uathed n-, *LU.* 98 a; "Táin Bó Reg. Egert."; *g.* huathid, *Cr.* 33 b.

UATH, fright; mor n-uath, *W.* and "L. macc n-Uisnig."

LUAD N-, rumour, discourse, "L. na gCeart," 170; "S. na Rann," pp. 53, 144; "Félire Index"; perhaps a U-stem.

BRODSCUAD, brodscoad, *ap.*, *quiscilia*, *Tur.* 2 c, 4 a; "O'Dav." 56.

DEAD N- (déad n-), end, *Sg.* 162 a; *d.* déud ("Táin óB Fróich," 144), déod, diud, *W.*; *Tl.* 72.

REUD (?), reoth, reuth; gl. *pruina*, "Cod. Hampt." 56 a.

ꝼleuchuꝺ, rain: a ꝼleuċuꝺ ꞅin, *Ml.* 83 d; *g.* ꝼlechuıꝺ, *W.*

aeꞇıuꝺ, eꞇıuch (?), *ds.*, raiment, *Wb.* 10 d, 29 a; perhaps *infin. masc.*; *ns.* ın bıaꞇhaꝺ ocuꞅ a n-eıꞇıuꝺ, "Laws," ii. 168, *bis.*

ocbaꝺ n- (ócbaꝺ n-), warriors, *ns.* "C. R. na Ríg," § 33.

ochbaꝺ (?), ochꝼaꝺ, sighing, groaning, *LL.* 29 a, 51 a.

ꝼıꝺbaꝺ (?), bill-hook, "Laws," iv. 72.

ꝺuıneꝺaꞇh (ꝺuıneꝺáꞇh) (?), *mortalitas*, "L. na gCeart," 184, "Four Masters," ii. 578; *g.* ꝺuıneꝺaıꞇh, "Cormac," 40.

ꝺeꞃbaꝺ: a nꝺeꞃbaꝺ, *certitudo*, *Z.* 222, 801, *W.*; but *nm.* ın ꝺeꞃbaꝺ, *Ml.* 19d; perhaps the a n- in *Z.'s Gl.*, *Sg.* 90 a, 3, = their, of them, as the *infin.* in -aꝺ is *masc.*

ımbeꝺ, ımmeꝺ, ımmaꝺ, *multitudo, copia*, *Z.*, *W.*; *ap.* ımbeꝺ, *Ml.* 56 b, 64 c, 93 b; *g.* ımbıꝺ, *Ml.* 68 c; *d.* ımbıuꝺ, ımbuꝺ, ımmuꝺ (*Ml.* 23 a, 45 c, 56 a, 64 c, 93 b, 94 b); *d.* ımboꞇh, "Echtra Nerai," ımmbuꝺ, *LB.* 214 a; ꞃoeımbeꝺ, *Tl.* Index.

caınımbeꝺ, *benedictio* (*Ml.* 105 a), *i.e.* good abundance.

ınꝺıuꝺ (?), *ds.*, *emphasi*, *Ml.* 23 a.

ꞇınꝼeꝺ, ꞇınꝼeꞇh, *inspiratio, spiritus*, is *neut.* in *Z.* 225; a ꞇ., *Sg.* 6 a, 9 a; *d.* ꞇınꝼıuꝺ; *g.* ꞇınꝼıꝺ, *Sg.* 9 b.

alꞇꝼaꝺ m-. *LU.* 106 a; alꞇꝼaꝺ mbꞃochbuaꝺa, *W.*, pride.

boꞃꞃꝼaꝺ, a mboꞃꞃꝼaꝺ, indignation, *W.*; boꞃꝼaꝺ and ꝼoꞃꝼaꝺ, *LU.* 111 a, 105 b; boꞃꝼaꝺ, swelling (of tongue), "Lismore Lives," 43.

bꞃaꝼaꝺ (?), twinkling (of an eye), *W.* = bꞃaꞇhaꝺ, a U-stem.

aꞃaꝺ n-, *dual.* ꝺá n-aꞃaꝺ; *g.* aꞃaıꝺ, warning, notice, "Laws," ii. 146, 148; iv. 14, 22; i. 284, 262, 100; *dp.* aꞃꞇhaıb, "S. na Rann," p. 48; also U-stem, *qv.*

ꞃobaꝺ (?), *g.* ꞃobaıꝺ, warning, *LU.* 57 a, 87 a; ꞃobuꞇ́, "Cormac."

nemeꝺ, *sacellum*, *Z.* 801, Welsh *neuad*, gl. *aula*, Gaulish *nemeton*; *g.* nemıꝺ, *Tl.* 240; *d.* nemıuꝺ; *ap.* nemeꝺa, "Gog. G." 40, 138; .ı. nemıaꞇh, "Cormac," 31.

ꞅennemeꝺ, ꝼıꝺnemeꝺ, old grove, sacred grove, "Amra Ch. C." § 4, "Ann. Ult." ann. 995.

ıumaꞇ n-, amount, muchness, *H.* 3, 18, 611 b.

cumaꞇ: a c. n-, the amount, "Laws," ii. 364.

ᴅeʀ-meᴛ (ᴅéɼ-meᴛ), ᴅeɼmeᴛ, ᴅeɼmaᴛ, gl. *oblivio; d.* ᴅeɼmuᴛ, *Ml.* 124 c, 32 d; *g.* ᴅeɼmaiᴛ, *Ml.* 23 d, a nᴅeɼmeᴛ, *Z.*

ꝼó-meᴛ, a ꝼoɼmeᴛ, memory, *Z*; aiᴛhmeᴛ, "Fél. Index."

ꝼoɼaiᴛhmeᴛ n- ꝼoɼaiᴅmeᴛ, *recordatio*, memorial, *Ml.* 92 c, 123 b, 61 b; *Wb.* 24 c; *d.* ꝼoɼaiᴛhmuᴛ, "Stowe Missal," 64; ꝼoɼaiᴛhmiuᴛ, *Ml.* 115 b, 56 d, 27 b; *g.* ꝼoɼaiᴛmiᴛ, *Ml.* 17 b.

ꝼoɼmeᴛ, ꝼoɼmaᴛ, ꝼoɼmaᴅ, *Ml.* 43 a, *invidia, emulatio*, envy; *d.* ꝼoɼmuᴛᴛ, *Wb.* 6 b; *d.* ꝼoɼmuᴛ, *Wb.* 12 c; ꝼoɼmeᴛ, a ꝼoɼmeᴛ, *memoria*, *Ml.* 23 a.

immꝼoɼmaᴛ, great envy, "S. na Rann," p. 142.

ᴛaiᴛhmeᴛ, ᴛaiᴅmeᴛ, gl. *mentio*, *Z. Wb.*; 3 c, b; *LU.* 104; *cf.* na ɼo-ᴛhaiᴛhmen, that he did not mention, *LB.* 33.

comét (?), a guard; gender or *gen.* not given in *Z. W.*; *g.* coméᴛa.

ᴀiʀeᴅ, aiɼeᴛ, aɼaᴛ, eɼaᴛ, eɼeᴛ, space (of time or place), *intentio*, iɼɼeᴅ eɼeᴛ, iɼɼeᴅ á eɼeᴛ, eɼaᴛ, *Ml.* 33 a; an-aiɼeᴛ, *Tl.* 254.

ᵹɼan-aiɼeᴛ; *d.* ᵹɼanaiɼiuᴛ, "Bk. of Armagh," and "Táin Bó Cualnge."

ꝼaiᴛɼ-eɼaᴅ (?), nearness, "S. Rann," p. 137.

eiʀʀeᴅ ɴ-, *W.* "Irish Texte," i. 80; eɼɼeᴅ, array, harness.

ᴅeʀeᴅ ᴍ-, gl. *finis*, *Ml.* 44 a, 10 b; ꝼoɼɼa nᴅeɼeᴅ, "Fragm. of Irish Ann." 236; ᴅeɼiuᴅ n-, *g.* ᴅeɼiᴅ, "Cormac," 15, 18.

ꝼuiʀiʀeᴅ ɴ-ᴀiᵹeᴅ, supplying, feeding guests, "Laws," iii. 18.

ᴛᴀiʀʀeᴅ ɴ-, journey, Crowe's "Siab. Ch. C." p. 384.

ꝼoʀiᴅ (?), *gs.*, *phari*, *Cr.* 33 d.

ꝼuʀᴀᴅ ɴ-ᴀiʀᴄᴅiᴅi, silver rampart, "Fled Bricr." pp. 178, 144.

ꝼuʀeᴛh, wall, enclosure, "Fled Bricr." 213.

ꝼoʀeᴛh (ꝼóɼeᴛh), gl. *vadum;* but *ap.* ꝼóiɼᴛhiu seems *masc.*

ᴛoʀᴀᴅ, fruit, produce, *g.* ᴛoɼaiᴅ is *neuter*, *Z.* 223; *nap.* S-stem: ᴛoɼᴛhe, ᴛoiɼᴛhe, "Amra Ch. C." p. 14, "Echtra Nerai"; *dp.* ᴛoɼᴛhib, *LB.* 211 ba; but *np.* ᴛoɼuᴅ, *Ml.* 46 c.

loɼᴛhoɼaiᴅ, *gs.*, abundant produce, "Topogr. Poems," 20.

lánᴛoɼaᴅ, full produce, "S. na Rann," 143.

lamᴛhoɼaᴅ, hand-work or produce, "Man. & Cust." iii. 115; *g.* lamᴛhoɼaiᴅ, "Laws," i. 150, *LU.* 49 b.

ᴛORᴀᴅ—*continued.*

muıpᴛhopaᴅ, mupᴛhopaᴅ, *fructus maris*, "Bk. of Fermoy," 24; *LU.* 121 a; "Stokes' Bodl. Cormac," 34; "Bk. of Balymote," 144 bb, núaᴛhopaᴅ, new fruit, *LB.* 214 a.

boppᴛhopaᴅ, great fruit, "Man. & Cust." iii. 532, *LL.* 138 a.

pígᴛhopaᴅ, royal food, "Man. and Cust." iii. p. 540.

Reb-Raᴅ, tricks; *g.* pebpaıᴅ, *LL.* 344; *g.* pebapᴛha, *LL.* 230 a.

ᴛReb-Raᴅ (?), assonance; *g.* ᴛpebpaıᴅ, "Thurn. Versl." 137.

mac-Raᴅ, disease, *as.*, "Laws," ii. 164.

ᴅec-Raᴅ (ᴅéc-paᴅ) (?), group of good people (?), *ds.*, "Bk. of Armagh."

ᴅRochRaᴅ (?), *ds.* wickedness, bad people (?), "Félire," 204.

FReach-Raᴅ, fpoechpaᴅ, heath, *ds.*, "Irische Texte," i. 106.

aıg-Reᴅ, ice; *g.*, oıgpıᴅ; *d.* aıgpıuᴅ, *W.*; from aıg, ice.

Lıg-Raᴅ (líg-paᴅ), brightness, *LU.* 99; *das.*, *W.*, who does not give the gender; I have seen, however, lígpaᴅ óıp.

FuRg-Raᴅ, remains; *g.* fopgpaıᴅ; *ap.* fupgpaᴅ, *Wb.* 10 b, *Ml.* 48 d, 57 d.

Fıaᴅ-Raᴅ, deer, *as.*, "S. na Rann," pp. 92, 137.

RuᴅRaᴅ (?), collection of things (?), *LB.* 104; *but* blushing, "Félire," 193; .ı. poᴅupaᴅ, "Cormac," 39.

Fıᴅ-Raᴅ N-, a collection of wood (?), *LL.* p. 187; *d.* fıᴅpuᴅ, "S. na Rann, p. 61; ᴅuıllepaᴅ (?), foliage, *LB.* 109 b.

FıᴅRaᴅ (?), alliteration, "Thurn. Versl." 30, 122.

meᴛh-Raᴅ (méᴛh-paᴅ), méaᴛhpaᴅ, fat, *as.*, "Fragm. of Irish Ann." 124.

Suıᴛh-Reᴅ, group of venerable persons, *ns.* to plural verb, "S. na Rann," 187.

Luaıᴛh-Reᴅ, luaᴛhpeᴅ, ashes; *as.*, *Ml.* 49 c, 118 d, "Maelduin's Cur." 478; *Ag.* marks it *neuter.*

SRuıᴛh-Reᴅ, collection of venerables, "S. na Rann," p. 151.

FoRaᴅ (?), fopuᴅ; *g.* fopaıᴅ, seat, throne, "L. na gCeart," 136, 142; *d.* fopuᴅ, shelf, *LL.* fol. 79 a.

eRRaᴅ, eıppeᴅ n-, armour, battle-dress, *W.*; see *supra.*

FaRRaᴅ (?), company; *ds.*, *Cr.* 33 b.

ᴅaRauᴛh (?) gl., *quercetum; Sg.* 53 a; for ᴅaɼ-ɼaᴅ, ᴅauɼ-ɼaᴅ(?).

eᴛ-Raᴅ (éᴛ-ɼaᴅ) (?), *neut. Z.*, lust; *g.* éᴛɼiᴅ, éᴛɼiᴛh, eᴛɼaiᴅ; *d.* éᴛɼuᴅ; *Sg.* 68 b; *Cr.* 6 c; *Wb.* 9 d, 9 c, 22 b; *Ml.* 71 c.

seᴛ-Raᴅ (ɼéᴛ-ɼaᴅ) (?), group of jewels or treasure.

seᴛ-Raᴅ N- (ɼéᴛ-ɼaᴅ n-), a kind of verse, *LL.* 33 a, also ɼeᴛɼaiᴅ n-, "Thurn. Versl." 177, 156; *np.* ɼéᴛɼoᴅa, ɼéᴛɼoᴛha, *ib.*

caRaᴛ-Raᴅ, friendship, charity: a c.; *g.* caɼaᴛɼiᴅ; *Ml.* 58 b, 61 c, 29 c, 30 d, 90 d; *Wb.* 27 a.

cuiᴛ-Reᴅ, a triad.

peRchuiᴛReᴅ, husbands allowance, *Tl.* xiv.

sLaiᴅ-Reᴅ, admixture (?); ɼlaiᴅɼeᴅ n-aiɼᵹiᴛ, *reprobum argentum*, *Ml.* 85 b; *cf.* ɼlaiᴅe, *Ag.*

Liᴛ-Reᴅ, letter-group, *Sg.* 144 b. loᴛ-ɼaᴅ, "Cormac," 27.

iL-LiᴛReᴅ, great letter-group, *Tur.* 72 a.

ᵹaRᴛ-Raᴅ (?), "S. na Rann," p. 52.

bRechᴛ-Raᴅ, mRechᴛ-Raᴅ, variety; am mɼ-, *Sg.* 197 a, *Ml.* 122 d, *Wb.* 15 c; *gs.* mɼechᴛɼaiᴅ, *Ml.* 90 c; *Sg.* 197 a; see *Z.* 856.

iL-mRechᴛRaᴅ, much variety; *ds.*, *Sg.* 29 b.

ᴅiuchᴛ-Raᴅ, state of waking, *Z.* 856; prob. *masc.*

mes-Reᴅ, feeding with acorns, "L. na gCeart," 28; meɼɼɼaᴅ, *das.*, feeding on acorns, "Cormac, in O'Don. Gram." p. 294; *g.* meɼ-ɼaiᴅ, assessment (?), "Man. & Cust." iii. 511.

cLess-Raᴅ, *ds.*; *pl.* cleɼɼɼaᴅa, arms of dexterity, *LL.* 84; *ds.* cleɼɼɼaᴅ, *W.*

es-Raᴅ (?), littering of pigs; *d.* eɼɼuᴅ, "Laws," ii. 366, 372, 414.

Luss-Raᴅ (?), herbs, *ds.* "Félire," p. 143.

Lias-Raᴅ (liaɼ-ɼaᴅ) (?), herding *or* folding sheep; *d.* liaɼɼuᴅ, "Laws," ii. 360, 372, 414.

asReuᴅ (?), *fuga*, *Ml.* 63 c.

puL-Reᴅ, blood; *d.* pulɼiuᴅ, *W.*, *LU.* 109 a; puilɼeᴅ, "Fragm. of Irish Ann." 66.

puaL-Reᴅ (?), "S. na Rann," p. 4; pual = water, *Sg.* 32.

ciaLL-Raᴅ (ciall-ɼaᴅ), "S. na Rann," p. 92.

ball-rad: richballrad, .i. corra rada, long legs, "MS. Mat." 506; *gs.* ballraid, limbs, *LU.* 82 b.

arm-rad, *ds.*, arms (?), "S. na Rann," l. 6958.

mil-rad (míl-rad), venison, "L. na gCeart," 2; hunting, "Bk. of Fenagh," 178.

dam-rad, company, retinue, party, *das.*, "Laws," ii. 386; "Man. & Cust." iii. 510; but *gf.* damraide, *LL.* 247 a.

glam-rad (?), clamour, "S. na Rann," 140.

sam-rad, summer; *g.* samraid; *d.* samrud, *W.* "Laws," ii. 252; *LU.* 100 a; *W. Ag.* mark it *neuter;* like gaimred. bithsamrad, lasting summer, "S. na Rann," 126.

gaim-red, gemred, a ng., *Wb.* 31 d, winter; *g.* gaimrid; *d.* gemrud, gaimriud, *Z.*, *W.*; *LU.* 109; "Man. & Cust." iii. 492, 498.

cnaim-red, heap of bones, "C. M. Tured," 45.

gnim-rad (gním-rad), work, *na.*; *g.* gnímraid, "Laws," ii. 392; i. 168, 180, 226; *dp.*, da gním-rathib, "Cambray MS." 37 c; *ds.* gnímrad, "Laws," ii. 392; *np.* gnímrada, *LU.* 59 a.

langnim-rad (lángním-rad), full work, "Laws," ii. 410.

macgnimrad (macgnímrad): *np.* na macgnímrada, *LU.* p. 59 a; *dp.* deggnímarthaib, "Gildas' Lorica."

lom-rad (?), fleece, "Laws," i, 186; *cf.* lomrad, a shearing.

sain-red n-, sainrech n-, *proprietas*, *Sg.* 26, 27 a; *W.* does not give the gender.

sundred, *d.* sundriud, specialty, *Tl.* 126.

broen-rad (bróen-rad), drops (?), "S. na Rann," p. 129; *cf* broen, a shower, "Bodl. Cormac," 22.

indrad n-, plundering, án indred, gl. *vastitas*, *Ml.* 102 a; "Four Masters," ann. 804; *g.* indrid, *d.* indriud, *Ml.* 43 d, 48 d, 53 d.

cund-rad (?), gl. *merx.*, *masc.* in *Z.*; *as.* cundrud, "Laws," ii. 294.

menmannrad, *g.* -aid; *d.* -ad, mind, thought, "S. na Rann," 145. Note—The *gen. dat.* or *acc.*, &c., shows some collectives in rad to be *fem.*: macrad, echrad, &c.

polad, polud n-, *substantia, summa, vis;* a p., *definitio*; *Sg.* 3, 9 a, 27 a; *Ml.* 36 a; *g.* polaid; *d.* polud, *Ml.* 22 d, 25 d, 92 a.

ilpolad, *Sg.* 28 b; rainpolad, *Z.*; *gp.* polad, wealth, "Laws," ii. 314; frithpholad, wages, "Lismore Lives," 393, "O'Davoren," 47.

anpolad; *g.* anpolaid; *pl.* anpolta; disqualification, "Laws," ii. 318, 324, 326.

intled, *ap.*, *insidias*, *Ml.* 29 d, intleda, *Ml.* 28 c, 31 c.

scemled, *pl.*, battlements.

diablud N-, the double, "Laws," i. 68, 280, ii. 58; *g.* diabulta (?), see U-stems.

collud N-, neglect, "Laws," i. 176, 180.

comallada, acomallada, *ap.*, events, *Ml.* 122 d.

belat (bélat), *compitum*, pass, *Sg.* 24 a; *d.* belut, "Bk. of Armagh"; *np.* bélat, belota; *ap.* bélata, belota, "Laws," i. 160, ii. 270, "Chron. Scot." 333; *gs.* belait, *LB.* 205; *gp.* bélat, *LL.* 303.

dillat N-, *ns.* a cloak or covering, *LU.*, "Táin Bó Cualngi"; *ac.* dillat, "Bk. of Armagh"; *as.* díllat, "Brocan's Hymn," 84; *pl.* dillata, "O'Donovan's Suppl."; Welsh, *dillat* = *vestis*, *Z.*, 154, 840, *pl.*; dillata, "Man. & Cust." iii. 487.

alath (álath), for a n-álath, *Sg. incant.*

caemchlod N-, change, *bis*, *LB.* 208 b.

comcet (comcét) (?), concert.

coiced (cóiced), a fifth (part), a province; *g.* cóicid; *d.* coiciud, *pl.* cúiceda, "Laws," i. 80, is *neuter*, *Z.* 310, is *masc.* in *W.* and in "C. M. Rath": *np.* cúigid; but *neuter* tri chóicet, *LL.*, fo. 45 and 129.

gaisced, *np.* gaisced, gasced, *W.*, seems *neuter*, means arms, armour; but *np.* gaiscid, *LU.* 107 a.

riched, *g.* richid; *d.* richiud ("Amra Ch. C." § 6, "Brocan's Hymn"), is *neuter*, *Z.*, *W.*; kingdom, heaven; so ardriched, high heaven.

fortched N-, fortched ngalann, "C. M. Rath." 170.

drochet (?), bridge, *Sg.* 46 b; *as.* drochet, "Irische Texte," i. 160.

machad N-, *LL.* 160 b, 166 b, for machdad (?).

eitged mbriathar, *turpiloquium* (?), crime *or* offence of words, "Laws," i. 92, 90; *cf.* étig, gl. *turpe*, *Sg.* 38.

dliged (dlíged), dligech n-, *np.* dliged, *Ml.* 32 d, *Wb.* 5 d, *Sg.* 2 b; *ap.* dligeda, *Sg.* 207 a, *Cr.* 6 a; dligetha, *Wb.* 6, 10 d; law, dues.

fírdliged, true law or reason.

slándliged, degdliged, *Cr.* 3 c, *Ml.* 16 b; indliged, andliged, unlawfulness; dá n-indliged, "Laws," iii. 26; urdliged, liability, "Laws," ii. 342.

imtelgad m-, support, "Laws," iv. 22.

argat, silver, a n-argat n-, *Ml.* 31 d, "Bodl. Cormac," 10; *g.* argait, airgit, argit, "Bk. of Armagh"; *d.* argut, "Siab. Ch. C." 388.

anad N, a stay; *nap.* anta, "Laws," i. 212, 262, 282, 284, a U-stem (?), *qv.*

inad, place, site; tuc do a n-inud, *LB.* 28; Maelduin's Curach, p. 470; *g.* inaid, *pl.* inata, *W. Ag.* mark *masc.*

cined, *voc.* a chined n-, O race! *d.* ciniud, *Tl.* 154, 204.

dunad (dúnad), camp, host in camp or on march; an dunad, *LU.* 19, 63; *d.* dúnud, "Mesca Ul." 40, 48; *LU.* "Táin."

bunad, *origo*; *g.* bunid; issed bunad, *Wb.* 5 b, 5 a.

cetnad (cétnad) n-uisse, incantation of . . . .

cetnad n-, kind of verse, "Thurn. Versl." 53.

sétnad n-, kind of verse, *gs.*; *ap.* setnatha, "Thurn. Versl." 20, 156.

sénnath, kind of verse, *ib.* 118.

sennad (sénnad), a sennad, gl. *denique*, *postremo*.

imthanad, gl. *alternatio;* an-imthanad, *Ml.* 68 d, *Wb.* 13 a; *ap.* imthanad, *vices*, *Ml.* 93 c; but *asm.* imthánad, *Sg.* 181 a.

torbanad (tórbanad) (?), utility.

aicned, nature; *d.* aicniud; *g.* aicnid, *Cr.* 3 c; *as.* tri an aicned, *Ml.* 125 d, 67 c, *Sg.* 217 b.

suaicned, good nature. nimnid (?), *gs.* poison, *LL.* 129 b

dechnad N-, a kind of verse; "Thurn. Versl." 9, 10, 24, 25, 40, 151; lethdechnad, meddechnad, sneddechnad, *ib.* 137.

aelned, gl. *illuvies*; *d.* elniud, but *g.* óelniuda, *LB.* 33; *neut.* *Z.*

truailned (truáilned), corruption; *d.* truáilniud, *LB.* 33.

imned, *tribulatio;* an i., *Ml.* 44 d; *d.* imniud, *Ml.* 44 b, 103 b, *Wb.* 16 a; *ap.* imned, *Ml.* 21 c; imnetha, *Wb.* 14 b, 23 b, 10 b.

mennat (?), mansion; *d.* mennut, "Bk. of Armagh"; *ap.* mennata, *W.*; the *gs.* mendota (*Tl.* 210) points to a U-stem; *d.* mennat, "Sick-Bed of Cuch." 388.

toiniud n-, (tóiniud n-), *defectio*, *Wb.* 26 a; toined, *tractatus*, *meatus*, *Ml.* 42 c; its *gen.* is toiniuda, *Ml.* 42 c.

fuasnad, *g.* fuasnaid, *turbatio*, *Ml.* 16 b; *masc.* (?).

othathnat (óthatnat) (?), *dimin.* of óthad, *Sg.* 42 a.

tirthat (tírthat) (?), *dimin.* of tir, *Sg.* 47 b.

fuined (?), *occasus*; *g.* f-id; *d.* f-ud, *Cr.* 33 b, 18 c, *Ml.* 94 b, "Fiss Adamnáin."

osnad (?), *ap.* osnada, *Ml.* 31 c.

condid, *gs.*, firewood, dry-wood, *Cr.* 24 b; *d.* condutch, *Tl.* 14.

maided, *clades*, *Z.* marks it *neut.*

cothud (?), *g.* cothaid, good cheer, "Cormac," 12.

istad, istud, treasure, *arca*, see etsud.

michostad (?), commotion, "Four Masters," an. 1160.

essid n- (essíd n-), *exitium*, *Ml.* 48 d, 67 c; *gs.* esíd, invariable in all cases; a n-esíd, *Ml.* 15 d, 34 a, 48 d, 73 a, 67 c. 50 b; *d.* esíd, *Ml.* 36 d, 46 c; essad .i. ní síd, "Cormac," 18.

etsud n-, ecnai, autsud n-, treasure of wisdom, *Tl.* 25 b, 641; etsad n-, *thesaurus*, *Ml.* 51 d.

immetsad n-, treasure, *Ml.* 51 d, great treasure.

sossad, station, *Wb.* 64; sossuth, *Z.*; *d.* ossud, cessation of arms, *W.*

nasad, nassad n-, festival, "S. na Rann," pp. 32, 40, 146; *LL.* 211 b, 10; ba hed nasa, *LL.* p. 194 a; hence *g.* Lugnasaid, *LU.* 52 a, "Bodl. Cormac," 8; .i. oenach, cluiche, "Cormac," 26.

sasad n- (sásad n-), *LL.* 121.

drummut (?); *ds.* "Bk of Armagh."

DECHMAD, *np.* dechmada, tithes, "Laws," i. 50; *fem.* in *LB.* 214 b.

SECHTMAD N-, the seventh part, "Laws," i. 180.

ORD, order; dá n-ord, *LB.* 72, *Ag.*, p. 625 (it is *masc.* in "Ascoli"; and int ord, *Wb.* 9 c, and ordd, *Sg.* 4 b, 23 a); *npm.* uirt, "Four Masters," i. 134; *d.* urd, urt, *Z.*

ORDD (?), *malleus*, *Sg.* 49 a.

DORD (?), murmur, basso, *LL.* "Ch. of Usnech"; *neut.* *W.*

ANDORD.

FODORD (?), *g.* foduirt, murmur, *Wb.* 11 a.

CENNBART, a c., gl. *capitulum*, *Sg.* 47 a (?).

ARD, dá n-ard, assonance of two verses, "Thurn. I. Versl." 137.

ARDD, *g.* Aird, *Altum*, *Altitudo*, "Bk. of Armagh," 238; Ard m-Breccáin; see U-stems.

CETHARAIRD (?), square, *Tur.* 46; *ds.* cethairaird, *LU.* 49 a, *Tl.* 238; means the four quarters.

ART (?), a stone; art, *junctura*, is *masc.* in Cormac.

ADART (?), pillow; *g.* adairt, "Four Masters," ii. 786; da adart, *W.*

ANART (?), *linteum*; *as.* "Bk. of Armagh"; *pl.* línanarta, *W.*

TROST (?), *trabs*, *Sg.* 70 a; *np.* trosta, *Sg.* 33 b.

TROSTAN (trostán), a staff, *W.*

DISERT M-BECC, a ndisert, hermitage, *LU.* 15 b; but *masc.* in *LL.* 280; *g.* dersirt, "Charters of Bk. of Kells"; see U-stems.

TUAISCEART N-, north quarter, "Fragm. of Irish Ann." 14, *LL.* 304 b.

ESCART (?), *peripsema*, *Wb.* 9 a.

FERT M-, mound, *Tl.* 38; see U-stems.

FERT N-, *ap.* fert, *Z.* 228, a miracle; *np.* ferta, "Bk. of Hymns," i. 57, *Tl.* 60; but *apm.* firtu, *Wb.* 32 c; this last seems a U-stem; *ns.* firt n-, *LB.* 259.

NERT N-AILL, ised an nert, *Ml.* 29 d, 35 a, 115 b; *Wb.* 11 c; *Sg.* 215, 222 b; *nap.* nert, *Ml.* 108 c, and "St. Patrick's Hymn" *gs.* neirt, *Ml.* 48 c, nirt, "L. na gCeart," 80; strength, force; so mor-nert and dínert, great power; fóirnert, violence; amnert, weakness.

AIRMERT (?), *d.* airmiurt, airmbiurt, *Ml.* 98 a, 40 d, 65 a, *armorum instructus apparatus.*

alt n-, shore, "Maelduin's Cur." 478; *pl.* állta, "Tog. Troi," p. 139; alt, .i. teaċ, "O'Davoren," 54.

allt, cliff; dá n-allt, a wooded vale, "Bodl. Cormaċ," 20.

dialt n-etarléime, "Bk. of Balymote," 325, a syllable, *Z.* 981; *np.* dialta, diailt, *Z.* 981; *np.* dialt, dialta; *g.* dialta, "Thurn. Versl." 129; see U-stems.

lecht, dentar an lecht, "Irische Texte," i. 122 (but *np.* lechtai, *ap.* lechtu, "Bk. of Fenagh," and "Fél. Index"), grave.

toracht, *proventus, eventus, successio; ap.* torachte, *Ml.* 81 b.

act, *np.* acta, the Acts of the Apostles, *LB.* 101.

cosc n-, *Ml.* 51 b, isred mo chosc, "Siab. Ch. C." 394; *g.* coisc, *Sg.* 36; *d.* cosco, *Wb.* 9 a; *dp.* coscaib, *Ml.* 111 b; *correptio, castigatio, elementum.*

inchosc, *g.* inchoisc, *significatio, Z., Sg.* 32b.

tinchosc, *institutio, Z.*; as cosc, écosc, técosc are *neut.*, so seem all in cosc.

imchusc, *ds.* correction (much correction ?), "Siab. Ch. C." 385.

tecosc, instruction, *W.*; *g.* tecaisc, "Pass. & Hom."; *np.* tecusca, "Man. & Cust." iii. 542; "L. na gCeart, 50; *np.* tegasc, "Mac Daire's Tegasc Flatha," l. 174; Atkinson makes it *masc.*

briathar-thécosc, oral instruction, "Serg. Con. C."

écosc n-, *Ml.* poem, issed a écosc, "Táin Bó Fróich"; *dp.* ecoscaib, *Wb.* 11 c, expression, look, form, *habitus*, .i. cuma, *Sg.* 23; a ecosc, a chongraim, *LU.* 105 b; *g.* ecuisc, "Bodl. Cormac," 32; bahead écosc, "Cormac," 20.

sainécoscc, *species particularis, Wb.* 5 a.

aestóasc, estosc (*Z.* 887); *g.* estoisc; *Sg.* 30 b; *Ml.* 120 c, *expressio, pressura.*

aithesc, an athescc, *sententia, responsum, admonitio, Z., Wb.* 9 d; *Ml.* 51 b, 35 d, c; *g.* aithisc, *Ml.* 35 c; *ns.* aithiusc m-, a n-aithesc, "C. M. Rath," 30; *Tl.* 172; "Táin Bó Fróich," 146; "Bodl. Cormac," 4; "Lismore Lives," 12; *ap.* aithusca, *W.*

taithesc, *responsum, Wb.* 27 c.

claithesc (?), a Cl. .i aithesc, "Lismore Lives," 64.

duiresc (?), "O'Dav." 61.

cumusc n-, *commixtio*, *confusio*, four times in "Laws," i. 304; *n.* cumarc; *g.* cumirc, cumairc, *Ml.* 58 b; *Wb.* 13 d; but *nm.* in cumarc; *Sg.* 197 b.

drindrosc, *np.* (wishes ?); *d.* drindrursc, *W.* p. 847.

arosc n-, *n.*, "Lismore Lives," 123, proverb; *np.*, "Man. & Cust." iii. 542.

comarc, question: comarcaib ⁊ aithercaib, *LB.* 211.

tochmarc n- (Emire, *LL.* 151 a; *LU.* 130 b, 131), the questioning, asking, courting of E.; *g.* tochmairc, "L. na gCeart," 242; *d.* tochmurc (*Ml.* 127 d), *procatio*; *n.* tochmarc, *Tur.* 2 a.

immchomarc n-, imchomarc, imchumarcc; án i. (*interrogatio*, *salutatio*), *Sg.* 27; *Wb.* 7 b, 31 a, 32 b; *Ml.* 46 a, 54 c, 72 c, 77 a; *g.* imchomairc, *Ml.* 107; *d.* imchomurc, *Ml.* 77 a; *Sg.* 27 a.

aidchomarc, *requisitio*; *g.* athchomairc, appeal, suit, "Laws," i. 258, 272, 352; ii. 94; *dp.* aidchomarcaib, *Wb.* 9 d.

ginathcomarc, "O'Dav." 54; luathcomarc, *LB.* 214 b.

ferchomarca, *pl.*, "Thurn. Versl." 31, *Sg.* 34.

fochmarc, inquiry, *W.*, "Thurn. Versl." 58.

dichomarcc, *g.* dichmairec, non-asking, "Laws," i. 173; "Man. & Cust." iii. 542; "Laws," ii. 352, 124.

iarcomarc, end of poem, foot of three syllables, "Thurn. Versl." 170, 29; "Bk. of Balymote," 307 b.

récomarc, foot of two syllables, "Félire Index."

frecndairc, a f., the present, *Sg.* 167 a, is an *adj.* used as a *subst.*

diuderc n-der (díuderc n-dér), long, tearful look, *LU.* 7 b.

olc, evil, *d.* ulc, *ap.* olca, *Ml.* 87 d; is used substantively.

tatalc, *ap.*, *fomenta*, *Ml.* 144 c.

condelc, condelg, *g.* condeilc, *d.* condiulgg, *comparatio*, *Z.*; is *neuter*: condelg n-aga, *LL.* 57 b, "O'Dav." 84.

arag, security; *np.* arag, "Laws," i. 260, 274.

sluag (slúag), host, *ap.*, "C. R. na Ríg," 51, and mod. version, 26.

ag (ág), *g.* áig, contest, *Wb.* 25 a; *ngp.* ag, "Laws," iii. 286.

cuimrech, bond, fetter, *d.* cuimrich, *Wb.* 32 a, 30 a; *pl.* cuimrecha, cuimrega, *Z.*, 626, 656, 633; *dp.* cuimrigib; seems *neuter*.

toiḋreċ (?), daybreak; *d.* toiḋriuch, "Laws," i. 66.

fintech (?), *d.* fintiuch, kindred, "Laws," ii. 332.

comtherchomrac, *ap. conventicula, Ml.* 37 c, *bis;* but *apm.* comtherchomracu, *Ml.* 37 c, and *nsm.* int uile comthirchomrac, *Wb.* 7c; comrag n-, "O'Dav." 65.

airec, *d.* airiuc (*Wb.* 3 d), aithairec (*Ml.* 42 c), fuirec ("L. na gCeart," 24), are *neut.* or *masc.*

scel (scél), story, tidings, a scél-sa, is-ed scél, *Ml.* 23 c, 55 c; "Bodl. Cormac," 24; *ap.* scél, *Ml.* 35 b, "C. M. Rath," 68.

airscel, irscél, fair tale.
cáinscel, good news.
mórscel, great tidings.
cridiscél (heart news), joy, "Serg. Con. C." 378.
binnscél, pleasant story, *Sg.* 25.
findscel, finscél, romance.
fisscél, message, tidings, *LB.* 217 b.
rémscél, preliminary tale.
laemscél, famous story, "Bk. of Fenagh," 340.
soscel, Gospel.
cétscel, first tidings.
aithriscél, narration.
foscél, minor tale.
prímscél, an important story.
gúscel, goscél, ráibscél, false tidings.
drogscel, míscél, bad news.
badbscél, tale of war or horror, *LU.* 109.
rígscéla, royal tales.
sos-scel, judgment.

cel (cél) (?), augurium, *Z.* 18, 32.

cenel (cenél), genus, *gens; nap.* cenél, *Ml.* 72 d, 67 b, *Sg.* 167 a, *Tl.* 126; *gs.* cenéuil, *Sg.* 31, 32; *n.* and *voc. pl.* cenéla, *Ml.* 67 b, 26 b; *ns.* cenél n- (see my *Preface*); *gs.* nephchenéil, *nongentis, Wb.* 5 a; echtarchenél, foreign tribe; dochenél, bad stock; dagcenél, *LL.* 27; *g.* sochenıúil, of good stock, "Bk. of Armagh"; echtarchenela, foreign tribes, *np., Tl.* 170; saerchenél, noble stock; senchenél, old tribe; senchenéla, *Tl.* 126; comceníúil; *gs.* equal stock, "Man. & Cust." iii. 500.

Nel (nél), cloud; á nél, *Ml.* 82 d, but *masc.* in nél, *Ml.* 83 a; and *ap.* níulu, *Z.*; *masc.* in *W.*

Míl (míl), beast; *gs.* míl, "Bk. of Hymns," ii. 129; *ns.* am míl, "Táin Bó Fróich," "De Chopur in da *M.* 242; míl m-, *LU.* 128; *anp.* míla, *LU.* 11, "Siab. Ch. C." 386; fermíl, male animal, "Laws," iii. 40; bledmíl and míl mór, whale, "Bk. of Hymns," ii. 269, muirmíl, whale; fiadmíl, wild beast, game, stags; *np.* fiadmíla, *Ml.* 121 c; geirrmíla (= míla maige?), hares, "Maelduin's Cur." 472; cendmíl, head ornaments (of a horse); túagmíla, loop animals, trappings, Man. & Cust." 160, 190; "Siab. Ch. C." 376; "O'Dav." 61, 103; corrmíl, gnat, *LU.* 98 b..

Síl N- (síl n-), seed, *Wb.* 4 c; *Cr.* 18 a; *Ml.* 44 a; *LL.* 313, 314; "S. na Rann," 119; "Irische Texte," i. 179; *gs.* síl, *Wb.* 15 d; *np.* síla, "Nennius," 66 (see my *Preface*).

hsíl (?), progeny; *dp.* silaib, *Tl.* 10, 70.

Il, many (things); *d.* ilib.

Rechol m-, "Laws," i. 26.

Col, *ap.* morchol, *scelera*, *Ml.* 91 a; *gs.* cuil, *piaculi*, *Ml.* 16 c.

Ol (ól), drink, drinking; a n-ol, *Z.*, *W.*; *gs.* óil, *W.*, "L. na gCeart," 114; *d.* oul, *Ml.* 94 c, 129 d; ol n-, *LU.* 23 b, "Táin Bó Fráich," 144; míodóil, *gs.*, mead-drinking, "Hyfiachrach," 216; fledól, carousing, *Tl.* 52; comól, carouse; *g.* comóil, "L. na gCeart," 72, 86; imrool, imról, great drink, abundance (*Wb.* 12 a, 23 c, *Ml.* 12 a), unless it is connected with tinól; sainól, soól, special drink, good drink; *np.* óla, *LB.* 217 c, 215 a.

Tinol (tinól), tinóol, imthinól, comthinól, lérthínol (*LL.* 301 b); *congregatio*, gathering, are *neut.* or *masc.*; athtinól, gathering, *LB.* 20 ba; *g.* comthinóil, *Sg.* 222 a.

Ceol (céol), song, music; *ns.* á ceul; *np.* ceul, *Ml.* 126 c, 115 b; ceol n-, "Maelduin's Cur." 488; *gs.* ceóil, ciúil, *W.*; *np.* céola, "Táin Bó Fróich," 150; *ap.* ceula, *Tl.* 114.

Seol N-, career, "Nennius," 279; seól n-, "O'Conor's Scriptores," i. pars 2, xxxii.; seol n-, guide, "Chron. Scot." 70; seól n-, veil, "Four Masters," i. 694; seol n-, scarcity, "Laws," v. 52; seol n-, *LL.* 127 b.

ᴅᴀʟ (ᴅál), a division (or distinct family), "Cormac," who gives Ꝺal-Riata as an example, but ᴅál, division, is *masc.*, *LU.* 41 b; Beda (*L.* 1, ch. i.) agrees with Cormac: ᴅaal, *lingua Hibernor., partem significat;* O'Flaherty disagrees with both, and says it means *proles*, posterity, hence Ꝺál (n-Araide, n-Aulum, gCair), &c., *LL.* 331, "Bk. of Balymote," 182; "Four Masters," iii. 22; "Nennius," 264; "O'Heerin," 122, &c.; *g.* ᴅail, *Tl.* 164, 168. (See *Preface*); ᴅál n-, "Cormac," 14, 20.

RIGDAL (ríg-ᴅál), royal assembly, "Fragm. of Irish Ann." 126.

ELL N-AILGEN, *LL.* gait, expression (of eye); *np.* ella airlinge, *LL.* 308 a.

DI-ALL (ᴅí-all), *deviatio, declensio; n.* a ᴅíall n-, *Sg.* 4 b, 158 b; *g.* ᴅíil; *d.* ᴅíull, *Sg.* 75 b, 50 b, 90, 91, *Ml.* 119 b; nepᴅíall, non-declension, *Ml.* 75 b, *Sg.* 75; roᴅíall, decline, "Amra Ch. C." 31; aᴅ-all, *transitus*, visit; *g.* aᴅíll, aᴅaill, *Ml.* 102 b, *Wb.* 14 a (*dp.* aᴅallaib, horse-bits (?) "L. na gCeart, 156); taᴅ-all, *transitus*, visit, *Ml.* 25 a; *gs.* taᴅill, *Wb.* 27 b; taᴅall, attempt: ní beriᴅ anaill, *LL.* 96; rechm-all, *Ul.* 70 b; *g.* rechmaill, *præteritio*, *Ml.* 102 a; tóchell n-, a journey, *migratio* (?), *LU.* 131; *d.* tochull, *Ml.* 82 d.

TOCHELL N- (tóchell n-, *LU.* 130 a, a stake (put down against one already offered at game), *W.* p. 830.

TOICHELL (tóichell), journey, *LU.* 34 a, *cf.* *LL.* 115 a.; tair-tell (?), *gs.* tairtill, a march, "L. na gCeart," 260.

TRIALL (tríall) (?), journey, going, *Tl.* 256; comthriall, "Four Masters," ii. 632, an. 1094. airmṫriall, "G. Corca Laide," 344.

IMRALL, *g.* imraill, *deviatio*, error, *LL.* 303 a.

IMROLL, a miss, a mistake, *das.*, *LL.* 63 a, *LU.* 60 a.

POINDEL (?), *pervagatio*, *Ml.* 121 d; *d.* paeniul, "Laws," i. 212, ii. 356. inᴅeal n-, "Cormac," 5.

PUIDELL (?), leavings, "Fragm. of Irish Ann." 68, *LU.* 114 a.

NUALL (núall), cry, howl; *pl.* núalla, *W.*; nuall n-, "C. Findtragha," i. 74; a nuall-sa, "Felire," 193, 202; *ap.* nualla, *LU.* 30 a.

TRELL (?), time; *gs.* trill, *LB.* 221 b.

DIABUL N-, ᴅiabol n-, the double, "Man. & Cust." iii. 490 *bis*; "Laws," ii. 306, 308, 332; see U-stems.

ubull, *ap.*, apples; *np.* ubla, *LU.* 48 b, 105 b.

cetal, cetol, cetul, a song, *canticum;* issed a c., *d.* cetul, *Ml.* 60 b, 33 b; *dp.* cetlaib, *Tl.* 254.

airceṫal, aercheṫal, aircheṫal n-, a poem, "L. Gabala," 212, "Bk. of Fenagh," 194, 274, *LB.* 104; trisyllabic poetry, "Thurn. Versl." 127; *g.* aircheṫail, *LL.* 38 a; *d.* aircheṫul.

clasceṫul, claſſcheṫal, claisceṫol, choir-singing, chanting, "S. na Rann," 32, "Fis Adamnáim," "Fiac's Hymn": from clas.

cóceṫal, coceṫul, *concentus*, harmony, *Z.*, *Ml.* 145 c; coiceṫtal na ccuach, "Adamnán's Columba, 275; cocceṫal, the clashing (of swords), "Cog. G." 180; .i. comcheṫul, "Cormac," 14.

díchetal, incantation, "Laws," i. 38, "Bodl. Cormac," 8, *Tl.* 56.

doceṫul, music, "Arma Ch. C." ch. 6.

dromcheṫal, a poet's song, "Amra Ch. C." ch. 7; *cf.* drumiu, more poetic, *ib.*

forceṫal, forciṫal, *monitum*, *eruditio*, *doctrina*, *Z.*; a forciṫal íccas, *Wb.* 13 b, 25 d; *nap.* forciṫal, *rudimenta*, *imbumenta;* *dp.* forceṫlaib, *Ml.* 47 d, 107 b, 14 b.

saebforceṫul, evil suggestion, "C. M. Rath," 167.

soḟoircheṫal, good teaching, "Lismore Lives," 400.

rocheṫal, great song; *np.* rocheṫal, rocheṫla, "Thurn. Versl." 60.

saercheṫal, free or noble teaching.

salmceḋal, psalm-singing, "C. M. Rath." 12.

tairceṫal, tairchiṫal, téirciṫal, gl. *vaticinium*, *Z.*, *Ml* 94 a, 64 c, *Wb.* 5 a; *g.* tairchiṫil; *d.* tairceṫul; *np.* téirciṫla, *Ml.* 89 b, 55 d, 19 b.

remṫhairceṫal, gl. *præsagium.*

tairmchiṫal, gl. *vaticinium.*

timcheṫol, some kind of song or music; I have lost the reference.

tincheṫal, gl. *incantatio;* *ap.* tinchiṫla, *Ml.* 76 b.

tindsceṫul, tinnsceṫal; gl. *inceptio*, *principium*, *Z.*

intinsceṫul, *inceptio;* *ds.* *Ml.* 15 a.

tobcheṫal, trumpet-sound, *Ml.* 120 c, *bis;* is ed tobcheṫal, *Ml.* 40 d.

caustal (?): ı caurtul ppı cner do, next his skin, "Mesca Ul." 38; *gp*. penchurtul, "Fragm. of Irish Ann." 84.

tocustal N-, a muster, *LL.* 94; tınol ⁊ tochurtal, *LB.* 227 b; tóchorta pledı, tochartal lochta.

tuaristal, wages; *g.* tuarırtaıl; *np.* tuarırtal, tuarırtol, tuarırtla, "L. na gCeart," 80, 50, 70, 118, 146, 63.

prestal (?), attendance; *d.* prertul, *Ag.*, *W.*

tul, taul, a boss; tul n-óır, *LU.* 81, 129; perhaps tul, forehead, front, is the same word.

toll, a hollow, hole, *W.*

trell (?), space of time; *g.* trıll, *LB.* 221 b.

all, rein; da n-all, *UL.* 106 a, 105 b, *W.*

all N-, gl. *saxum, petra; g.* aıll; *as.* all, *W.*

alt, da n-alt, *W.* p. 462.

comal, comol, comul, comoll, gathering, union; camal n-, "Four Masters," i. 30; *LL.* 57 ab; "Amra Ch. C." l. 30; "S. na Rann," p. 130; "Fragm. of Irish Ann." 222.

comall, observance, fulfilment, *LL.* 82 a; comul n-, "Four Masters," i. 30; ii. 572, 596; comol .ı. nert, "O'Dav."

míchomall, non-observance, non-fulfilment, bad performance.

comoll n-, compact, "L. na gCeart," 220; .ı. cengal, "O'Dav." 72.

accomol, acomol, *unio, conjunctio, synæresis*, *Sg.* 54 a, *Wb.* 23 a; *g.* accomuıl, acomuıll, accomaıl; *d.* accomul, *Ml.* 210 a, 15 b, 58 b, *Sg.* 212 b.

nephaccomol, *g.* nephaccomoıl, *Sg.* 7 b, *Z.* 861.

comaccomol, comacomol, comaccumul, (*animi*) *conjunctio, adjunctio*, a conjunction and subjunctive (in grammar); *g.* comaccomuıl, *ap.* comaccomla, *Z.* 988; *Ml.* 61 a, 62 a; *Sg.* 203 a, 212 b; *Cr.* 60 b; *Ml.* 28 a; but *np.* comaccomuıl, "Amra Ch. C." ch. 1, *LL.* 26 a; comacolma, *ap.*, enclitics of *Z.* 714, should be, I think, comaccomla.

coaccomal, a conjunctive or subjunctive.

roaccomol, *subjunctio, constructio*, subjunctive, *Z.* 656, *Sg.* 154 a.

comal—*continued.*

ꝼo-comul, comfort, *as.*, "Laws," ii. 362.

deg-accomul, goodly comfort, "Laws," ii. 362.

er-chomul, gl. *lucar*, *g. lucaris*, *Sg.* 126 b; money payed to play-actors, *θεατρικὸν ἀργύριον*, *i.e.* goodly comfort or a douceur given to them, = ꝼoaccomol, degaccomol; the Irish glossarist took it for *lucellum*, a small profit: *lucelli aliquid dare, facere aliquid lucelli, tecum partita lucellum* of Cicero and Horace. Dr. Ascoli omits the word in his "Glossarium," pp. 113, 114, 115.

aurchomol, erchomol, fetter of two fore-feet, "Bodl. Cormac," 10; urchomul, .i. ꝼeiτir, glar na nGall, "Cormac," 26.

auraccomol, fetter for the two fore-feet, "Bodl. Cormac," 10.

ꝼorcomol (?), imprisonment, "Táin Bó Flidais," 46.

bledmall (?), sea-animal, whale (?), *g.* bledmaill, *W.*; it is *masc.* sometimes.

temel (?), darkness, *d.* temul, *Z.* 998; *Ml.* 16 c: tri themel, *per tenebras.*

anacul, *salvatio*, *g.* anacuil, *d.* anacul, *W.*; *as.* anacul, "Bk. of Armagh"; *Z. W. Ag.* do not mark gender; *cf.* adnacul n-.

idnacul, escorting, *LU.* 42 b, *LL.* 114 b; cf. *tradere*, *traductio*, tidnacul, adnacul, and ídnaicer, which leads or conducts, *Ag.* I think all these in cul are *neut.* as adnacul.

tidnacul, tindnacul, tinnacul, *traditio*, *remuneratio*; *das.*, tinnacul, *Wb.* 4 b, 9 b; *Ml.* 97 a, 124 c; *g.* tindnacuil, *Wb.* 33 a, "Nennius," 26.

comnacul, *facultas*, *possessio*, (*conditio*) (?); *cf.* coemnacair, *potest*; comnacal, necessaries, "Lismore Lives," Index.

é-comnacul, lack of possession or property.

adnacul: a n-adnacul n-erctoilcthe, the open grave, *Ml.* 22 ba; *g.* adnocuil; *d.* adnocul, *Ag.*; *ap.* adnocla, *LB.* 211 b, ꝼír-adnacla; *d.* adnaclaib, *Ml.* 83 d, 69 a; an a, "Cormac," 21.

com-adnacul, co-sepulture, common grave, *Wb.* 27 a.

ꝼoscul N-, ꝼoꞅcul nꝺíꞅeċ, a straight drive, *LL.* 263 b, and *LU.* "Táin."

mascul: a maꞅcul, the masculine gender, *Sg.* 66 b.

banꝺscal: a mbanꝺꞅcal, the woman, *LU.* 22 a; *cf.* German, *das Weib.*

airecul, aıꞅeᵹal, a chamber, "Sergl. Con. C." 382.

ꝺorochol (?), *foramen*, *Sg.* 54 a.

sercol, *as.* ꞅeꞅcol, *W.* "Amra Ch. C." 73; *np.* ꞅeꞅcla; gl. *irritamenta gulæ*, *Sg.* 63 a; the *as.* and *np.* show a *neuter.*

saiᵹul (ꞅáeᵹul), ꞅaeᵹal, time, life-time; *g.* ꞅaeᵹuıl, *Ag.* makes it *masc.*, but it is *neut.*, a ꞅaeᵹul, in l. 7791 of "Pass. & Hom."

ᵹell, ᵹıall, gl., *pignus*; a nᵹell n-, *nap.* ᵹell, *Wb.* 14 c; *Ml.* 27 a, 123 c, 58 d; *g.* ᵹıll, *d.* ᵹıull, *ap.* ᵹella, "Laws," i. 50, 281.
 aıchᵹell, M'Dare's "Tegosc Flatha," l. 175.
 ꞅmachꞇᵹell, "Laws," i. 276.
 ꞇaıꞅᵹell, a fine.

ꝼorᵹell, ꝼoꞅᵹall, a ꝼoꞅcell, a ꝼoꞅcal, gl. *attestatio*, *testimonium*; *g.* ꝼoꞅcıll, ꝼoꞅcaıll; *d.* ꝼoꞅᵹull, ꝼoꞅcull, *Z.*, *Wb.* 25 d, 28 b, 14 c; *Ml.* 44 c, 46 c, 131 a, 42 d, 46 c, 35 b.
 caınꝼoꞅᵹall, fair testimony, "Colman's Hymn."
 ꝺubꝼoꞅᵹell, false testimony, "Laws," i. 176.
 ᵹuꝼoꞅcell, false testimony, *Wb.* 13 b; *np.* ᵹuꝼoꞅᵹell, "Laws," ii. 328; *gs.* ᵹuꝼoꞅᵹaıll, *Tl.* 8.
 ꝼuᵹell (?), ꝼuᵹall, gl. *judicium*, *Z.*; *d.* ꝼuᵹıull, *LB.* 33; *g.* ꝼuᵹıll, *W.*; *Z.* doubts of the *gender*, but *ap.* ꝼúıᵹle of *Ag.* seems to show a *neuter* which passes to the S-declension in the *plural.*

sraiᵹell (?), ꞅꞅáıᵹell, ꞅꞅoᵹell, a scourge; *g.* ꞅꞅoᵹıll, *Z.*; *np.* ꞅꞅaıᵹle, "Bk. of Hymns," ii. 156, seems *neuter*; it is *fem.* in *Ag.* *dsf.* ꞅꞅoᵹıll, *LB.* 218 b; *neut.* "S. Celt. Decl."

saiᵹul (?), age, life, *Wb*; *g.* ꞅaıᵹuıl; *as.* ꞅaıᵹul n-, *Ml.* 119 b; probably *masc.* as ꞇempul.

ubul, apple; ubul n-óıꞅ, "Táin Bó Fróich"; ba heꝺ uball, "Fragm. of Irish Ann." 92, 202; *np.* ubla, "Hyfiachrach," 284 *W.*; *npm.* ubaıll, *Ag.*

ımbel, border, rim: ımıol n-, "C. M. Lena," 146; *g.* ımbıl, *d.* ımbıul, *W.*; ochaṗımmel, achaṗımlıb, "Tog. Trói," l. 1131, *LL.* 267 b.

·caıssel N-, a stone structure, *maceria:* caṗṗel n-Oenᵹuṗa, *LL.* 211 a, "Bk. of Hymaine," R.I.A., fol. 145–6; perhaps caıṗle of *W.* 412 is its plural of S-declension; *g.* caıṗṗıl, "Lorha Cumthach"; *d.* caıṗṗıul, "Bk. of Armagh"; *gp.* caıṗṗel, *murorum*, "O'Sull. Hist. Cath. Compendium," 136.

·clausul (?), *ds. clausula*, *Ml.* 41 a.

tuısel (?), a fall, case; *npm.* tuıṗıl, *Sg.* 71 a, 188 a; Ascoli does not give the gender.

ᵭeıssel (?), right-hand or south side; *d.* ᵭeıṗṗıul.

temel (?), *d.* temul, darkness, *Ml.* 16 c, 30 a.

ᵹemell (?), ᵹemel, fetter; not neuter in "Circ. of Ireland," 34.

ᵭaer, ᵭéṗ, tear; *np.* ᵭaeṗ, *Ml.* 23 a; *ap.* ᵭéṗa, "Four Masters," ii. 618; it *sgf.* na ᵭéṗe, *LU.* 45 a and *W.*, yet *as.* ᵭéṗ, *W.*

·aer (áeṗ) (?), áıṗ, *vituperatio*, *Z.*, áıṗ; *Wb.* 16 a; *g.* áıṗe, *LL.* 81 a; aıeṗ, aıṗ, is *masc. Ml.* 72 c.

tathaır (tathάıṗ) (?), gl. *reprehensio*, *Z.*, *Wb.* 16 a; *d.* tathaıṗ, *Ag.*

·combaır N-, "Laws," i. 180, for combaṗ, meeting (of waters, &c.); *na.* Combaṗ, Combuṗ; *g.* cumbıṗ, *Tl.* 238, 350, and "Bk. of Armagh."

teoaır (?), *gs.* contemplation, *Wb.* 12 a.

ṗer (ṗéṗ), grass; *g.* ṗeúıṗ, *Sg.* 68 b; *np.* ṗéṗa, *W.*

·ar (áṗ), áṗ n-, "Four Masters," ii. 596, i. 330; *g.* áıṗ, *Ml.* 113 b, *Tur.* 50; *dp.* áṗaıb, *Ml.* 33 d, 34 a; ṗıoḋ-áṗ, destruction of woods, "Four Masters," an. 1121.

·or (óṗ), gold; óṗ n-, "Carm. Paul." *W.*; *g.* óıṗ, *Z.*, *W.*; *W.* and Ascoli do not state the gender.

bán-óṗ, bright gold, *LL.* 266 a; ᵭeṗᵹóṗ, red gold; ṗíṗóṗ, pure gold.

ᵭıor (ᵭíoṗ) (?), *gl. abriza*, *Sg.* 73 c.

mor (móṗ), móṗ n-eṗbaıᵭ, much loss, móṗ nᵭuba, much sorrow, *LL.* 334, "Félire," 201.

ṗormor (ṗoṗmóṗ), uṗmóṗ, chief part, the most; *g.* uṗmóıṗ, *Ag.*

ᏆOR, tower; τop mbpeᵹoin, "Nennius," 240.

LER (?), sea; is *neuter*, says Stokes, in "Félire Index"; is *masc.*, says *W.*; but there is no proof given by them; however, *ap.* lipu *W.* favours *W.'s* view; *g.* lip; *d.* liup, *W.*

MUR, rampart; am mup, "Maelduin's Cur." 476; mup n-Ollomon, mup mbpaiᵹτhoch, "S. na Rann," 15, mup n-olloman; *np.* mupa, *LU.* 211 a; but *npm.* muip; *ap.* mupa, *W.*, *Ag.*

LAR (láp), gl. *solum*, floor; al lap, *Ml.* 89 d; 108 d, *LL.* 292 b; *g.* laip, *Ml.* 34 d; *da.* láp, *W.*; Stokes doubts of the gender in "Félire Index"; coppláp, centre, "G. Corca Laide," 344.

CERTLAR (cepτláp), the very centre, "Circ. of Ireland," 42.

FOSSADLAR (foppablap), station, "Lism. Lives," 392.

ITHLAR (iτhláp), area, corn-floor; *g.* iτhláip, *Sg.* 68, *Ml.* 137 a; cf. *ds.* iτh-lainn; gl. *areâ*, *Sg.* 68 a.

ORLAR (opláp), gl. *vestibulum*, "Mediev. Tract on Lat. Decl."; also upbáp, a floor, area, level ground, as ppaτh an uplaip, Stranorlar, "Joyce's Names of Places," ii. 425.

CLAAR, cláp, gl. *tabula*, board, plank, *Z.*; cláp nbapa, oak board, "Man. & Cust." iii. 480; *d.* claap, *Z.*; *np.* clápa, *Ag.*; it means also a flat surface; cláp an eubain, the forehead; hence pianchláp, *W.*, lmchlaip, *gs.*, *Tl.* 170; lubenchlap, "Thurn. Versl." 48; baile an chláip, Clare Galway; see "Joyce's Names of Places," i. 427; maᵹ cláip = *campus planus*, "Trias. Thaum." 184.

ᵹALAR, sickness, distress, *dolor corporis vel animi;* ᵹalap n-, an ᵹᵹalap (for a nᵹalap), *Z.* 1005, "Cambrai MS." 27 d, *Ml.* 61 c; ᵹalap n-eclip of *Wb.* 29 a = disease of languor or weakness (of stomach), *cf.* éiᵹlibe, languid, "O'Begley's Engl.-Ir. Dict.": *dp.* ᵹalapaib, *Ml.* 107c; *ds.* ᵹalup, *W.*; *g.* ᵹalaip, *np.* ᵹalpa, *Ag.*, *LB.* 111 b.

cennᵹalap, headache, *Wb.* 17 d.

cliabᵹalap, chest disease, *LB.* 219 a.

cpebemᵹalap, "S. na Rann," 132.

cpiτhᵹalap, ague, *Tl.* 160.

bianᵹalap, languor, "Colman's Hymn," "Gildas' Lorica,"

τpomᵹalap, heavy sickness or grief.

OLOR N-, olor n-olar, drink of drinks (?), gravy of gravies (?), *g.* olair, *LB.* 217 c, *LL.* 210 b; Olor (*LL.* 24 a) is the name of the river Sixmilewater.

MONAR N-, monor n-, monur n-, work, occupation, *LL.* 395; "Bk. of Hymns," ii. 129; *LB.* 11 b; "S. na Rann," 145; "Circ. of Ireland," l. 195; "C. M. Rath," 132; "L. na gCeart," 8; lethmonur, "Cog. G." 192; but *nm.* in monur, *LL.* 234 a; a monar aidche sin, that was his night-work, *W.*; it appears chiefly in chevilles.

TOR N-, tower, "Nennius," 240.
nemthór m-bodba, "C. M. Rath," 170.

NEUTOR, neutar, *g.* neutair, *Sg.* 206 a, 39 b, 90 b, the neuter.

LESTER, lestar n-, vessel, *d.* lestur, *Z.*; lestar n-, "Codex. S. Pauli," *W.*, *ap.* lestra, *W.*
fidlestar, vessel, "Man. & Cust." iii. 576, *W.*
tuslestar, *thuribulum*, *Sg.* 3 a.
laechlestar, a warrior's boat, *LB.* 215 b.
uirciléstraib, *dp.*, *hydris*, "Bk. of Hymn," ii. 154.
marlestar, large vessel.
minblestar, small vessel; *dp.* minblestraib, "Laws," iii. 192, ii. 366.
fidlestar, findlestar, "Man. & Cust." iii. 495.
soilestar, *gladiolum*, "Med. Tract on Celt. Declension."
mac-lestar, a second vessel, "Fragm. of Irish Ann." 26.

ASTAR (?), journey; *g.* astair, "Bk. of Fenagh," 366; "L. na gCeart," 153.

ALLTAR, the other world, yonder side, *W.*
altar (?), fosterage, *ap.* soaltar, *g.* comaltair, "Laws," i. 168, 190, ii. 160.
centar, this world, this side of the country, *W.*
echtar, *pars exterior*, *Z.*
anechtar, the outside; *g.* anectir, *Wb.* 10 a.
immechtar, imechtar, the outside, *Z.*; da n-imechtar, two extremities, "Fis Adam." *LU.* 28 b; .i. forcenn, "O'Dav." 97.
íchtar, the lower part; *ds.* íchtur, *Cr.* 33 c; Ascoli does not give the gender.

aLLtaR—*continued.*

uachtap, óchtep, óchtap, the upper part, top, cream; *gs.* ochtip, "Bk. of Armagh"; Ascoli does not give the gender; cream, "Laws," ii. 254; *d.* uachtup, "Irische Texte," i. 34.

caRachtaR N-, letter, *Z.* 228; c. n-aill, *Sg.* 4 a, 5 a, 6 b, 7 a, 7 b; *d.* cap(ach)tup, *Ml.* 34 a; *ap.* cápachtpa, *Sg.* 3 b, 9 a.

cechtaR n-ai alaill, each of them.

cuchtaR, kitchen, *neut.* (*Z.*), but *fem.* in *LB.* 218 b, "Laws," iii. 192, "L. na gCeart," 36.

mialtuR (?), bad fosterage, "Laws," ii. 164; cf. *p.* poaltap.

lathaR N- (láthap n-), lethap, a láthap; *d.* lathup; *ap.* lathap; *dispensatio, dispositio*, "S. na Rann," 143, *Ml.* 51 c, 42 c, 44 b, 103 d, 42 b, *Wb.* 5 c, *Sg.* 154 a, *Ml.* 91 d, *LL.* 203 a; eplláthap, gl. *dispensatio.*

lathaR N-, *temptatio*, seems *neut.*, *Z.*, *Wb.* 9 d.

lathaR N-, "S. na Rann," p. 143.

laitheR presence; eplathap, presence, *LB.* 251.

saithaR (páithap), paethap; *g.* páithip, labour, *Z.*; a pái-thap n-, *Wb.* 11 a; *Ml.* 24 d.

RuathaR N-, "Bk. of Balymote," 45 b, "Four Masters," i. 562, "Fragm. of Irish Ann." 198, "S. na Rann," pp. 148, 71, "Hyfiachrach," 182; *g.* puathaip, rout, career.

depgpuathap, *ap.* red or bloody rout, *LL.* 78 a, "C. M. Rath," 212.

echpuathaip, *gs.* horse-race, stampede, "S. Bodleian Cormac," 39; *dp.* puathpuib, incursions, "Laws," i. 226; piathop, *torrens*, is *masc.*, *Ml.* 134 b.

iNathaR, *pl.*, *viscera interiora*, *Z.* 781.

taRthaR, *terebra*, seems *neut.* *Z.*

aRathaR, ogn-apathap; *g.* apathaip, plough, ploughing, "Man. & Cust." i. 486, 479; "Fragm. Irish Ann." 16; *ap.* apathpa, "Bk. of Lismore," 45.

cuathaR, sieve, seems *neut.*, *Z.*; is not *neut.* in "C. Bern." 34 a.

ETHAR, boat, *Sg.* 35 a, seems *neut. Z.*, but *mnp.* ethair, "Four Masters," i. 354, and "Voyage of Snedgus."

CLITHAR (?), shelter, *as.* clithar, "Circ. of Ireland," 44, *LU.* 496.

LOTHOR (lóthor), lóathar, *pelvis, alveus, canalis*, seems *neut.*, *Z.*; *g.* lothair, "Four Masters," i. 198, *Cr.* 39 c, *Sg.* 676.

LOTHAR (?), *gs.* lothair, garment, "C. M. Rath," 186; *dp.* lothraib, *LL.* 274 b.

MOTHAR N-, mothar n-aidche, darkness of night, "O'Davoren," 105; darkness, "Four Masters," i. 562; mothor (?), mothor mara, *LL.* 135 b.

MOTHAR (?), stone fort in ruins (O'Donovan), a cluster of trees or bushes, "Joyce's Names of Places," i. 298; *dp.* mothraib, tufts (of beard), "C. M. Rath," 184.

OTHAR (?); *g.* othair, a wound, "L. na gCeart," 164.

OTHAR (?); *dp.* othraib, wages, "L. na gCeart," 134.

CATHAR MELA, a honey comb, (?).

PARTHAR (?), drink, .i. cuirm, "O'Donovan," 94.

SRATHAR (?), *stragulum*, seems *fem.*, *Sg.* 221; airther, east; *d.* airthiur, is *masc.* in *Sg.*; riathar, *torrens*, is *masc.*, *Ml.* 134 b; airer, *g.* oirir, *pl.* airera, seems *neut.*

CORRTHAR (?), fringe, "L. na gCeart," 154.

ILAR N-, *g.* ilair; *d.* ilur, multitude, many (of persons, animals, things), *Ml.* 48 c, 131 d; ilar n-, six times in p. 13 of "S. na Rann," not only in chevilles, but beginning of lines; in chevilles, p. 142, &c.; hilar neutair, the plural of the neuter, *Sg.* 39 b.

OENAR (óenar) (?), *d.* óinur, one (person), *Sg.* 215 b, "Siege of Howth," 60; triar, three (persons); *g.* triir, trír, "Man. & Cust." 519; "Maelduin's Cur." 490; *n.* triaur, "Laws," i. 288; *cf.* ilar n-, and *p.* noinbar.

cethrar, four (persons); the gender of ar group is *neut.* or *masc.*

cóicer, five (persons); cuicer, 5th generation, "Laws," ii. 152.

séiser, sésser, six (persons).

mórsésser, móirsesser, morfesser, seven (persons), *i. e.* a big seven.

oenar, etc.—*continued.*

ochtar, eight (persons); *g.* ochthair, "Man. & Cust." iii. 519.

nonbar, nonbur, noenbur, noenbor, nine (persons); *ap* trí noinbar, "Fragm. of Irish Ann." 218; nonboru, *W.*

dechnebar, deichnbor, ten (persons).

oirer, abundance.

forar (?), *gl. finis, Ml.* 56 b.

diror (?), *gl.* nasturtium, *W.*; *g.* dioraír, "Four Masters," i. 430.

comrar (?), casket (is *fem.* in "Four Masters," i. 360, ii. 600).

celtar (?), a cloak of disguise, *LU. Tain.*

celar (?), concealment, "Siab. Ch. C." 378.

murear (?), *g.* muirir, a good number, company, offspring, "Four Masters," ii. 968, "L. na gCeart," 158, 206, 266.

tasgur (?), a fleet, .i. coblach, "Four Masters," i. 124.

fogur, a fogur, the sound, *Sg.* 30 b, but a may be the pronoun "its."

crindar (?), *d.* crindur, a fall, falling, "O'Dav." 65.

accobor, an accobar, the desire, *Wb.* 3 d; *ap.* accobra, *Wb.* 30 c, *Ag.*; cobre domunde, wordly desire, *Wb.* 29 c., connected with this, and is, perhaps, feminine.

comaccobar, gl. *concupiscentia; g.* comaccobuir, *Wb.* 3 c. 13 d; a n-uile comaccobor, *W.* 11 c.

uabar (úabar) (?), uabar, obar, pride, *Z.*; *g.* úabair, *W.*, *incerti generis*, says *Z.*, but is not *fem.*

membur, memmur, *np.* membur, a member, *Z.*; *ap.* meamra, "Laws," ii. 278.

ambor (?), ammor, a bathing tub, font, *W.*, is, I think, *masc.* in Middle Irish; *np.* ommair, *LL.* 54 a.

combar, (?), combur, *g.* cumbir, "Bk. of Armagh," *Tl.* 164; confluence of water, is probably neuter, as is inber, inlet of water, with which it seems etymologically connected; see comair n-, *above*, p. 155; Duibchommuir, *LL.* 129 b.

inber n-, *ostium fluminis*, river-mouth, (river, in "C. R. na Ríg"; and "Laws," i. 122); *ns.* inbep n-, "Laws," i. 68, 70; "Táin Bó Fróich," 156; "Táin Bó Regamon," l. 10; "Bk. of Ballymote, " 408 a, 355 a; "O'Davoren's Glos." 62, 100; see other examples in *Preface;* an inbep, *Tl.* 448; *g.* inbip, "Laws," i. 122; inbbuip, "Cormac, 15; *d.* inbiup, "Nennius," 248, *Tl.* 34; *nap.* inbepa, "Bk. of Fenagh," 204, *Tl.* 150; *g.* Apbinbip, *LL.* 127 b.

indber (?), a spit, *LL.* 292 b; *g.* indbip, *Tl.* xxii., *LB.* 215 b.

aithber (?), imaithbep, reproach, *LB.* 111 b.

fobar (?), a fountain, spring, or flow of water, "Four Masters," iii. 23; *g.* fobuip, "Bk. of Armagh"; it means "a well" in "Hyfiachrach," 477.

robar (?), a great flow; robap fola, a flux of blood, "S. na Rann," p. 148; U-stem: *g.* roboptha, abundance, "O'Dav." 113.

adbar, cause, matter; *as.* an adbap, *materiam*, *Ml.* 138 c; ippeb adbap, *Ml.* 71 c; *g.* adbaip, *Ag.*, *np.* adbapa, *LL.* 218 b; it is *masc.* in *W.* and *Ag.* It is connected with inbep, combap, fobap, robap (?).

comadbur, materials, *W.*

deithbir n-, cause, reason, "Laws," ii. 138; it is an *adj.* used substantively; *cf.* in-deithbip, gl. *merito*, *Ml.* 47 b.

arbar (?), *g.* apbip, gl. *cohortis*, "Bk. of Armagh"; *d.* apbup, *cœtu*, *Ml.* 55 b, 121 c; *ap.* (?), apbap, *Ml.* 62 b; *dp.* apbpib, *Ml.* 63 c; apbup, *g.* apbuip, .i. slóg, "O'Dav." 50.

scibar (?), pepper, *Z.*

ribar (?), sieve, *Z.*; .i. cpíathap, "O'Dav." 115.

argetbor (?), "Bk. of Armagh"; *cf.* dechnbop.

doburbur (?), *ds.* "Bk. of Armagh."

duillebar (?), foliage.

clamar (?), satire, "Irish Metr. Glosses."

clochar (?), clochep, a stony place; *g.* clochip, clochuip, *d.* clochup, "Bk. of Armagh," *Tl.* 158, "Adamnan"; in "Adamnan" the Lat. *ns.* *Clocherum* reflects the Irish neuter; it seems a collective noun.

TOCHAR N- (tóchar n-), causeway; *g.* tochuir, "Bk. of Armagh"; tochar n-glonda, "Mac Gn. Find," p. 38, 2nd ed.

SALCHAR, a collection of filth (from salach), "Laws," ii. 160; *nda.* salchar, filth, *Ag.*

FINECHAR (fínechar) (?), relatives, a "fine" group.

CENDAR, group of heads, "Mesca Ul." 32: for cendar na nonbor.

NASCAR (?), bundle, .i. naidm.

DORAR N-, "Thurn. Versl." 33; but dorar, *d.* dorair, conflict, difference, is clearly *feminine.*

NEIMER (?), a stony place; *g.* neimir, "Four Masters," ii. 968, from nem, a stone.

BRUAR (brúar), breakage, fragments, "Fragm. of Irish Ann." 74.

BRISCBRUAR (briscbrúar), a heap of fragments, *LL.* 710 b.

BUAR (búar) (?), cattle; *g.* búair, "Fragm. of Irish Ann." 40, 74, 82; buar, .i. buinnech, "O'Dav." 61; *masc.* in "Diarm. 7 Grainne," *W.*

TUAR (túar) (?), manure, "Laws," 200.

MAGAR (?), *d.* magur, depth (of the sea), "Bodl. Cormac," 30.

AIRER (?), *d.* airiur, *ap.* airera, territory, "S. na Rann," p. 126; harbours, *LL.* 305.

COR n-delend, a cast of a spear, "Táin Bó Cualnge," and *LU.* "Toch. Emere."

COR N-, turn, circumstance, "Four Masters," ii. 612.

ACCUR (?), ease (?), *Wb.* 29 d; anaccor, difficulty.

IMMORCHOR n-delend, a carrying back, turning about, *LL.* 236 b, and *LU.* "Táin," "Táin Bó Cualnge," "Mesca Ul."; immarchor n-, "Man. & Cust." iii. 372; immarcor n-, voyage, "Bodl. Rawl." B. 512, fo. 57.

URCHOR N-, irchor, erchar, *g.* aurchir, a shot; urchor n-aigh, "Ch. of Lir," § 20; *d.* erchuraib, *telis*, *Ml.* 34 c; but *ap.* urchoru, "Gildas' Lorica."

CRANCHUR, *sortes*; *nap.* inna cranchur, *Ml.* 81, 37 d.

DECHOR, difference; dechor n-, *Sg.* 38 a, 41 b; arn-ed dechur, *Ml.* 24 d; a ndechur, *Wb.* 33 b, *Ml.* 114 a; dechur n-, *Ml.* 114 a; *dp.* ildechraib, *Ml.* 125 d; *gs.* dechuir, *Sg.* 212 a.

ᴅUChUR, ıꞅ eᴅ a nᴅuchuꞃ ꝼıl, *Ml.* 115 a.
ꝼORChOR, violence.
ꞇeRChOR, mishap, *LB.* 33.
aꞇhChUR, aꞇhchuıꞃ n-, a returning, "Laws," ii. 338.
ꞇaꞇhChOR, ꞇaꞇchoꞃ (?), return, removal; *asm.* ın ꞇaıᴅchuꞃ, *Ml.* 47 c; *g.* ꞇaıᴅchuıꞃ, *Ml.* 62 bc.
ꞇaChOR, combat.
ꞇROꞇChOR, combat, feat, *masc.* (?).
ꞇıNCOR, ꞇınchoꞃ (?), supply, furniture, *g.* ꞇıncaıꞃ, "Man. & Cust." iii. 499; *d.* ꞇıncuꞃ, "Laws," ii. 356.
aıReCUR n-aꞃaᴅ, meeting or combat of chariots, *LL.* 91; aıꞃcuꞃ, *pressura* (*Ml.* 38 d), is *masc.*
ꞇROCUR, *np.* "Laws," i. 280.
eCUR N-, putting in (of stock), "Laws," ii. 306.
SOChaR (?) revenue, *ds.*, "L. na gCeart," 96.
ROSSaR n-ᴅíꞃech, "Nennius," 244, direct narrative (?).
aeS, *g.* áıꞃ, aıꞅꞅ, age, aeꞅ n-eꞅcaı, "Nancy Gl."; comaeꞅ, *ap.* (?), *coetaneos*, *Wb.* 18 c; aeꞅ n-, folk, "G. Corca Laide," 12, 22.
eSS N-, vessel, "Second Battle of Moytura," p. 60.
OS, wild boar (*or* deer?); a n-oꞅ, "Irische Texte," i. 34; ᴅa n-oꞅꞅ, *LL.* 246 b; "Brocan's Hymn," l. 57; "De Chopur in da M." 245; *g.* oıꞅ, deer, "Laws," i. 272.
ꝼeSS, *nap.*, *scita*, *Cr.* 39 b; *Ml.* 73 b, 128 d.; *g.* ꝼıꞅꞅ (?), *Sg.* 2 a.
aNꝼıSS, *gs.*, ignorance, *Wb.* 13 b.
baS (báꞅ), báꞅꞅ, death, báꞅ n-, a mbáꞅ n-, *Z.*
combáꞅ, joint-death, *Wb.* 24 a.
eꞃnbáꞅ, *g.* eꞃnbáıꞅ, death by the sword, *LL.* 5 b; "Sanctan's Hymn."
ꞇıuᵹbáꞅ, final death, "Four Masters," i. 534.
ᴅLUS N-, closeness, "Man. and Cust." iii. 448; *LL.* 59 b, 60 a, *six times.*
ROS, *g.* ꞃuıꞅ, ꞃoıꞅ, flax, is not *masc.*, "Laws," ii. 368.
ROS, ꞃoꞅꞅ, wooded promontory: Roꞅꞅ n-, *LL.* 297 b, 297 b, 298 b; "Nennius," 258; "Bk. of Lismore," 1474; *gs.* ꞃuıꞅ, ꞃ̇uıꞅꞅ, "C. Ruis na Ríg"; *ap.* ꞃoꞅꞅa, *Tl.* 146; *LB.* 208 a; Iꞃ-ꞃuꞅ, *g.* Iꞃꞃaıꞅ, "Nennius," 248.
NOS (nóꞅ) (?), custom; *np.* nóꞅa, "Hymany," 62; *d.* nouꞅ, "Laws," i. 12.

ass (?), *g.* aırr, milk, *LU.* p. 256; "Táin Bó Fróich," 144.

cobas, *compages*, *Z.*; *Sg.* 2 b, "C. Ruis na Ríg, § 3, 34.

cambas (?), "Bk. of Armagh."

amus, *temptatio*; *np.* aımre, seems an S-stem.

INDas, ınnar, manner, kind; *Wb.* 33 c, *bis*; *g.* ınDír, ınnır, *Ml.* 36 a, 35 c; ırreD ınDar, *Ml.* 35 c.

auiss (?), *gs.* "Bk. of Armagh"; ırreD auırr, that is a dwelling, "Bodl. Cormac," 18.

buas m-, *gs.* "O'Conor's Rer.Hib. Script." i. pars 2, lvii.

soas N-, roar n-aırcheDaıl, "Cormac," 8.

eulas (?), *g.* eulaır; *d.* eulur, knowledge, *Ml.* 63 a, *Sg.* 209 b.

bernas (?), *gap*; *g.* bernaır, *d.* bernur, bernor "Bk. of Armagh," "L. na gCeart," 18, 38.

anfos (anfór) (?), restlessness, "Cormac," 1.

meDtos N-, *libripens*, *Sg.* 114 a.

urrathas, aurraDur, *np.*, "Laws," i. 260, 274, *passim*.

allas (?), sweat, "Paris' Eutychius."

eclas (?), galar n-eclır, *Wb.* 29 a; *cf.* eıgliDe, faint, "Coney's Dictionary."

aingcess, aıngcherr (?), anguish, *LB.*

eres N-, heresy, "Stowe Miss." 65 a.

eruus (?), a meeting, *LL.* 58 a.

arus (árur), dwelling; *g.* areır, araır, "Bk. of Armagh," "L. na gCeart"; *np.* aırıre (S-stem); *ap.* aırura, "Bodl. Cormac," 16; *np.* arura, "Cormac," 29; *d.* ır-arur, "Fragm. of Irish Ann." 142; *cf.* forur, "Laws," i. 298.

aros, *ap.*, *munilia*, &c., "Bk. of Armagh."

Dorus, Doror, door, *Z.*, *g.* Doruır, "S. Maelduin's Cur.," 488; *d.* Dorur, *Ml.* 131 c; *gp.* Dorur, "S. Voyage of Snedgus," 24; *ap.* torur, Doırre, Dorre, *Ml.* 98, *LL.* 114, "Siab-Ch. C.," 386; *np.* Dóırre, Dóırrea, *Z.*; *nagp.* Doırrea, *Ml.* 46 a; *voc. pl.* Doırrea, *Ml.* 98.

forDorur, lintel, *LU.* 105 b.

rtuagDorur, archway, "Tog. Trói." p. 139.

a n-ımDorur, *LU.* 112 a; "Táin Bó Flidais"; *np.* ımDoırrea, *claustra*, *Ml.* 92 d.

eross (?), *d.* erur, *puppis*, "Bk. of Armagh."

FORUS, *d.* forur, forar, *processu*, "Baeda Cr." 36, 6, *Wb.* 15 d; irred forur, "Yellow Bk. of Lecan," 217; "O'Dav." 93; *ap.* forur, *profectus*, *Ml.* 104 d; *gs.* foraır, *Ml.* 94 c, 131 c; *g.* béim forır, *Wb.* 9 c, 13 a, 11c, 25 c, 28 a; *Sg.* 13 a; forár (?), *nds.*, *profectus*, *proventus*, *propagatio*, *Wb.* 11 b, 18 c, *Ml.* 69 a.

FORUS N-, pen, pound, house; *g.* foruır, *ap.* forura, *dp.* forrıb, forruıb, "Laws," ii. 10, 10, 10, 116; i. 302, 292, 298, 266, 268; in "Fled Bricr." forur seems = a rest, or back seat of chariot; forur does not eclipse in "Laws," i. 292.

INTURAS, *ap.* *incursus*, *Ml.* 35 d.

MITHURUS (míthurur), *np.* mıthururra, unfortunate expeditions, *LU.* 111 a.

GRAN (grán), grain; *ap.* grán, *Sg.* 184 b.

LAN (lán): al lán, the whole, *LU.* 108 a.

SLAN N- (rlán n-), safety, security, "Laws," i. 230, 232, 246, 250, 281; *np.* rlána, sureties, "Fourth Charter of Bk. of Kells."

LOCHAN (lochán) (?), small lake, "Circ. of Ireland," 50.

AN (án) (?), drinking vessel; *pl.* ána, "Cormac"; ıan, a vessel, is *fem.*

CRIDECAN (crıdecán), little heart, "Carm. Paul.," is *neut.*, as crıde.

AISLEAN (aırleán) (?), *ds.*, *articulus*, *Ml.* 132 d.

TOEBAN (tóebán), little side.

MORAN (morán), much, many; beccán, a few, a little.

CRIDIN (crıdín), gl. *corculus*.

BIRIN (bırín), a dartlet, *LU.* "Táin Bó Cualnge."

ETHIN (*ap.* ?), *hederas*, or *baccar*, *Sg.* (diminutive of ıth ?).

MIAN N- (mían n-), desire; *Ml.* "Carm." 1.

TRIAN N- (trían n-), a third (part), "Laws," i. 272, 274; ii. 56, 362, 364; "O'Dav." 100; "Siege of Howth," 60; "Cog. G." 136; dá d-trían, "Keating & O'Donovan's Grammars," 372; "Cog. G." 204, 206; *g.* trín, "Four Masters," ii. 568, 1175; *d.* trıun, "Laws," ii. 252; "Broccan's Hymn"; but *ns.* ın trían, already in *LL.* 262 a; da d-trían, "Laws," ii. 156.

TRIAN—*continued.*

Duibthrían, *g.* Duibthrín, *d.* Duibthriun, Dufferin (Black Third), "L. na gCeart," 164, 168, 156.

leith triun, half a third, "Laws," ii. 390.

FUAN (fúan), *tunica*, *Z.*; fuan n-, *LU.* 106 a, "Táin Bó Fróich," "Ir. Metr. Gloss."

LOAN (lóan) (?), *adipem*, *Ml.* 39 d.

LIN N- (lín n-), *g.* lín, *rete*, *cassis*, *Wb.* 29 b, *Tur.* 46 b, *Sg.* 63 a; *np.* lína, *Ml.* 39 d; lín m-beind, *LU.* 102 a.

LIN (lín) (?), *g.* lín, flax, *W.*

LIN (lín), number, is *masc.*, *W.*, *Z.*, *Ascoli*; but I find lín n , *W.*; issed a lín, *Wb.* 12 c, *Cr.* 42 a, *Sg.* 30 a; and *np.* lína, "Laws," i. 194.

DIN N- (dín n-), protection, "S. na Rann," 65, 134.

IARN, ernn, *ap.* ernna, irons, implements, "Laws," i. 482, 486; *np.* erna, "Cormac," 14.

FEMUN, *ds.*, the feminine gender, *Sg.* 75 b.

LOMAN, *ap.*, *sphæras*, "Leyden Gl.," but is *fem.* in "Ascoli" and *W.*

IMBRESAN, *contentio*, *altercatio*, *d.* imbresun, imresun, *Wb.* 11 c, 30 c, *Ml.* 132 c; *np.* imbresna, *Wb.* 30 b, 29 b; *g.* imbresnae *as.* imresain, in *W.* is *fem.*

CRANN, *arbor*, a crand, forsa crand, "Bodl. Cormac," 324; *g.* cruinn, *d.* crunn, *Sg.* 65 a, is *masc.* in *Z.* 226, 1002, and *W.*; but a cocrann and *nap.* cranna, cammchranna, *trabes*, *Ml.* 37 b, 92 d, *Sg.* 189 a, "Bodl. Cormac," 24, *neuter*; it is *masc.* in *Ag.*: *np.* craind, *ap.* crannu.

CESADCRANN (césadcrann), cross, *LB.* 214 b.

LAMCHRAND, fore-pillar of harp, "Man. & Cust." iii. 358.

LOMCHRUND, *ds.*, *LU.* 111 a.

BASCRAND, a rattle, hand-clapping.

MURCHRANN, mast, "O'Dav." 106.

SEOLCHRAND, mast, "O'Dav." 106, "C. R. na Ríg."

OLACHRANN, olive tree, *Wb.* 5 b.

COCRANN, *sors*, a cocrann, *dp.* cocrannaib, *Ml.* 37 bd.

IALLACRAND, *np.*, sandals, "S. Maelduin's Cur." 65; but *npm.* iallacraind, "Man. & Cust." iii. 158; this is from iall-acrand; acrann is *fem.*, *Ml.* 56 b.

SLOND, *d.* slund, *significatio*, is perhaps *neut.* like tórand.

FOND, *np.* "Toch. Emere," l. 27, bottom, land (?).

TORAND (tórand), toorand, toorant, gl. *figura, significatio, definitio*, *g.* tóraind, *Sg.* 3 b; *d.* toorund, "Bk. of Armagh"; tórunt, torrund, *Z.*; *np.* tóranda, *Sg.* 4 a; *as.* tóirand, "Incant. Sg." *Sg.* 9 b.

FERAND, land, issed ferand, *LU.* 416; *nap.* feranna, *Ag.*, "C. M. Rath," 222, "Fragm. of Irish Ann." 154; ferann, *g.* ferainn, *ager*, *Wb.* 19 d; *d.* ferund, *W.*

INTINSCANN (?), beginning, a n-intinscann, *Sg.* 148 a.

ECHTRANN, a foreign thing; *np.* aechtranna, foreign things *or* parts, *Ml.* 28 c.

FOTHRAND (?), noise, "Fled Bricr."

TORAINN N-, "S. na Rann," 153.

OFFREND (?) offering, Mass, *g.* oiffrind, *d.* offriund, "MacCarthy's Stowe Missal," "Amra. Ch. C." § 10; Ascoli does not give the gender; Stokes and *Ag.* mark it *neuter*.

DILGEND (dílgend), dílgent n-, gl. *deletio, exterminatio*; *g.* díl-gint, dílgind; *d.* dilgiund, dilgiunn, *Ml.* 53 d, 64 r, 48 b, 33 c, 112 d; *Sg.* 52 a, 148 a. *Z.* 487 says it is *masc.*; *W.* does not give gender; but n- shows the *neuter*.

OGDILGEND (ógdílgend), *internecio*, *Sg.* 52 a, utter ruin.

LEGEND (légend) (?), a legend, *lectio*, *Ml.* 84 d; *Sg.* 59 b; *g.* légind, *Ml.* 31 a; *d.* legunn, *W.*

AIRLEGEND (airlégend), reading aloud, = German, *vor-lesen*.

SCRIBEND (?), *scriptio, scriptum*; a scribend, *Sg.* 119, 195 a; gebend, prison, a word of like termination, is *fem.*: *d.* gebind, *LL.* 5 b.

ATHSCRIBEND (?), rescription, re-writing, copying.

FORBANN, order, mandate, severity (of Jewish *or* Pagan law); *ap.* forbanda, *Z.*, *Wb.* 18 c, 21 c, 7 c; *g.* forbaind, *d.* forbunn, *Ag.*, but in forbann, *Tl.* 38.

nemforbann, "Lismore Lives," 396.

COMMANT N-, *professio*, *Ml.* 78 b d; *d.* commund, *conjuratio*, *Ml.* 44 d.

CAILEMENT, gl. *calamentum*; an cailement, "Stokes' Irish Materia Med." 228.

DIUMAND (?), *d.* diumund, contempt, "Laws," ii. 336.

TALLAND, *d.* tallond; *ap. deg-tallanda*, *Wb.* 12 a, 17 c, *Ml.* 69 c.

ECOMLONN (écomlonn) (?), battle, unequal fight; a n-écomlonn, "Táin Bó Reg."

CILORNN (?), *urceus*, *Sg.* 49 a; perhaps *fem.*, as lochann.

INUNN, an inunn, the same (thing), "Bed. Cr." 34.

CAINGEN n-gle, business, "S. na Rann," 129; a chevile, but *daf.* caingin, *Z.*; some of these chevilles may be *gp.* (?); *gs.* (?) caingne, "Cormac," 11.

CENN, head, end; a cenn, *ap.* cenna, *four times* in "Bodl. Cormac," 53; *Z.* makes cenn, *g.* cinn, *d.* ciunn, *masc.*, but he gives no mark of gender. The following compounds that end in cend here point to *neuter*; *np.* cind, *ap.* cinnu, of *W.* show *masc.* in Middle Irish; but *ap.* cenna, *LU.* 89 a.

AIRCHINN, airchind fore-head, front-end, front of house as opposed to cóib, side, in *Wb.* 21 c and "Laws"; da n-airchind "Laws," i. 274; it is wrongly rendered by *principium*, *Z.* 868; Mr. Stokes translates it correctly, and might have omitted the query. After "front" *Wb.* says, "As Jesus Christ is the corner-stone, side and front (cóib ⁊ airchinn) are contained in him," as a corner-stone unites at the corner two walls of a building. "Laws," i. 260, 274, fri da taeb ocus fri da n-airchind, on the two sides and on the two ends of his land, *i.e.* in fada ocus in gairid, in length and breadth. So airchind seems front and rear walls of a house, etc. Perhaps from air-chenn, fore-head, = façade, *frons ædium*, and also *posticum*, "the back *front*," as "Smith's Dictionary" renders *posticum*.

FORCENN (?), forcend; *g.* forcinn; *d.* forciunn, forcunn, end, *Ml.* 19 c, 56 d, 59 b; *Sg.* 148 a b, 188 a, 169 a, 203 b, but *nm.* in forcenn, forcan, *Ml.* 22 d, 89 c, 91 a; *Z.* does not mark gender; *W.* and *Ag.* mark it *masc.*, but yield no evidcnee thereof; *cf.* cenn and tarmorcenn.

TARMMORCENN N-, tarmmorchenn, *g.* tairmorcinn, *d.* tarmoirciunn, *ngp.* tarmmorcenn, end, *Sg.* 111 a, 62 a, 166 a, 33 a, 43 a; tarmforcend, "Thurn. Versl." 130; *np.* ré tarmmorcenn, *Sg.* 166 a; tarmmorcinn; *d.* tarmorciunn, *Sg.* 62 a, 33 a. Hence we may conclude that tarmforcend and forcend, *etc.*, are *neuter*, yet *apm.* tairmoirciu.

MUIRTCHEND (?), carrion, "Bodl. Cormac," 16; moirtchenn, gl. *subfocatis*, i.e. *morticinium*, "Bk. of Armagh."

SESCENN (?), sescend, *d.* sescunn, "Bk. of Armagh," a (dry) marsh, *dp.* seiscennib, "Fragm. of Irish Ann." 162.

ESCANN (?), a water-can, "Cormac," 18.

FOCHANN (?), cause: issead fochann an chatha, "Four Masters," i. 160; fochonn, fochunn, *occasio*, is not neuter in *Wb.* 26 b, 27: dus̃r indip fochunn ícce; *g.* fochuinn, *Ml.* 35 b; *nm.* isé f. in *Ag.*, *W.*

MIND n-óir, "Amra, Ch. C." 6, *LU.* 105 b, "Man. & Cust." iii. 160; a mind, gl. *diadema*, *insigne*, "Turin," 3, 96, *Ml.* 129 c; *np.* minda, "Bec Fola"; *np.* inna mind, gl. *insignia*, *Ml.* 18 d, *Wb.* 20 d, *Cr.* 41 c; *gp.* mind, "Four Masters," ii. 1158.

RIND, star; ar rind sin, gl. *vesper*, *Sg.* 70 b; *ap.* rind, rinn, gl. *signa*, *Ml.* 2 a, 145 d, "Bed. Cr." 18 b; *dp.* rendaib, *Cr.* 18 c, gl. *sideribus*; its *gen.* renda, *Sg.* 73 a, shows it to be also of the I-declension.

DA ERREND (da érrend) (*acc. Wb.* 20 d), *stigmata*; if neuter it should be dan-érrend.

RINN, *ap.* promontories, is of this declension, "Laws," i. 160, 270.

ASCLANG (?), load, *g.* asclaing, *LU.* 111 b.

FULANG (?), *d.* folung, fulach, *toleratio*, *Wb.* 17 c, 26 b.

LAIDENG (láideng), *np.* galleys, "C. R. na Ríg," § 8, seems *neuter*.

FOIMTHARRUṄG N-, putting off (of clothes), *LL.* 63 a, 65 a.

DRONG N- (*bis*), "S. na Rann," l. 6279.

TECMANG (?), *g.* tecming, *d.* tecmung, an event.

OG (óg), the whole of a thing; a n-uag, a n-og, "Félire," 200; da n-óg, *Sg.* 98 a.

SLUAG (slúag) (?), host; *ap.* slúag, "C. R. na Ríg," in old and modern versions; for the usual slúagu.

AIRTHICC (?), *gs.*; *d.* airthiuc, "Bk. of Armagh."

SETHNAGA (?), *ap.*, *toros*, *Cr.* 26 b.

AIREC (?), *inventio*, *g.*, airic, *d.* airiuc, *Sg.* 5 a, 5 b, 106 b, *Wb.* 3 d; perhaps *masc.* if aithirciu, gl. *argumenta* (*Ml.* 31 a), is its *ap.*, and if *argumenta* means *inventiones*. If so, fuirec seems also *masc.*

COMRAG N-, a meeting, "O'Dav." 65.

ᏏeC N-, bec n-étaig a little of clothing, *LB.* 215 a.

ATRAᏏ, aitreb, *Sg.* 38 b, *Wb.* 3 d; a atrab, a n-atrab sin, aitreb n-, *Wb.* 27 b, *Ml.* 17 b, *LB.* 276; *g.* atraib, *Sg.* 190 b, 209 b; *d.* atrub, *Ml.* 126 c, *Sg.* 198 b; dwelling, *possessio.*

bithaitreb, bithaittreb, "Lismore Lives Index," and "Félire."

comatrub, *ds.*, *cohabitatio*, *Ml.* 47 c.

síratrab, long residence, *Wb.* 3 d.

ᎠITHRAᏏ (díthrab), desert, *Ml.* 98 d; *d. neuter*, dithrub, *Z.*

TREᏏ (?), tribe; *d.* triub, *Ml.* 73 b; *ap.* triub, *Ml*, 101 c.

INTREᏏ N-, furniture, "Laws," i. 122; *g.* intreib, "Laws," ii. 358.

FOINTREᏏ, furniture, *Sg.* 113 a, *Tl.* 10.

TREᏏINTREIᏏ, *gs.*, house furniture, "Laws," ii. 358.

ᎠEINTRUᏏ, good furniture, *LU.* 99.

ᎠEᏏ M-, variation, *Ml.* 40 a.

INᎠEᏏ, *lucrum, stips, pecunia, quaestus, adquaesitio;* coror hed mo indeb, an indeb, *Wb.* 23 d, 28 c; *g.* indib, *Ml.* 125 d, 73 a; *d.* indiub, *Wb.* 10 d, 45 a.

FORGAᏏ, *d.* forgub, thrust, "Man. & Cust." iii. 507, also forgam.

ᎠUᏏ, ink; *ns.* a ndub, *Sg.* 248 b, *Ml.* 13; *d.* dub, *Wb.* 15 a.

drochdub, bad ink, *Sg.* 217.

dub, *g.* duib, *d.* dub, *fel*, *Cr.* 35 a, *Wb.* 15 a; "S. in Celt. Decl." p. 14, calls dub, ink, a U-stem; as this would involve a *gen.* duba or dubo, and as these words seem the *adj.* dub, *g.* duib, used substantively, they seem O-stems; Dub, the river, is *masc.*, "Ann Ult." an. 859, but *fem.* or *neut. ds.* Duib, *Tl.* 146.

CRUMᎠUᏏ (?), a dunghill, .i. otrach, crumduma, "O'Dav." 63.

FOᎠᏏ, *g.* fuidb, *ap.* fodba, spoils, *Ml.* 92 d; but *ap.* fodbu, *W.*; fodb, a felling axe, *LL.* 59 b.

FERᏏ (?), a word.

AM (ám), a n-ám, *g.* aim, *d.* am, hand, *manus*, *Ml.* 36 c, 33 d, 134 c, 134 d.

AM: a n-am, time, *W.* 632, col. 1.

ᎠAM ndartaide, an ox, "O'Clery."

ꞇoem (ꞇóem) n-ᵹlé.

ꞇolam (ꞇólam): a ꞇólam, gl. *diluvium.*

arm, weapon, *np.* aꞃm, aꞃma, *Sg.* 33 a, *Wb.* 22 d; *ap.* aꞃma, *Ml.* 55 c, *Sg.* 35 a, 33 a; *gs.* aıꞃm, *Sg.* 104 b.

ꞇorm (= ꞇuꞃma (?)); ꞇoꞃm n-ᵹle, "S. na Rann," "Bk. of Balymote," 374 a; ꝺın, "Fragm. of Irish Ann." 190.

ꝼorum N-, ꝼoꞃom n-, achievement, "C. M. Rath," 246, *LL.* 203 a, "S. na Rann," p. 139.

ꝼorꞇhrum N-, rustling, "C. M. Rath," 184; tumult, "Fragm. of Irish Ann." 190.

ꞇorruim N-, reckoning, "Laws," i. 288; may be S-stems.

aıream N-, a reckoning, "L. na gCeart," 74, 74.

ᵹaınem, sand: a nᵹaınem, *LU.* 26 a.

ꝺernum (?), *detrimentum*, *Wb.* 8 d; *i.e.* ꝺeꞃ-nom, great destruction; *cf.* "O'Reilly," *v.* nom.

membrumm (?), a membrane, *g.* membꞃuımm, *d.* memꞃum, *Z.*, "Cormac," 9, 10.

IV.—O-Stems *ending in* -ach.

Many of these conform to the S-declension and end in **-aige** *in nap.*, **-aigib** *in dp.*

cuach, *g.* cuaıch, *np.* cua(ı)che (cup), *LU.* 113 b, "Stokes' S-stems."

mıach m- (mı́ach m-), sack, "Man. & Cust." iii. 486; but *np.* méıch, *gs.* meıch, "Laws," ii. 238.

allbach m-, allbach mbꞃaꞇha, *LU.* 106 b; *cf.* all, prodigious, *O'R.*, all, .ı. oll, móꞃ, *O'Cl.*

ꝼalbach, row, file, *ap.* ꝼalbaıᵹı, *LU.* 80 b; palisade or rampart (?), *np.* ꝼalbaıᵹe, *O'Cl.*; *cf.* ꝼal, a hedge.

murbach, *g*, muꞃbaıᵹ, low land by the sea.

ꝼoꞇbach (ꝼóꞇbach), *np.* ꝼóꞇbaıᵹe, sods, *LL.* 59, 265; *g.* ꝼóꞇbaıᵹ, turf, turf-cutting, "Laws," i. 164, 166, *LL.* 97 ab, 97 b, 120 a. *Cf.* "Stokes' S-stems," and "Zimmer's Kelt. Stud." iii. 11.

ꝼıꝺbach, some kind of corn, *LB.* 219 a.

cRuaᴅbach (?), hardness, "C. R. na Ríg."

combach, combaᵹ, *fractio*; *g.* combuıᵹ; *d.* combuch, combuᵹ, *Ml.* 126 a, "MacCarthy's Stowe Missal," 250, 251; "Bk. of Armagh"; *ns.* a combach, "Stowe Missal," 250, 264.

tobach, cutting, levying, distraint; *g.* tobaıᵹ, "Laws," i. 276, L. na gCeart," 136, 184; *d.* tobuch, *LU.* 126 a, is *neuter* (like combach), from ᴅoboŋᵹaım.

uRthabach, levy, cess, *LB.* 259 a; *cf.* tobach.

athbach (?), attack (?), compulsion; moŋ n-athbach; *g.* athbaıᵹ, "S. na Rann," 127; *cf.* athboınᵹıᴅ, a compeller, *W.*

uRbach (?), defence, "L. na gCeart," 130; perhaps eŋbach of "S. na Rann," 68, is the same word.

fobach, digging, "O'Dav." 88, 91.

buanbach (?), buanḟach, *g.* buanbaıᵹ, buanḟaıᵹ, *LL.* 71 a, *LU.* 121 b, some game of chess. See "Zimmer's Kelt. Stud." iii. 79.

mainbech, deceit; a maınbech, am muınbech, *LU.* 102 a, 100 b; also written muınmech, *W.*; maın, .ı. cealᵹ, "O'Cl."

biaᴅbach (bíaᴅbach) (?), food, "O'Dav." 50.

miᴅbach (?), barley; *g.* mıᴅbaıᵹ, "O'Dav." 104.

taiᴅbech (?), breaking up, abrogation; *d.* taıᴅbıuch, "Laws," i. 18, 52.

apach, entrails, *ngp.* abaıġe, apaıᵹe; *d.* apaıᵹıb, "Stokes' S-stems."

toRmach n- (tóŋmach n-), a toŋmach (*g.* toŋmaıᵹ, toŋmıᵹ, "MacCarthy's Stowe Missal," 169), *auctio, augmentum, auxesis*, *d.* tóŋmuch, toŋmuᵹ, *Z.*, *Ml.* 83 b, 97 c; *Sg.* 77 b; *Z.* was uncertain of gender, but n- and a, and *ap.* foŋtóŋmach, show *neuter*.

foŋtóŋmach, addition; *Sg.* 212 b; *g.* foŋtóŋmaıch; *ap.* foŋtoŋmach, *Ml.* 88 b, *Sg.* 221 b, 202 b, a.

ımthóŋmach, augment, increase, *LB.* 251, "Laws," i. 24; *dp.* ımthoŋmaıᵹıb, *LU.* 101 a.

mıthoŋmach, *decrementum*, "Med. Tract. on Celt. Decl." 28.

taiᴅmech (?), taıthmech, unloosing, explanation, analysis, *W.*; see taıᴅbech.

soinmech, *ap. proventus*, *Ml.* 81 b; adjective used substantively.

ᴅoınmech, *ap.* ᴅoınmecha; *gl. adversa*, *Ml.* 19 d.

ᴅoacaıᴅmach, *np.* ᴅoaccalᴅmacha, appellatives, *Sg.* 29 b.

ᴅrolmach (?), ᴅrolbach, vat; but *dsf.* ᴅrolmaıᵹ, *LL.* 34 a, is a crook; *nap.* ᴅrolmacha, handles of a drinking horn, "L. na gCeart," 158; *cf.* ᴅrol, .ı. lúb, hook, "O'Cl."

cumᴅach, cumthach, cumtach, covering, *Z.*, *ædificatio:* ıffeᴅ a c., *Sg.* 209 b; *np.* cumtach, *Ml.* 84 a; *ap.* cumthaıᵹe, *dp.* cumtaıᵹıb, *LB.* 73 a, 21ba, *LL.* 304 a, *LU.* 99.

aᴅchumtach, aıᴅchumtach, athchumtach, *instauratio*, *Wb.* 26 a, *Ml.* 135 a.

arcumᴅach, ornaments, *LB.* 209 b.

tlaıthcumtach, *g.* tlaıthcumtaıᵹ, "S. na Rann," p. 16.

etach (étach), garment, *Z.*; éıtach, *Wb.* 29 a, 27 b; *ns.* a n-étag, a n-étach, "S. Bodl. Cormac," 4; *g.* aetıᵹ, *Wb.* 12 b, *Ml.* 144 c; *np.* étaıᵹe, *W.*, *LL.* 97 b; *gap.* eᴅaıᵹe, "Laws," ii. 148, 146; *dp.* étaıᵹıb, *gp.* étach, "L. na gCeart," 266, 176.

ᵹerrétach, short dress, *LB.* 215 b.

tımthach, *np.* tımthaıᵹe, *dp.* tımthaıᵹıb, garments, trappings, "Tog. Trói," l. 596, "S. Bodl. Cormac," 32, .ı. éᴅach, "O'Dav." 119; *d.* tımthuᵹ, accompaniments, "Man. & Cust." iii. 484.

atach N-, a n-atach, *g.* ataıᵹ, *d.* atuch, *refugium, effugium*, *Ml.* 66 d, 40 b, 49 d, 54 b, 107 d, 121 c.

atach, prayer; ıffeᴅ attach, "Bk. of Hymns," ii. 123, *g.* attaıᵹ, *LL.* 280.

fuaᴅach N-, carrying off, "Laws," ii. 124, 266.

ertach, errᴅach, ıartach, ırtach, aurᴅach, *refectio*, feast; *ns.* a n-ertach, *Ml.* 121 b, *g.* ertaıᵹ, *Ml.* 118 c, *d.* erᴅᴅuch, "S. na Rann," p. 137; *np.* erᴅaıᵹe, *LB.* 73 a, 169 a, *LU.* 73 b.

anaurthaıᵹ, anerᴅaıᵹ, *gs.* great festival, "Félire," 194.

urthach, oath; a n-urthach, "Laws," i. 180.

ıartach (íartach), sequel, *np.* íartaıᵹe, mı-ıartaıᵹe, *LB.* 211 a; íarᴅaıᵹe, remnants, "Laws," ii. 282.

ecnᴅach (écnᴅach), écnᴅaᵹ, slander, *injuria*, *Wb.* 30 c, 1 c, *Ml.* 93 a; *ds.* écnᴅuch, *Ml.* 72 b, 29 a, *Wb.* 11 c; ecnᴅuᵹ, "Bodl. Cormac," 12; *np.* écnaıᵹe, *LB.* 111 a, 211 b.

preiteach N-, renunciation, "Four Masters," ii. 618; frecech, answer, *W.*; guarantee, atonement, "Laws," i. 62, 296.

andach (?), *d.* anduch, *malitia*, *Ml.* 134 d, .i. ferg, "O'Dav." 50; *g.* andig; *d.* andug, *Z.*

budech: a mbudech, *officium*, *Ml.* 73 a.

intech, *d.* intiuch, scabbard, *Z.*; *dp.* intigib, "Tog. Trói," l. 1716.

intech (?), *d.* intiuch (a day's) journey, *Ml.* 140 a.

diuthach (?), fraying of thighs in walking, "Cormac," 14.

etradach (étradach) (?), *prostibulum*, *Sg.* 53 a.

tarcadach: a t., the relative, *Sg.* 197 a.

aitrebthach, the possessive, *Sg.* 32; but lechdach, a liquid, is *fem.*, *Sg.* 5 a.

errethech (érrethech), érredech, *np.* érrethcha, érredcha, *redditiva*, *Sg.* 27 a.

deainmnechtach, deainmnechtech, the denominative, *Sg.* 2 b, 29 b.

erthuaiscertach, *euro-aquilo* ("Bk. of Armagh"), iarthuaiscerdach, gl. *etesiarum*, *Z.*; ichtardescardach, lower right-hand portion, íchtarthuaiscerdach, lower left-hand portion, "Mac Carthy's Stowe Missal," 257.

cathach, trespass, *pl.* caithche, "Stokes' S-stems," p. 9.

ethech (?), *g.* ethig, perjury.

etiuch, *ds.* refusal, "Man. & Cust." iii. 569.

fothach (?), *d.* fothug, attack, "Amra Ch. C." § 5.

sidach (sídach), elf, *pl.* sídaige, *W.* (hill fairies), *LU.* 50 a; *gp.* bansídaige, banshees, *LL.* 23b.

fidach (?), brushwood, *g.* fidaig, "Lismore Lives Index."

lathach (láthach), puddle; *W.* does not state gender; *np.* lathach, "Irische Texte," i. 190; *d.* lathach, "Topogr. Poems," 72; it is *fem. da.* lathaig in "Charters of Bk. of Kells," "Four Masters," iii. 244.

belach, pass, *compitum*; *g.* belaig, *Tl.* 46; *np.* beilge, "Cog. G." 116; *ap.* belgi, *LB.* 206 b; *ds.* beluch, *dp.* belgib, *LU.* 39 a, *LL.* 93 a.

ᵹenelach, generation, pedigree, *as.* ᵹenelach, *Ag.*; *np.* ᵹenelaiᵹe, "Laws," i. 44, 156, ii. 160, *LL.* 230 b; but *np.* ᵹenelaich, *LL.* 144 b.

mullach, top, crown of head; a mullach, a mullaᵹ, "Bodl. Cormac," 3, 4, 14, 40; *d.* mulluch, *W.*, *Ml.* 58 c; *np.* mullaiᵹe, "Stokes"; *Ag.* is right in calling it *neuter*; *W.*, and "Nigra's Glossæ," 68, do not determine the gender.

cennmullach, *d.* cenꝺmulluch, head-top, *LB.* 218 b.

pirmullaᵹ (ṗírmullaᵹ), the very top, "Bodl. Cormac," 40.

ellach (?), *unio, junctio*, *g.* ellaiᵹ, *d.* elluᵹ, elluch, *Z.* 660; ic ellach ocuꞅ ic tinól, *LB.* 208 a; *cf.* immellaiᵹe; iꞅ cuma ellaċ ⁊ tellaċ, "O'Dav." 82.

immellach, *np.* immellaiᵹe, out-houses, out-works, adjoining houses (?), "C. R. na Ríg."

ollach, enlargement, *np.* ollıᵹe; *cf.* ollaiᵹim, *amplio.*

brollach, bosom, *as.* bꞃollach; *d.* bꞃolluch, *dp.* bꞃollaiᵹib, "Stokes' S-stems."

connlach (?), stubble, from connall, gl. *stipula.*

tenlach, fire-place, hearth, *Tl.* 14; *g.* tenlaiᵹ, *d.* tenluᵹ, "Laws," iii. 190, *LU.* 19 b, "Mesca Ul." 50, *W.*; tenlach, gl. *tolletum*, *Sg.* 36 b, points to a *neuter*, and so it must be, like tellach.

tellach, fire-place; a tellach, *Tl.* 14; *g.* tellaiᵹ; *a.* tellach; *np.* tellaiᵹe, *W.* *ap.* tellaiᵹi, "Bk. of Fenagh," 158, show *neuter*.

tellach, household, race, people, = teᵹlach, the hearth, for the people of the "hearths and homes"; Tellach (nᵹoꞃmᵹaile, n-Oꝺꞃain, &c., mꝺꞃaonain, mbꞃeaᵹꝺa, mꝺꞃaonain). "Bk. of Fenagh," 384, "Hy Maine," 24, "O'Dugan's Typogr. Poem," 24; tellach mꝺꞃuinain, "Cambrensis Eversus," i. 242; O, ꞅíl, clann, cinel, mac, muinteꞃ, tellach, *vel quid cognatæ significationis familiarum satoribus adjici solet tum ad familias, tum ad terras ab iis insessas denotandas*, "Ogygia," p. 361; *np.* tellaiᵹi, ꞅꞃímtellaiᵹi, septs, "G. Corca Laide," 28.

bantellach (?), *g.* bantellaiᵹ, taking possession of property by women, "Laws," i. 14 b, 148, may be a comp. of tellach.

ᴛellach—*continued.*

ᴛeᵹlach, family, household (house-load) (?), *familia, familiares*, *g.* ᴛeᵹliᵹ; *d.* ᴛeᵹluᵹ, *Z.*; *d.* ᴛeᵹluch, *LU.* 112 b; a ᴛeᵹlach n-, *LU.* 107 a, "Táin Bó Fróich," *W.*; *np.* ᴛeᵹlaiᵹe, "Ir. Texte," i. 96; *gp.* ᴛeᵹlach, "Four Masters," ii. 652. Zimmer, in "Kelt. Studien," ii. 25, makes it *masc.*, perhaps wrongly.

ppímᴛheᵹlach, chief household; *g.* ppímᴛheᵹlaiᵹ, "Cog. G." 70; pialLaiᵹe, *np.*, troops (= pianlaiᵹe ?), "Ann. Ulster," 817.

luchᴛlach, load (of boat, pot, gridiron), hence crew, &c. *Z.* 855 translates anachᴛ Nóe a luchᴛlach, *servavit Noe et ejus familiam*; but literally it means, Noah saved his boat-load; by supplying ip, "and," the metre and sense are preserved, and we read, *Rex regum, qui servavit Noe et* (*Arcæ*) *onus*, i.e. *vectores*. Ippeᴅ ba luchᴛlach, a luchᴛlach, *LL.* col. 777, "Siab. Ch. C." 388, "Colman's Hymn," l. 22; *dp.* luchᴛlaiᵹib, "Tog. Trói," p. 138: *cf.* luchᴛ, what is cooking on a gridiron, "Bodl. Cormac," 30.

marcᴛlach, horse-load, *dp.* mapᴄᴛlaiᵹib, "Lismore Lives," 47, *W.*

uᴛlach, lapful; *g.* uᴛlaiᵹ, *Tl.* 10; *np.* uᴛlaiᵹe, uᴛlaiᵹi, Stokes' "Irish Ordeals," 226.

urᴛlach, lapful; *np.* upᴛlaiᵹe, "Félire," p. 32.

ᵹoiᴛhlach (ᵹóiᴛhlach), ᵹáeᴛhlach, marsh, *palus*, *Z.*; *d.* ᵹóiᴛhluch, *Ml.* 33 c; *cf.* ᵹóiᴛhlachᴅe, *paluster*, *Sg.* 54 b; *np.* ᵹáeᴛhlaiᵹe, *Palus Mæotica*, *Z.*, "Tog. Trói," p. 138; *gp.* ᵹaeᴛhlaiᵹi, "C. Findtragha," 1; *dp.* ᵹaeᴛhlaiᵹib, "Nennius," 236, "O'Conor's Rer. Hib. Script." i. pars 2, xxxv.; *LB.* 227 b; *cf.* ᵹaeᴛh, a stream.

airᵹeᴛlach (?), *g.* aipᵹeᴛlaiᵹ, silver-mine, "Laws," i. 166, 170.

ceᴛlach n- (?), "S. na Rann," 73.

maslach (?), dung, "Laws," ii. 200, *cf.* ochᴛpach.

brochlach (?), a cooking place; *cf.* ᴛenlach.

broᴛlach (?), *pl.* bpoᴛliᵹi (?), *vestimenta*, "Zimmer's Glossæ Hib." 218.

caᴛlach (?), caᴛhlach, *universitas*, is *fem.*, *Wb.* 7 c, 33, 44; is *masc.* according to Zimmer in "Kelt. Studien," ii. 25.

cobLach, fleet; *g.* coblaig, "L. na gCeart," 170, "Tog. Trói," 138; *d.* cobluch, *Tl.* 66; *dp.* coblaigib, "Four Masters," i. 564.

murchoblach, sea-fleet; *dp.* murchoblaigib, *Tl.* 206.

cobLach; *dp.* coblaigib, tackling (of a harp), "Amra Ch. C.," § 1.

ORDLaCh, inch; *np.* orlaige, "Laws," iii. 334, ordlaige, *W.*

INDLaCh: a n-indlech, *gl. interreptione, corruptionem, Ml.* 32 a, 64 a; *g.* indluig, "Bk. of Fermoy," 26 a.

TaIDLeCh, tindlech, *satisfactio:* a taidlech; *g.* taidlich; *d.* taidliuch, *Ml.* 23 a, 32 a; taithlech, peace, quiet, "Félire"; bright, *Ag.*

cáintaidlech: a cáintaidlech, *satisfactio; d.* cáintaidliuch, *Ml.* 32 a, b.

aSLaCh, *persuasio, seductio, suggestus, deceptio; d.* asluch, aslug; *ap.* aslach, *Ml.* 141 d, 26 c, 109 b, *Wb.* 30 c.; *ap.* aslaige, "Félire," 194; *dp.* aslaigib, "St. Patrick's Lorica," *Tl.* 50.

CRaISLaCh, crislach, girdle, border; *d.* crisluch, womb, cavity, "S. na Rann," 134; *np.* crislaige; *dp.* crislaigib, "Tog. Trói," l. 1659 and Index.

CRaeSLaCh, maw; *d.* craesluch, "S. na Rann," 132.

mImaSLaCh (mímaslach) (?), *gl. cardo.*

PUaLaSCaCh, *vitulamen, arbustum; g.* poalascich, "Bk. of Armagh"; *np.* púaláscach, *Ml.* 48 c, "Southampton Psalter," 58 a; *ap.* pualascacha, "Bk. of Hymns," i. 231; *dp.* pualascachaib, *Ml.* 48 c; but *nm.* in pualascach, *Sg.* 65 a.

maThaRLaCh (?), matrix, *Sg.* 69 a.

COILaCh (cóilach) (?), cailach; *g.* cóelig, *LL.* 198 a, *LB.* 238 a.; *d.* caeluch, rods, "Lismore Lives," 47.

ImbLeCh N-, border, "Táin Bó Dartada," 205; *d.* imbliuch, "Bk. of Armagh"; imliuch, *Tl.* 68,152; the *g.* imlecho, imlecha, of "Ann. of Ulster," years 533, 687, 736, show a U-stem.

aILeCh (?), *g.* Ailich; *d.* Ailiuch, *Tl.* 152, 80, "Circ. of Ireland," 24, 54, "Four Masters," an. 1094.

LUgaCh m-: lugach mbeg, little finger, *O'Cl.*

NeCh, *g.* neich, *Wb.* 26 b; *nap.* neiche; something; *pl.* neiche, "Laws," i. 66, 268" iii. 180.

ainech, einech, honour, *g.* éinich, "Táin Bó Flid." l. 10, *LL.* 247.

enech, front, face, *ap.*, *Ml.* 100 b.

airenach, forefront, *d.* airenuch, "MS. Mater." 506, "Tog. Trói," p. 138; *g.* airinig, *np.* airinigi, "Stokes' S-stems"; but *np.* airinich, airinig, *LU.* 107 a.

dedenach (déidenach), the last.

enach n- (énach n-), a swamp, *see* Preface; *d.* enuch, *Tl.* 184; éanach n-dubáin, "Hyfiachrach," 284; *g.* eanaig, "Topogr. Poems," 26; *g.* enaig, *pl.* enaige, fen, pond, way, "O'Don. Supplement"; enach n-, "Hyfiachrach," 282.

oinach (óinach), oenach, a fair; *agon regale*, "Bk. of Armagh"; ferthair an óenach, *LU.* 43, "Sick Bed of Cuch."; issed oenach, "Man. & Cust." iii. 538; *ns.* aenach m-, "L. na gCeart," 86, 90, 227; *np.* oenaige, "Man. & Cust." iii. 542, "Laws," iii. 346, "Scél na Fírflatha" of Stokes, p. 185, "Fair of Carman, p. 542; óenach n-uirc tréith, "Bodl. Cormac," 26.

immedonach (immedónach), the intestine.

tegnach: a tegnach, *LU.* 107 a.

imnach n-, garment, "Bodl. Cormac," 32, 33.

domnach, a church, Sunday; D. n-Airne, and *np.* domnaige, *Tl.* 250, 138, *LB.* 47 a; *d.* domnuch, and *dp.* domnachaib, *LU.* p. 25 b, domnaigib, "Amra Ch. C." § 6, "Fragm. of Irish Ann." 184; *d.* domnuch, "Bk. of Armagh"; *g.* domnich, *d.* domnuch, Sunday, *Wb.* 14 a, *Ml.* 45 d, *Tl.* 124.

fendomnach, "Bk. of Armagh."

muinnech, deceit; a muinnech, *LU.* 101 b, for muinbech, *qv.*

cennach (?), *np.* cennaige, coffins, "Bk. of Fenagh," 200.

cennach n-, "S. na Rann, p. 52; cendach ndaim, "Bk. of Balymote, 298 ab.

sondach, sonnach, palisade of wood or iron over a múr; *ns.* arsondach, "Fled Bricr."; *np.* sonnaige, sondaige, fences, "Maelduin's Cur." 480; but *masc.* "Siab. Ch. C." 386.

echainiuch (?), *d.*, "Bk. of Armagh."

annach (?), wickedness, *LB.*, *d.* anduch, *Ml.* 48.

uisniuch (?), *ds.*, "Bk. of Armagh."

mianach (?), mine, metal, *g.* mianaig, "Cormac," 36.

caichach n- (cáichach n-), trespass, "Laws," iv. 96.

ASNACH (?), *ds.*, gl. *costas*, or *ap.* donarnach, "Gildas' Lorica."

CRINACH (crínach) (?), firewood, withered wood, *g.* crínaig, *Tl.* 10, 12, "Cormac," 20, *as.* crínach, *W.*

DIUNNACH N-, "Cormac," 20, washing (?).

EMNACH (émnach) (?), *dp.* émnaigib, twins, *LB.* 219 a, "Cormac," 17.

TAMNACH (?), *d.* tamnuch, *Tl.* 98.

TRACH N-, Trach mbendchuir, *litus*; it has same meaning as tracht, the *apm.* of which is trachtu, *Ml.* 121 a.

OTRACH, othrach, ochtrach, *stercus*; *g.* ottraig, *LB.* 218 b; "Cormac," 13; *d.* otruch, *LU.* 103 a, 111 a; *np.* ochtarche, *Wb.* 9 a, *Ml.* 129 c; *ap.* ochtrach, *Ml.* 129 c; *dp.* otraigib, "Stokes' S-stems," othraigib, *Ag.*; maelochtrach (*nomen viri*), in "Fragm. of Ir. Ann.," is no doubt *masc.*

AURDDRACH, phantom: *pl.* aurdraige; *dp.* aurdraigib, "Stokes' S-stems."

INDRACH N-, .i. eric, "O'Dav." 97.

TUDRACH (?), *irritamen*, *Sg.* 54 a, *as.*

TOIDRECH (?), daybreak; *d.* toidriuch, "Laws," i. 66.

FITHRACH (?), .i. duilesc, "O'Dav." 94.

LUTHRACH (lúthrach), bolt; *ap.* lúthraigi, *Ag.* and "Stokes' S-stems."

LATHRACH (láthrach) (?), a site; *g.* láthraich, "Four Masters," an. 788; *n.* láthrach; *d.* láthruch, "Bk. of Armagh"; *as.* láthrach, "Félire"; "O'Donovan's Suppl." makes it *fem.*, and *asf.* lathraig, *LL.* 305 a; but the *g.* is laithrig in "Four Masters," i. 856.

BROTHRACH (?), a spear of some kind; *nap.* brothraige, *Tl.* 72.

BROTHRACH (?), rug, *LL.* 258 b; *dp.* brothrachaib, *W.*, it is *fem.*

ARTHRACH (?), *dp.* arthragaib, ships, "C. M. Lena," 44.

SCIATHRACH (sciathrach), shield strap, *LU.* 129 *W.*, "C. R. na Ríg."

CUIMRECH, *vinculum*, bond, fetter; *d.* cuimriuch, *Z.*; *ap.* cuimrega, cuimrecha, *dp.* cuimrigib, *Wb.* 1 d, 27 c, 23 a, 23 b, 26 c; *g.* cuimbrig, *Ag.*; *g.* cumrig, "Félire Index," where it is styled *masc.* and *neuter*.

cuimrech—*continued.*

cúibrech, fetter; *g.* cuibrig, *d.* cuibriuch; *nap.* cúibrige, *Ag.*, where it is styled *masc.*; *gp.* cuibrech, "Félire."

au-chumriuch n-, ear-tie, ear-ring, *LU.* 64 b.

cainchumrech; *g.* cáinchumrig, *Wb.* 7 b, is perhaps for cáinchomracc.

rárchuimrech, over-fettering, "Laws," i. 168, 174.

glomrach, bridle-bit; *np.* glomraige, "Stokes"; *ap.* glomraige, *LB.* 232 b; *d.* glomraigib, *LL.* 110 a; *cf.* glomar, muzzle, curb, *W.*

tulrech (?), face, *das.*, "Laws," i. 66.

cuindrech, *correctio, castigatio, severitas; d.* cuindriuch, cuindriug, *Ml.* 22 c, 49 b, 114 d; *Wb.* 11 d, 19 c; *Ag.* makes it *masc.* without support from the texts, *W.* and *Ascoli* do not give the gender; but the *neuter* seems clear in á cuindrech, *Ml.*, gl. *castigatio;* if it were his or its (i.e. *peccati*), it would be a chuindrech; *g.* cundrig, cunnrig, *d.* cundriug, "Man. & Cust." iii. 502, 503; *g.* cuindrig, "Four Masters," ii. 602. This and arach are connected with adriug, atomriug.

arach, *g.* araig, tying *or* spancelling (of a cow), "Laws," iii. 228; árach, security, *Ag.*

buarach, cow-spancel; *dp.* buairgib, "C. M. Rath," 297, 316.

con-arach, a dog's chain *or* leash, *LL.* 63 b.

aurrach, levies, *np.*, "Man. & Cust." iii. 507.

cosrach (?), fetter (*O'R.*), for cos-arach (?); *cf.* glomrach, *etc.*; perhaps *dp.* cosraigib, of "Stokes' S-stems."

burach (búrach) (?), anger, prowess; *as.* a mbúrach, "Siege of Howth," 56; burach m-buaid, "Bk. of Lecan," 244; *d.* burach teneð, fury of fire, "Laws," i. 98, 166; it is *fem.* in "C. R. na Ríg."

buirech N-, "O'Dav." 99.

fuirech (?), fuirec, feast, ale, .i. cuirm, "O'Dav." 85, 91.

spuirech, (?), *fragmentum*, "Med. Tract on Ir. Declension," 23.

curach, boat; a curach, "Maelduin's Cur." 462.

curech (?); *g.* Curig, the Curragh, *LL.* 47 a.

errach (?), *g.* erraig, *d.* erroch, *W.*; errug, *Cr.* 87 a.

aithrech (?), *mutatio, Ml.* 98 d.

AITHIRRECH, return, repetition; a n-aitherrech sin, *Ml.* 94 a; *d.* aithirriuch, *Z.*; oitherroch, "Bk. of Armagh."

AITHIRRECH, *emendatio;* d. aithirriuch, *Ml.* 98 b, 22 d, seems the same as the preceding word; *cf.* adreig, *mutat*, *Wb.* 13 a.

DIRECH N- (dírech n-), fine, "Man. & Cust." iii. 489.

DIRECH N-, stripping, .i. nochta, "O'Dav." 72.

lándirech (?), full stripping, "Mac Carthy's Stowe Missal."

lethdirech (?), half-uncovering, *ibi.*; these seem connected with ní dérgamar, *non destituimur*, *Wb.* 15 b.

TOSSACH, tosach, beginning; is ed tosach, *Ml.* 27 d; *d.* tosug, tossuch, tossoch, *Z.*; tosuch, "Bk. of Armagh"; *Z.* marks it *neut.*

fortosach, beginning, "Fragm. of Irish Ann." 210; *cf.* for-thósmach.

FASACH (fásach), desert; *d.* fásach; *dp.* fásaigib, *LU.* 118 b; *ap.* fásaige, *LB.* 218 a.

FASACH (fásach), maxim (of law); *dp.* fasagaib, "Laws," i. 18, 228; *Tl.* 566; maxims, precedents, commentaries.

FALTACH, shed, *dp.* faltaigib, *LL.* 264 b.

V.—IO-Stems, *called* IA-Stems *by Windisch.*

IO-*Stems are masculine or neuter; the marks by which the neuters may be identified are stated in the Preface.*

DIBE (díbe), gl. *extinctio; cf.* bethi, gl. *feriendi*, *Ml.* 114 d; díbe, a refusal, *LL.* 188 b.

imdibe, *circumcisio;* an-imdibe, -i, -u, *Wb.* 2 a, 23 d.

nebimdibe, non-circumcision, *Wb.* 18 d.

clar-imdibe, *interfectio.*

etarimdíbe, eterimdibe, itirimdibe, *interfectio*, *Z.*; "O'Dav." 90.

etirbe, etarba, misfortune, "L. na gCeart," 20.

eterdibe, etardibe, *interitus; cf.* etirudib, *interemit*, *Ml.* 123 b.

dimdibu, *ds.*, circumcision, *Wb.* 10 a.

timdibe, gl. *deminutio*, ruin, "Fragm. of Irish Ann." 100; "Bk. of Fenagh," 246; curtailment, "Four Masters," ii. 614.

aiRDbe N-, apDbe, *interfectio, interceptio, internecio;* cutting, "Laws," i. 236, 230; ii. 252; *LL.* p. 70; *d.* apDbiu, aipDbiu, *Ml.* 14 a, 55 b, 80 b, 100; *g.* aipDbi, *Ml.* 41 c; ilapDbe, "Irische Texte," i. 60.

ecapaipDbe, *internecionem, perimere, Ml.* 123 b.

poipcbe, gl. *vastatio, Z.*; "Four Masters," i. 110.

aicbbe, (*maris*) *recessus, remeatus; d.* aichbiu, *Ml.* 34 c; "Bed. Cr." 34 c; aichpe, "G. Corca Laide," 348; cpénaichbe, *LL.* 129 b, strong ebb *or* cutting off.

eipe, eibe, epe, cutting, violation (of law), *ndas.*, "Laws," i. 282, 162, 260; ii. 140.

caipe, cepe, *excisio, concisio, επιτομη, Ml.* 14 d, 37 a; ceipi, cutting, "Laws," i. 202; aDbul-ceipe, "Laws," i. 202.

cobe (cóbe), cobe, cobae, *decisio, præcisio, incisio, Wb.* 2; *Ml.* 26 c; *d.* cóbu, *Wb.* 5 b; *Ml.* 37 d.

Damchóbae, gl. *βουταμων, Sg.* 68 b.

coipccobe, circumcision, *Wb.* 23 d.

nebchobe, nepchobe, nepchóbe, gl. *praeputium, Wb.* 1 d, 2 c.

achaubae (?), death, "Cormac," 4.

Diubae, *g.* Diubai, *d.* Diubu, cutting, digging, "Laws," i. 162, 202.

cuba n-, attack (by an army), "Laws," i. 298; digging, O'Dav." 119; accusing, *Ag.* and "O'Don. Suppl."

cuba n- ainme, giving a bad name, "Laws," i. 240.

pubae, *succisio, vitiatio* (vine-cutting), *Sg.* 26 a; *d.* pubu (attack and defence), "Laws," i. 230; ii. 270, 276; *np.* puba, *ibi.*, i. 160.

puba n-, charms, "Laws," i. 176, 180, witchcraft.

puba, act of scaring (horses), "Laws," i. 162.

poDiuba = puba ("Laws," i. 160, 298), attack, cutting down, *sg.* and *pl.*

pube, a cutting down, "O'Don. Suppl."; puba, *d.* pubu, *np.* puba, "Laws," ii. 270, 268, 276; i. 160, 230.

poDpúbu, delay, *ds.* (?), *Ml.* 22 a.

cuRba, *d.* cupbu, exemption, "Laws," i. 282; iii. 24.

aıchchumbe, a wounding; *g.* aıchchummı, *d.* aıchchumbu, "M'C.'s Stowe Missal," 251; laceration, "Laws," iii. 356; *ap.* aıchchumbe, gl. *cauteria*, *Wb.* 1 c, 1 b; *ns.* aɒcumbe, *concissio*, *Wb.* 23 d; achchuma, "Laws," i. 232.

aırba, breaking of a fence, "Laws," i. 174.

sıchbe (ríchbe) (?), horse-rod, "Siab Ch. C." 376; rıchbı n-, "S. na Rann," p. 62; *masc.* ın rıchbe, *LU.* 52 b.

fıdbae, woodman's axe, "Laws," ii. 140, 146; i. 166, 170; fıɒba, gl. *falcastrum*, "Tract on Latin Declension."

debe m-(b)ecc, a little difference, *Ml.* 40 a; *dp.* ɒebaıb, *simultatibus*, *Ml.* 19 c; ɒebe cıncuɒa, *Ml.* 46 c and *passim*.

guba, wailing, *d.* gubu, a nguba, "Irische Texte," i. 38; *d.* gubu, *Tl.* 202.

subae, *jubilatio*, *g.* ruıbı, *d.* rubu, *Ml.* 146 d, 47 d, 67 c, "Four Masters," ii. 594.

dubae, anxiety, may be inferred from ɒubach, *Ml.* 19 a, *LU.* 29 a; mór n-ɒuba, "Félire," 201; ɒuba, gloom, "Circ. of Ireland," l. 173; *d.* ɒubu.

torbe, carbe, utility, profit, *Z.*, *Wb.* 2 a, 14 a.

etorbu (écorbu), *ds.* unprofitableness, "Laws," i. 254.

forbe (forbae), *perfectio*, performance, finishing, *Wb.* 20; *d.* forbu, *Ml.* 55 c, 15 a, 55 a, *Wb.* 14 d; *d.* forbo, *Sg.* 151 a.

orbe, orre, orbbe, arre, orba, heritage; orba n-aıll, a n-orre, *Wb.* 27 c, *Ml.* 27; *g.* orbaı, *portionis*, *Ml.* 102 a; orrı, "Bk. of Armagh; ɒa n-orre, *Wb.* 2 c; ırreɒ a orbae, "Carm. Paul."

forba, heritage; but *d.* forbaıɒ, ground, *LU.* 117 b, *LL.* 222 a.

futhairbe (?), .ı. críoch no reranɒ, "Táin Bó Reg." l. 21.

indarpe, ınɒarrae, *exheredatio*, *repulsa*, *expulsio*, *Wb.* 10, 19, *Ml.* 23.

indarbe, *d.* ınɒarbu; gl. *jectu*, *exjectatione*, *repulsam*, *Ml.* 23 c, 85 c, 127 b; "Laws," i. 505.

foarbbe, a drive *or* ride (*or* its distance); fuıchaırbe, *LU.* 111 a.

airbe, *g.* aırbı, fence, "Laws, iii. 290; *gp.* aırbe, *ibi.* i. 98; but *np.* aırbeɒa, *LL.* 239 a.

iarbe, *dp.* ıarbaıb, gl. *lucis*, *Ml.* 99 d.

erbe n-druad, a fence or cutting (?), "Four Masters," an. 555.

imbe, *g.* imbi, *dp.* imbib, gl. *sæpibus*, fence; á n-imbe, *Ml.* 102 a, *maceriam*; *ns.* imbe, *np.* ime, "Laws," iv. 54, 72, 118, 24, i. 489.

immarbe, *as.*, falsehood, deceit, "Amra Ch. C." § 6.

taulchube (?), *g.* telchubi, gl. *cadi*, a vat, *Sg.* 180 a.

abae, gl. *alveus fluminis*, *g.* lech-abai, "Four Masters," i. 372 (?).

ruidbe (?), .i. biatha, "O'Dav." 113.

esce (éṡce), an aeṡcae, an éṡca, moon; *g.* eṡcai, éṡci, *d.* éṡcu, *Cr.* 3 d, 33 b, *Wb.* 32 a, "Nancy Gl."

cainéṡce, fine moon.

nueṡcae, new moon.

disce, diṡccae m-blechta, dryness of cows, "Laws," iv. 52.

dorche, *ngp.*, *tenebrae*, "Ascoli."

rucca (?), *n.*; ruccu, *d.*, *confusio*, *Ml.* 9 c, 55 b, *Wb.* 9 c; but *d.* ruccai, *Ml.* 27 c.

breinciu (?), *caries*, *ds.*, *Cr.* 34 b.

luge, luige, oath, *Ml.* 14 c, 36 a; *g.* lugi, *Wb.* 14 c; *d.* lugu, *Tl.* 180; a fírluge, fírluige, *jusjurandum*, *Z.*; *d.* fírlugu, *Ml.* 115 a, 36 a; *d.* comlugu, *conjuratio*, *Ml.* 44 b; *d.* lugu.

comluige, "Four Masters," ii. 786; luga n-, "Lismore Lives," l. 50.

lugu (?), *ds.*, smallness, "Amra Ch. C." § 6.

fortuge (?), garment, covering, *LB.* 43.

imthuge (?), garment is *fem.*: iṡṡí a imthuge, unless iṡṡi refers to *veritas*.

trichtaige (?), thirty days; *gs.* in áir trichtaigi, at the age of thirty, *LB.* 33; *d. fem.*, *Cr.* 3 c.

foscaigiu (?), *ds.*, *Ml.* 21.

muiragu (muirágu) (?), *maris fundo*, *ds.*, "Bk. of Armagh";

segi (?), *gs.*, "Bk. of Armagh."

lige, bed, *torus*, *lectus*, *cubile*, *Sg.* 52 b, 107 a; the gender not marked by *Z.* or *W.*, but appears from *nap.* lige; *d.* ligiu, *Ml.* 55 c; ligu, *LL.* 78 a; *nap.* lige, *Ml.* 76 d, 77 a; *ap.* ligaib, *Wb.* 27 b.

cobuige, *concubitus*; *dp.* cobligib, gl. *cubilibus*, *Wb.* 6 a; *W.* makes it *fem.*; *d.* coblige, cohabitation, *Ag.*

crolige (crólige), gore-bed, agony; *g.* croligi báir, a wound that remains till death, "Laws," iii. 138: *d.* crolige, "Fragm. of Ir. Ann." 96; cró, .i. bár, "O'Dav." 67, 68.

FOENLIGE (fóenlige) sick-bed, *LL.* 100 b.

FRESLIGE, *adjacentia*, lying close; *n.* frerslige, "Man. & Cust." iii. 489; *g.* frerligi, *Wb.* 3 d.

MOCHLIGE, early grave, "Ir. Texte," i. 81.

OTHARLIGE, sick-bed, *LL.* 121 b, "De Chopur in da M." 240, and *W.*

ROSAIGLIGE (?), a kind of verse; *gs.* "Bk. of Balymote," 289 a.

SERGLIGE (wasting), or sick-bed; *d.* serglighu, "Sick-bed of Cu." 376, "Ir. Texte, i. 208; serccliga, "O'Dav." 122.

SIRLIGE (sírlige), long lying, *W.*

RIGE (ríge), kingdom, kingship, rule, *Ml.* 14 a; not in *Z.* (!); Stokes says it is *neut.* or *masc.*; its gender not in *W.* or *Ag.*; *ns.* rige n-, *LL.* 106 a, "Bk. of Lismore," 749; "Bk. of Fenagh," 252; "C. M. Rath," 130; "MS. Materials," 572; *ap.* ríge, "Siab. Ch. C." 372; *g.* ríge, *W.*; *d.* ríghiu, *W.*, "Laws," i. 510; rígu, *Ml.* 71 c, Bodl. Cormac," 18, "Félire," 200.

AIRDRIGE N- (airdríge n-), "Bk. of Fenagh," 356, 366.

AIRRIGE (airríge), governorship, "S. na Rann," 126.

COMRIGE (comríge), joint rule, "Nennius," 70.

ENRIGE (énrige), sole sovereignty, *LB.* 206 b.

LAINRIGE (láinríge), full sovereignty, "Fragm. of Ir. Ann." 76.

ETTRIGI N-, *LL.* 208 a.

ERGE (érge), éirge, rising, *Z.*, *Ascoli*; *g.* aergi, *Ml.* 83 a; *d.* aergiu, *Ml.* 21 c.

esséirge, eséirge, *resurrectio*; *d.* esséirgiu, eiresgu, *Z.*, *Ascoli*; *d.* eirseirgu, *Ml.* 3 c, 13 b; esérgo, "Stowe Missal," fo. 64. It is *fem.* in *LU.* 33, and *passim.*

coméirge, comérge, the rising out *or* muster, *LU.* 111 b; "Bk. of Fenagh," 300, 360; "Fragm. of Irish Ann." 178; "C. M. Rath," 148; *d.* coiméirgiu, *Tl.* 4, 162, 46, 40.

comeiséirge, co-resurrection, *Wb.* 27 a.

immeirge, going off, flitting, "Lismore Lives," 394.

uréirge (rising before a person ?), full respect, homage, "Laws," ii. 196, 194, 354; "Lismore Lives," 403.

IARMEIRGE, iarmerge, midnight, nocturns, matins, *LL.* 282; "Amra Ch. C." § 21.

AIRGE MOR (aiрge mór) (?), great herd, *as.*, "Fragm. of Irish. Ann." 72.

DERGE (án déрge), déirge (*Ml.* 118 b, 111 b), *desertio; d.* déirgiu, dergu, *Ascoli; n.* á n-daerge.

nephdéirge, non-desertion, "Turin," 209 b.

indergе, innergе, desertions, *ap.*, "Laws," iii. 64.

ARGI (?), *gs.*, "Bk. of Armagh."

CORP-RIGE (?), *d.* Corrrigiu, descendants of Corp, in tribe names, "Bk. of Armagh."

-rige, *na.*; *g.* -rige, posterity in (Cat-, Ciar-)rige, (Bend-, Boon-, Cal-, Call-, Cer-, Ciar-, Greg, Sái-, Temen-)rigi, "Bk. of Armagh"; they are perhaps *neuter;* the *dat.* Cothrugu is there perhaps for Cothrigu, as Murcrigu, "Bod. Cormac," 34.

CUAILNGE (?); *d.* Cuailngiu, Cooley.

ASCNADIU (?), *ds.*, *probatio*, *Ml.* 53 b.

DEDE N- (déde n-), two (things), *Wb.* 25 d; *Ml.* 62 c; *d.* dédiu, *Wb.* 9 c; issed a n-dere, *Ml.* 100 c, seems for a ndede-se; in dede (!), *Ml.* 17 b.

trede, tréde, three (things); a trede sin, that (group of) three; *d.* trédiu, *Ml.* 60 b, *Wb.* 21 b; *np.* na trede, "Amra Ch. C." 21; *d.* tredaib, *Sg.* 10 a; a tréde, *Sg.* 220 b.

cethardae, cethardе, four things, *Wb.* 21 d, 32 c; a céthardе, the tetrad; ceṫarda also means "fourfold," "Laws," i. 274; *Wb.* 21 d.

sédе, six (things).

ADAEE N-, property, "Cormac," 3.

BLEDE (bléde) (?), goblet.

BUDE, buide (?), thanks.

DEBIDE N-, a kind of verse, "Thurn. Versl." 17, 45, 147; "Bk. of Balymote," 298 a, 303 a, 307 b.

CRIDE (críde), heart; *ds.* cridiu, *Wb.* 7 d, *Ml.* 37 a; *ap.* cride, *Wb.* 15 a, 29.

fírchride, the very heart.

timm-cride, cowardice.

beochride, a lively *or* merry heart.

luathcride, gl. *cardiacus*, quickness *or* panting of heart, "Pr. Leid." 266.

trommchride, tromchride, *jecur*, *Ml.* 65, *Sg.* 65.

michride, malice, *LB.* 211 a.

anchride, an-chride n-, *injuria*, wrong, malevolence, *Ml.* 93 d; 115 b, 23 d; *Wb.* 9 c, 96; *Tl.* 188; *g.* ancridi, *Sg.* 181 a; *Ml.* 38 d, 27 c; *Wb.* 96.

forcmachte: a f., *factitium*, *Sg.* 30.

cumscaigthe: a c., *motaria.*

nephescide, nefaiscide, *scotoméne*; *d.* nefaescidiu, *Ml.* 29 d, 30 a.

innaide: a n-innaide, *d.* idnidiu, *expectatio*, *Wb.* 23 b, 42 c; *as.* indnide, *Ml.* 42 c seems *masc.*

cetnide (cétnide), a cétnide, the primitive, *Sg.* 188 a.

todochide n-, a tothóchaide, the future, *Ml.* 61 a, *Cr.* 61 a; *g.* todochaidi, *Sg.* 191 b; *d.* todochidiu, *Wb.* 12 c.

fortchide (?), *d.* fortgidiu, moonlessness, darkness, *Ml.* 29 d, 30 a.

spirdide: a spirdide sin, that spiritual thing.

rangabalda: a rangabalda, the participle, *Sg.* 39 a.

forgnide (?), *d.* Forgnidiu, "Bk. of Armagh"; forgnaidiu, *Tl.* 82.

mide (?), Meath; *d.* midiu, *LU.* 129, "Ann. Ult." 713; *g.* midi, "Bk. of Armagh," *Tl.* 68, 76.

suide, seat, *sessio*, *sedes*, *g.* suidi, *d.* suidiu, *Z.*, who makes *neut.*, but does not give a reason therefor, nor does *W.*, or *Ag.*, or "Stokes' Félire"; but *ns.*, suide n-, *LL.* 308 a, and *np.* ríg-ṡuide, three times in *Ag.* show the *neuter*; *ds.* sudiu, *LU.* 111 b.

corrṡuide, round or smooth seat, arm-chair with arms like the beak or prow of a boat.

dálṡuidae, *forum*, *d.* dálṡuidiu, *Sg.* 57 a, 218 b.

impṡuide, *obsidio*, *obsessio*, *Ml.* 43.

impude, for impṡude, a seat, *obsidio*; *d.* impudiu, *Wb.* 9 b, 9c, *Ml.* 106 b.

imṡuide, besieging, *d.* imsuidiu, *vallando*, *Ml.* 123 b.

iúgṡuide, *Sg.* 50 a, tribunal; *cf.* iudic, judge, judgment, *Ag.*

prímṡuide, chief seat, *cathedra*; *d.* prímṡuidiu, *Tl.* 218, "O'Dav." 84.

suide—*continued.*

ríġṡuide, *thronus*, *d.* ríġsuidiu, *solio*, *Ml.* 114 d, 115 a, *Sg.* 50 a; *na. dual*, ríġsuide, *Tl.* 118; *np.* ríġsuide, *Ag.*

trebunṡuide *Sg.* 50 a, tribunal, a tribune's seat.

uide, *περίοδος*, *iter*, *cursus*, journey; *as.* uide, *Ml.* 60 a, "Laws," ii. 34; *d.* ar cach uidiu in n-aball, *Ml.* 60 a, 82 d; *ap.* uide laithi, *quotidianos progressus*, *cursus*, *Cr.* 31 c; *as.*, *ap.*, and *ds.* (latter omitted in "Ascoli's Gloss.") point to the *neuter*, as perhaps does a uide, *W.*; uide is in *Z.* 230, but not in the *Z.* Index; *W.* and *Ag.* omit gender; uide, ar n-uide, "C. M. Rath," 166, give *n.* and *as.*

guide (?), prayer, praying, *neut.* or *masc.*, *Z.*; *d.* guidiu, *Wb.* 29 d, "Laws," ii. 96; also *af.* guidi, *Wb.* 7 a; *df.* guidi, *Ml.* 73 b; it is only *fem.* in "Félire," *W.*, and *Ag.*, and in guidi of "Colman's Hymn"; *dsf.* poigdi, *mendicatio*, *Wb.* 26 b; *df.* digdi, *W.*, favour the *fem.* of guide.

muinde, *collarium*, from muin, *collum*, neck, *Sg.* 35 a: am muinde; it is an *adj.* used substantively.

linde (líndae) (?), *as.*, *linteum*, "Bk. of Armagh," an *adj.* used as *subst.* from lín, *linum.*

rinde (?), ar rinde, the spear-point, "Tog. Trói," l. 1552, or arrinde is one word; airrinde: for an airrinde, "Sg. Incant"; perhaps a large rent or gash, "Stokes."

arde, airde n-, *signum*, sign, *Wb.* 11 c, *Ag.*, "Four Masters," ii. 602; *np.* airde, *Tl.* 34, *Ag.*; *d.* airdiu, *LU.* 24 a, "Maelduin's Cur." 484; arde óira, *Wb.* 22 b, should be, I think, arde n-óira, *g.* airdi, *Tl.* 124.

comarde, *signum*, *signaculum*, *Wb.* 10 c, 21 a, 22 b; *ns.* comarda n-, *W.*

derbairde, sure sign, miracle, *Ag.*

sáibairde, saebairde, false sign or miracles; *ap.* *Wb.* 26 a.

sainchomarde: a sainchomarde sin, that special sign, *Wb.* 26 b.

comartha n-, sign, mark: c. n-echlaige sin, *LL.* 70 b; *nap.* comarthada, *Ag.* (!).

innchomartha, memorial, mark, fitting monument, "C. R. na Ríg," § 25.

cairdde, compact, "Nennius," 232; *nap.* cairde, *pacta*, *Ml.* 91 b, 104 a, 108 c, *LL.* 307 b; *d.* cairdiu, *fœdere*, *Ml.* 18 d, "Ir. Texte," i. 214; cairddiu, "Man. & Cust." iii. 497; *W.* does not give cairdiu of his texts, marks *fem.*; it seems *fem.* in "Félire"; and we have in cairde, *gl. pacta*, *Ml.* 91 c, which should be, perhaps, inna cairde; the *ds.* and *nap.* show the *neuter.*

aitherrechtaichthe: a aitherrechtaichthe, the patronymic, *Z.*

remeperthe, a r., the aforesaid thing, *Wb.* 32.

esngarthe, *edictum; g.* ersngarthi, *Ml.* 94 b.

diruidigthe (dírurdigthe), a derivative; *d.* dírurdigthiu, *Sg.* 188 a.

olfoirbthe (olḟoirbthe), pluperfect; *d.* olḟoirbthiu, *Sg.* 151 b.

sechmadechte, the past, the preterite; *d.* sechmadechtu, *Ml.* 122 b, *Cr.* 69 b.

guthaigthe, vowel, *Sg.* 53 a.

cuicthe (cúicthe), a space of five days; *g.* cuicthi, "Laws," i. 146.

cleithe, n-: Cimbaeth cleithe n-óc n-Emna, *LL.* 21 a; see next word.

cleithe: a cleithe; *d.* cleithiu, roof, "Mesca Ul." 48, but senchleithe, *d.* senchleithiu, a vassal, is *masc.*, I presume, "Laws," i. 226.

laithe, lathe, lá, lá, lae, day, are *nas.* and *nagp.*; *n. dual*, dál-lae; *gs.* laithi, lathi, lái; *d.* laithiu, lau, láo, lóu, ló (various glosses quoted in my Index to the "Bk. of Armagh"); *n.* a laithe, al laa n-, *Ml.* 21 c, *Wb.* 6 b; a cóicetmád lá, "Cormac," 10; *as.* al lae, a laa, *Ml.*15 c, *Wb.* 23 a; *n. dual*, dal-lae, *Cr.* 31 d.

cendla, *g.* cenlai (*d.* cendlo chásc, .i. lathe ḟledi Crist, "Cormac," 12), supper-day, Holy Thursday, *LB.* 63, 265, "MacCarthy's Stowe Missal," "Lismore Lives" Index.

líthlaite, festival day, "S. na Rann," 144; *g.* líthlaithi, *Tl.* 40.

laithe—*continued.*

medonlathe, medonlaa, mid-day, *Sg.* 66 b, *Z.*

nóilaithe, *np. nundinum*, *Sg.* 116 b.

óenla, one day.

sainlaa, *ap.* sainiláa, special days, *Wb.* 6 b.

samla, summer-day, "Bk. of Lismore," 48 b.

sithlaithe, long or peaceful day, "Fiac's Hymn."

tiuglaithe, the last day; *g.* tigláithe, "Four Masters," ii 618.

aithe, *talio*, *Wb.* 14 c; *g.* ind aithi, *LB.* 214 a; *neuter* (?).

suithe N-, *LL.* 246 a.

sathe (?), a thrust.

lutha N-, lutha n-eithig, "Bk. of Lismore," 50.

fotha N-, form, "Cormac," 16.

corthe, pillar-stone, *as.* a corthe; *np.* corthe, "Siege of Howth," 60; "Táin Bó Flidais," l. 97; but *nm.* in corthe, *LL.* 78 and *W.*; so are saithe, *masc.*, *Ml.* 90 b, glosnathe, *Ml.* 99 d, and morchute, "Fiac's Hymn."

cumachte, cumachtae, cumacte, cumactte: *ns.* a cumachtae, issed a cumachte, *Ml.* 16 a, 48 a, 68 a, 74 b; *g.* cumachti; *d.* cumachtu, *Ml.* 74, 81 a, *Wb.* 33 a; *nap.* cumachte, *Wb.* 6 a, 21 a.

techte (téchte), right; is ed a thechte, "Stowe Missal," 64; *Sg.* 117 a; *d.* téchtu, "Sergl. C."; *Wb.* 13 a; *as.* téichte, *Wb.* 6 a.

etechte (étechte), injustice, illegality; *d.* étechtu, "Laws," i. 254; "Sergl. C." 380.

sechte: a sechte, the (a group of) seven things, *Wb.* 26 d.

snechtae, snechta, snow; *g.* snechtai; *d.* snechtu; snectu is *neut.* says *Ag.*, but *as.* in snechta, *W.*; *nmp.* snechti, gl. *nives*, *Sg.* 8 a, 8.

milte (mílte), *militia*, *nas.*; *g.* mílti is *neuter*, *Z.*; but why not *masc.*?

leire N- (léire n-), completeness, "Laws," ii. 176; but léire, industry, is *fem.*, *Wb.* 13 d, *Ml.* 32 b.

ercһre (?), eɼchɼa, ıɼchɼe, *defectus, eclipsis; d.* eɼchɼu, ıɼchɼu, *Ml.* 31 a, 30 d, 58 b; *Wb.* 26 a; *g.* ıɼchɼı, *Wb.* 3 a; *Z.*, *W.*, *Ag.* do not give the gender.

acre (ácɼe), *reclamatio, reprobatio; as.* in *Wb.* 9 c; *n.* acɼae, complaint, *Tl.* 188; *n.* accɼa, plea, action at law, *Ag.*, which marks it *masc.*; but *W.* makes it *neuter;* and it, no doubt, was like the following words derived from ʒaıɼım.

ꝼuacre, ꝼócɼe, ꝼoccɼa, *monitio, indicare, arguere, Wb.* 3 a; ꝼuacɼae n-aɼaıꝺ, "O'Don. Suppl."; *d.* ꝼocɼu, *Wb.* 31 c; ꝼocɼa, disregard of laws (?), "Laws," i. 230.

ıɼꝼócɼe, aıɼócɼe, áıɼocɼe, *admonitio, Z., Wb.* 16 d; *as.* eɼꝼuacɼa, *LB.* 33; *ns.* ın ꞇ-eɼuacɼa, "Bk. of Hymns," ii. 172.

ꝼuɼꝼ̇ócɼe, ꝼuɼꝼ̇ocɼe, order, warning; ꝼuɼꝼ̇óʒɼa, advertisement, title of "Dunlevy's Preface to Catechism"; *ds.* ꝼuɼóʒɼu, notice, "Laws," i. 262.

ꝼanocre (ꝼánócɼe), croaking (of a raven).

ꞇeruacra (ꞇeɼúacɼa), summons, *W.*

uʒra (?), challenge (?), "Tog. Trói," 609.

ꝺıuccra (ꝺíuccɼa), ꝺıucɼe, ꝺıucɼae, ꝺıucaıɼe, clamour, *Tr.* 1 a. In "Stokes' Goidelica" it is marked *fem.*

ꝺoʒrae (ꝺóʒɼae), ꝺoʒɼa, lamenting; *g.* ꝺoʒɼaı, *d.* ꝺoʒɼu, *W.*; it belongs, I think, to the ʒaıɼım group.

aırcre, eɼcɼe, *interdictio; see* eɼʒaıɼe.

ꞇımcre, request, invitation; *see* ꞇımmʒaıɼe.

ꞇacre, ꞇaccre, *argumentum, Wb.* 25 a; *d.* ꞇacɼu, *Wb.* 25 b, *Tl.* 128; *np.* na ꞇacɼaı, *W.*

ꝺeʒꞇacrae, good argument; *np.* ꝺeʒꞇacɼae, *Tr.* 2 a, 3 a.

ꝼrıꞇһaʒra, arguing against, "Lismore Lives," 393.

ımꞇһaccra, great *or* mutual contentions; *np. LB.* 208 b. This word or ımꝼɼecɼa may throw light on ımmuɼ-ꞇecɼaꞇhaɼ, the obscure word of "W.'s Dict. and Texte," i. 262, l. 5.

ꝼrecre, ꝼɼeccɼe, answer; *n.* a ꝼɼecɼe, *Wb.* 25 b, *Ml.* 35 c, 62 c; *d.* ꝼɼecɼu, *Wb.* 30, *LB.* 33; *np.* ınna ꝼɼecɼa, *Sg.* 26 a.

coımꝼrecra, return, "Laws," ii. 314.

ꝺeʒꝼreccra, good answer.

IMFRECRAE, correspondence, *Ml.* 58 a; acá trá .i. etir inna cethri ferru; *g.* imfrecrai, mutual answering, *LB.* 33; imfreccra, imreccra, assonances, "Bk. of Hymns," i. 127; ii. 172.

LANFRECRA (lánfrecra), full answer, "Félire."

NEMFRECCRA (némfreccra), silence, *LB.* 211 a.

ESCONGRA, proclamation, edict, *LB* 33, *Ag.*

FORCONGRE, *imperium, mandatum;* forcongra, *LB.* 33; *d.* forcongru, *Ag.*

DIUCAIRE, *clamor, W., Ag.*, who do not give gender.

ERGAIRE, irgaire, urgaire, *interdictio, vetitum; n.* a n-irgaire, *Wb.* 3 c; *g.* ergairi; *d.* ergairiu, *Ml.* 35 d, 125 a.

INGAIRE (?), minding (sheep, pigs); *d.* ingairiu, *Tl.* xvi., *W.*

ESCAIRE, a proclamation: is an escaire dóib.

FORGARE, *imperatio, Z.*

FORNGAIRE, forṅgaire, *imperium, præceptum; a.* forṅgairiu, *Ml.* 120 c, 53 d, *Wb.* 31 c, *Z.* 461, .i. agra, "O'Dav." 86.

GOLGAIRE, weeping and crying: a n-golgaire, Táin Bó Fróich," 148, *W.*; *np.* golgaire, *W.*, who marks it *fem.*; from gol, .i. dér, "Cormac," 23.

CULGAIRE, rattling (of a chariot), "C. R. na Ríg"; *as., ibi.*, and *W.*, *LL.* 109 b.

BASGAIRE, clapping of palms of the hands, *as., W., Ag.*

BRANGAIRE, "O'Dav." 60.

SCRECHGAIRE, crying of infants, *as., Tl.* 160.

TAIRGAIRE, tairgire, promise; *d.* tairgairiu, tairgiriu, *Wb.* 19 c, *Ml.* 33 d.

TAIRNGIRE, promise: a tairngere, *Ml.* 122 d; *g.* tairṅgeri; *ap.* tairṅgere, *Wb.* 11 a, 33 b, *Ml.* 108 b.

GAIRE, cry, shout; *g.* gairi, *W.*; *as.* árdgaire, "Félire"; *nap.* na gaire, *Ag.*; *cf.* a ngair, the cry, *Sg.* 176 b.

ESNGAIRE, *ap., edicta, Ml.* 105 c.

ETARGAIRE, *LU.* 101 b.

TIMGAIRE, N-, recall, withdrawal, "Laws," ii. 308, 338; *np.* timgaire, "Laws," ii. 166, 164, *LL.* 270 b, *LU.* 125 b.

INGAIRE (?), *d.* ingairiu, herding; *Tl.* xvi.

IMBAIRE (?), ridge; *d.* imbairiu, *Tl.* 196.

ESCRAE, escra n-, a vessel, *LB.* 116.

COBRA N-GARG, "Ir. Texte," i. 107.

BELRE, bélre, béelre, language, *sermo*, *Z.*; *g.* bélri, *Wb.* 12 a; *g.* belrai, *Ml.* 42 c; see bérle, bélre n-echtrann, foreign language, *Wb.* 12 c.

il-bélre, *ap.*, many languages, *Wb.* 12 d b.

gnáthbelra, common speech, "Cormac," 32.

gall-belre, foreign tongue; *gs.* guillbelrai, "Bk. of Fenagh," 222.

iar m-belre (Bk. of Balymote," 326 a), 1°, an adverb; 2°, iron (*i. e.* hard) obscure expression.

senbélrae, old language, "Stokes' Bodl. Cormac," 22.

rem-belre, adverb.

ANRE (?), gl. *colirio*, "Cod. Cantab." p. 156, "Zimmer's Gl."

AMRE, amra, *portentum*, *prodigium*; *g.* amri; *d.* amru, *Ml.* 17 a, 67 b.

adamre, adamra: a n-adamre, a wonder, *portentum*, *Ml.* 61 a, 63 c; *np.* adamrae, *Ml.* 115 b.

DAIRE (?), an oak-wood; *d.* dairíu, "Bk. of Armagh."

dairbre n-, a n-dairbre n-oll, great oak-wood, "W. Texte," 105; dairbri, *gs.*, oak-wood, "L. na gCeart," 46, 74.

CAERI, *gs. d.* Caeru (?), "Bk. of Armagh."

POOLIRE, *pugillare*, "Bk. of Armagh"; *np.* pólaire, *Tl.* 190, 655.

DIRE N- (díre n-), a fine, "Laws," i. 66, 481, 512, where (p. 489) dírech n- seems a mistake for díre; *g.* díre, *ibi.* 511, 178; conid ed treś dire, "O'Dav." 99; *d.* díriu, "Man. & Cust." iii. 477, 512, 503, 484, 497.

comdíre, equal fine.

coirpdíre, body fine, lethdíre, lan n-díre, "Laws," i. 40, 176, 66, 274, ii. 66.

FELIRE (félire), an félire, "O'Dav." 75.

AILLE, praise, prayer, Stokes in "Félire"; but *asf.* ailli, in "Bk. of Armagh"; *fem.*, *W.*; *adf.* ailli, *petitio*, *Wb.* 16 d, 28 c.

CAILLE, caille, *pallium*, *Z.*, *Wb.* 11 c; *as.* in "Bk. of Armagh."

caille finda (?), gl. *cella vinaria*, *Sg.*

caili (?), *gs. pudoris*, *Ml.* 55 b.

saile, *saliva*, *sputamen*; an saile, an sele, "V. of Snedgus," 16; "Yellow Bk. of Lecan," 391; *d.* sailiu, "Sg. Incant."; *ac. dual.* and *pl.* sale, *Z.*, *W.*; *d.* selib, *Z.*

sele (?), the River Blackwater in Meath, *gs.* in "Bk. of Armagh"; but *g.* séili, *Tl.* 106.

air-scele (air-scéle), famous tale, great report.

so-scele, so-scéle, the Gospel; *g.* soscéli, *d.* soscélu, *Wb.* 32 a, 26 a, 18 c; *gs.* soscelai, *Ml.* 42 b, *Tl.* 28.

a cenele n- (a cenéle n-), cenélae, cenelae, *genus*; cenele n-diumai, *Sg.* 8 a, 46 b, *LB.* 211; *g.* cenéli, *Wb.* 26 d; *d.* ceneliu, "Bodl. Cormac," 12; cenele n-echa, gl. *far*, *Sg.* 57 a; *np.* cenéle, "Cod. Cambr." 38 a.

il-chenéle, *np.*, many kinds, *Wb.* 12 d.

sain-chenelae, special kind.

berle (bérle), language, *g.* bérlai, "Amra Ch. C." 2; *g.* bérli, *Z.* 626; *d.* bérlu, "Nennius," 228.

combérla, common speech, "S. na Rann," p. 131.

sobérla, eloquence, "C. R. na Ríg," § 27.

iarm-berla, an adverb.

iarbérla, kind of verse, "Thurn. Versl." 37.

rembérla, adverb.

bile (?), a tree; *voc.* bile, "C. M. Rath," 214; is *masc.* in Middle Irish; *d.* biliu.

dorbile n-, a spreading tree, "Four Masters," i. 152.

tairgille n-, *g.* tairgilli, additional pledge, "Laws," iv. 114.

tolae n-, *Ml.* 93 b; tola n-glé; a tóla, *Cr.* 61 a; *d.* tolu, *exundantia*, *Cr.* 39 a; tola tuile, a flowing flood, "Four Masters," ii. 586; tolu n-, "S. na Rann," 153.

tuile, a flood, "Beda Cr." 25 a c; *d.* tuiliu, *Ml.* 51 b.

authuili (?), *gs.*, "Bk. of Armagh"; *g.* tromtuili, "Man. & Cust." 536.

uile, an uile, all, the whole.

buale (búale) (?), bovile, *bualium*.

TUTHLE (?), *gibbus*, *Cr.* 9 a.

EGLI, aigli (*Mons?*), *gs.*, "Bk. of Armagh."

CERTLE (?), *glomus*, *Sg.* 70 b.

COCHE (?), *d.* cochu, *clunis*, *Sg.* 67 a.

LUE (?), a kick, *calx*, *Sg.* 50 a.

LUE (?), lua, *splen*, *lien*, *Sg.* 63 a, 63 b, 93 b; seems to be a t-stem, from lue liach, l. liad of

LUAE (?), *ap.* or *gp.*: inna luae, gl. *juncturas gubernaculorum; as.* loí, *LU.* 68 b; lae, *LL.* 44 b; lui, *LB.* 217 b; *g.* lui (?), *Ml.* 59 b, which Ascoli renders by *ramus* (better perhaps *remus*); cf. *ds.* lúich, lúid, a steering oar, "Bodl. Cormac," 32.

DUMA, *agger* (tumulus, "Bk. of Armagh"); *cf.* fodumaigertar, *exaggeravit*, *Ml.* 55 d; duma (ndrena, ndur, n-Gobla, n-Eirc), *LL.* 211 a; "Bk. of Hy Maine," fo. 145–6; Preface to "Fiac's Hymn"; "Bk. of Balymote," 189 b, 352 b; *g.* dumi, "Bk. of Armagh"; dumai, "Four Masters," i. 398; "Laws," i. 170; *d.* dumu, *LL.* 127 a; "Nennius," 208; *ap.* adnocla no duma for marbu, *LB.* 211; dumu, gl. *cervos*, *Ml.* 48 d, should be damu, or dumu, .i. *acervos*.

cruimduma, *ngs.*, a dunghill, "Bodl. Cormac," "Cormac," 13; *lit.* worm-heap (?), .i. otrach.

treduma, triple-mound, "Petrie's Tara," 117.

INDSMA (?), fixing, mounting, "L. na gCeart," 266.

NII (níi), ní, a thing; *d.* níu, *Ml.* 47 b, *Wb.* 11 d; *dual*, da ní, *LB.* 216 a.

nephní, neṗní, nemní, nothing; nempni, *Tl.* 180.

AIRNE (?), *g.* Airni, *d.* Airniu, "Bk. of Armagh"; the plain about Knock, Co. Mayo.

EILNE (?), *g.* Eilni, *d.* Eilniu, a plain near Coleraine, *LA.*

LATHARNA (?), *d.* Latharnu, *Tl.* 164.

AITHGNE,* aidgne, *notis*, *cognitio*, *recognitio*; *g.* aithgni, *a.* aithgne, *W.*; aidgne, *Wb.* 19 d; *d.* aidgniu, aithgniu, *Wb.* 1 c b, *Ml.* 42 c.

écne, aecne, aeccne; *g.* écni, *d.* écnu, *Wb.* 7 c, 8 a, *Ml.* 128 a, *W.*; *as.* an ecne, *Wb.* 8 a.

anécne, ignorance; *g.* anécni, *Wb.* 17 a.

---

* The words of this -gne group are marked *neuter* by *Z.*, *W.*, and others: an écne, cetna n-etargnae, a mbérna, point to *neuter*.

aithgne—*continued.*

digna, contempt; *d.* dignu, "Laws," ii. 320, *W.*; .i. drochgne, dimicin, "O'Dav." 75.

engne, *d.* engnu, *scientia*, *Wb.* 2 a, 14 c, *Ml.* 14 d.

ingnae, *intelligentia*; *g.* ingni, ingnai; *d.* ingnu, *Wb.* 11 b, *Ml.* 89 b, 14 c, 140 b.

comgne, learning, *LB.* 215 a; *g.* coimgni, .i. senchas, "O'Dav." 60.

ergnae, eirgne, irgne, *intellectus*, *Z.*; *g.* ergnai, "Toch. Emire"; earnae, *Ml.* 113 b, is perhaps for ergnae.

etersce, etarsce, knowledge, *intellectus*; *g.* etarsci, *d.* etarscu, *Wb.* 26 cd, *Ml.* 42 cd, 59 a, 140 b.

etarscaib, *experimentis*, *Ml.* 72 c.

nephetarscae, *stultitia*, *Ml.* 58 a.

etargnae, etargne, etergne, etargna, *g.* etargni, *Wb.* 8 c, 26 c, *experimentum*, *sapientia*, *notio*, *Wb.* 21, *Cr.* 6 a; *n.* etargnae n-, "Félire," *v.* écna; is écna n-etargna, *Sg.* 197, shows *neuter.*

besce (bésce), bésgne, .i. dligedh, "O'Dav." 59; behaviour, *Wb.* 14 c; a mbésca, the usage, *mos* (*Tl.* 34) = *regulam*, "Bk. of Armagh," fo. 6 ba; *g.* bésci, *Wb.* 24 b; *d.* béscu, "Félire," p. 199; *ap.* bésgna, *disciplinas*, *Cr.* 13 d; *as.* bésce, *Z.* Stokes marks *masc.* in "Félire" Index.

degbaesce, *propositum*, *ritus sacer*, *Ml.* 85 d, 105 bd; *g.* degbescai, *d.* degbéscu, *emendatione*, *Ml.* 85 d, 87 d, 105 b.

drochbésce, *g.* drochbésci, bad manner of life, *Ml.* 118 a.

brogne (?), *d.* brognu, dearth, "Four Masters," i. 408.

lugna (?), moon, "Stokes' Metric. Glosses."

aithne, *d.* aithniu, knowledge, "Four Masters," i. 308; *d.* aithniu, observation, "Laws," i. 238.

aithne, *depositum*, *Z.*; *ns.* a n-aithne, *np.* aithne, *Sg.* 6, 66, 203 ab.

aithne, command, commendation: a n-aithne, *pl.* na haithne, "Laws," iii. 218, 220; "Turin Gl." 203 a.

uaithne (úaithne) (?), úatne, pillar; *d.* úaitniu, *neut.* or *masc.*, "Félire" Index.

soithne (?), *d.* soithniu, *fax*, *fomes*, *Ml.* 97 b, 104 b, 131 d.

ᴄımne, ᴄımnae, ᴄımpne, ᴄınne, *mandatum, præceptum;* a ᴄımne, *Z.*; *d.* ᴄımnu, *Ml.* 114 b, *Wb.* 4 d, 6 d; *nagp.* ᴄımnae, *Ml.* 45, 51 b, 58 a, 115 c, *Wb.* 2.

ᴅamna n-, ᴅ. n-apaıᴅ; *materies*, makings, "Laws," iii. 78.

seımne (?), *d.* Seımnıu, Island Magee, *Tl.* 164.

alMNE (?), almne glunae, *geniculum.*

caemna (?), good cheer, *LL.* 279 a; "Cormac," 12.

gıbnae (?), gıpne, *cirrus.*

comalne (?), *interous.*

cuaılnge (?), *d.* Cuaılṅgıu, "C. R. na Ríg" Index; *nomen viri* in "Four Masters," i. 26.

buınne (?), tube.

ᴅıne (ᴅíne) (?), generation, *W.*

saıne n-, paıne nᴅıgla, "Bk. of Fenagh," 234.

ceᴄna: a céᴄna, the same thing, *LU.* 101 a, "Bodl. Cormac," 4, 12.

ana n-, delay, respite, "Laws," i. 282 and often; for anaᴅ n- (?).

ᴄarsno: a ᴄappno, the thwart-piece; *d.* ᴄappno, "MacCarthy's Stowe Missal," 256, 257.

ıᴅna (?), weapon; *d.* ıᴅnu, L. na gCeart," 6; *ap.* ıᴅna, ıᴅnu, *W.*

fıaᴅnısse, *testimonium:* a fıaᴅnıppepın, *Wb.* 18 b d; *pl.* ınna fıaᴅnaıppe, *W.*; *d.* fıaᴅnıppıu, presence, *Tl.* 198.

gaufıaᴅnuıppe, gufıaᴅnaıpe no gufopgell, false witness, "Laws," i. 58; ii. 320, 322; "Man. & Cust." iii. 493.

núefıaᴅnıppe, nufıaᴅnaıppe, núıeᴅnıppe, nueᴄhnıppe, nuaıᴅnıpe, New Testament; *ns.* an nuıeᴅnıppe, an núıaᴅnıpe, *Wb* 15 b, *Ml.* 2 d; *g.* núıeᴅnıppı, nueᴅnıpı, núıaᴅnıppı, nuaıᴅnıpı, *Wb.* 15 a, 26 a, 27 a, *Ml.* 17 d; *d.* núıeᴄhnıppıu, nufıaᴅnıpıu, *Wb.* 10 d, *Ml.* 35 b.

ermaısse (?), *d.* epmaıppıu, hitting, attaining, *Ml.* 2 d, where it seems to mean *collineare, attingere, assequi;* seems connected with the obscure word epmaıg, of *W.* (?); it is, doubtless, with po epmaıpeᴄap of *Ag.*; *d.* eapmaıppın, *LL.* 144 a.

maısse (?), food, "Fiac's Hymn"; maıppe, beauty, is *fem.* as appears from maıppıu, *pulchrior*, of *Z.*

nasa: ba heᴅ napa loga, *LL.* 194 a, perhaps for napaᴅ n-, *qv.*

fortse (?); *g.* fopᴄpı; *d.* fopᴄpıu, south-side of a house, "Man. & Cust." iii. 509.

VI.—I-Stems.

I-Stems are of all genders; the Neuters are known by the marks given in the Preface. It is hard to tell whether some of the following words are U, I, or S, or even O-Stems.

PICh m-, Pích mbuana, *bis* in *LL.* 166 b.

ICh m-, ích mbuana, "Bk. of Balymote," 405 b.

ICh N- (ích n-), ích n-erred, a hero's bound, *LU.* "Táin Bó Cuailnge"; the *as.* is in *W.*, coriech n-erred, "Man. & Cust." ii. 372.

TRAIG (tráig), strand, = *litus*, "Bk. of Armagh"; *n.* traig n-, *Sg.* 130 b, Tráig mbaile, "MS. Materials," 473; *as.* a traig, "Maelduin's Cur." 462, 462; *g.* trága, "Hyfiachrach," 116, "L. na gCeart," 188; trago, trégo, in air-thrago, magtrégo, *qv.*; *d.* tráig, "C. M. Rath," 34, *Tl.* 98.

AIRTHAGO, fore-shore (?), "Adamnán," 178.

FINNTRAIG, Ventry; *g.* Findtrága.

MAGTRAIG, *g.* Magtrégo (?), "Four Masters," i. 300.

MURTRAIG, sea strand, "Lismore Lives," 396.

GRAIG N-, graig ngabor, *LU.* 48 a; *np.* grega, gregu; *d.* graig; gl. *equitium*, *W.*; but *np.* graige, *LL.* 304 a, *Tl.* 46; *ap.* graige, "Siab. Ch. C." 380, 382, *LU.* 2 b, 2 c, point to an S-stem; *ap.* grega, *LL.* 304 a.

serr-graig, young stud-horses, *LL.* 103 b.

GELGABARGRAIGE, *LB.* 207 a, *gp.*

BUAID (búaid), búaith, victory, prerogative; *ns.* a mbúaid, *Wb.* 11 a; a búaid n-, *LL.* 273 a, *LU.* 100, 121 b, "Toch. Emire," "Bk. of Fenagh," 370, "Siab Ch. C." 390; "Félire"; *voc.* a buaid n-, *LU.* 100 b; *g.* buaide, *Wb.* 24 a, "Félire"; buada, W., "Félire"; *nap.* buada, *W.*, *Ag.*; *gp.* buade, "Félire."

bánbuaid, "S. na Rann," 127.

braenbuaid, *ibi.* 128.

dimbuaid, ill-luck, disaster, *LU.* 109, "C. R. na Ríg," "Bk. of Fenagh," 362.

glanbuaid, "S. na Rann," 140, "Félire."

mórbuaid, "Bk. of Fenagh," 224.

carabuaid, caraway: an carabuaid, "Stokes' Ir. Materia Med." 23; of course I do not mean to look on it as a compound of buaid.

ᴅebuɪᴅ (?), ᴅebuɪᴛh, ᴅebaɪᴅ (?), fight, *rixatio*, *Z.*; *g.* ᴅebᴛha, "Laws," i. 176; *fem.* in *Z.*, *W.*; but *Ag.* does not mark the *gender;* there is no sign that is *fem.* unless it is ᴅe-baɪᴅ, like ceᴛ-baɪᴅ; *g.* ᴅebᴛha, *W.*; *np.* ᴅebᴛha, *Ag.*

ᴅechubaɪᴅ N-, a kind of metre, "Thurn. Versl." (what declension ?).

ꝼorcraɪᴅ N-, excess, "Laws," i. 280, "Man. & Cust." iii. 492, *W.*, *Ag.* (what declension ?).

ɪarꝼaɪᵹɪᴅ, inquiry; a n-ɪarꝼɪᵹɪᴅ ꞅɪᴅe, "Siab. Ch. C."; it is *fem.*, *Ml.* 35 c, 20 c; *gf.* ɪarꝼaɪchᴛheo.

sɪᴅ (ꞅíᴅ) (?), ꞅíᴛh, fairy seat or hill; *g.* ꞅíᴅo, ꞅíᴅa (ꞅɪᴅuɪ, "Echtra Nerai"), *W.*, "Egerton," 1782, fo. 71; *viri side sunt aerii spiritus, quorum habitacula sunt in collibus amœnis*, "Ogygia," 200; *gp.* ꞅɪᴅe, "Bk. of Armagh"; ꝼɪꞃ ꞅíᴛhe, no ꝼanᴛaɪꞃꝼɪ, *Tl.* 100; *W.* does not give the gender, but his examples show *masc.* or *neut.*; the *gs.* in ᴛ-ꞅíᴅe, *LU.* 99 a; "Sergl. C." 110; cluaɪn ꞅíᴛhe, ꞃaᴛh ꞅíᴛhe (unless these two are *gp.*), of "Four Masters" Index, point to a neuter S-stem; *ns.* ꞅɪᴛh Aoḃa, "Four Masters," i. 70; *am.* coꞃɪn ꞅɪᴛh hɪ ꝼ̇ɪl ꞅɪᴛh, "Amra Ch. C." § 22.

sɪᴅ (ꞅíᴅ), ꞅíᴛh, peace; *ns.* ꞅɪᴅ n-ᵹlé, "S. na Rann," 110; éꞃ-ꞅíᴅ, war, "Ir. Texte," i. 75; ꞃoꞅ̇íᴅ, good peace, "S. na Rann," 150; *g.* ꞅɪᴅa, *W.*, in ᴛ-ꞅ̇íᴅa, *LU.* 63 a, 86 b, "Bk. of Lismore," 206; *Ag.* and *W.* mark it *masc.*; but ꞅíɪᴅ, *g.* ꞅíᴅe, *Wb.* 27 c, 20 d, is either *neut.* S-stem or a *fem.*; in the "Félire Index" it is *masc.* or *neut.* The modern ꞅíoḋ, *g.* ꞅíoᴛha, shows a U-stem.

ᵹrɪᴛh (?), aꞃmᵹꞃɪᴛh, shout, clash of arms, *LU.* 77 b, "C. M. Rath," 184; *gs.* ᵹꞃeaᴛha, "Nennius," 228, "Four Masters," ii. 596; ᵹꞃeᴛha, "Félire"; *np.* ᵹꞃeᴛha, "Félire," Jan. 25; it is *masc.* or *neuter; as.* ᵹꞃɪᴛhmóꞃ.

crɪᴛh (?), quaking, *nds.*, *W.*; *g.* cꞃeᴛha (?).

ɪᴛh (?), corn; *g.* eᴛho, "seems neuter," *Z.*; *g.* aᴛho, "Cod. Bern." 34 a; eᴛha, *LU.* 24 a; *gp.* eᴛhe, *Sg.* 60 a, 70 a; *d.* ɪᴛh, *W.*

nɪᴛh (níᴛh) (?), conflict; *g.* níᴛho, *Tl.* 92; *as.* nɪᴛh, *Z.* 1005, *W.*; *cf.* ꞃo nɪᴛhaɪᵹeᴅ, *Ag.*; *g.* níᴛha, "C. R. na Rig."

MUIR, sea; *ns.* a muir, "Siab. Ch. C." 388; am muir, *Tr.* 4 b, *bis.*; am muir n-, "Félire," 189, "O'Dav." 62; *g.* mora, *Sg.* 94 a; mara, *W.*; maro, "Maelduin's Cur." 478, "Siab. Ch. C." 242; *np.* mora, *Ml.* 3 a; mara, *W.*; *ap.* mure, *Ml.* 122 a; *gp.* muire (in salmuire, "Félire"; ilmuire, "Cormac," 13).

bennmuir *pinna*, *Sg.* 67 a.

glasmuir, green sea, "L. na gCeart," 2.

linnmuir, "S. na Rann," 144.

mórmuir, bog, "Irish Metr. Glos."

romuir, great sea, ocean, "S. na Rann," 144.

salmuir, salt-sea; *gp.* salmuire, "Félire."

téchtmuir, *LB.* 208 b, the frozen ocean or sea, from téachtaim, I condense, congeal.

SRUTHAIR (?), sruthra, *da.* sruthair, Shrule, "Four Masters," iii. 339, 414; "Ann. of Loch Cé," ii. 13, 208; it means a stream in "Joyce's Names of Places," vol. i.

CUAIRT N-, "Cormac," 9, 22, *gs.* cuarta, *npl.* cuarda, *W.*, a circuit, visit; *Ag.* marks it *fem.*

GLUAIR, kind; gluair n-glé, "S. na Rann" Index (what declension ?).

LIN (lín), number, lot; *ns.* lin n-, *LU.* 102 a; an lín, "Maelduin's Cur." 460, 462; al lín, "Yellow Bk. of Lecan," 644; lín mband, *W.*; *g.* líno, lina, "Ascoli," who, as well as *W.*, marks it *masc.*; but *Ag.* does not give gender; it is *neut.* in "Félire Index"; lín, a net, is *neut.* O-stem.

LIN (lín), class (of people), side; *np.* lína; *d. dual*, dib linaib, *Ag.* (what declension ?). *W.* marks this *masc.*

GEIN N-, birth, child; a ngein, *g.* gene, *W.* 632, 590, seems an S-stem; it is *fem.* in *Ag.*; aithgin, *as.* seems to mean renaissance, regeneration, "Pass. & Hom." l. 3812.

GUIN, *vulnus*, a mortal wound; a nguin, *Z.*; *gs.* gona, *Sg.* 57 b; *ap.* gona, *W.*

CONGUIN: a conguin, *expunctio*, which the glossarist mistook for *punctio*, *compunctio*; a conguin cridi, *aculeum doloris*, *Ml.* 23 a, 32 c.

IMMLIND, navel; a n-immlind, "Gildas' Lorica."

AITHGIN N-, restitution, "Laws," i. 168, 174, 170; *gs. np.* aithgina, 142, 172, 260, 272, *etc.*; aithgin mbetha, "Félire" Index.

RINN, rinn, star, *signum, sidus;* ar rinn, a rinn, *g.* renda, *np.* renda, rinn, "Ascoli's Gloss."; *np.* renna, *W.*; rinnd, *aculeus,* is *masc.*, *Wb.* 13 d.

ERREND (érrend) (?), *stigmata, signa, Ascoli;* but in da érrend shows that it is not *neut.*; perhaps we should read in da n-érrend.

TUAISRINN, *gp.* tuaissrenn, northern stars, *Ml.* 94 a, or *Tr.* (?).

AIRCHIND, front; da n-airchinn, front and rear walls (of a house), "Laws," i. 274; of this declension (?).

MUIRN N-, troop; muirn n-uabair, "L. na gCeart," 158; of this declension (?).

TORAIN N-, "S. na Rann," 153; of this declension (?).

DRUIMM, *g.* drommo, back, ridge; *six times* in "Bk. of Armagh"; Noindrommo, *Sg.* 226 a; *see* ANN-stems.

AERAIC, aeraic mbriathar, *Ml.* 59 a.

AES N-, age; *n.* aes n-esci, age of the moon; *g.* aiso, *d.* ais, *voc.* áis, *Ascoli;* it is *masc.* when it means age *or* class of men; *neut.* when = age of the moon; but also *neuter* in aes mberri, aes mbeire.

FOROIL (foróil). *abundantia, Z.*; a foróil, *Wb.* 16 d, *Ml.* 16 (?)

DEROIL (deróil) (?), *nihil, Wb.* 18 a; these are probably adjectives.

VII.—U-Stems.

These are Masculine, Neuter, and Feminine. Neuters may be known by the marks given in the Preface.

LOCH N-, lake; not in *Z.*; *n.* loch n-, *LL.* 167 a, *bis; LU.* 98 a; "Bk. of Lecan," 250 b; "Bk. of Balymote," 391 a; and ten instances in our Preface; *g.* locho, *bis* in "Bk. of Armagh"; *gs.* and *g. dual,* locha, "Félire"; *np.* locha, *W.*

brenloch, *LU.* 33 a.

clóenloch, *LL.* 169 b.

dubloch, *g.* dublocho, "Bk. of Armagh."

iarsloch.

Magloch, Fourth Charter of "Bk. of Kells."

Morloch, "Four Masters" Index.

muirloch, *salsugo,* "Southampton Gl."

munloch, puddle, *LB.* 414.

turloch, dried-up lake, *LL.* 158 b, 291 b; but *ns.* turloch Airt.

ımbleċh N-, now ımleach; *ns.* ımlech n-, ımblıuch n-, *LB.* 216 a; "Táin Bó Dartada," p. 297; *g.* ımblecho, *d.* ımblıuch, "Bk. of Armagh"; *g.* ımlecho, ımlecha, "Ann. of Ulster," 523, 687, 736; Imlech of p. 85, "Lismore Lives," should be Imlecha; but *g.* Imlıᵹ in Seventh Charter of "Bk. of Kells"; *g.* ımblecha, *d.* ımblıuch, ımlıuch, land bordering on a lake, "Félire"; ımlıoch n-eaċ, "M'Firbis' Pedigrees," p. 216; yet Imlech Onanḋ, *Tl.* 94.

ᵹRAD (ᵹrádḋ) (?), love; *g.* ᵹrádḋa, *Ag.*; *W.* marks it *neuter.*

RAċh N-, stock; *gs. ap.* racha, "Laws," iii. 214, 226, 340, 300. ḋaerrach, daer-stock, *ibi.* 217.

RAċh (?), *np.* racha, pledges, guarantees.

RAċh, grace; *gs.* racha; *np.* racha, *Ag.*; rach n-, luck, "Bk. of Fenagh," 312, 408; *np.* prímrácha, *LB.* 219 b; what declension? mírach, bad luck; ríᵹrách, royal grace, "Lismore Lives," 398; amrach, nemrach, "Cormac," 1.

CRAċh (trách), trach, canonical hour; *g.* tracha; *ap.* tracha, trach; *gp.* trach, *W.*; *gp.* tracha, *Ag.*; *W.* and *Ag.* mark it *neuter;* why? *ap.* tracha, *LL.* 305 a; trach, *LU.* 28 a; mochtrach, early dawn.

Aċh N- (ách n-), *LL.* 60, 303 a, "Bk. of Balymote," 397, 398; "Mac Gniomh. Finn," p. 38, 2nd ed., *bis.* a ford; aach, *Tl.* 198; *as.* tar an ách, *H.* 2, 12, *bis*, *g.* ácho, "Ann. of Ulster," 627, 737, 760, 78; *ns.* ach, *Tr.* 53 b; *ap.* acha, acho, achu, *W.*, who marks it *masc.*, which it perhaps generally is.

FAċh (fách), cause; fách n-eıdıᵹ, "C. M. Rath," 54; but ın fach, "Félire" Index and *Ag.*; and ır é tra fách is common in Middle Irish.

bRAċh (brách) (?), judgment; *g.* brácho, "Bk. of Armagh"; *g.* bracha, *W.*, *Ag.*, who mark it *masc.*; why?

DAċh N-, colour; *g.* dacho, *Wb.* 5 c; *np.* dacha, *LU.* 99, *LB.* 108; *np.* dach, "Ir. Texte," *T.* 71; *ns.* dach n-; *gs.* dacha, *W.*, who marks it *neut.*; *Ag.* marks it *masc.*; líᵹdach, rodach, "Félire."

meċh N-, failure, decay—now meach; *g.* mecha, "Laws," i. 232; mech n-, *W.*

AeD, fire; dá n-aed, .ı. da ḟúıl, Amra Ṡenáın, cf. *g.* and *voc.* Aıdo, "Bk. of Armagh."

SUTh, *fœtus*, *fructus*; *g.* rotho; *np.* rothe, *Z.*, who marks it it *neut.*; *np.* rothe, *Sg.* 64a; *ap.* ruthu, *Ml.* 39 cd; *W.* and *Ag.* do not give gender. I find no sign that it is *neuter* except its likeness to rruth.

LANSUTh (lánruth), "Southampton Glossary."

SRUTh N-, "O'Dav." 56, *Ag.*, *rivus*, *flumen*; *g.* rrotho, rrotha, *Sg.* 35 b, *Wb.* 32 c; *Z.* says *neut.* or *masc.*; *np.* rrotha, *W.*

camḟruth (*cf.* Welsh, *camfruth*), *fluvius curvus*, *Z.* 147.

imḟruth (counter-tide, *O'R.*), "Bk. of Armagh"; *flux* (*ventris*), "S. na Rann," p. 61, l. 4160; *np.* imrrotha, great streams, *LU.* "Táin Bó Cualgne."

ríġrruth, "S. na Rann," 148.

BRUTh, glow, ardour, bruth n-, brud n-, *LU.* 104 a, 125 b, *W.* 590; "Fled. Bricr.," "Toch. Emire"; *g.* brotha, *W.*, who does not give gender; bruth n-armach, "O'Dav." 56.

FRIThBRUTh (?), "O'Dav." 83, refusal, rejection.

LANBRUTh, *g.* lánbrotho.

LONNBRUTh N-, fury, "MS. Mater." 506.

MURBRUTh N- (mórbruth n-), *LU.* 106 b, *W.*

bruth (?), bruth, .i. dermut, "O'Dav." 58.

GRUTh (?), curds; *g.* grotha.

UNBLUTh (anblúth), anbluth n-én, ornament or part of chariot, *LU.* 106 a, *bis.*

LUD, lúud, *velocitas* (*alacritas* ?), *Z.*, *as.* luth, "Félire"; comluth, comlud, "L. na gCeart," 4; luth n-, "S. na Rann," 44; cétlúd, "Cormac," 9, 10.

INDRUTh (?), foray; indruth n-, "Man. & Cust." iii. 508.

RET N- (rét n-), a thing; *LU.* 26 b, *g.* réto, *Z.*; *Z.* and *W.* mark it *masc.*, and it is *npm.* ind reta, *Sg.* 148 a; gach rét mbeg, "O'Dav." 77.

REUD, **REUTh** (?), *ds. gelu*, *pruina*, *Z.* What gender and declension?

MID, now mioḋ, mead; *n.* am mid; *g.* meda, *W.*; *Z.* is doubtful of the gender. *Cf.* Gaul. *medu.*

FID, now fioḋ, wood; fid n-gabli, *LL.* 159 a, 216 b, "Bk. of Balymote," 357 b; fiod ndorcha, "Four Masters," an. 1166; *g.* fedo, feda, *Z.*; in *Z.* and the glosses it is *masc.* in fid, *Wb.* 5 b; *d.* friuth, *ter* in *Tl.* 194; *gp.* fede, "Cormac." 16.

allfid, "Cormac," 12.

anad N-, stay, delay; *gs.*, *nap.* anta, "Laws," i. 146, 148, 262, 264, 282, 284.

arad N-, arud n-, notice; *g.* artha, *d.* arud, "Laws," i. 120, 146, 230, 256, 284; *n. dual*, da n-arad, 262.

miad N- (míad n-), honour; dímíad, *g.* dímíada, "C. M. Rath," are U-stems (*see* under O-stems).

diablud N-, *g.* diabulta, the double, "Laws," i. 114, 158, 160, 280, ii. 66, 212; "O'Dav." 60.

urad (?), *gs.* urtha, charm, spell, "Laws," i. 180, 176; *neut.* or *fem.*(?); *ap.* urtha, *W.*; *g.* ertha, *LB.* 217 b.

luad N-, talk, "Félire Index"; what declension?

mennat (?), abode, *g.* mennato, "Bodl. Cormac," 36; *d.* mennut "Bk. of Armagh"; *gs. ap.* mennota, *W.*

aided N-, death, *LU.* 38 a; *g.* aideda, *obitus*, "Ogygia," 385, *Ag.*; *as.* aiged, for aided, *W.*; however, *dasf.* aidid, *LL.* 127 a; *Tl.* 224, 250; "C. Finntragha," 76.

audsud N-, etrud n-, treasure, *arca*, *Tl.* 62, 256, 461; etrad, *Ml.* 51 d; irtud, *Tl.* 482; irtadluc, treasury, *LB.* 219 a; *np.* irtoda, "Man. & Cust." iii. 511 (?); artuda, of *LU.*, means reins.

ucht N-, ucht n-ornae, "Cormac," 44; but ucht ornae, *LL.* 144 a.

recht N-, racht n-, cid a recht, "Laws," i. 230, 260, 160, iii. 28; *LB.* 211 a; *g.* rechto, *Wb.* 31 d; it is *masc.*, *Wb.* 1 d, 4 d, 13 d *bis*; *Ml.* 46 c, 86 a; but ar recht, the law, *Ml.* 77 a, is *neut.*, and yet na tri recte, *Wb.* 29 a, which *Z.* took for *np. neuter*, is, I think, the *gp.* governed by *testibus* (or *testimonio* understood).

anrecht, ainrecht, illegality, "Laws," ii. 272, i. 256; "S. na Rann," 126.

dithrecht, *np.* dithrechta, .i. dirrectad, "O'Dav." 76.

oigrecht, full right.

desimrecht N-, dermrecht n-aill, example; *gs. ap.* derim-rechta; *gp.* derimrechte, *Sg.* 66 b, *Wb.* 26 b, 30 c, *Sg.* 214; drochdermrecht, bad example, *Ml.* 118 a.

landirech (lándírecht) (?), lethdírech, full uncovering, half uncovering; *cf.* durig, *nudat*; of this declension (?); *cf.* direch n-, O-stems.

AIRECT, airecht (?), *curia*, a meeting; *gs. np.* airechta, "Eutych. Vindob." *LU.* 27 b a; *d.* airiucht, *LL.* 308 a, *LU.* 27 a, *Tl.* 138; but *gf.* na hairechta, *LL.* 115 a, not *neut.*: da airecht, "Rawl." 487, fo. 14 b.

FULRACHT (?), bloodshed.

ICHT (?), .i. cenel, "Cormac," 18.

SLICHT N-, sliucht n-, track (also version, story), "S. na Rann," 60, 150; *gs. ap.* slechta, "Laws," i. 282; *ap.* slictu, *Z.* the modern *gen.* is sleachta, *Ag.*

DRECHT (drécht) (?), dreecht, *pars, portio*, *Wb.* 4 d, 5 c.

DRECHT (?), .i. imat, eolus, "O'Dav." 74.

CECHT (cécht) (?), power, *salus*, "Cormac," 16.

BRICHT (?), spell; *np.* brechta, *Tl.* 50; *gs. np.* brechta, *W.*; *Ag.* marks it *masc.*

TRACHT (?), strand, shore; *ds.* *Tl.* 98, and Index to "Four Masters"; I have met Tracht mBenchuir; *np.* inna trachta; *gp.* trachtae, *Ml.* 67 d; *ap.* trachta, *LB.* 218, trachtu, *Ml.* 121 a.

ECHT (écht), deed; echt n-oll, "Harl. Gloss." 354; *np.* na héachta; *LB.* 276, "C. M. Rath," 210; *ap.* banéchta, *ibi.* 212; *g.* échta, *W.*; *np.* échta, "G. Corca Laide," 162.

FECHT, journey, time; nach fecht n-aile, "Slab. Ch. C."; fri fecht n-ega, on the death journey, "Cormac," 3, 382, a fecht sa, this time, "Fled. Bricr." *W.*; *gs.* fechta, *Wb.* 23 a; gl. tursas, *O'Cl.*

HUATHFECHT (?), "Cormac," 3.

DIALT, syllable; *g.* dialta, *np.* dialta, dialt, "Thurn. Versl." 129, "Cormac"; *v.* deach; *np.* dialt, *bis*; *g.* dialta, *bis*, "Cormac," 16, 17.

ARD N- (árd n-), ardd, *altum*, *altitudo*, "Bk. of Armagh"; Ard mBreccain, "Bk. of Balymote," 51 a; *g.* ardo, arda, "Four Masters," i. 11, 26; "Fragm. of Irish Ann." Sixth Charter of "Bk. of Kells"; "O'Conor's Rer. Hib. Scrip." I. pars i., clxv.; *g.* arda, "Mart. of Tallacht," Aug. 23; "L. na gCeart," 128; six times in "Mc Firbis' De Episcopis," p. 86; airdo, "Ann. of Ulster," 689; also an O-stem, "Bk. of Armagh."

lethárd, a sloping height, "Joyce's Names of Places," vol. 1.;
imárd n-, "Laws," i. 26.

NERT N-, *Sg.* 215 a, *virtus, vis*, strength, *Z.*, *W.*, *Ag.*, and "Félire Index," mark it *neuter; gs.* nerta, *d.* neurt, *Wb.* 31 b, 6 d, 18 b, *Ml.* 46 d; *np.* neurta, *Tl.* 50; *ap.* neurta, nerta, *W.*, *Ag.*; *gp.* nertae, *Ml.* 34 d, *exhortationem;* as to gender, *cf.* firt; *gs.* neirt, "Ann. of Loch Cé," i. 190.

FIRT, *virtus, miraculum; g.* ferto, *ngp.* ferte, *ap.* morfferta, *Z.*; *Wb.* 8 a, 12 a, 12 b; *Z.* and *W.* omit gender. *Ag.* marks it *masc.*, and "Felire" Index, *neuter;* in "Félire," *gs.* ferto, *np.* ferta; *ap.* firtu, *Wb.* 12 a, 8 a, 12 b, 26 a, *Ml.* 16 c, 17 c, 69 d; *ns.* in fiurt, *W.*; *as. neut.* an ḟirt, *Ag.*; firt n-, *LB.* 259; *gs.* ind ḟerta, *Tl.* 92,

sáibfirt, *ap.* sáibfirtu, *Wb.* 26 a; wrongly marked 26 c in *Z.* 858.

FERT N-, mound, grave; fert mbecc, *Tl.* 138; an feurt, "Bodl. Cormac" (3 ?); *nas.* fert, firt, *LL.* 97 a b, 120 a; probably an O-stem; *g.* firt Aeda, "Four Masters," i. 400; *ds.* fiort, *ibi.* 160; fert, "Mart. of Tallaght," Jan. 1; it is also *fem.* IA-stem in "Bk. of Armagh," and often in *Tl.* and elsewhere.

DISERT (dísert), a ndísert sa, *LU.* 15 a, hermitage; *d.* dísiurt, *Tl.* 266; *LU.* 15 b, marked *neut.* in "Félire" Index; *n.* in disert, *g.* díserta, *LB.* 217 b, 218 b; *g.* dísirt, "Four Masters," i. 428.

BIR, biur, now bior, a spit, *n.* or *ap.* beura, *sudes*, *Sg.* 67 b; *gs.* bero, bera, *d.* biur, *gap.* bera, *LU.* 92, 69 b, "Stokes' Celt. Decl."; *nap.* bera, *LB.* 217 a, "Laws," i. 178; but indber, a spit, *LL.* 292 b; *g.* indbir, *Tl.* xxii, is an O-stem.

SMIR (?), marrow, *g.* smera, now smior.

PUDAR (?), hurt, harm, *nas.*, *W.*; *g.* pudra, "Laws," i. 178.

FIUS (?), fiuss, fiss, knowledge: a fius sin, *Wb.* 10 b; *g.* fesso, fessa, *Wb.* 14 d, 26 d; the form fius, now fios, shows U-stem.

remfius, prescience, *ds.*, *Wb.* 31 a, also an O-stem; *g.* fiss, *ap.* fess, *Z.*, who marks it *masc.*, as do *W.* and *Ag.*

CLESS, feat, trick; dallcless n-éoin, "Fled. Bricr.," "Siab. Ch. C.," 378; a toraindcless, *LU.* 37 a; cless n-éoin, *W.*; *g.* clessa, *W.*, who marks it *masc.*

ꞇes, heat, *g.* ꞇeꞅa, *neut.* according to "Stokes' Decl." 14; but *am.* ın ꞇeꞅ, *calorem*, *Ml.* 42 c; *g.* ꞇeꞅa, *Sg.* 5 a; *W.* and *Ag.* mark it *masc.*, but give no reason therefor.

memꞇhess (?), *g.* nemꞇheoꞅꞅa, nemꞇhıuꞅa, a charm, *LB.* 264, *LL.* 187 a.

less (?), leꞅ, advantage; *g.* leꞅꞅa, *np.* leꞅꞅa, "Laws," i. 236; *na.* less, *Z.*; *neut.* or *masc.*

les, léꞅ, light, *ns.*; *as.* a ꝼoꞃléꞅ, a ꝼoꞃleꞅ, the roof-light, "Táin Bó Fróich," 140.

ᵹles (ᵹléꞅ) (?), tuning, preparing (a harp); *as.* ᵹleꞅ, "Man. & Cust." Index; *g.* ᵹléꞅo (an instrument of any kind), a pen *or* stylus, "Bk. of Armagh"; *gp.* ᵹleꞃe, weapons, "C. M. Rath," 144; *gs.* ᵹléꞅꞅa, *W.*; it is now ᵹleuꞃ, manner, *etc.*; aıꞃ ᵹleuꞃ ᵹo = so that, *see* "Coney's Dict."

ᵹless (?), *ap.* ᵹleꞅꞅa, gusts of wind, "Four Masters," i. 524.

ᵹus (?), .ı. ᵹnıoṁ, ꝼeaꞃᵹ, "O'Clery," a brave deed; *n.*, aꞃꝺ a nᵹuꞅ, great the (their ?) deed, "Nennius," 276; *g.* ᵹoꞅꞅa, "C. M. Rath," 136; *gp.* na nᵹuꞅ nᵹalmaꞃ, *LL.* 25; *ap.* ꝼoꞅꞅa, *W.*; as it appears in names of men, Ꝼeꞃᵹuꞅ, Ꝼeꞃᵹoꞅꞅo, *etc.*, it may be *masc.*

cambas (?), camboꞅ; *g.* camꞅa, "Bk. of Armagh" Glossary.

cenondas (?), *g.* cenannꞅo; *d.* cenınnuꞅ, "Bk. of Armagh," "Ann. of Ulster," 806.

sians (?), ꞅenꞅ, *sensus*, *Z.*, *g.* *senso*; *gp.* ꞅenꞅe, *Wb.* 23 b, "Bk. of Armagh."

ᵹnim (ᵹním), now ᵹnıoṁ, deed; ᵹním nᵹlé, "Bk. of Fenagh," 326, 360, five times in "S. na Rann" Index, once in *Ag.*, once in "O'Conor's Rer. Hib. Scrip." ɪ. pars ii., xxxv. It is *masc.* in *Z.*, *W.*, *Ag.*; *gs.* ᵹnímo; *pl.* ᵹníma; the *neuter* form is found in chevilles, and may contain the preglossarial gender.

maichim n- (?), maıꞇhem n-, pardon, *LL.* 358, *LB.* 215 a; *d.* maıꞇhem, "Félire," 86; where we find also *af.* maıꞇhım; but *a.* maıꞇheam, *Ag.*

comram: a comꞃam ꞅın, *LU.* 107 b; *g.* comꞃama; is *masc.* in *W.*, trophy, competition, *LL.* 79 a b.

deichthriub (?), ten tribes, *ndas.* *Ml.* 100 b, 137 c, 67 a; *g.* ꝺeıchꞇhꞃebo, ꝺeꞇhꞃebo, *Ml.* 100 b, 106 d; cf. *gp.* (?) ceꞇhaꞃꞇhꞃebe, "Fiac."

LINN, linn, liquor, drink, beer, *potus*, now lionn, (in Munster, liúnn); ir hed ar linn, *as.* frirra linn, *Wb.* 13 c, 7 d, an linn, *Tl.* 54, al linn, *W.*; *d.* linn, *Z.*; linn, "Laws," i. 2; *g.* lenna, lenda, *Ml.* 129 d, *Wb.* 7, *LL.* 63 a, "Mesca Ul." 44, *Tl.* 236; *ap.* lenna, "Bk. of Balymote," 252 a; the compounds are deglinn, braichlinn, blaithlinn, (*LU.* 107 a, "Man. & Cust." 37) good malt, mellow liquor.

deglinn, good drink; *g.* deglenda, "O'Dav." 55.

DINN (dionn, "Four Masters" Index): a ndinn, *oppidum*, *Sg.* 63 a; *g.* denna, *LU.* 9 a, *LL.* 175 a; deanda, "Fragm. of Irish Ann." 38; *ap.* dinna, "Four Masters," ii. 570; *d.* for dinn, for dinn, "Félire,"80; dinn Tradui, .i. dún Tradui, *Tl.* 570; in Modern Irish dionn shows a U-stem.

GLOSSARIAL INDEX OF THE LL. TEXT.

N.B.—The numbers refer to the paragraphs; the asterisks to the words and forms not (or not explained) in Windisch's Dictionary. The cases, genders, and numbers are marked by their initials, thus, *dasm.* = dative and accusative singular masculine; *N., D., Ag., S., W., Z., BA.*, are for *neuter, dual*, Atkinson's *Glossary*, Stokes, Windisch's *Dictionary*, Zeuss' *Grammatica*, and *Book of Armagh*, respectively.

a', his (its); proleptic in § 51: a airm sénta Conculaind.

a, her (its).

a n-, their (twelve times); = al- before l, 8, 8, 8, 22; am- before labial, 9; a triar bráthar (their trio of brothers), the three brothers, 57.

a, which, 25, 25; a n-, that which, 29, 29.

a n-, the, is *neuter* in a ní, the thing.

a = as, out of, 6; from 3, 5, 8, 8, 10, 11, 12, 38.

a = ó, from, 19, 22, 38, 53, 54.

á', a' = ó a', from its, 25.

a (eight times), O! an interjection; it aspirates; but does not asp. the possessive mo: a mo phópa.

ahain* = ó ḟain (?), from that, thence (?). *Cf.* óḟain ille, *LL.* 191 a; ó hḟain, "S. na Rann," l. 2381; ohein, *Tl.* 216.

abaind,* 28, 52; *dasf.* of ab or abann, a river; *np.* aibni,* 6; *n.* aband, "B. of Lismore," 70; *LL.* 198 a; abonn, "B. of Fenagh," 208.

abba,* cause, reason: mór-abba.

abbrai,* 27; *2d. sg. pres. ind.* or *subj.* of atberim, 5; *depend. form*, in n-abbrai, sayest thou, *or* wouldst thou say?

abóind, 25 = ar abaind, or ar a bóind, or ar a bond (boind), by its bottom, "Where the river was deeper than anywhere else by its bed." The text seems corrupt if bóind is not *dsf.* here.

abram,* 7. mac Romrach.

ac, 5, 7, 9, at; *idiomatic* with gabaim, 22, 25, 47; by *after passives*, 2, 17, 17; acum, 5, at me; acut, 14, with thee; acaind, with us, 4; to us, in our presence, 23; by us, for us, 23; acaib, among you, 25; ac, do, la designate the agent *after passives;* accu, 2, 8, 13, 19, 29, at them, by them: rocomairleced accu.

acallaim, 19, *dsf.*, to speak, address.

accaill breg,* 23; *asf.*, the hill of Skreen; acail .i. tulach hiril Sgrin Choluim Cille indiu, *LU.*, p. 50; *n.* achall ar aicce Temuir; *g.* aichle, *LL.* 161 a; "Sench. M." III. 82, aicle, "Ogygia," 341.

accill,* 9, 9, *dsf.*; i n-accill seems synon. with i n-airichill (9), in readiness for, *or* for; for accill do mharbhtha, in wait to slay thee, "Mac-Ghníomh. Find," § 32; *cf.* "Cath. Fintraga," p. 91, ed. by Dr. Meyer; *cf.* an-fochill, *incuriam*, *Ml.* 117 b, 127 c; ic faichill, preparing, "C. M. Rath," 154.

a-chétóir,* 25, at once (at the first moment), = fochetoir in *Z.*

acht, 8, etc., but; act, 44; acht mad, 27, unless it be; act mani, 11, unless, after a negative; acht, 27, marks transition rather than antithesis.

acus,* and; *in full*, 7, 11, and *LL.* 91. in § 51 used idiomatically in descriptions; inund acus, 44, the same as; acus *aspirates*, 12, *as in Sg.* 33 a, 10; ocus, *Z.*; ocos, "7th Charter, B. Kells."

admolta,* 3, 15, *gsm.*, of eulogising, of eulogy; *np.* 13, 23, 24.

aed,* 8, *nsm.*; son of Conall Cernach.

aed,* 32, *nsm.*; son of Conad Buide.;

áes, aes, 46, 3, 15; *nasm.* folk; aes ciúil, musicians; aés óchbad, 34, youths, young-folk, or warriors.

aesam, 44; oesam, oesum, 38, 40, 41, 42; *das.* protection, defence; ḟaesam, *LL.* 268 b; bar th'(ḟ)oesam 7 bar do chommairge, 38. *g.* faesma, exemption, protection, "Laws," I. 100, 200. *Cf.* mac faesma, child of adoption, "Man. & Cust." III. 587 a.

ágaib,* 48, *dp.*, limbs, fragments (?); con-daralsat é na ágib, *LL.* 169.

aibbgetus,* 8, *ns.*, maturity, i.e. good quality of drink; synon. with gléire, *ib.*

aíbniusa, 13, *gsm.*, delight, pleasure, merry-making; *n.* aibinnius, "Atkinson's Gloss." Note that the emph. particle follows first of two gen. connected by acus.

aichnid, 11, known, *an adjective, nsm.*; su-aichnid, distinguished, *LU.* 110 a.

aicned, 25, 26, 27, *nsm.* or *N.*, mind; *g.* aicnid.

aidble,* 4, *npm.*, vast, great; aidlib, *dp.* 5, *ns.* adbal; ind-adbol, gl. *valde, Z.*; it is like uasal, uaisle; may be *nsf.* of a noun; *as.* aidble remend, *W.* and "Adamnan," 274; aidble uird, "O'Hartigan."

aidchi, 15, 16, *asf.*; *np.*, 6, night; inn-aidchi sin, 53, on that night is *acc.* or *dative*; *ns.* adaig, *g.* aidche, *LU.* 48, 58, 102 a, 128, 118.

aided, 46, *as.*; *g.* aideda, (violent) death *here*, and so is bas; *ns.* aided, *np.* oitte, *LL.* 189 b.

áig, 11, *gsm.* or *N.* of ág, war, danger; *ds.* ág, contest, *Wb.* 25 a; benaim bemend ágmara, I strike brave strokes, *LU.* 76 a; *g.* aig, "B. of Fen." 226; agmar, valorous, "B. of Fen." 398; *g.* ága, *LL.* 88, 81.

aiged, 36, *nsf.* before infinitive; *das.* 13, 21, 22, 44, face, front: in-agid, towards, to meet, against, 13, 22; *gs.* aigthi, 17, and *LL.* 114 b.

aigsem, 6, we shall drive (?); shall go, fear (?); *cf.* is aichthi, it is to be feared, *Sg.* 33 b.

ro-s-ail, 2, *pres.* (made *past* by ro) with infixed pron. s, who nourished him; ailebthair, he shall be nursed, "Ch. of Uisnech," notail, he feeds thee, *Z.*

áil, 15, 23, *ns.*, pleasant, pleasure (?) ros ail damsa, cid ass áil latt? = as adlic let, *LU.* 108.

aile, 9, 9, 10, 10, other; *ap.* 31; seems *gp.*: for seilb neich n-aill n-aile, 43, on the possession of any other nobles (?).

ailella, 11, *gsm.*, of ailill, father of Sencha, and son of Culclan, "Sench. M." I. 150.

ailill, 3, 5, 16, 17, 19, 23, *nda.*; son of Ross Ruad and consort of Queen Medb, and brother of Cairpre Nia Fer (King of Tara) and Find File (King of Ailenn or Ailiu); ailill *in full*, 23, and *LL.* 170 b; mac Matach, "Sench. M." I. 150.

aill, 43; seems *gp.* of aill, a nobleman, "O'Davoren," p. 49; aill, some, others, *LL.* "MS. Mat." 507.

aim, 1, 6; in-aim (in [the] time), when, as in tan and in-tain, they seem *def.*; in aim rancatar, *LU.* 109 b.

ainm, 25, *nsN.*, name.

áin, 55, *gs.* of ár, gl. *strages.*

airáibniusa,* 11, *gsm.*, great pleasure; *see* áibniussa; air is intensitive, as in ur-árd telcha, on the very top, *LL.* 97 b.

airchind, 36, *npm.*, *præcipites*, headlong, forward, fleet; *Z.* translates is airchenn ṁ-bes salt, *est indubium esse saltum;* the word is not in the Index of *Z.* It may mean "determined;" the noun aircind means a front (of a house or chariot), *LU. Táin;* tóib 7 erchinn (side and front?), *Ml.* 131 e; fri da taeb (sides), fri da n-airchind (fronts), "Laws," i. 274.

airchisis, 3, *s-pret.* of airchisim, I pity, spare; it takes *do* after it.

airdairc, 54, *ns. N.*, notable.

airdi, ardí, 15, 3; compar. of árd, high.

airderg, 6, *nsm.*, seems = airdairc; as it stands it means "very red," *præruber;* cf. airdérgud, *propositum*, *Z.*

airecht, 22, *ds.* airecta, 18, *np.*, courts, assemblies; *ns.* airecht, *gs.* airechta, *LL.* 115 a; = *eiriott* in Anglo-Irish; to await, "L. na gCeart," 4.

airet, 17, *as.*, time, space; in n-airet, so much, so long; ind-airetsa, gl. *tamdiu.*

airfiti, 3, *gs*; *np.* 13, 23; amusement, amusing compositions; cantar ciúil 7 airfiti 7 admolta.

airfitid, 15, *gs.*; *np.* 24; *ns.* airfitiud or airfited, *delicias*, *Tl.* 6; airfeided aon uaire, the pleasure one hour, *LB.* 152; *g.* oirfitid, "B. of Fen." 206.

ra-airgestar, 4, 3 *sg. dep. pret.* of airgim,* or ergim,* she ravaged (it ?); ro airg, *LB.* 207 b, 208 a.

airgni, 3, 15, *npf.* of argan, *as.* argain, 4; *ap.* airgni, 22; plundering, ravaging, havoc; *ns.* argain, *np.* airgne, *LL.* 190 a; argni, airgne, "B. of Fen." 398, 284; *ap.* oirgne, "F. Mast." i. 260.

airichill, 9, 9, 11, *def.*, expectation or preparation: in-accill 7 in-airichill Conaill, 'n-a remur 7 'n-a airichill dam; airichill, *LL.* 106 b (*bis*); airichligis, *LB.* 116 a; ro hairichlit, they were prepared, *LL.* 268 a (*bis*); airchlis, he met, "Mesca Ul." p. 6; oc erochill, awaiting, expecting, *LU.* 31 b; *tuum usum*, Mac Daire's "Teg. Flatha," l. 174; *cf. LB.* 207 b, 210 a; "Cormac," 12.

airidni, 3, 15, *npf.*, outhouses, offices; a. 7 immellaige, a. 7 urbada, half a house, "Petrie's Tara," 203; it contained eight couches; *ds.* airidin, "Petrie," p. 203. *Cf.* udnucht, palisade (?), *Goidelica*, 177–182, "O'D. Suppl."; airidi, a dairy (?), "Man. & Cust." iii. 488.

airm, 3, 7, 8, 8, 12, 19, 22; *asf.*, a place, co h-airm.

airm, 51, *npm.*, *gp.* arm, 14; *dp.* armaib, 51; arms, weapons; *nsN.* in O. Irish, arm, *pl.* arma.

airthiur, 25, 25, *ds.*, east quarter; perhaps *neuter*.

áisi, 14, *gs.* of áes, age; seems *fem.* here, and different from áes ciuil, etc.

aiss, 37, *ds.*, back; ría n-ais, (they brought) back or on their back.

aissec, 17, 17, 19; *ndsm.*, repayment; aiscis, he gave, restored, *LL.* 358.

aitecha, 34, 34; *napm.*, youthful; *gp.* aitedach, *LL.* 266; *ds.* áitiu, youthfulness, *LB.* 236 b; *n.* óitiu, *d.* óitid, *W. Cf.* óitidchi, younger, *LL.* 58 aa.

aitheo, 7, *dsm.* flight; *n.* aitheo, *np.* aithio, *LL.* 190 a.

aith-ger, 39, *asm.*, very sharp; or from aith-gep, axe-sharp. *Cf.* oe-aith, *bipennis*, *Sg.* 67 a.

aitib, 13, atib, 15; *dpm.*, apartments, buildings, as the triplet shows; *nv.* aite, *W. & Ag.*

aithli, aithle, 6, 13, 25: a'haithli, arr a haithle, afterwards; ar t'aithli, after thee, "B. of Magh Rath," 170.

Álaib,* 10; = Olaf, the most prominent name among the Vikings; Olaf invaded Ireland in 852, "Ann. of Ulster," .i. alainn, "O'Dav." 50.

alban, 7, *gsf.* of alba, Scotland; *a.* Albain, "Marian. Scotus."

ale, used with ap, bap, pap, to signify "replied"; perhaps it is the ale, ille, = here, hither.

ale ar, 42, and *fo.* 90 a; ale bap, 7, 23, 23, 27, 27, 40; ale bap, "B. of M. Rath," 306, 308; ale pap, § 11 of our text; see note 2 to § 7.

algessach, *ns.*; *voc.* algerraig, importunate: see athepne.

alind, 57, *dsf.*, seat of the Leinster Kings, near (and north of) Old Kilcullen, Co. Kildare; *g.* ailend, "Man. Materials," p. 492; also *g.* alinne.

alle, 11, *ap.* of álainn, beautiful.

allib, 42, *dpN.* of all, cliff.

allud, 25, 26, *ns.*, fame; *gs.* allaid, *LL.* 217 b; *n.* alla ("B. of Fen," 228) should be, perhaps, allad; inallaid, famous, "B. of Fen," 380; *ds.* allud, *LU.* 102 a.

alt, 39, 40, 42; *ns.*, act (effort?).

alt, 12, 34, 36, 38; *das.* juncture (of time); alt, form, frame, "B. of Fen." 374.

ám, am, indeed; occurs 13 times.

am, 6, time.

am(al), 10, as; amal, *Wb.* 3 b, 6 a.

amargin, 30, *ns.*; *g.* amaipgin, 9, 40; perhaps *n.* amapgen. Conall Cernach and Ansruth were sons of an Amergin.

ámlaib,* 7, grandson of Inscoa.

amlaid, 3, 5, 6, 8, 19; amlaid rin, like that, so, 34.

ammaig, 51, outside.

amne, 5; thus, so; amne, gl. *ita; or pudor, cf.* er-amni, gl. *impudentia;* amne, bap Cuil Sibrilli, so indeed, quoth C., *LL.* 58 b; or *gen., cf.* pat aipgne, "MS. Mat." 492; er-aimne, fearlessness.

amra, 19, 19, wonderful, famous.

an, 6, 7, 2 *sg.*, *imper.* wait; anad, 6, 30, 36, to wait, waiting, halt; anand, 22, 3 *pres. depend.*; anat, 22, 3 *pl. pres.*, po anrat, 31, 32, *pret.*, they stayed at rest; po anratap, 36, they halted; pa anratap, 52.

an-air-tuaid, 16, from nor-east, i.e. southwestwards.

anam,* 5, 12, 28, 40, *vs.*, life, soul; *ds.* anmain. *Cf.* "Cath Finntraga," 9.

and, 11, 12, in it, therein; into it, 25; then, 3, 8, 9, 13, 23, etc.; there, 8, 11, 12, 13, 14, 15, 23; thither, 11, 18, 26; and-rain, 23, there; and-rin, 3, 8, 9, 11, then; there, 8; in that, 7; and-ro, 23, 55, 57; and-rút, 12, 33, 8, yonder, in it yonder; aith and, 23, good then! = maithm ám, 48, and elsewhere.

andá, 38; anda, 17, 25, than (is); andathi-ri,* 48, than ye are.

andar, 28, it seems; andap let, thou wouldst fancy, *LL.* 55 b.

anfaid, 10, *gsm.*, of a surge; *ns.* glarranfud, 10.

anglonnach, 31, *ns.*, mighty; glonn .i. gnim; *but* anglonnar, crime, "Laws," ii. 168, 170.

aní, 1, 17, 53, the thing; *neuter of* inti.

an-íar, 4, from the west.

anim,* 22; blemish, reproach; *as.*

anocht,* 38, *ds.*, to succour, protection.

anró,* 4, 5, trouble; not in *W.*, *Ag.*, or *Z.*; ánnró, persecutions, S. Mark, x. 30.

ánruth, 40, *voc.*, ánraid, 40, son of Amargen; ánruth = poet of second rank; anraid = warriors, "Magh Lena," 44, "Hyfiach." 230; da n-anraid, two soldiers, "B. of Magh Rath," 176, anrata, valiant, anroth, hero, "L. na gCeart," 130; *ib.* 188.

an-uair, 22, when.

an-úas, 17, from above: fair anuas = over and above, like modern do bárr air.

aperóil, 6, *gs.*, April; *g.*, Appril, "F. Mast.," i. 560.

apraitis, 20, 2 *sg. pres. enclit.* of atberim, *qv.*, they might say.

ar,* us, *infixed pr.*, rarmetairni.

ar, 6 etc., our; ar n-, 3, 3, 15, 15; ar m-, 5, 5; ar . . . ni, 22, our, *with emph.*

ar, 5, 9, 35, 47, on; at, 52; by, 5, 5; on (expressing state of mind), 56; on (after gabaim), 34; (after verb of watching), 25; in addition to, 11; by reason of, 27.

ar n-, 1, 8, 13, 14; after, upon (of time); ar cur catha; ar-sain, 25, thereupon, after that.

ar, 3, 9, 15, 18, 30, 43, 52, said, quoth; ar se, 15, said he; see bar, for.

arabóind, 25; *scribal error for* ar boind, *or* ar abaind (?).

araile, 34, 45; *agsm.*, the other, each other.

ard-feirt,* 56, *ds(f?)*, high hill or tumulus.

arfiadat,* 29, they relate, = atfiadat, 29.

arget, 4, *asm.*, silver; *neut.* in O. Irish.

aris, 57, again.

armach, 45, *gpm.*, armed; *but* ármecha, numerous, *LL.* 232 b.

arnabarach, 13, 14, on the morrow.

ar nad, 44, on whom it is not (?).

artuir,* 7, *gsm.*, Arthur?

ar-metair-ni: see rarmetair.*

ás, 20, 23; as, 26, over, above, as, *LU.* 69 a; "Ir. Texte," i. 213.

as, **ass**, 27, 23, *rel.* form of is, which is; it aspirates.

ass, 34, out of it; assa, 13, 25, 39, out of its; assa n-, 15, out of their: assin, 5, 38, 44; as governs *dative.*

assu, 38, easier, *comp.* of asse, *Z.*

ro-t-astraig,* 15; *3rd sg. pret.*, has brought thee on a journey; from astrach, travelling, *LU.* 47 a; astar, a journey, *W.*

at, 6, 6, 6, 28; they are.

atá, 29, 33, 52, is; atát, 29, they are.

ro-ataim, 1, 1, 2; *pret.* he confessed, admitted; atmaim, I confess, "F. of Carman," p. 538; adem, gl. *agnoscere*, *Ml.* 71 *b*; ataimet, gl. *profitentur*, *Z.*; mani atma, if he does not acknowledge, "Sench. M." ii. 308; admas, who professes, "B. of Fen." 320.

ra-ataithé, 24, 3 *pl. pret. pass.*, were kindled; ataither, is lighted, *LL.* 179; ataifes, who will kindle; átúd, kindling, *LL.* 287 b, 75 a.

atberim, 5; atbiur, 20; atdiur, 28, 46; atuir, 11, 38; atdir, 8, I say; atdir is a scribal error for atdiur; *t-pret.*, atbert, 3, 5, 6, 19, 57, he said; atrubramar,* 40, we said; ebber, 14, *depend. fut.* 1 *sg.* *Cf.* atiursa, tiursa, I say, *LL.* 91 a, 93 a, 96 a.

atchloss, 39, *pass. pret.*, was heard.

atchondairc, 44; atćonnairc, 43; atconnairc, 41, 42, he saw; *pret.* of atchíu.

atchuas, 1, 19, *perf. pass.*, was told; so in *LU.* 196.

atetha, 27, goes at, takes, brings; atethad, would bring, "Laws," i. 250; ethaid, he takes, *LL.* 124; atetha lóg, *LL.* 54 b; atethatar, are brought, *LL.* 96 a, 97 b; eithaid 7 beirid, *LL.* 124 a. *Cf.* donetha, *infra;* etha .i. luid, atethar, is brought, "Sench. M." i. 64, 250; adetha, is got, *Tl.* 246.

atfiadat, 29, they relate; 3 *sg.* atfet, "H. of Fiac."

atfua, 17; at-fua, very good, *or* they are good (?). *Cf.* ferb fua, of good cows, *LL.* 77 a; fó = good: "fó limsa ón, ar medb," *LL.* 57 a; adfenar fo fio, "Laws," i. 256.

áth, 28, 52, *ds.*, ford.

athar, 53, *gsm.*, father.

atherne algessach, 44, *ns.*; atherni, 30, 43; *va.* atherni, 43; = calf, *LU.* 8 a.

athisc,* 19, 19, *gas.*, address, answer, *Ml.* 51 b; *neuter n.* aithesc, in old glosses; proposal, words, *np.*, aitisga, § 11, "Mod. Text."

atraacht,* 10, 34, 52; 3 *sg. t-pret.* of éirgim (from atomriug, *me erigo,* "Ascoli"); 3 *pl.*, atraachtatar, 10; atractatar, 34; *s-fut.* atrái, thou shalt rise up = rise up, *LL.* 94 a, 119 a; attraiged, he was standing, "B. of Hymns," ii. 204; but atraigset, they raised (the ire), *LL.*, p. 134 a; atriug, I rise.

a-túaid, 25, from the north.

ba, 8, 8, 13, 27, 36, 37, 55, 55, 56, 57; was, it was; cona raba, so that there was not, 34.

ba, 11, 17, 22, 25, will be, *fut.* of is.

bad, 2, 3, 3, 5, 5, 7, 8, 11, 11, 15, 15, 36, 55, 56, 2*ry fut.*, might, should, would be; would have been, 55, 56; it aspirates in 2, 8.

bái, 1, 1, 1, 2, 5, 8, 11, 12, 19, 22, 34, 56; bo, 4, 5, 15, *pret.*, was; rabái, rabe, rabúi, rapo, rapa, rap, rop, ropo, ro-bái (that) he was, 26, 8, 48, 17, 53, 30, 36, 13, 57, 36, (*its nominative is plural,* 30); bamar, we were, 55, 56; batar, 57; ro-batar, 8, 12, 27, 46; rabatar, 15, 15, they were; beind, 8, I should be, 2*ry fut.*; beit, 22, they shall be; beith, beth, bith, 23, 48, 51, 25, 62, to be, being; bes, 11, 11, who *or* that are, as shall be, 17; nabeth, 3 *sg.* 2*ry fut.* for nobed; betis, rabetis, 9, 36, 3 *pl.*, 2*ry fut.*; bí, 53, 54, *imperat.* 2 *sg.*; biat, 22, 1 *sg. fut.*; bid, 22, 3 *sg. fut.*; bíth, 2*ry pres.*; rop, 15, 26, 2, it was, it were; ropad, rapad, 18, 56, 11, would be, would have been.

ba, 10, under, *gov. dat.* for fo; *so* "B. of Fen." 324, and *LL.* "MS. Mat." 507.

ba chota,* 53; ba chuta, 43, 44; he obtained (?). *Cf.* atcotedae, "B. of Arm."; fort chotaċ, by thy friendship, *LU.* 74.

ro-s-bae,* he slew them, *or* that slew him; to benim, 3 *pl.* robéotar, *LU.* 62; béo, I slew, "Frag. of Ir. Ann." 108.

ro-báded, ro-baded, 25, 25, *pret. pass.*, he was drowned.

bágach, 22, *nsm.*, contentious.

báig, 46, 57, *asf.*, strife, war; *gs.* báige, 12, valour, "B. of Fen." 320; *gs.* bága, *LL.* "MS. Mat." 492, 506.

báire,* **báre**, 10, 17, *man's name.*

balc, 57, *nsm.*, force, strength, resistance, *or* the strong, *LU.* 100 b.

bále,* 10, *man's name,* "MS. Mater."

bale, 11, *ns.*; *gs.* baile, 53; *dp.* balib; place, residence, home; *as.* bail i ṅ-gebad, 20, where *e* is elided; or is bail *af.* of bal, a sister form of bale?

ro-s-banaig, ro-t-banaig, 2, 3; *pret.* of bánaigim; whitened him, thee; made him pale.

ra-bansatar, 37, *pret.* of bánaim, they grew white.

ban-solus, 20, *dsN.*; ban-folais, 16, 23, 25, *dasf.*; ban-foilse, 25, ban-folsi, 26, *gsf.*, white-bright; *ns.* bán-folus.

bar, said, 24 *times*; bar é-sium, 26, quoth he.

bar, on, upon, 16 *times*; *idiomatic* after celim, 20, condaigim, 51, and verbs of watching, 25; barsin, 5, 18, barsna, 39, on the.

bar, 15, 15; bar n-, 11, 19, 19, your.

barbarda, 47, barbarous, fierce.

barécaim, barrécaim, barrecaim, 51, 36, 23, 36, 38 (*s-pret.*, 3 *sg.*, of forécmaing, it happens), fell out, fell in with; ol do-n-ecmaing, because it happens, falls out, *Pr. Sg.* 40 a; arrecaim, *LL.* 53 b.

bar-rionachtatar, 8, *t-pret.* of for-ionacaim; they announced *or* gave out, communicated.

bar-ro-eblangair, 25, *redupl. perf. depon. form.* of for-lingim, he leaped; forroebling, he leaped, *LU.* 29; but our word seems an impersonal pass. past tense: ní hed barroeblangair dorum etir ón, acht ro lingestar saebléim isin bóind," it [the water] was not jumped [over] by him at all; but he leaped a false leap into the Boyne. *Cf.* do-eirbling, do-arblaing, foroiblang-sa, gl. *desilit, præveni*, "Tur. Gl." 1 d, *Ml.* 95 d. co raeblangtar, *LU.* 102 a.

barraebris, 3, *redup. pret.* of forbrisim, for for-ro-be-bris, broke, won; forbrissset comlund, they will win the fight, *LU.* 81; gor roebris, so that he broke, *LL.* 60 aa; *see* brisiud, *infra.*

barulngither, 34; forulngither, 25; *pres. pass.* (with past meaning from the infixed ro) of foloing, gl. *sustinet*; was suffered, tolerated; *the* f *aspirated by* ro has disappeared.

bás, 46, *asN.*, death.

ra-s-básaig, 23, *pret.* of básaigim, it mortally wounded him, brought him to death's door. *Cf.* Anglo-Irishism, "I'm kilt."

basc-bémnech, 53, *as.*, red-striking (of hoofs); barc, red, "Cormac," *O'Cl.*, "O'Dav."

batnoathar, 21, 3 *sg. pres. pass. or depon.*; batnoathar dóib na scelasain, these tidings are manifested, made known to them (*or* by them to him), *or* he relates, *etc.*; condnoathatar, 8, *pret.* (they made known, told), suggests that batnoathatar is the true reading of 21; see note 5, § 8; atnói, gave, *Tl.* 140.

bebsat, 6, *red. s-fut.*, they shall die; or *s-pret.*, bebais, he died, "Felire"; bebsait, they died, *LL.* 270 a; *red. perf.* ro-m-bebe, *Z.*

bec, 19, 42, *as.*, little, small; *sm. voc.* bic, 42.

béim, 44, 46, *asN.*, a blow, stroke.

-béimnech, -bémnech, 55, 53, *as a noun or adjective*, striking, reverberating. *Cf.* "Frag. I. Ann." 122.

beind, 5, *dual* (?), horns, *n.* bend.

beir, 53, 54, 2 *sg. imper.* of beirim, take, bear; rabert, 44, *t-pret.*, he gave, made; *inf.* breith, 8, 38, *ds.*; robretha,* 8, *present; or preter.* in A., he gave; it seems ro + bretha. *Cf.* nochara; berthai, 46, ye bring, bear.

bél, 12, *asm.*, lip, mouth; bél-átha, ford, 6; *np.* beóil, lips, *LL.* 55 b.

bélscáláin,* 23, 24, *npm.*; *ap.* bélscálánu, 20, huts; *ap.* botha 7 bélscálana, "F. Mast." III. 311. *Cf. LL.* 57 a.

RO-benatar, 37, *pret.* of benaim, they cut; benaid, he strikes, *LL.* 122.

bennacht, 54, *as.*, a blessing.

bennachtain, 55, *asf.* of bennachtu, a blessing.

beó, 17, 17, 19, *nds.*, *adject. used as a noun*, a living (thing); *np.* bí, *LU.* 99; beo, cattle, *O'Cl.*

berba,* 16, *dsf.*, the Barrow; *gsf.* berba, "L. na gCeart," 202; Berua, *fem.*, "Cambrensis," 30.

bern,* 57, *nsf.*, a gap; *ns. LL.* 115 b, 83 b, 96 b; *n.* berna, *LL.* 18 b; *ds.* beirn, "B. of Fen." 376.

RA-bertaig, 51, *pret.* of bertaigim, he brandished, shook; rodom-bertaigedar, he shook it, *LL.* 113.

biad, **bíad**, 1, 1, 2, *nsN.*, food; *g.* bíd, 23, 24.

bidba,* 18, *ns.*, foe; *gp.* bidbad, 6, 9, enemy, "Sench. M." III. 198; I. 208: bidbad 7 námat, *LB.* 208 a.

bith, 18, 6 (?), *da.*, world.

bith, 26, to be; was slain (?), 54.

blad, 19, 19, *nsf.*, renown, *O'Cl.*; atá slighe an ionruic deunta go bláith, the way of the righteous is made plain, Prov. xv.; *g.* bloide and blaith, famous, "B. of Fen." 312, 368.

blae, 3, *ns.*, breast, *O'R.*; blái, of a beard, O'Curry's "Ch. of Uisnech," 78; blae, a green, "Trip. Life."

bleith, 25, to grind, turn a mill; *verb. noun* of melim.

bliadna, 11, *gsf.* of bliadain, a year.

bó, 17, 3, 4, 4, 5, 5, 17, 6, 18, 17, *ngsf.* and *gp.*, a cow.

RA-boc,* 51, he showed, *or* waved: r. 7 rabertaig; bogad, tossing, Eph. IV.; bocad, he shook, *LB.* 235 b.

bodba, 39, 40, 41, 43; *gs.* of bodb, war, danger, dangerous, "O'D. Suppl."; "Mesca Ul." 14, 26; "F. Mast." I. 508; martial, "Frag. of Ir. Ann." 164; mist, steam, fog, "O. B. Crowe," and "Siab. Ch. Conc." 424; *as.* bodb, "F. Mast." I. 300; (of trumpets), "Frag. of Ir. Ann." 164; b. = cruechta, "O'Dav." 63.

bognitha, 26, 2 *sg. pres. pass.*, was made, for dognithe; *or* bognith a guin, his wound, a being proleptic, and dognith *pret. pass.* (?).

bói, 25, 46; ro-bói, rabói, 3, 12, 26, 55, 6, 35; 3 *sg. pret.*, was; *see* ba.

bóind, **boind**, 20, 23, 25, 26, 29, 56; *daf.* of Boend, "Adamnan"; *g.* bóinne,* boinne, 18, 27, 55, the Boyne; *n.* bóand, *LL.* 194-5; boandus, "Cambrensis," 31.

borb, 3, *nsm.*, stubborn, violent; *gs.* buirb, 2.

borulngither, 48; *see* barulngither.

botha,* 20, 23, 24, *napf.* of both, a hut.

bothait,* 5, he fell; *s-pret.* of tuitim.

brágit, **bragit**,* 17, 18; *das.* of brage, neck.

brat, 4, *as.*, *a collective*, captives, *or* a garment; *da.* broit, captivity, in *W.*; *ns.* in brat, the captives, *Tl.* 164.

bráth, 54, *asm.*; bratha, 36, *gs.*; doom (destruction ?).

brathair, 19; *gp.* brathar, 57; *dp.* brathrib,* 57, brother.

breg, 22, 23, 28, 57, *gp.* the Brega of Mag-Breg, between Dublin and Drogheda.

brethir, 8, 11, 20, 44, 46, *asf.* of briathar, a word; atiurra brethir, I vow, 11; briathra, 3, 5, 6, 19, 57, *nap.*

bríg, 22, *gsf.* brige, 12, power, force.

brissiud, 5, *ns.*, to break; barroebris, he broke, 3.

broddor fuít,* 7.

broddor roth,* 7.

brón, 4, *gsm.* of brón, sorrow.

brotha, 12, *gsN.* of bruth, vigour, glow, fury; bruthcha, gl. *furiales*, *Ml.* 16 b; buden bruthmar, *LL.* 97; bruth fola, "B. of Magh Rath," 170; Londbruth n-, *LL.* "MS. Mat." 506.

brotla,* 22, *nsm.*, bold (?): in sluag brotla bágach; *LB.* 36 b: brotla no beoda no sulbir; brotla, fiery (phalanx), "Cath. M. Rath," 214; perhaps akin to broithleog, noise, *O'R.*; *ap.* brodla, saucy, mischievous, "C. M. Lena," 118, 121 (brotbla, garments, "B. of M. Rath," 186); applied to reins, *LL.* 144 a; to blows, "C. Finntraga," p. 100; bith-b., "Thurn. Versl." 56.

bruide,* 7, *gs.*, a man's name.

bruiden, 13, *nsf.*; *as.* bruidin, 15; palace, mansion; *gs.* na bruidne, *LU.* 97; at 15 it is written for *acc.* bruidin.

(nír)brulngither,* 45, *pres. pass.* of fuloing, *sustinet* (with ro infixed) = it was not endured; nírborulngither, 48, *qv.*

brunni, 3, 51, *nas.*, breast, bosom.

buadach, 3, *ns.*, victorious.

búain, 10, Bále's father; *gs.*

buale, 6, *nf.*, cowshed, *LL.* 225; a palisade for defence, "C. M. Lena," 78; .i. dún, "O'Dav." 57.

buan, 25, 57, lasting, steadfast.

búar, 4, *asN.*, kine; *collective from* bó.

bud, 22, it shall be, was, would be; 25, forms a superlative.

bude-chaiti,* 14, *npm.*, contented with eating, satiated; from bude, contentment, and caithim, I consume; or possibly budech-aiti, from ait, pleasant; ro chaemchaith, he happily spent, "B. of Fen," 88; *pl.* buidi; gl. *contenti*, *Ml.* 115 b.

buden, buiden, 47, 30, 31, 49, *nsf.*; budin, 49, *as.* (= with a band); *dp.* buidnib, 57; company, squadron.

buide, 32, *gsm.*, yellow.

buinne, 36, *ns.*, a branch: doss diten 7 buinne bratha.

búraig,* 40, 41, 42, 43, *asf.* of búrach, .i. borrágh, great exploit, "O'Clery"; a charge, "Cog. G. re G." 174; burach teine, "Laws, I. 166, 170, fury of fire; búrach beathraige, a man of lowing herds (!), "L. na gCeart," 200; prowess, S. "Siege of Howth," 54, 56; bellowing, "Mesca Ul." 32; *as.* buraig, vengeance, "C. M. Rath," 298.

ca, 3, 3, 29, what? *inter. adj.*

ca, 3, 5, 6. 26 = oc a, at its; cán, 19 = oc an-, at their; ca, 11 = co a, to its (?).

cach, 6, 17, *etc.*, every, *ns.*; *gsm.*, 13, 17, 17, 17, 23; *gsf.* 13 (?), *gsm.*, cacha, 20, 31; *gsf.*, 17, 17; every, each, cach oen, 35.

cách, 34, 39, 54; cach, 25; everybody.

cadd (*inis*), 7, *g*; insi Gaíd, *LU.* 112 b.

cade, 5, 30, what is it?

chael, 34, slender.

caem, 8, handsome.

cháep,* (chǽp) 12, *nsf.*, clot, lump; in cháep chró 7 fola . . . in loím 7 fola, *dual*, di chaep criad, *AG.* *Cf.* caebb oo, gl. *jecur*, *Sg.* 6 b; caép cro, *LL.*, p. 85 b.

chain, 4, *dsm.*, fine, famous.

cairell* coscarach, 32, *nsm.*

caIRn, 22, *gsm.* (*tumuli*, "Cambrensis," 140), of Carn, i.e. of Carn Macha. *Cf.* a Chongal mullaig macha, "B. of M. Rath," 172; ba nia in chairn Cormac mac Chonchobuir, "T.C.D. H." 3, 18, p. 594; .i. chairn na forairе ar Sliab Fuaid, *LU.* 78 a b; it guarded the pass to the palace of Emain, and was near Newtown-Hamilton.

caIRpRe nIa-feR, 45, Cairpre nia-fer, 16, 21, 19, 22, 45, 54, *nsm.*, King of Tara and son of Ross Ruad; the "Book of Lecan" says he was King of Temair Broga Nia in Leinster, not of Temair Breg, "B. of Magh Rath," 139; he was King of Leinster, "Ogygia," 281; arorí na nGaidel, "MS. Mat." 515.

cáIt, 20, = ca áit, where.

Ro-caItheD, 24, was consumed, eaten, *perf. pass.*

calma, 19, brave; chalmu, braver, 48; chalmacht,* bravery, 47.

cammaIn, 11, also, however, = cammaib (?).

can, 4, 4, *etc.*, without, Old Ir. cen, *gov. acc.*; before *infinitives* = not to, 17, 20.

can, **chan**, 22, 19, whence. *Cf.* ciachuin, whence, fanchan, *undique*, *LB.* 55 a.

chanaD, 7, *gs.* or *pl.*, taxes; *n.* cáin, *g.* cána, *LL.* 300.

Ro-canaIt, 13, 24, *pass. pret.* of canaimm, were sung; cantar, *imperat.* 3 *pl.* 23.

canas, 19, whence? *Cf.* can.

cano gall,* 8, *nsm.*, cano = a file of the 4th degree.

caRaIt, 11, 12, 12, 14, *np.*; *dp.* cairdib, cairdib, 7, 8, friends; *ns.* cara.

caRpat, 53, *gp.*; carpait, *np.*, 13, 13; *dp.* cairpdib, carptib, 35; *ns.* carpat, chariot. *Cf. carpentum Gallorum*, "Florus," Lib. I. c. 18.

caRpRe, son of Daurthacht, 31.

caRptIg, 30, 30, *gsm.* and *np.* of carptech, *LL.* 67, a chariot warrior; the *np.* is put for *ap.* here. *Cf.* traigthech, gl. *pedes*, *Sg.* 50 b.

caRRaIc, 9, 10, *dasf.* of carrac, rock, "F. Mast." I. 26.

caRRaIc muRbuIlg,* 9, 10; in Dál-Riada, near Murlough Bay, Co. Antrim, "F. Mast." I., p. 10.

cath, 1, 3, 40, *etc.*, *passim*; *ndasm.*, battle; in cath fo, 30, *acc.* of thing referred to; catha, 1, 25, 26, 31, *passim*, *gs.*

catha, 29, 50, *gs.* and *np.* of cath, battalion; *dp.* cathaib, 39.

cath Ruis na Ríg,* 1.

cath na tána, 1; fought at Gairech and Ilgairech in the present Co. of Westmeath, where Conor defeated Medb.

cathaIgthe, 25, 26, *gs.* of cathugud, fighting.

cathbath, 12 times; never in full; *n.* Cathbadh, *LL.*, p. 93; *na.* Cadbad in *LL.*, pp. 106 and 311, 3rd col.; *gs.* Cathbad, Cathbath, Cathboth in "B. of Armagh," the *ns.* of which would be Cathbu or Cathba. It seems to be of the O or 1st decl. in *LL.*; the voc. *must* be a Chabaid in last line, § 5.

cath-buaDach, 7, battle-victorious; *cf.* cloidem cathbhuadach, *gladius prœliaris*, "Ogygia," p. 296.

cath-eRReD, 34, *as.*, battle-dress.

cath-mIlID, 34, *npm.*, battle-warriors; *n.* cathmíle or catmil.

ce m-, 5, though; it does not usually eclipse.

ro-s-ceastar, 12, it tormented him; *dep. pret.* for ro chéss, he tormented.

cebé, 54, whatever it be, whether there be; ce be, cen co be, whether or no, "Sench. M." iii. 192.

cech, 25, *ns.*; *gsm.* 17, 37, every, each; *gsf.* (?) cecha, 30.

cechtarda,* 39, *adj. dpm.* on each side.

nír cheil, 20, *pret.*, he did not conceal, takes dar (on, *i.e.* from), after it.

céile, 11, *ds.* ceili, 25, fellow, match: on chinn . . . ca chéile, from one end to the other; mar a bói inber dub domni a cheli, where the inber was deeper than elsewhere.

ceilg, 29, *dsf.* of celg, concealment, ambush, deceit.

céill, 27, *dsf.* intelligence; *n.* ciall, sense.

céim, 6, *as.* or *ds.*, step.

cheithern,* 19, *voc. sg.*, a soldier-band, soldiery; .i. cuire armide, "Cormac"; *asf.* cethirn, *LL.* 134 a; Cethern is a proper name, *LL.* 90.

celg,* son of Romrach, 7, *nsm.*

celtchair, son of Uthechar, 9, 27, *nsm.*; *n.* Celtchar, *LU.* 101 a.

cen co, 18, although not (without that).

chena, 5, already, forthwith, 7.

chenandain,* 10, *np.*, some sea animal. *Cf.* d'éirig suas an fiad druimionn ceannon donn, "Siamsa an geimrid," p. 15; I know only two words like it: cenannas, cenondas, Quenvendani, "Inscrip. Brit. of Hübner."

cend, 5, 11, 37, 46, 49, 51, 51, *nas.*, head, end; ar cend, to seek, *or* for, 5; i cend, against, towards, 37, 46, 49; *see* cind; a g-cionn, at the end of, Job xxviii. 3.

cend-find, 21, white-headed; *cf.* cennindán, little white head, "Tripartite Life," p. 162.

chend-róit,* 28, *npm.*, highways; *ap.* rotu, "Felire"; atáit il-anmanna for conairib, .i. sét, rót; lam-rotae, tuad-rotae, cenn bothar .i. b. coitchenn, "Cormac," 22.

cerchaill, 6, *nsf.* pillow; *gs.* cind-cherchailli, *LL.* 53; gl. cervical; *ap.* cercailli, "Man. and Cust." iii. 499; *dp.* cercaillib, couches, "Laws," ii. 358.

ro-cherddaind, 40, ro-cherdain-se, ro-cherddain-se, 42, 43, 40; *2ry pres.*, I might cast; *for* focherdaind, *see* fochera, 57; note the absence of the d before se.

cernma,* 54, *gs.* for southern half of Ireland, over which Cernma ruled; his seat was Dún Cernma on the Old Head of Kilsale, *see LL.*, p. 127, and the "Four Masters."

cernach, 9, *d.*; *gs.* Cernaig; surname of Conall; cern, .i. buaid, "Metr. Gl." 34.

chert, 22, *ns.*, right, *adjective.*

ra-chertaig,* 51, *pret.* of certaigim, he poised (it?); adjusted (corrected, in "Atkinson's Gloss.").

nir cheiss, 27, cess, 25, 26, *s-pret.* of cessim, he suffered, grieved, chafed; takes for after it; rochess, he suffered, *Tl.*, p. 16; cessit, they ask, "O'Dav." 69.

cet, 22, son of Maga, Carn Ceit, now Carnket, in parish of Baslick, Co. Roscommon, called after him, "O'Don. Supp."; *v. LL.* 79 a b.

cet, 7, 10, *as.*, son of Romra.

cét, 49, *gs.*; 45, 32, 31, *ngp.*; 30, *g. dual; dp.* cetaib, a hundred.

chetamus,* 7, 8, = cét-tomus, first measure (?); bad chotamus don chetamus; = measure for first measure, tit-for-tat; or cot-amus, an attack for a first attack (?).

chethir-ríad,* 13, 14, *Ngp.* and *np.*; *dp.* cethirriadaib, 13; four-wheeler; carpat cetarriata, *LB.* 234.

cétna, 26, 27, cetna, *gp.*, 26, same.

cethri, 3, 5, 15, 16, 17, four; *g.* cethri, 32.

cethramthanaib,* 47, *dp.* of cethramthu; quarters, pieces, *Z.*

cia, 1, 2, 8 × 2, 12, 18 × 2, 19, 27, who (?), always, *n.*

cían, cian, 11 × 2, 30, far, distant, long (of time), *ds.* dochéin; *dp.* a cianaib, 38, 46, by far, long ago; also a noun, do chéin mair, *LL.* 86.

ciar,* 4, 5, = cia-r, though it were (?); cerram, though I am, "B. of Fen." 224; ciarbat, *LL.* 344 a.

ciar-banriad,* 4, though it were a woman's ride or raid (?), *or* of dark-white (grey) chariots (?).

cid, 1 × 2, 2, 3, 11, 18, 23 × 2, what is it? 25, 33, 46, why?

cid, 18, 36, though.

cid tra acht, 12, 34, 39, 40, 44, however.

ciis, 3, *s-pret.* of ciim, he wept; cithech, gl. *flebilium*, *Ml.* 65; cí, weeps, "Frag. of Ir. Ann." 214.

cind, 9, 10, 11, 15, 22, 23, 25, 29, 42, 53, 55, *gd.*, *sg.*, *np.*, head, end; i cind, at the end, 53, 55; against, 26; for do chind, ahead of thee, before thee, 23, 29; cindu, 46; cind is *np.* to tuargabtar, 15, their heads rose, or for cindu, they raised their heads; for ar cind, ahead of us, before us, 29.

cinnas, 28, how?

cipé, 19, ciped, 4, whatever it be, what there was.

cipp,* 18, *gsm.* of cepp (stock, fetter); *cf.* cip, cipia, *LA.*; cep, a stock, "Hy Many," 165; *LU.* 112.

chisa, 7, *gs.* of cís, tribute.

ciuil, *gs.*, 3, ciúil, 15; *gsN.* of ceól, music, tune; *np.* 13, 23, 24.

claideb, 38, 39, 53, *as.*; *gp.* 38, 39, 53; *g.* claidib, 17, 39, 39, 39, 45; *d.* claidiub, *LU.* 69; *ap.* claidbi, *LL.* 109 b.

claideb-derg, 7, red-sworded.

chlaideb-ruaid, 5, *voc. sg.*, red-sworded.

claifiter,* 22, *fut. pass.* of clóimm, they shall be defeated; rodo-s-cloe, 56, he defeated him, *pret.*

clainne, 29, *gsf.*; *dp.* clannaib, 16, 17, 19; clann, children, clan.

clár, 29, flat surface; *nN.* clar n-dara, "Man & Cust." III. 480; clár-siss,* *ds.*, 56, wide experience (?).

clé, 54, left-handed, left; *dsm.* chliu,* 29.

cless, 54, *gp.*, feats.

chlessamnacht, 27, *ds.*, dexterity; *cf. ap.* clessrada, arms for feats of dexterity, *LL.* 84.

chliab, 51, *ds.*; *gs.*, chléib, 8, chest (of a man); basket, cradle, "Laws," I. 166-8.

chlidna,* 16, *gs.*, a strand near Clonakilty, "MS. Mater." 306, "Magh Lena," 95; *cf.* Tond Cliodna, *LL.* 168 b; Touncleena, Glandore Harbour, Co. Cork, Index of "Four Masters"; *n.* Clidna, *LL.* p. 168.

rodos-cloe, 56, defeated him; *pret.* 3 *sg.* = ro chlói, *Ml.* 37 a.

cloen, 56, oblique, squint-eyed.

clos, 45, *pret. pass.* of cluinim, was heard.

clothra,* 7, *nsf.*, daughter of Conor; *g.* clothrann, "Ogygia," 288-9.

cned, 3, wound, *nsf.*; *g.* cnedi,* 2; *dp.* cnedaib, 6, a sigh.

chnedaib,* 6, *see* cned.

ra-t-cnedaig,* 2, 3, *pret.* of cnedaigim; has wounded thee; *from* cnedach, wounding, "B. of Fen." 318.

co, 1, 2, 3, 4, 7, 8, 12, 13, 22, 23, 52, &c., to, unto, until.

co, 1, 4, 5, 47, before an adjective forms an adverbial locution.

co n-, 5, 16 × 3, 19, 57, with; con-a', with his, 57.

co n-, 10, 14, 18, that; 3 × 2, 25, 26 × 2, so that; 11, 25, 30, until; 4, 15, so that, until; 14, 15 × 2, in order that; co, 4, *is idiomatic for* ano, ano ro.

coblach, 10, 12, *ns.*, fleet.

cocao, 54, (the making of) war.

cocetal, 45, cocetul, 39, *nas.*, music, clang, ring.

cocthaig, 54, 2 *sg. imper.*, make war.

choibsegud,* 2, to heal; coibregud no richugud no cnearugad, *H.* 2, 15, p. 120; or *cognoscere*, diagnose the disease, from cubur.

cóic, 47, five: cóic cét déc = of 1500.

coicait, 14, *np.* of cóica, for *accusative.*

coiced, 11, 21, 52, *ns.*, *ds.* 4; *gs.* cóicid, 19, 38, 20; *d.* coiciud, 4; *np.* coicid, 5 (*for acc.*), a fifth, province; cacha coicid, 19, in every province.

coiced emno, 4, Ulster.

coic fiur,* 11, (with) five persons; *d.* in form, but seems for *n.* coicer.

coicthiges, 1, 2, 3, *gpm.*, fortnight, *gsm.* cóicthigir, 11; cf. *gp.* trí cóicthiger, "Laws," II. 240, "L. na gCeart," 134, 138.

chóir, 2, 4, 5 × 5, 27, just, right, honest, *voc.* 4.

coirthi,* 40, *das.* of coirthe, pillar-stone.

colaind, 22, *dsf.* of colann, body; used for plural here for sake of rhyme.

colomda,* 8, column-like, stout (?); *cf.* columrach = *columnaris*, "Ogygia," 117; "dove-like" would ill suit our text; do cholomnaib ferb, of hides of cows; colluma, columns, *LB.* 209 a.

choma, 17, *nsf.*, condition, terms; *das.* comaid, 17, 20; *np.* na coma, comada, 19, 19, "request;" "C. M. Rath." 306; *cf.* "C. M. Lena," 106, 64; ní maith cach gan chomaid, *ib.* 62.

comair,* 30, 31, 32, 33, *ds.*, presence, company; i comair, *gl.* a farrad, "O'Dav."; cen chomair n-dae, gl. *præter Dominum* (*Ml.* 51 b) = without God; where Ascoli integrates comairle, *perperam*, I think; fa chomair = for, 1 Cor. xvi.; 2 Cor. xii.

comairle, 5; comairli, 6, 9, 14, 15, 17, 27, 30, 31, *nds.*; *as.* and *np.*, comairli, 17, 17, counsel.

ro-comarleiced, 17, 19; comarliced, 2; *pret. pass.*, was allowed, i.e. was agreed on; ro chomairléic, he decided, "Mesca Ul." 8; but he permitted, "F. Mast." III. p. 2272; conrairléiciur, gl. *commisi*, *Ml.* 74 c.

comardda,* 44, *np.*, signs, level (?).

combad, 14, 15, 19, that it may be; *see* ir, ba.

combága, 15; combaga, 15; combáge, 17; *gsf.* of combág, contention, hostility; *dsf.* oc combáig, gl. *certans*, *Z.*

comchuibdi,* 44, *np.*, even, level (?); comardda comchuibdi.

comfeng, 5, intense wrath; *as.* comferg, "B. of Magh Rath," p. 160.

comleithet, 17, *ns.*, equal area, extent; *ns.*, *LU.* 19 b.

comlond, 26, combat, conflict; *g.* comlaind, comlainn, 25, 34; *da.* comlund, 25, 52. *Cf.* comlunn, gl. *pares*; *n.* comlann, comlond, (deed of) battle, "B. of Fen." 324, 312.

commaidmech, 7, boastful, glorying.

chommain, 11, 11; *gs.* of comman, favour, bestowal, communication; in *Wb.* 6, 25, the *ndf.* is commain; but it is gov. by febur, excellence, in our text.

chommairge, 4, 38, 40, *das.*, protection; *d.* commairgi, 40, 41, 42. *Cf.* a chomairce na b-peacthach, *Refugium peccatorum*, "Litany of B.V. Mary."

commorais*, 49, *pret.* 3 *sg.*; ra-chommortatar, 46, 3 *pl.*, kept up.

chomnaide, 30, delay; chomnaidi, 31, *nsf.*; *dm.* comnaidiu, 29 (to rhyme with chliu; waiting, delay: c. 7 irnaide.

chomnaidi, 31, 32, *see* comnaide.

comnaidiu, 29, *see* comnaide.

comnessam, 37, nearest.

comrac, 55, 56, *ns.*; *gs.* comraic, 26, 34, combat, strife. *Cf.* comraigit, they fight, "B. of Fen." 324.

comrád, 13, conversation.

comterbtis,* 57, 2 *sg. pres.*, they performed, perfected; or shared (their deed) (?).

con-, 6, 9, 20, 38, so that: con-bad, con-fáitte, con-topacht.

chonair, 23, *dsf.*, path; *n.* conar; *g.* conaire, *LL.*, p. 30; for conair, on the march, "B. of Fen." 358.

conall, 7, 8 × 4, 36, 40, &c., *ndas.*; *gs.* Conaill, 8, 9, 27, 45; *voc.* 38; C. Cernach, 8.

conall* anglonnach, 32.

conbad, 20, 38, that it be; combad.

conchobor, *as.* 22 (in full, elsewhere last syllable or last two omitted), *n.s.*, *passim*; *gs.* Conchobuir, 5, 7, 10, 19; son of Fachtna Fathach; in *LL.* 106 a, he is called son of Cathbad.

condalb,* 22, *nsf.*, .i. duchus no gael no imarbaig, *H.* 3, 18, p. 286. *Cf.* connailbe, friendship, *O'R.*

condnoathatar,* 8; *see* batnoathar; they announced it.

confáitti, 9; *see* fáitti.

confingi,* 11, *ap.*

congaib,* 57, *ds.*, grasp, seizure; *see* note; or *dp.*, straits, "O'D. Suppl."; perhaps, cumgaib, straits or difficulties, *LB.* 74, *Ml.* 112 a; or congaib, *dp.* of cuing, prop of battle, "C. M. Rath," 312.

congaile,* 14, 27, *gsm.* of Congal; as *g.* Dungaile, Dúnlinge.

conid, 52,

conna, 1, 2, 8, 9, 20, that (in order that) not.

connach, 3, 6, 15, 20, so that not.

connacht, 16, 21, *gp.*; *dp.* Connachtaib, 57; *np.* Connachta, Connachtmen, Connacht.

connaid, 32, *gsm.*, a man's name.

ra-chonnairc,* 40; ra-chonnaic, 38,* he saw; 3 *pl. pret.* rachoncatar; 1 *sg.* atconnac, "Mesca Ul." 38.

connar, 1; connar' chotail, that he slept not.

connatacht, 53; *t-pret.* of condaigim; he asked.

connici, 26, 27, unto.

conricci, gl. *pertinguens usque ad*, *Wb.* 33; *now* conuige.

contopacht, 51; ocus contopacht, and he cut off, *or* and so he cut off.

cor, 23, unto; cor-Ross.

cor, 55, turn, condition, affair, means, *LL.* 268 b; *d.* chur, 6, 17, 18, occasion: don chúr-sain.

chóra, 19, *voc. sm.*, valiant, *O'Cl.*; or *gs.* of peace used as adjective, as fíre; coru, .i. cuice is coir, "Laws," 384.

corbo, 3, 12, that it was; corbat, corbdar, 13, 44, that they were.

corcar-glana, 11, *ap.* of corcarglan, purple-bright.

coro', 6, that it may be.

corop, 6 × 4, 13, that it may be; so that it was, 25, 53; until it be, 14.

corp, 51, *nsm.*, body.

chorr-cind,* 10, *np.* (round-, beak-crane-)heads; corrcend, *LL.* 164 a.

corr-gabla,* 11, *ap.* (round or smooth) forks, yard-arms (?), spars (?); .i. croiceann, "O'Dav." 63.

coscor, 27, *ads.*; coscur, 4, *das*, triumph, slaughter; .i. buaid, "T.C.D. H." 3. 18, 603; coscarach, coscorach, triumphant, 7, 32.

coscorach, 7.

cosindiu, 48, till to-day.

cossin, 56, *sg.*, to the; *dpl.* cusna, until the, 22.

cot, 7, unto thy.

nír-chotail, 1, 1, *pret.* of cotlaim, he slept not; corochotlur, *LU.* 104.

cotal-tigib,* 13, *dpN.* of cotal-tech, sleeping-house or cubicle.

chotamus, 7, 8, *ds.*, equal measure (?); *see* cetamus.

cotut-chend,* *as.*, 51, hard-headed.

cráet,* 15, what (thing)?

craib, 52, *asf.* of craéb, *LL.* 111 a, a branch, *or* a wood.

cráo,* 12; cró, 12, *gs.* of cró, gore.

crecha, 22, *np.* crech, plundering.

crí,* 19, *ns.*, body, frame, shape; mo chrí, *LL.* 307 a; "F. Mast." II. 582, 616, 892, 898; indeclinable.

crích, 54, *gpf.*; crichi, 17, 11, *gs.*; *dp.* crichaib, 6, 7, 8; end, region.

chride, 5, 12, 51, *nda.*; cridi, 8; *np.* crideda,* 39, heart.

crig,* 28, *das.* of crich, territory.

crithail,* 57, *ns.*, litter (?).

ro-chrithnaigsetar,* 16, *s-pret. dep.* of crithnaigim, they shook, reverberated.

cró, 12, *gs.*, blood. *Cf.* cró, *dp.* croaib, death, "Sench. M." I. 186.

chróda, 19, valiant, gory.

cro-derg, 22, blood-red.

ra-chroth, 51, 52, *pret.* 3 *sg.* of crothaim, I shake, brandish; *s-pret.* 3 *sg.* crothais, 51.

crú (?), 15, blood, death; but *ds.* crud, *jumenta*, "Nennius," 80.

chruachain, 19; *dsf.* of Cruachu; *g.* Cruachan, *LL.* 170 a.

cruachan-ráith,* 16, *das.*, Rath-croghan; *da.* raith in "B. of Armagh"; *d.* Cruachan-ruith, *LL.* 53 b.

cruadbach,* 5, *ds.*; ar cruadbach, ar comfers, *for* hardness *or* steel-bit; it seems synonymous with comfers. *Cf.* fót-baige, bits, sods of turf, *LL.* 59; cruadbać, victory, success, "B. of Fen." 282.

cruadín,* 51, *as.*; Cu Chulaind's claideb, *LL.* 268 b; it means the little hard or steel thing. Cf. Whitley Stokes on "Irish Ordeals," pp. 199, 227; O'Cl.; "Man. & Cust." II. 322.

cruaich,* 57, *dsf.* of Cruach; i.e. Cruachain, cruaich, rick, *Tl.* 114.

crúaid, 8, 19; cruaid, 5, 8, hard, stern; crúas, hardness, *LL.* 62.

cu, to, *gov. dat.*, 14; *see* co.

cu mór, much, 25, *adverb. prefix*; *see* co.

ra-chuala, **rochuala**, 45, 48; *perf.* 3 *sg.* cluinim, I hear; cualabair-si,* 15, have ye heard? 3 *pl.* ra-chualatar, 39, 53.

cualnge, *as.*, 6, 8, 7, not once in full; *gd.* Cualngi, *LU.* 65 b, *LL.* 56 b; *d.* Cualngiu, *LL.* 262 b; "Cooley," *n. viri*, "F. Mast." I. 26.

cuani,* 22, *pl.*, hosts, bands, = buidne, *O'Cl.*; "L. Gabala," p. 17; cuan, a troop, "B. of Fen." 374.

ro-cuas,* 16, *pret. pass.*, was sent.

cubaid, 22, fitting, proper.

chucaind, 6, 15; chucainni, 15, 21, to us; cucu, ćuccu, to or against them, 36, 15; cucut, to thee, 19.

ra-chuclaigetar,* 39, *pres. pass.* with ro; they shook, quaked; see note, § 39; ro chichlaig, he shook, Stokes' "Lismore Lives," Index.

cú-chulaind, 44 [*W.* for *A.*]; Cu-Chulaind never in full; *da.* Coin-Culaind, 51, 55. Cf. *nsm.* (son of) Cauland, *LU.* 60; *g.* Con Culaind, 51, 55: *da.* Coin, 54; see *LL.* 63 a.

cuing (?), company, following, followers; *d.* congaib, *q. v.* *Cf.* "Stokes' Met. Gloss." 54.

cuir, 54; 2 *sg. imper.* of cuirim, I put; *pret.* 3 *sg.* ros-cuir, 47, he put them.

cuirp, 24, *npm.* of corp, body.

cuit, 17, share, part, *nsf.*

cul-gaire, *as.*, 53, chariot-noise *or* clatter; cul, .i. carpat, *LL.* 109 b, *LU.* 6, "Cormac," 13.

cuman, 5, *ns.*, recollection, remembrance; ni cuman lim, gl. *nescio*, *Wb.* 8 a; nirbo chumain leiss, *LU.* 50 b.

cumma, 26, *das.*, manner, fashion.

cunnis,* 51, *s-pret.* of condaigim, he sought; nad-cuinnius, *s-fut. and subj.* 1 *sg.*

curaid, 34, *npm.* of cur, caur, cura, champion, *LU.* 109 b.

co ro-chuiriur,* 26, *pres. dep.* 1 *sg.*, with *subjunctive* or *fut.* meaning, I may put. *Cf.* digiur; 2*ry fut.* 1 *sg.* cuirfind; 3 *pl. pret. pass.* racuirit*; *inf.* cur, putting, giving (battle).

curu, 11, *apm.* of cor, or cur, *LL.* 268 b, security, surety, covenant.

chuta,* 43, 44, seems synon. with daic, opposed to daiċ, bad (?).

chutul-sa,* 12, it pleased; 15, pleasure, satisfaction (?); codul, .i. cairde, comdal, *O'Cl.*; = bad, *O'R.*; nimdéni cutal, "Ir. Texte," I. 98.

d', 4, 17, 18 = do, to; 4, 11, 18, 18 = de, of; da', 5, 14, 17, 25, 44, to his, its; dá', of its, 17; da n-, 14, 18, to their; dá n-, da n-, of their, from their, 28, 6, 22, 34; da n-, to which, 15; da n-, da m-, of which, 7, 8, 11, 22, 54; da = do before bar, 15, 15.

da, 5, two; *dp.* dib, 26.

dacia, 7.

dachuatar, 29, who went; 3 *pl. perf.* dochóad, I want.

dadluig,* 4, *pret.* 3 *sg.*, whom she cleft down, laid low; dluig in crand, split the tree, "Felire," p. 73; rodluigset, they cleft, *LL.* 58 b a; dedlaig, he split; *red. perf.* of dlugim, "S. na Rann," p. 133; *inf.* dluige, "F. Mast." an. 1121; *LB.* 212 a.

dafaethais,* 54, 2 *sg. fut.* of (do-fuitim) tuitim; 3 *sg.* dofaeth in *W.*; *pres.* dofuitet, dothuitet, *LU.* 97.

daic,* seems synon. with cuta, 43, 44; = do aic, for a request; aic, a bond, "O'D. Suppl."; or = do-aic, for a 'no' or refusal. *Cf.* saic; daig, he found (?), "B. of Fen." 402.

dáig, 3, 7 × 2, 17, 18, 19, 20, 22; daig, 6, 23, for, since, because.

daigi* mac dega, 26, *nsm.*

dail, 13, *as.* of dal, a distributing (of drink).

dairbre, 37, oak branches, *ap.*; *gs.* darbri, oakwood, *LL.* 253; *nN.* dairbre, *W.*

dáire, 4 × 2; a chieftain of Cualnge; *g.* Daire mic Fiachna, "Y. B. Lecan," col. 648; lived at Glaiss Cruim, in Cooley, p. 241 of "De Chopur in da M." *Cf.* *LL.* 54 b, 158 a, "L. na gCeart," 6.

dairecht,* 22; to the assembly.

dait, 19; duit, 6, 23, to thee.

ᴅál, 39, meeting; *as.* ᴅail, 5; in a ᴅail, towards it, "B. of Fen." 234; *ns.* ᴅail, a fact, "B. of Fenagh," 350.

ro-ᴅáleᴅ, 13; 3 *sg. pret. pass.* of ᴅálim, I distribute.

ᴅalemain,* 13, *npm.* of ᴅálem, a distributer (of drink).

ᴅam, 4 × 3, 5 × 2, 17, bull, ox; *gs.* ᴅaim, 4, 5, 17.

ᴅam, 3 × 2, 11 × 6, 14 × 2, 18, 19 × 2, 22, 23 × 2, 46, to me, for me.

ᴅam,* 19, to my.

ᴅamait,* 22, 3 *pl. pres.* of ᴅamaim, I grant, yield; nír ᴅam, ᴅamatar, "B. of Fen." 312, 258: ni ᴅamaiᴅ cert, "B. Lecan," fol. 183; na ᴅaim cert, who has not yielded justice, "Sench M." i. 268. *Cf.* nír ᴅam Conall cóir na cert ᴅo bioḃaiḃ, "B. Fenagh," 312.

ᴅána, 11, 30 × 2, 46; *gs.* of ᴅán, art, science.

ᴅano (always da*no*), 2 × 2, 3 × 2, 8 × 2, 12 × 2, 14 × 2, 15 × 2, &c., too, then, however, (particle indicating sequence).

ᴅar, it seems.

ᴅar, 8 × 3, 12, 25 × 2, 29, 39, 51 × 2, 52, through, across, over, past; ᴅar ᴅo, 51, in two; ᴅar (a) air, 38, 39, 40, behind him; ᴅar a n-eir, 52, behind them.

ᴅarach, 18, 37, *gsf.* of ᴅair, an oak.

ᴅarach, *gsm.*, 18, Oak, name of a warrior.

ᴅariacht, 11, *t-pret. sg.*, who reached (it agrees with *pl.* antecedent); 3 *pl.* ᴅariachtatar, 46, 47; ᴅa-m-riachtatar, 3, they reached me; ᴅoriacht, *LL.* 116 b, he came.

ᴅarónait, 9, 3 *pl. pass. pret.* of ᴅognίu; were made.

ᴅatha, 22, *np.* of ᴅath, colour.

ᴅaurthacht, **ᴅurthacht**, 31, 31, *gsm.*, father of Eogan, king of Farney; *g.* ᴅurthachta, *W.*

ᴅe, 7, 26, of, from.

ᴅe, 4, 5, 26, 51, 52, from, off (him, it) thereof.

ᴅeaᴅ, *gs.* merr ᴅeaᴅ; ᴅé, *LB.* 218.

ᴅeḃaiᴅ, 22, *dsf.*, strife; *n.* ᴅeḃaiᴅ, gl. *simultas*, *Ml.* 19.

ᴅec, 30, -teen.

ᴅechain,* 55, *ds.*, to see, examine; ᴅéchair,* 40, *s-pret.*, he scanned.

ᴅechsum,* 15, *s-fut.*; co n-ᴅ., that we may go; go ᴅech ré, that he go, "B. of Fen." 356.

ᴅeᴅaᴅ,* 16, 17, *gsm.* of ᴅeᴅa (?), whose clan was about Sliab Luachra; Cúroi was their chief.

ᴅeg-áesa, 11, *voc. sg.*, goodly folk; ᴅeg-aera, 30, *gs.*

ᴅegaiᴅ, 22 (in phrase i nᴅegaiᴅ = after, behind).

ᴅeg-amra, 2, 3, 27, 30, *nsm.*, right-wonderful.

ᴅeg-ḃaleᴅa, 3, 15, *nap.* of ᴅegḃale, a good *or* strong place; synon. with ᴅunaiᴅ here.

ᴅeg-láith, 34, *np.*, goodly heroes, champions; *gp.* lath n-gaile, *LU.* 63a, 90a. *Cf.* ᴅaglaich 7 ᴅegóic, *LL.* 99 a, 97 b.

ᴅeg-mathi, 51, *npm.*, good chiefs.

ᴅeg-thír, 4, *dsN.*, goodly land.

ᴅeich n-, 45, 47, 50, ten; *np.*, ᴅeich cét, 47, 50, ten hundred.

ᴅeireᴅ, 14, *asm.*, end, last part.

ᴅeirg,* 16, 19, 29, *gsm.* of ᴅerg.

ᴅéis, 45, *dsf.* of ᴅíar, blade (of sword).

ᴅelga,* 11; **ᴅelgga**, 9, *gs.* of ᴅelga; ᴅún ᴅelga = Dundalk; *d.* ᴅo ᴅelga, *LU.* 68 b.

ᴅemin, 36, certain.

dena, 54, 2 *sg. imper.* or *subj.* of dogníu, make, do; dénam, denam, 8, 6, to do, doing; *imper. pass.* 3*rd*, dentar, 23, 23; dernad, 18, *pret. pass.* dependent; dernat, *pret.* 3 *pl.* depend. form, *fut.* 1 *sg.* dogen, 9 × 3; 3 *pres. ind.* do-m-gni, dotgni, 5, 3, makes me, thee; 3 *sg. pres. pass.* donither, do-n-ringni, has done to us; doringned, doronad, *pret. pass.* 3 *sg.*, 2, 24, 55, 8; 3 *pl. pret. pass.* doronait,* 24.

deór,* 3, *ds.*; *ap.* déra, 3, a tear.

derb, 5, 54, certain.

dercis, dercais, 38, *s-pret.*, he looked, glanced; ra-dercastar, rodercastar,* 3 *sg.* 39, 42, 40, he looked.

derg-ór, 17, *ds.*, red-gold.

descad, 8, *gpm.*, dregs, leavings; leaven, *Wb.* 96; *np.* descaid.

desciurt, the north, *as.*

dessi, 13, *gsf.* of días, a couple, two persons.

di (i.), 5, 51, from her, it; with it, 51.

di, 28 = de, from.

dia, 4, if.

dia m-, 11, while.

di-airm, 38, *ns.*, unarmed, much-armed (?).

dían-loscud,* 4, act of making burn fiercely; dian, gl. *celer*, *Sg.* 64 b.

diarmait* duanach, 46, *nsm.*

díb, i., 12, 15, 22, 26, 39, 44; dib, 10, 20, 25, of or from them: *note*, díb, 15.

di-cheillid,* 47, insensate, mad.

di-chor, 56, act of displacing, repelling, laying aside.

dichra,* 38, earnestness, fervency; dichra, fervent, *W.*; but it is a noun here.

di-chur,* 14, *ds.* of dichor, to lay aside, displace.

dígail, 5; digail, 7, 8, vengeance, avenging; *dasf.* of dígal; díglaind,* 46, 1 *fut.* 2*ry*; ra-díglais,* 5, *s-pret.*, thou hast avenged.

digiur,* 14, *subj. pres.*; con-digiur, that I may go; dig,* 25, 26, 3 *sg. s-fut.*; digset* (that) they shall go, 21. *Cf.* 3 *sg.* digset, *LL.* 114 b; coro chainiur, *LL.* 117 a; nach digis, that thou mayest not go, "B. of Magh Rath," 160.

dílsib, 16, *dp.* of díles, own, native.

dím, 44, from me.

dimbúaid, 38, 39 × 2, *ns.*, defeat, disaster, ill-luck, "B. of Fen." 362.

din, 46, of the, with the; for the, 6.

dind, *N.*, *oppidum*, *Sg.* 63 a.

dind ríg,* 16, *asN.*, *now* Burgage Moate, Co. Carlow; *g.* Denda.

dindgna, 6, *gp.*, hill, fort; *ns.* dindgna in dunaid, *LL.* 253, fortresses, "Fragm. of Ir. Ann." 82; do dindgnaib doss, from tops of bushes, *Sg.* 203.

dinn* na bóinne, 25, *as.*, the Hill-fort of the Boyne; dindferta, a hill, *LU.* 64 a, ll. 11, 15; dind, .i. *arcem*, "Nennius," 92.

díriuch, 52, straight[way], direction, *d.* or *as.* of díriech; *np.* dirge, *LB.* 18.

dírrám,* 23; dirram, 23, *ns.*, great number.

díten, 36, *gsf.* of ditiu, ditu, *Sg.* 66 b, *teges.*

do, 1 × 2, 2 × 2, 3, 5 × 2, 8 × 4, 11, 14, 17 × 3, 18, 22, 27, 56, to, for; 55, for, as (do mnái = to wife); 16, 18, by (of agency, after *passive* or *infinitive*); 1, 2, 17, 25 × 2, 39, joining *infin.* with *noun* on which it depends.

do, 10, 11, 16, 17 × 2, 19, 26, 47, 54, = de, of (*partitive*), from.

dó, 1 × 2, 3, 8 × 2, 17, 18 × 2, 19, 23, 25 × 2, 48, to, for, of, &c. (him or it); do, 8, 12; by *after passives*.

do, 5, 11, 12, 19, thy.

dó, 51, two; *see* da, dib.

dobbrónach,* 3, sad; usually dobr-; perhaps for dub-bronach.

doberim, 44, I give, put, cause, bring; 3 *sg.* dobeir, dober, 11, 18; 3 *pl.* doberat, 52; 3 *sg. fut.* dobera, 21, 44; 3 *sg.* 2*ry fut.* doberad, 20; dobert, 39, 45, 46, 48, 51, *t-pret.* 3 *sg.*; 3 *pl.* dobertatar, 52; 3 *pl.* 2*ry pres.* dobertis, 57; dobretha,* 8, 8, 53, *pres.* 3 *sg.* (?), he puts *or* gave; *W.* calls it a *pret.* in ta; *imperat.* 2 *sg.* tabar, 13, 14, 2*pl.* tabraid; *infin.* tabairt, 36, 38, *ds.*

docuas,* 17 was told, *pret. pass.*; see atchuas; docuas = *itum est*, *Tl.* 228, 184, "Bodl. Cormac," 28.

dochum, 53, towards, *gov. genitive.*

dogebad* sib, 46, ye should find or get; 3 *sg.* 2*ry pres.* or *fut.* of dogabim, fogabim.

dogar,* 39, *as.* (written dogar), sorrow; perhaps we should dogra, anguish.

dóib, 8, 10 × 3, 13, 19, 21, 25, 46; doib, 15, to *or* for them.

dóit, 45 × 2, 48 × 2, 51, *ndasf.*, hand.

dol, 23, act of going, = dola, 23 × 2; dul, 5, 14; *cf.* techta = techt, *infra*, *n.* dula, *W.*; dola, "Frag. of Ir. Ann." 73, 136.

dolaid,* 11, *gs.*, injury, loss, *O'R.*; *cf. ns.* dolod and solod, "Fled Bricr." 90; dolad, distress, discomfort; *cf.* folad, solace, "Felire"; *rather* charge, load, impost (*see note*).

dolluid, 10, 26, 51, he went; 3 *pl.* dollotar, 10, 52.

dom, 23, 43, to my; dol dom chonair, 23, to go my way.

domenmnach,* 3, dispirited.

domna,* 4, causes, matter, materials. *Cf.* rígdamna, the makings of a king.

domni,* 25, deeper; or *pl.* deep.

don, 7, 8, 17, 18, for the.

don, 5, from the.

dond, 4, 17, brown; *np.* duind, *LL.* 259 a.

dond cualngi,* 17, the Brown (Bull) of Cualnge.

do-n-ethe,* 15; do-n-ethea, 14, that it may go on, proceed; *pres. subj.* of do-ethaim. *Cf.* atetha, *supra.*

do-n-rat, 1 × 2, 2, that made him; dorat, 52, he gave.

donti, 17, to the person.

doragad, 8 × 2, 18, 19, 26, 27, 2*ry fut.* 3 *sg.*, would, should go; *see* ragat.

dorn,* 18, Fist, *ns.*, name of a warrior.

dornaib, 37, *dp.* of dorn, fist.

dorosset,* 26, *fut.* of doroichim, they will arrive; *see* torset, torocht.

doss, 36, *ns.*, a bush; *gp.* dindgnaib doss, from tops of bushes; *sg.* 203.

dot, 7, to thy.

dothaet, 12, goes, = dotéit, *Wb.* 25 d; "Bodl. Corm." 36.

drech-solus, 9, 11, *nds.*, bright-faced.

dreich, 13, *dasf.* of drech, face: fa dreich, for, in preparation for.

dremun, 47, furious.

drúi, 2, 3, 27, 30, *nsm.*, druid.

druim, 51, *asN.*, back.

duaibsech, 51 × 2, gloomy, dreadful (stubborn, "Frag. of Ir. Ann." 72), darksome, *LU.* 64 a, 60 a.

duanach,* 46, songful.

duit, 6, 23; *see* do (I.) and tú.

dulig,* 55, *ns.*, grievous, sad.

dún, 4 × 4, 9, 11, 13, fort, castle, *naN.*; *d.* dún, 9, 11, 13; gl. *arx*, *Sg.* 61 b.

dún (II.), 5 × 3, 6, 7, 30, 54, to, for us.

dunad, 6, *gpN.* or *m.*, fortification; *npm.* dúnaid,* 3, 15; *d.* dúnud, 7, 10, a fort; also a force (on march), *LU.* 63, 65.

dún delga, *as.* 4, 13, *d.* 9, Dundalk.

dungail,* 7, *gs.*

duni, 18, person, *nsm.*

dún daire,* 4, in Louth.

dun sescind,* 4.

dún sobairge,* 4, *now* Dunseverick.

é, 2, 5, 10 (*idiom*), 14, 19 × 2, 21, 26, 45, 47, disjunctive form of sé, he; é, him, 47; é-side, 45, that.

ech, *gp.*, 36, 53, of horses; *np.* eich, 36, 36.

echach, 4, 5, *gsm.* of eochu.

ecairther,* 13, *subj. pres. pass.* of ecraim, may be prepared, put in order; *pret. pass.* 3 *sg.* ra hecrad, 11, 13.

ecal, 18, *ns.*, causing fear, dangerous; *np.* ecil, *Z.*

ecla, 20, *asf.*, fear; *ds. LL.* 67; *d.* ar m'ecla, *LL.* 67.

eclach, 51, fearful; ecl. in the *ms.*; eaglach, fearful, timid, Job ix., Matth. viii.

echlach, 7, horse-boy; .i. giolla cursais. *O'Cl.*

écmais, *dsf.*, 26, absence; *gs.* écmaisse,* 7, 8; écmaissi, 7; écmairi, 11, 12; the *gen.* is used *adjectivally.*

ecrait,* 56, *np.* or *ns.*, enemies (?); *ap.* ecrata, *LL.* 58 b; but *cf.* ar écraitib, sluagedaib, cursaib, *LL.* 265 b, = cavalcades (?); but ecraitte, strife, "F. Mast." III. 1766; ar cach n-ecraiti, from every disaster, "F. of Carman," p. 530.

echtra,* 19, *as.*, adventures, expeditions; rachaid cethri echtra, "B. of Fen." 282.

echtrand, 6, 6, 9, *gp.*, foreigner; *np.* aechtrinn, *Wb.* 12 c, 21 b.

ed, 5 × 2, 18, this, that.

éicne,* 3, *gsf.*, security (?); écen, *da.* écin, violence, "Ascoli." *Cf.* écne, wisdom.

einech, *nas.*, 45 × 2, 48, face.

éirge, *gs.*, 13, act of rising, or going forward; *pret.* 3 *sg.* ro-éirig, 10, 14; 3 *pl.* ra-ergitar, 10, 13.

éis, 25; eis, 52, *d.*, track; dar éis, behind, 52; da éis, 34, behind it; da n-éis, 34, behind them; di éis, *retro*, *Z.*

éisteacht, 48, *ds.*, act of listening; ní éistenn, he does not listen, *LL.* 367 b.

heit(er),* 17, possible: sir ba heit,* who could.

elga, 6, *gs.*; ellga, .i. herend, *LL.* 45 a; *d.* elga, "Nennius," 142; elga, .i. uasal, Joyce's "Keating," p. 4: *n.* elga, *O'Cl.*

ro-hellamaigit,* 8, 3 *pl. pret. pass.*, were prepared; ellam, gl. *præparatio*, "Ascoli's Glos."

élúd, 7, escape; *infin.* of élaim; elathar *is* escaped, evaded, *LL.* 266 a; dan-elat, if they elope, "B. of Fen." 366.

ém, 26, indeed, etc.

émain, 1, 2, 22, *dsf.*; *g.* emnó,* 4; Navan Fort, near Armagh; *g.* na emna, *LL.* 63 a.

enecl(ann), 11, *nsf.*, amends; .i. eraic, *O'Cl.*; *gs.* eneclainne, honour, "Sench. M." I. 174; tribute to a king for protection, "L. na gCeart, 98.

eochaid eolach, 46, *ns.*; eochaid iúil, *W.*

eochu,* 16, *ns.*; *ds.* 17, 17, son of Luchta; *g.* echach, 4, 5.

eogan, 31, *ns.*, King of Farney, and son of Durthacht.

eolach, 46, *ns.*, learned.

eóluis,* 8, *gs.* of eólas, the knowledge (of the road). *Cf.* chaill sé an t-eolus, he lost his way.

erc, 53, 55, *nas.*, son of Carpre and Fedelm; he stands for two persons in D'Arbois and Windisch's works.

erdarcus, 25, *ns.*, notability.

erdorn, 17, *ns.*, hilt; er, *intensit.* as ur-árd, the very top (?); ó thul co aurdornd, from face to croup, "L. U. Táin."

heriu, 11, 12, 57, *nsf.*; *g.* her(end), 3, 5, 7, 11, 15, 16, 17, 44; *d.* herind, 20, Erin.

herling,* 7, *gsm.*

errach,* 6 × 2, *nsm.*, spring-time; *d.* errug, "B. Cr." 37 a.

errid,* 28, *np.*, array, dress; *ns.* rian-erred, *LL.* 76 b; *d.* erriud, *LL.* 266 a; *as.* cath-erred, 34. *Cf.* errad, to arrange, *LL.* 268 b; *cf.* cath-erred, erred airderscoir, erred Patraic, "B. of Fen." 80, 198, 286.

esbach, 55, wanting, vain, *ns.* espa, a vain thing, "B. of Fen." 208.

esbaid, 4 × 2, want.

escomol,* 56, profitless, nonfulfilment.

ess-airm,* 38, *ns.*, disarmed. *Cf.* di-airm, *supra.*

ess-arcain, 42, *dsf.*, act of striking, killing.

et, 1, 3 × 3, 6, Latin = and, *for* acus.

etar-lén,* 9, *ds.*, mutual sorrow, concern; etarlén, great hurt, "S. na Rann," p. 137.

eter, 47, 55, between.

etir, 12, 25, at all.

ra-étlaiché,* 34, *2ry pres.* 3 *sg.* of étlaim (és-tallaim), would be cut.

éttaid, 28, *np.* of éttad, armour, "B. of Magh Lena," p. 20, 70; *as.* éidiud, "B. of Magh Rath," 68.

fa, 36 (that) was.

fá, 14, 45; fa, 13, 52, 54, under, against; among, 54.

facca, 11, *pret.* 3 *sg.*, *depend.* of atchíu, I see; 3 *pl.* faccatar, 30; *2ry *fut. pass.* faicfithe, 36.

faccíail* (?), 38, to see; or for facbáil, to leave.

facsin,* 15, *ds.* of facsiu, seeing; for acsin, *W.*

ra-facctha,* 34, *2ry pres. pass.* of fácbaim, would be left (were seen?).

facctna, fachtnai, 25, 17, *gs.* of Fachtna Fathach, Conor's father.

fadb,* 18, *ns.* = Knot, *O'Cl.*; a weapon. "B. of Fen." 376.

fadéin, 3, 50, 51, own.

fades, 21, 52, southwards.

faebra, 6, *n.* or *ap.* faebra = weapons, "Mesca Ul." 32. Perhaps an error for ferba, cows (?); *depen. pres.* 1 *sg.*

fagaim,* 26, I find, *depend. pres.*; 1*st pl.*, fagum,* 25, of fogabaim,* I find.

fail, 3, 7, 14, 18, 28, 44; fil, 36; fuil, 7; ro-fail, 3, 4, 23, is, there is, which is; 3 *pl.* failet, 12, 25; ro-failet, 14; ron-fuilet, 23, are; not used with *adjectives.*

fair, 7, 8, 17, 20; fair, 53, on *or* for him, it; *idiom.* 20, 53.

fairggi,* 22, *as.* of fairgge, the sea; foirrce, gl. *thetis.*

fáitbiud,* 18, *ns.*, laughter, smiles; fo-r-aitbi, gl. *subrisit.*

fáitte,* 7, 9; faitte, 8, *perf. pass. pl.* of fáidim, were sent; *imperat.* 2 *sg.*, 7; fáitti, 7, faitti, 14; *part. necessit* (?), are to be sent; used as *imperat.*; fóitte techta, messengers were sent, *LU.* 55; confáitti, 9, seems *hist. pres.*, he sent.

falluid, 16 × 2, 19, *pret.* for fo-n-luid, so he went.

ra-falmaiged,* 13, the *pass. pret.* of falmaigim, I evacuate, empty; folam, empty; folmaiged, laying waste, *Ag.*

fáilte,* 8, *asf.*, welcome, joy; *cf.* feraid l. faelti friu 7 ferri in bentrocht uli 7 férais f. dano faelti, "Serglige Conch." § 35.

fanna, 6, *np.* of fann, weak.

far,* 11, = bar, said; so *LL.* 268 a.

far,* 22, 34, 40, = bar, for, on, upon; *idiom.* 34.

far n-, 11 × 2, 22, 30, 46, = bar, your; far m, 46.

farggaib, 4, *depen. pret.* of facbaim, she left.

farrad, 34, *as.*, neighbourhood; im-farrad, with me, *LL.* 115 a.

farroeblangatar, 15, *pret.*, they overleaped; forruleblangtar, *subsiluerunt*, *Ml.* 129 c; *see* bar-roeblangair.

farsin m-, 38, on the; *pl.* far na, 40.

fath, 5, *ns.*, cause, matter (?); *cf.* arapa a fath, for this cause, *LL.* 74; fath-comairle, wise counsel, "B. of M. Rath," 296; instruction, *O'Cl.*, .i. fis, "O'Dav." 88.

fata, 30, 52, long.

fathach, 19, foreseeing, sage, clever, *O'Cl.*

fathaig, 17, *gs.* of fathach.

fathúaid, fathuaith, 19, 25, 26, 38, northwards.

febra, 6, *gs.*, February.

febus, 11 × 2, *n.* or *d.*, excellence.

fecht, 15, *na.*; fect, 14, 15, journey; f. 7 sluaged, hosting, *LL.* 55, 57; expedition, army.

feda gabli, 52; feda gaible, 19; *gs.* of fid gaible.

fedma, 39, *gsN.* of feidm, effort.

fégais,* 38, 41; fegais, 43, 46; *s-pret.* of fégaim, he scanned, looked at.

feib, 20, 39, 48, as, when.

féic,* 25 × 2, *ns.*; m. follomain m. faichtna fathaig.

feidilmi, 53, *gsf.* of feidelm, daughter of Conor.

féile, 29, *gsf.*, honour, gl. *honestas*, *Z.*

féin, 5, 54, own, self.

feirt, 56, *dsf.*, a height, mound; *d.* firt, *LL.* 97; *fem.* fertae in "B. of Armagh."

feithen,* 41, 42, *nam. voc.* fethin, 41, son of Amergin.

nitfeltaig,* 18, *np.*, they are not deceitful; *cf.* fell, contention, deceit.

fer, 19, 26, 30, 44, *ns.*; *as.* 44; *gp.* fer n-, 7, 17, 33, 45, man; *d.* feraib, 44; fir, *gs.*, 17, 22, 37, 39, *np.* 6, 11, 29; *ap.* firu, 13; *ds.* fir, 25, 26.

feraind, 17; ferainn, 11, *gs.* of ferann, land.

ferais, 8, *t-pret.* 3 *sg.* of feraim, I make, pour, = firis, *LL.* 92; ro-ferrsata comlanna, they fought this battle, *LU.* 97.

feránach, 6, grassy.

ferggach, fergach, 52, wrathful.

ferge, 40, *gsf.* of ferg.

fergus,* fianach, 46, *as.*; Fergus, mac Róig, 18; slain by Ailill, *LL.* p. 25; Ulster hero.

ferr, 11, better.

fessa, 7 × 2, 8, 9, 14, 17, *np.*, intelligencers *or* messengers.

fessa* (II.), 8, 9, *npf.* of fess, a feast.

ro-fessa* (III.), 17, *pl. pret. pass.* (were known) here = were sent; ro fessa fessa, from faidim.

fetar,* 3, 48, I know, knew; 2*ry fut.* festa-su, 4, thou wouldst know.

fíamach,* 19; *cf.* fiam, .i. long, *O'Cl.*

fianach,* 30, 46; Fergus F., a poet.

fichit, 11, 50; *ds.* and *np.* of fiche, twenty.

fid, 37, *das.*, a wood; *g.* feda, 34, 19, 52; feda gaible, 19, 52.

fidach* fergach, 19, 52, *nsm.*, wooden (?).

filid, 46, *np.* of fili, poet.

find, 16, 19, 21, 52, 57, *nsm.*, King of the Galian, his palace at Ailenn; son of Ross.

finnchad,* 8 × 2, *ns.*, son of Conor.

finnchorad,* 57, *gs.*, battle of Findchora; mentioned in "D'Arbois' Catalogue."

finnmór, 7, 10, *ns.*, son of Rofer.

fínscoth,* 55, *nsf.*, daughter of Cuchulaind.

fintan, 49, *nsm.*, son of Níall.

fír, 29; fir, 29, true, truth.

fir* **catha**, 22, *ap.*, true battalions; or *as.*, in the truth of battle.

fír-glicc, 19, truly acute(-minded).

fis, 29, *ds.*, knowledge; do chlár-fiss, 56, of plain, wide knowledge (?).

fithal, a famous Brehon, "Sench. M." iii. 30.

flaith, 22, *ns.*, a chief; 13, prince *or* beer; *cf.* "Cormac," 19.

flaith, 54, *dsf.*, reign.

flath-briugaid,* 23, *ns.* or *pl.*, chief yeoman; *gs.* and *pl.* briugad, *W.*; *cf.* "Laws," i. 248.

fled, 9 × 3, 13; banquet, *nsf.*; *ac.* fleid, 8; fled, 9; *g.* fledi, 14; *dp.* fledaib, 22.

fliuch, 3, *ns.*, wet, moist.

fó (i.), 14; fo, 8, 45, under, throughout, among.

fó, 17, under his.

fochera,* 57, *3rd sg. pret.* (or *fut. redupl.*?) of fo-chrenim; he fell, docer, *Z.*

fodalta, 47, *dp.*, divided, distributed.

fodectsa, 23, at present; fodechtra, now, *LU.* 113; fodesta, *LL.* 84.

fodéin, 47, own.

foen-glinni,* 23, *ns.*, feeble security.

foillged,* 34, *ds.*, cutting; faillgim, *sarpo*; foalgaim, *prosternor*, *Z.*

foirne, 5, on us, *idiom.*

foirtched,* 34, *ds.*, act of destroying; d'foirtchead, to be destroyed, "B. of M. Rath," 248.

folcmara,* 3, *ap.* of folcmar, abundant. *Cf.* falc, shower, "Hy-fiach." 28 b; falc, flood, *O'R.*; folc, to sleep, "Laws," 240.

follogod,* 28, 139, act of neglecting; fullugim, gl. *abdo;* follaig = the gl. *neglecta*, *Z.*

follomuin, *gs.*, 25; *cf.* follamnuiger, who rules, "B. of Fen." 392.

folluid, 16, *perf.*, he went, = fo-n-luid (?).

fón, 37; fon, 26 (*idiom.*), under the.

for, 3, 9, 43, said; *see* far, bar, ar.

for, 11, 12, 13, 17, 18, 25, 28, 43, 54, on, over; *see* bar, far; form, 3, 44, on me; fort, 17, on thee; foraib, foirb, 11, 46, 33; foraind, 52 (*idiom.*); forainne, 55, 56, against us; forni, 5, on us; forro, forru, 13, 45, 46; forthu, 11, 25, 26, on them.

for-aire, 6, *das.*, act of watching.

forbbaid,* 11, *gs.* of forbbad,* land. *Cf.* forbe = orpe, heritage; *ds.* forbaid, *LL.* 117; orbaid, *LL.* 222; *d.* forbad, accomplishment, "B. of Magh Rath," 168.

for-dergad,* 51, *as.*, wounding.

forithin, 21 × 2, 46, *nds.*, help, succour; furiuth, gl. *succurro*, "Félire"; or from fóirim (?).

for-ruada,* 3; *ap.*, very red; *cf.* *np.* for-derga, very red, *LL.* 67; forruaid, crimson (sea), "B. of Fen." 824.

fortacht, 46, *ds.*, aid; furtacht, 21, 21.

fossugud, 38, act of arresting, to stay, check.

fot,* 6, *ds.*, watching, heed; an-fot, heed-lessness, *LL.* 125 b, 171 b, 263 b.

fót,* 6, *nm.*, sod of earth, gl. *cespes*, *Sg.* 66 b; *np.* fóit, "Siab. Ch. C. 376.

fothrucud, 4, act of bathing (the body); folcad (of the head); fothraiccthi, gl. *balneum*.

fothuaid, 34, northwards.

fr[eccomas] (?),* 56.

freccomas,* 6, *ds.*, watching, warding; (.i. comed no frairfaighe, *O'Dav.*), frithaire, *Tl.* 254; = frith-con-mer; *see* midem.

fri, 8, 13 × 2, 39, 42, 45, 48; towards, against, for the purpose of; *gov. acc.*; it is often ri in our text; *gov. dat.* 42.

fris, 56, against him; frind, 54; friu, 18, against them.

frithálter,* 14; 3 *sg. pres. pass.* of fri-álim, be feasted, tended.

frith-beirt,* 54, *asf.* of frithbert,* opposition; frisbiur, gl. *obnitor*, *Z.*

frith-rosc, 39, counter-charge; rurg, skirmish, *O'Reilly;* tarla frithrusc fergi eturro, "Lism. Lives," 393.

fua, good; at-fua, *cf.* fó, good, "Laws," I. 256; = bec, "O'Dav." 92.

fuar, 17, cold.

fuatecht,* 25 (= fuadach), act of pursuing, to run away with; fúaitgid, *W.*, he runs away with.

fuidb, 39; *gs.* of fodb, arms, spoils; fúdbai, *spolia*, *LB.* 206 b.

fuil, *ds.*, 4, blood; *g.* fola, 3, 12; *dp.* fuilib, 6, wounds *or* bleedings; *np.* fuili, *LL.* 90 b.

fuilt,* 24, *npm.* of folt, head of hair; *d.* fult, *LL.* 68.

fuligud,* 51, act of bleeding, a wound. *Cf.* forfulig tractad fola fair, *LL.* 72.

fulngidi,* 30, 30, 31, 33, *np.* of fulngid, supporters. *Cf.* tuirthi fulaing catha, "B. of Magh Rath," 162.

furáil, 5; furail, 11, = furóil, 5, gl. *magnum*, *Wb.* 10 d, excessive. *Cf.* deróil, small; furóil, *LL.* 64 a; "O'Dav." 94.

furic, 8, *npm.*; fuireca, 9, *ap.*, feasts; *n.* fuireag, *O'Cl.*; *d.* oc fuiriuc, *LL.* 57 b.

fus, *see* hi-fús.

gab, 27; ro-gab, 22, 25, 34 × 2, 45, 47, 51, 52; 3 *sg. s-pret.* of gabaim, he took to *or* began, took, went; followed by ar, 34; gabsat, 57, 3 *pl.*; na-gabad, 34, 2*ry pres.* 3 *sg.*; gabai, 20, 2 *sg. pres. indic.*; gabáil, 17, *def. infin.*; rogabait, 13, 15, *pass. pret.* 3 *pl.*; gabar,* 23, *imperat. pass.* 3 *sg.*; rogabtha,* 17, 2*ry pres. pass.* 3 *sg.*; gabthar,* 14, 3 *sg. subj. pres. pass.*; 3 *pl.* gabtar,* 13, 15; geb, 20, 1 *sg. fut.*; gébaid, 25, 3*rd sg. fut.*; gebad, 20, 2*ry fut.* 3 *sg.*

gábae, 8, *gs.*

gabalta, 6, *np.*, taken up, engaged. *Cf.* gabáiltoch, *captus*, gabáil dunaid, encamping, *LU.* 76 a; sogabalta (horses), easily-yoked, "Siab. Ch. C." p. 376.

gabra, 13 × 2, *npf.* of gabair, horse; *gp.* gobar, "B. of Fen." 366; "Fled Bricr." 96.

gach (?), 6, every.

gaetha, 6, *npf.* of gáeth, wind; *d.* gaith, *LU.* 118.

gaethach, 6, windy.

gaible, 19, *gsf.*

gáine,* 31, *nsm.*, son of Daurthacht; *cf.* gaoine, .i. maith, good.

gair, 39, shouting, *ns.*

gairdi, 6, 22, *np.* of gairit.

gáire, 18, *gs.*, laughter.

ro-gairset, 25, 3 *pl. s-pret.* of gairim, they shouted; gairfit, 6, *fut.* 3 *pl.*

gal, 19, *nsf.*; *gp.*, 4, (deed of) valour; *g.* gaile, 34, 35; *da.* gail, *LL.* 344, *LU.* 124 a; *dp.* galaib, *LU.* 77; *d.* congail catha, "Frag. of Irish Ann." 166; gleógal, "F. Mast." I. 438.

gal[ann], 26; *cf.* doṙigned guin galann de, *LL.* 258 a, "C. M. Lena," 142; galand, .i. gaisced, no namad, *O'Cl.*

galaig, 29, *voc. sg. m.* of galach,* valorous.

galar, 3, *nsN.*, disease, distress; *g.* galair, 2. *Cf. dolor, vulnus.*

galían, *ng.*, 11, 16, 23, 50; *ds.*, gal-ian, 48, 52; Leinstermen, "Laws," I. 70.

gall, 8, *ns.*, 7, 8, 11, 12, 14, *gp.*, foreigner.

gallecda, 7, 8, 11, 12, *dp.*, Gallic (= Norse ?).

gall-iathaib, 7, 8, 11, 12, *dp.*, foreign lands.

garba, 6, *np.* of garb, rough.

gascedach, 27, 52, skilful at arms.

gascid, 14, *gsm.*, gasced, practice of arms; *nd.* gasced, arms, *LL.* 84; *d.* gascid, *LU.* 124; *np.* gascaid, *LU.* 64 b.; *i.e.* sword, shield, etc., *LU.* 102 a.

rogeisestar,* ro-géisestar, 48, 35; 3 *sg. pret.* géisim, I moan; 3 *pl.* rogéisetar, rogeisetar, 48; ní ra geis, *LL.* 268 b, it did not resound, no geissed, which resounded, "Nennius," 200.

geiss, 23 × 2, *ns.*, a magical command or prohibition; *dp.* geissaib, 54.

geltaib,* 38, *dpm.* of gelt, madman, "Mesca Ul." 20.

gessaib, 54, *dp.* of geiss.

gillai, 34, *npm.* of gilla, a page, attendant; *dp.* gillaib, 34; gil-(laib), 28.

gillanrad,* 38, pages, followers; a *collective, nsf.*

glainidi, 11, *ap.* of glainide, glassy, crystalline.

glan-fothraicthi,* *gs.* of glan-fothracud, clean-bathing; fo-thairethib, gl. *balneis*, *Z.*

glas-darach, 37, *gsf.* of glas-dair, green oak.

glas-gesceda,* 37, *ap.* of glas-gésca (?), green boughs.

glas-láth,* *ns.*, 36, *collective*, green *or* young warriors; *np.* glasláith, recruits, "Ann. of L. Cé," I. 410.

glass-anfud, 10, a green surge, storm; *cf.* glasmag, sea.

-glassi, 8, *gsf.* of glass, green, or glaisse, greenness.

glé, 5, clear; good, *O'Cl.*

gléire,* 8, *ns.*, choice, abundance, *O'Cl.*

gleó, 57, strife; *np.* gleoithi, "B. of Fen." 218; *g.* gliad, "Hyfiach." 294; mell-gleó, a fight with stones, *LL.* 92; gleo, .i. cath, "Ode to Brian O'Rorke"; mell-gleo n-illiach, *neuter*, *LL.* 92 a, 92.

ra-glinnigit,* 8, *perf. pass.* 3 *pl.* of glinnigim, I make secure; glin-nigthi, 23, *pass. part. pass.*, secured; rodglinnestar, he strengthened her, *W.*

gló-béim,* 45, *nsN.*, a straight (?) blow; gló-snathe, gl. *norma*; perhaps gleó-béim.

glond[beimnech], 53, *ns.*, a striking deed (?), *or* deed-striking; glond, deed, crime, "B. of Fen." 64; "F. Mast." I. 170; gloinnbéimnech na gcloídemh, "Frag. of Ir. Ann." 122; glond, fame (?), *LB.* 217 c, .i. guin duine, "O'Dav." 94.

glun-gil, 29, *voc. sg.* of glun-gel, white-kneed.

glunmar, 27, 52, large-kneed.

ro-gniad,* 9, *perf. pass.* of gníim, was made, held; ro-gnithea, 3 *pl.* 24; gniter, 23, 3 *pl. imperat. pass.*

gnim, 57, *nms.*, act, action.

gnúis, 36, 38, *nasf.*, face; gnúsi, 39, *np.*; gnúsib, 39, *dp.*

gobann, 18, *gsm.* of goba, smith.

goin, 18, *ds.*; guin, 26, *nsN.*, act of wounding mortally; a death-wound, "B. of Fen." 374.

ᵹó-lam,* 17, *nsf.*, false-hand (?), *or* falseness of hands.

ᵹorma, 11, *ap.* of ᵹorm, blue.

ᵹothia, 7.

ᵹraiᵹib, 28, *dpN.* of ᵹraiᵹ, horse-team; *gp.* ᵹreᵹ, of horses, *LL.* 59, 61; *ap.* ᵹraiᵹe, gl. *equitium.*

ᵹretha,* 24, *np.* of ᵹrith, ardour, "Mesca Ul." 36; *or* preparations; la méc ᵹretha, with much *éclat*, "Nennius," 228; ᵹrith, .i. ᵹaire, *LB.* 35 b; *gs.* ᵹretha, clash of arms ("F. Mast." II. 596) = arm-ᵹrith, *LU.* 77 b; *pl.* ᵹretha, shouts, "Fél." Jan. 25; ᵹrith, spiritedness, "C. M. Rath," I. 184; ᵹreathaim, I prepare, winnow, *O'R.*; ᵹrith sleᵹi, *LL.* 267 c.

ᵹrianan, 17, summer-house, bower; palace (of heaven), "F. Mast." II. 930; *gs.* ᵹrinain, 17.

ᵹuaillib,* 35, *dp.* of ᵹuala, shoulder (*syncopated*), for ᵹualnib, ᵹualannaib; so in "B. of Magh Rath," p. 140; *dp.* mid-ᵹuaillib, *LU.*, *Táin*; ᵹúallaib 7 sliastaib, *LL.* 85 b.

i n-, 1 × 2, 4, 6 × 4, 7 × 4, 8 × 2, 13 × 3, 17, 20 × 2, 22 × 2, in (govs. *dat*); 10, 21, 23, into (govs. *acc.*); i n-a, 39, into his; 'n-a, 11 × 2, 26, in his, its; i n-a n-, 14, 47, 57; 'n-a, 21, 57, in their; 'n-ar, 21 × 2, in our.

i n-, 3, 7, 8 × 2, 12, 15 × 2, 19, 20 × 2, 25, 36, 45, in which; *see* i n- (I.).

i, 30; **hí**, 6, 13, her, it (*fem.*).

hi n-, 6 (nihinam), not in the time of (?).

.i., 1, 7, 16, abbreviation for ed ón (in Latin, *id est*), that is, *i.e.*

***ro-íad**, 51, *pret.* of iadaim, he clasped, closed.

iaram, 18, afterwards; íarum, *Z.*; iaram : iar n- : : riam : ria n-.

ro-iarfach,* 12, *perf.* of iarfaiᵹim, he asked; iarfaiᵹid, 22, to ask.

iarfat,* 11, *fut.* of iarraim, I shall ask, seek; *infin.* iarraid, 5; is followed by for, 11.

ian-lebur,* 39, *asm.*, very long.

iartain, 13, 51, thereupon, afterwards.

iarthur, 25, *ns.*, the west.

iat, 3, 11 × 3, 12, 13 × 2, 14, 15 × 2, 20, 31, 32, 52, they (*disjunctive*), *nap.*; bar iat, said they, 15, 20.

iathaib,* 6, 7, 8, 9, 11; íathaib, 12; *dp.* of iath; lands, countries; iath, .i. ferand, *LU.* 7 b; *ap.* iathu, "Man. & Cust." 514.

ibair, 18, *gs.*, yew.

ic, 7, at; icom, 25, 26, at my.

ícc, 17, payment, to pay.

ict, 7, *gs.*, muir n-icht, the English Channel.

idna,* 11, *ap.*, arms, spears; *m.* idnu, *W.*; iadna, .i. arma, Mulconry's "Ode to Brian O'Rorke."

i-fus, 56, hither, here, on this side; *ds.* of fos; see *W.*; i fos, here (on earth), "B. of Fen." 2.

il, *for* in; il-lármedón, 50.

il,* 7, *as.*

íle,* 7, *as.*, Islay in Scotland; ilea *insula*, "Adamnan"; *as.* ile, "Nennius," 146.

il-ᵹaire,* 4, much (or varied) shouting *or* laughter; *as.*

ili, 6, *np.*, many, multitudes (?): ile, .i. iomad, *O'Cl.*

iliach, 32, *gsm.*, Connad's father.

ill-dathacha,* 11, *ap.* of il-dáthach, many coloured; the second l is due to contact with d.

il-ríana,* 10, *np.*, many *or* great water ways; rian, .i. span, sea, *O'Cl.*; *see* renaib.

im, 5, 54, 57 × 2, about, around, in connexion with.

im', 22, 38, in my; im' oenur, 38, I alone.

imdádaib,* 13: imdadaib, 15; *dp.* of imda, couch; *gp.* imdad; *gs.* imdad, *LL.* p. 29; *d.* imdaid, "C. M. Rath," 296; *LL.* 29; *n.* imdae, *LU.* 99.

im-denam, 17, reparation, restoration, making good (?), usually ornamenting; *ns.* immdenam, gl. *limbus*, *Z.*

-im-gén, 27; imgen, 26, very long (géin, long, *O'R.*), great birth *or* fact (?).

im-luad, 19, *as.*, to move, moot; ro-t-im-luaid,* 15, *pret.* of imluadim; has moved thee.

immach, 10, 36, 51, outward.

immar, 8, 54, as, like; immar ubull, like an apple, *LL.* 90.

imme, 16 × 2, 34; immi, 19, 25, 26, about him.

immellaigi,* 3, 15, *npN.*, connected premises, outhouses. *Cf.* imbel, imblech, and imb-ellach, circumjunction; *cf.* iomallaiche, *Scotch Bible*, Numbers xxii. 41.

ra-immir,* 51, *pret.* of immrim, he played, plied; followed by *for*.

immoro, 14, indeed, however; written in full, *LL.* 238 a.

-impá, 52, *pret.* of impóim, he turned; sóit, they turn, *LL.* 259 a.

im-theit, 29, which goes round, surrounds.

im-thúsa, 23; imthusa, 45, *np.*, events, proceedings, performances. *Cf.* i. 7 imthecta, *LU.* 65 b; imthus, history, "B. of Fen." 258; rémimthus, the going before, "L. na gCeart," 126.

in, 6, the; *as.* in n-, 15, 16, 17; *ns.* inn, 10, 30, 31; *gs.* in feda, 35.

in, 19, 22 × 2, 25, 26, 27, *interrog. particle.*

in, 7 × 2; in n-, 57 (?), *art.* or *prep.*

inad, 17, 20, 36, 39, *ndas.*, place.

inber, 10, 25, 26, *nas.*, river (mouth); *g.* inbir, 16, 25; *d.* inbiur, 9; *npN.* inbera, "B. of Fen." 204; river, "Laws," I. 122; Inber Linni Luachainne, 10, 11, 14, 15, at Dundalk; Inber Semni, 10, Larne, Co. Antrim.

inchaib, 7, *dp.*; con inchaib órdaib, with gold facings, *LU.* 94 a; ar i. a einig, under his protection, "C. M. Rath," 248; i n-i., in the face, front, "Laws," I. 176; ar i. Eremóin, in presence of E., *Ms.* H. 4, 22, p. 120; protection, presence (?); tiomnaim mo chorp 7 m'anam ar ionchaib do thrócaire, "Parrthus an Anma," p. 294; ar a inchaib, for his front, "Man. & Cust." III. 506; di inchaib, from face, honour, *ibi*, 493; inchaib, *ds.* (?), honour, *LL.* 115 a; dot inchaib, for thy honour's sake, "Siege of Howth," 48, 52; *LB.* 219 a; "Laws," I. 232, inchaib, .i. aigid, "Cormac," 19.

innchomartha,* 25, sign, *ns.*

indiu, 15, to-day.

ro-indlit,* 13, 15, *pass. pret.* of indlim, were yoked; indil, .i. cengal, "Félire."

indliter, 13, 15, *pres. pass. imper.*, let them be yoked, got ready.

indmassa,* 11, *gs.* of indmass, wealth, treasure; *gp.* inmass, 27.

ingen, 4, 5, 7, 55, *nsf.*, daughter; *g.* ingini, 53.

innaigid, 25, 26, 30, 39, 40, 42, *ds.*; in phrase, da n-inn. d'a inn. in his direction, towards him, them; *see* innsaigid.

inneoin,* 36, according to their will; d'aimdeoin, in spite of, O'Begley's "Dict."; deóin, *d.* deonaib, will, *LL.* 193 a, 164 b; inneoin = a support *or* a prop in "Hyfiachrach," 254. Is it the meaning here?

inniasat,* 25, 26, *fut.* of innisim, I will tell; ro-innisetar,* 19, *pret.* 3 *pl.* *Cf.* indesat, I will tell, "B. of Fen." 292, 350.

innithim, 26, 27, *nsm.*, thought, meditation.

innóchάin, 35, *nsf.*; innochain, 48, Conor's shield.

innocht, 20, to-night.

innossa, 25, 38, 48, now; indossa, *LL.* 279 b.

innund, 25 × 2, 26, from here, over.

inrim,* 6 × 2, incursion. *Cf. g.* indrid, gl. *vastatio*, *Ml.* 27 a, imrim?

insaigid, 17, 31, 51 × 2, *ds.* against; = innaigid, *supra*; *cf.* saigid, to attack, *LL.* 92; "da insaigid," innsaigthech, aggressive, "B. of Fen." 398.

inscoa,* 7, 10, *gsm.*, father of Amlaib.

insi, 7, *gs.* or *pf.* of inis, island; *dp.* insib, 7 × 2.

intí, 57, the person: *see* í (iv.).

intib, 37, in them.

intig,* 39, *dsN.*, a scabbard; *see* note.

inund, 44, same, identical.

ir, *for* in: ir-Ros, ir-robadud, 25, 36, 45, 48.

irdarcus, 26, glory: = airdarcus, gl. *claritudo*, *Z.*

irgalach,* 14, 27; *nsm.* irgal, fervour, *Z.* 627; irgal, *g.* irgaili, conflict; *np.* irgala, gl. *arma*, *Wb.* 6 b, *LL.* 268 b; *voc.* irgalaig, 27, son of Macláig.

irgnam,* 23, preparation (of food); aurgnaid, prepare ye, *LL.* 249; = ergnam, *LL.* 125.

irial, Iriel, 27, *nsm.*; *voc.* Iriel, 28, 29; son of Conall Cernach.

irnaide, 30, 31, 32, delay, waiting. *Cf.* furnaide, to wait, "B. of Fen." 284.

ro-sn-irthócaib, 2; *s-pret.* of irthócbaim, who raised, reared him, *qui l'éleva*.

is, *passim*, it is; iss, 3, 5, 8, 12, 15.

is, 18 × 2, who is, *rel.* form of is (= as); iss, 3, 5, 8, 12, 15, it is: iss-and, iss-ed, iss-í, iss-íat.

is, 4, 5, 19, *for* acus. *Cf. W.*

isin, 25, issin, 15, 29, in the, into the.

itegaid,* 23, = it' degaid, behind thee.

itir, 25, 27, 45, at all.

itradsa, itrathsa, 40 (= in tráthsa), this time, at present; ittraithe, forthwith, "B. of Fenagh," 116, is a different word.

l, *for* n: ro-l-luid, 11; il-lár, 50.

l, 4 × 2, stands for *vel*, nó, or.

la, 9, 13, with, by; *gov. dat.* 9.

lac, 29, *ns.*, weak, trifling.

laech, 6, 48, *gp.*, warrior; *gs.* laich, 4; *voc.* láich, "B. of M. Rath," 172; *np.* laich, "Laws," iii. 14.

laeg, 51, *ns.*; *g.* láig, 14; mac Riangabra, Cú's charioteer; *voc.* láig, *LL.* 263, 75 a.

láeg, laeg, 3, 5 × 3, calf.

lagen, 11, 48, 52, *gp.*; lagin, *np.* Leinstermen.

láideng, 8, *np.*, galleys, vessels, boats; *ap.* laidenga suaighte, "C. M. Lena," 44; ceithri longa re laidhing, four ships with a boat, "L. na gCeart," 260 ("F. Mast." iii. 2272: *gp.* laoiding.)

láifeit,* 4, *fut.*, they will put; laait, they utter (a wail), *W.*

lais, 1; leis, 11, 12, 45, 47; leiss, 27, by, with him; laisium, 34; emph. form of lais; lé, 4, with her.

láith gaile, 3, 4; *npm.*, heroes; *n. dual*, lath gáile, *LU.* 37 a; *gp.* lath ngaile, *LU.* 99 b; hence lathus gaile, bravery, *LU.* 112 a.

laithe, 56, *asN.*, day; la, 36; lathi, 55, 56, *as.*; *gp.* lathi, 53.

lám, 36, *nsf.*, hand; *das.*, láim, 8, 37, 46, 51; laim, 11; *pl.* lama, 6.

ro-lam, 36; *pret.*, he dared.

lamach,* 22, throwing [javelin]; *g.* lamaig, "B. of Fen." 356.

lám-deirg, 19, *gsm.* of lám-derg, red-handed.

lán, 28, full.

lán-chalma, 48, *gp.*, full-valiant.

lár, 7, 34, *ads.*, middle; 51, *as.*, ground floor; *N.* = forrال lár, *LL.* 292.

lár-medón, 47, 48, 50, *ds.*, the very middle.

lassair, 29, *asf.* of lassar, 28, a blaze.

lassait, 29, 3 *pl. pres.* of lassaim, they blaze.

lat-su, latt, letsu, lett, 11, 13, 15, 23, with thee.

lathir, *asf.*, 25, 26, place, station; lathar, *gp.* lathre, "B. of Fen."; *d.* cathlathraig, battle-field, "C. M. Rath," 262.

leirg, 29, 56; leirgg, 28; *dsf.* of lerg, hill-slope, "C. M. Lena," 92, 146.

leith, 56, *dsN.*, leth, side; *d. dual,* lethib.

lem, 5 × 2, 14 × 2, 54, by, with me; = lim, 4, 14, 17, 22, 28, 46.

ro-lenastar, 52, *pret.* of lenaim, he followed.

lenna, 23, 24, *gsN.* of linn, liquor, drink.

leo, 3, 8 × 2, 9, 14, 15 × 2, 24, 47, 57 × 2, with, by them; 57, theirs.

leódús, 7, leodús, 8, *gs.* of Isle of Lewis, "Cog. G."

leriti,* 3, 15, the plainer, more abundant, conspicuous.

lia, 28, stone, flag.

lia, 4, *ns.*, more, greater.

ligi, 14, *dsN.* of lige, lying, repose.

lín, 23, 29, *nam.*, number.

lind, 25 × 2, pool, water; *gN.* linni, 10, 11, 14, 15, 25.

lind, 30, 54, by, with us; of ours, 30.

lind féic, 25.

lind luachainne,* 10, 11, 15, 25, the R. Lagan (?), "Circ. of M. Mac Eirc," 31.

ra-lingestar, 25, 25; *dep. pret.* of lingim, he leaped.

lochlaind, 7, 10; *dsf.* of Lochland (Sweden *or* Norway), *g.* Lochlainne, 7, 10; *as.* Lochlaind, *LU.* p. 114 a; crích lochlann otha innsib Orc co gothia, *LB.* 65 ab.

locht, 22, fault, blame.

loegaire buadach, 9, 32, *nsm.*

loim, 12, *ns.* drop, clot; gl. *gutta, Cr. Prisc.* 9 b; loimm chrú, gory liquid, "Bodl. Cormac," 25: *cf.* "Ir. Texte," I. 104; lom, a clot (of blood), "M. Ulad," 20.

longa, 8, 11, *nap.* of long, ship.

longport, longphort, 14, 20, *nas.*, camp.

lonti,* 8, *np.*, provisions, *Ag. v.* lón.

lór, 18, 22, enough.

lorg, 52, *asm.*, track.

lorg-fertais,* *dsf.*, 44, 46, spindle club; *ap.* fertsi, *LU.* 63 b; *nf.* fertas, a pole, *LL.* 61 a, 71 d.

ra-loscit,* 3, 15; *pret. pass.*, they were burnt.

luachainne,* 10, 11, 14, 15, *gsf.*

luachra, 16, *gs.* of Luachair.

lúagni,* 48, (lu-), 50; in 47, 50 it is *dative; dp.* luagnib, 16; luaigne na temrach, 23, a people of the Barony of Lune in Meath, "F. Masters."

luaithiu, 36, *compar.* of luath, quicker.

ra-luamnaigsetar,* 39, *pret. depon.* of luamnaigim, they fluttered; ar luamain, rolling (eyes), "Loch Cé," I. 412 (?).

lucht, 18, for lucht, people.

lucta,* 16, 17; lucca, 17, *gsm.*, father of Eochu.

lucht-lethna,* 11, *ap.* of lucht-lethan, folk-ample, *i. e.* well manned.

lugaiti,* 11, *compar.*, the less; lugu, less.

luið, 25, 27, 49; raluið, roluið, 3, 12, 26, 51; ra-luið, ral-luið, 15, 25 (rol)luið, 11, he went; 3 *pl.* lotar, ralotar, rolotar, 34, 8, 19, 37, 21, 22, 53.

m', 5, 12, 38, for mo before vowels.

ma,* 10 × 4, = fa (*cf.* co ma thri = co fo thri, "B. of Fen." 354; "C. M. Lena."), under, 10; *or* about, *i.e.* with; it gov. *dat.* ima, "B. of Fen." 324.

ma,* 4, 11, about which (?).

macha, 1, 2, 22, *gs.*, Armagh, a royston crow, a milking yard, "Laws."

machaire, *gs.*, 34, field, plain.

macc, 4, 7, 16, &c.; *g.*, *voc. sg.*, and *np.* meicc, son, 5, 7, 22, 53, 57; *dp.* maccaib, 10, 7.

maccláig, 14; macclaig, 27, *gsm.* of macclách (?).

maccraide, 57, *gsf.* of maccrad, young folk.

mad, 8 × 2, 11 × 2, 18, 21 × 2, 22, if it is, if it were; madiat, if it were they, 11.

mael, 7, *as.*; *g.* maile, 10.

mag, 13, *nsN.*, plain; *g.* maige, 13; *d.* maig, 5.

mag murthemni, 13, the plain of Louth.

magach, 22, *gsf.*; Cét was her son, and mata (5) her daughter, *LL.* 54 a.

maidm, 29, 38 × 2, *nsN.*, rout; *g.* madma,* 39.

maig, 5; i.e. mag in Scáil in Connacht, or mag Aí.

máile, 10, *gs.*, of the Mull of Cantyre.

maimthi,* 6; mam, .i. cochur, "O'Dav." 105.

máini, 11, 27, *gs.* of main, wealth. *Cf.* main, .i. celg, "Irish Ordeals," 223.

maith, 11, 14, good, *adj.*; 57, good, *subst.*; 3, 5, 11 × 3, 12, 21, 38, &c.: as *interjection*; *np.* mathi, 13; *dp.* mathib, 8, 10, 13, 14, chiefs; also maith sin, "C. M. Lena," 50.

máitis, 4, 2*ry pres.* of máidim (?), they were boasting *or* breaking.

man, 5, about the; man, 4, about which; cid ma n-denai, *LL.* 56 a.

manip, 11, unless it is.

mar, 25, 29, govs. *acc.*, as, like; mar oen ra, 37, along with; mar sain, mar sein, like that, that being so; 40, 42; *see* immar.

mara, 7 × 2, 8 × 2, 10 × 2, *gsN.* of muir.

marb, 5, dead.

marta, 6, *gsm.*, March; a hocht Cailne marta muaid, on the 8th of the Cal. of March, "F. Mast." ann. 926.

marthanach, 25, long-lived.

mat, 5, about thy; or mat-rúanaid, hand-strong.

matae, 5, *gsf.*, mother of Ailill and Cairpre Niafer ("Ogygia," 269, 278) and daughter of Maga, *LL.* 54 a; matai, .i. muicci, *LU.* 109 a.

máthair, 7, mother.

medb, *passim*, 3, 4, 5, 16, 18, 22, *nsf.*; *da.* meidb, 5, 17, 18, 19 (*cf.* Medu, a woman's name, "F. Mast." 8), Queen of Connacht; *g.* meidbe, *LL.*, p. 125.

medar-cáini,* 13, *np.*; see medarcháin, nice and merry, mellow; medair, pleasant, "B. of Fen." 416; *g.* medarmesca, *LL.* 268 b; *ns.* mesc medarchain (*LL.*, fo. 57 a), drunk and merry, "Nennius," 87: medar, utterance, "S. na Rann," 145.

meicc (?) ($\overline{\text{mc}}$. *or* $\overline{\text{m}}$.); *gs.* 5, 7; *np.*, 22; *vs.* 53; see macc.

meir, 5, for mar, as, *or* mairg, woe (?).

RO-MEMAID, 34; ro-mebaid, 12; *red. perf.* of maidim,* he, it burst, broke; mebais, 5, 18, 3 *sg. pret.* and *fut.* *Cf.* memais forraib, ye shall be routed, *Tl.* 138.

MENBAD,* 46, 55, unless it were, were it not that.

MEND, 18, 19, "Mac Salcholgan"; *g.* mind, *LL.* 169 b; *i.e.* the Dumb, *LL.* 75 a; great, noble, "B. of Fen." 334, 374.

MENI,* 5 × 2, unless.

MENMA, 25; m(en)ma, 15, *ns.*, spirit, courage.

MERDRECH,* 17, *voc.*, *meretrix;* but hardly more offensive here than "bold woman!"; *see* note.

MERGGIDA,* 11, *ap.* of merge, banners; *np.* meirce, *LL.* 265 b.

MERTAIN,* 5, *asf.* (?) of mertan, cowardice, weakness.

MES DEAD,* 39, *nas.*; *voc.* meis Dead, 40 (*cf.* fer Dead); mess D. m- Amirgin 7 daltadochoin-chulaind, *LL.* 115 a; *ns* mess Dia, *LL.*, p. 161 a.

RO-MESC, 26, *pret.* of mescaim, he plunged; *see* note; measgas iad fein air muir, "Three Shafts," 262; in the glossary it is rendered "mix with;" mescaid, *Tl.* 70.

MESCA,* 13, *np.*, drunk; *cf.* buadir-mesca (*LL.* 54), turbulently drunk.

MESSI, 14, *emph. form* of me, me, I.

MESTI,* 14, the worse.

MÉT, 11, 12, *ns.*, amount, extent, greatness.

RAR-METAIR-NE, 5, has ruined us (?); met, .i. milliud, *O'Cl.*; for ra n-metair (?); rar-medrann, it confuses us, "Frag. of Ir. Ann." 218; rotmedair, it has confused thee, "S. Boroma," p. 44; *v.* note.

MIAD, 29, *ns.* (*neuter*, "B. of Fen." 314, 338, 350), honour; so in *LL.* 109, 268 b.

MIDE, 28, *gs.*, Meath.

MIDEM,* 25 × 2, 27, *ds.*, act of contemplating, reconnoitering, view do mes, *ad examinandum*, *Ml.* 15 d; *cf.* midemnas, meditation, *O'Cl.*; midiur, *puto*, *Z.*; do mide-main an t-slóig, "F. Masters," IV. 988.

MID-LÁN,* 11, *ns.*, mid-full, half-full (?).

MID-UACTUR, 8, *dsN.*, mid-upper part. *Cf.* mid-ais, middhage, *LB.* 71; midlae, midnoct, midchuairt.

MILA, 6, *npN.* of mil, animals.

MÍN, 4, 34, smooth, fine, small; co mín, gently, as she pleased.

MÍN-ETROCHT,* 1, *dsf.*; min-etrocht, 2, smooth-bright.

RA-MIN-GLANTA,* 24, *perf. pass.* of min-glanaim, they were smooth-cleaned.

MINTA,* 47, *dp.*, fine, small; *a participial form.*

MI-RUN, 5, *nsf.*, an ill-design; but *g.* mirúin, "B. of Magh Rath," 168.

MÍS, 11, *ds.* of mí, month.

MITHIS, 5, *ns.*, time(ly); mithig, time, *O'Cl.*

MNÁI, 55, *dsf.* of ben, woman; *ds.* *LL.* 287.

MO', 3, 4, etc., my.

MÓ, 4, 5, 18, 25, greater; used as *noun*, 4; is mó, most (*adverb*), 18; moti, 3, 15, the greater.

MO, 10, = fo, ma, immu, about, under.

MO, 6, more, *or is verb prefix* (?); mo aigsem.

MOCH-TRATH, 14, at an early hour.

MOD,* 7, *as.*, a man's name.

MÓR, 10, 12, 25, great; *gms.* móir, 23, 23; *vocative*, 40, 41; *np.* móra.

RO-MÓR,* 49, *pret.* of móraim, he held, prepared; *see* note.

MÓR-ABBA, 3, *ns.* (mor-), 3, 18, great cause. *Cf.* 'ar aba,' because of; mórabba, *LL.* 55 a, 55 a, 56 a, 67 b.

mór-adbul, 9 × 2, very great; *gsN.* móradbuil, 10.

morc,* 6, *gp.*, hogs; .i. torc, *O'Cl.*; or for marc, steeds; Morc is the name of a man, Dr. Joyce's edition of "Keating," 90.

mór-cháin, 9 (mor-), 9, very handsome. *Cf. LL.* 97 a.

mór-descain, 25 × 2; mor-descin, 26, 27; *ds.* of deicsiu, act of reconnoitring.

mór-dílind, 40, *ds.* of mór-dile, great flood.

mór-fairge, mór-fairgi, 8, *gsf.*, great sea, ocean.

mór-longphort, 20, great camp.

mór-muman, 11, *gs.*, of Great Munster.

mor-rígain, 5, *das.* of mór-rígan, great queen.

mor-slúag, 34, *nsm.*, great army; *gs.* mór-sluaig, 53.

mor-thechiud, *ds.*, great flight.

moti, 3, 15; the more, the greater.

muadmuirn,* 53, noble band; muad .i. mór, muirn .i. buiden, *O'Cl.*, *LB.* 207 a b; clamour, "Frag. of Ir. Ann." 190; "C. M. Lena," 104; "F. Mast." *an.* 1504; hilarity, heartiness, "L. na gCeart," 128, 146; "C. M. Lena," 80.

mucci, 57, *gsf.* of mucc, a hog; mucál, a swine litter, "O'Dugan's Top. Poem," 10.

muile, 7, *as.* the Mull of Cantire.

mulind, 25, *gs.* of mulend, a mill, *molina.*

mumni, 11, *np.*, the Munstermen; for Mumnich.

munbad, 56, unless it had been.

muncind,* 8 × 2, *asf.*, surface (side?); *gs.* na muinchinde, "Ann. of Loch Cé," II. 659; muincind in murtrácta, *LB.* 215 a; M. Mara Romuir, "S. na Rann," l. 3987; muincenn muiride n-Gadanta, Straits of Cadiz, "Frag. of Ir. Ann." 160, 162.

munud, 8, *ds.*, act of teaching.

múr, 4 × 2, *asm.*, wall, a mound of defence, "C. M. Lena," 78.

murbuilg, 9, 10, *gs.*; Muirbolc, ("Adamnan," 40), Murlogh Bay, Antrim, "F. Mast." Dunseverick was in Murbolg Dalriada, "F. Mast." I. 26; i taeb sleibi Slánga, *Tl.* 120.

muride, muridi, 10, 12, *ns.*, seafaring, marine.

munir,* 11, *gs.*, family, breed, "O'Dugan's Poem," 6; *pl.* muiréir ("Nennius," 140), families; *d.* muiriur, "B. of Ballymote," 382 b; *LL.* 156 b; *g.* muirir, company, "F. Mast." II. 968.

murisce, 5, *gsf.* of muiresc, *LL.* 168 a, Murrisk, Westport.

murthemni, 13, *gs.*, in Louth.

na, 54 × 3 (do) not.

na, 3, 11 × 2, 25, 28, 33, = nach, that not, *q.v.*

na, 4, 5, in which not.

na, 4 × 2, 22, 26, 28 × 2, nor.

na, 1, 15 × 3, = na; *gp.* 7; *g. dual*, 5; the; for inna, as in *LU.* 122 a.

na,* 4, 44; ná, 36; for indá.

na, 48, = nó, or, *q.v.*

n-a, 4, 34, 46, 51, for i n-a = in *or* into (his, its, their).

na, 20, 22 × 2, 34, 45, in phrase na co = no co, until.

nach (I.), 5, 11 × 2, 15, 19, 28, 46, that not, who is not, which not (is sometimes understood), written ná, 19, 44.

nach (II.), 15, *neg. interrog. particle* = *nonne*, etc.

nad, 17 (?), 44, that it is not.

nad-fetar, 11, that I know it not. [na = that not: -d- = it: fetar = I know.

nad-orgenamar-ni,* 17, 33, *qv.*

namait, 20, *da.*; namat, 9, *gp.*, enemy; *n.* náma.

nar (I.), 29, = na (II.) + ro(p), that would not be.

'n-ar n- (II.), 4 × 2, = in our; *for* i n- and ar n- (our).

nas,* 3, 15, = indár (oldaar), than is (are).

nech, 2, 17, 25, 36, 44, one, a person, anybody; *g.* in nech, the person, 2; neich, 40, 42, 43, *gs.*; neoch, 1, 2, 11, 17, *ds.*; do neoch, 11, 17, whoever.

néill, 49, *gs.*, father of Fintan.

nert, 51, *as.*, strength; nert gaile, *LU.* 124 a.

nessa, *gsf.*, mother of Conchobor; ba neas ingen echach a máthair, "B. of Ballymote," 247.

ní, 7, 14, 17, 25; ni, 4 × 2, 6, 14, 18, 22, not; ní heo, it is not it *or* so, 25.

ní, 18; ni, 54, anything.

-ni, 17 × 2, 21, *emph. suffix*, 1 *pl.*

nia fer, 19, *ns.*; *g.* niod fer, *LL.* 121 b; nioch, "B. of Armagh."

niam-glonnaig, 49, *gsm.* of niam-glonnach,* of bright deeds; the full form is in *LL.* 91 a.

ní clé, 54, anything sinister (?).

nimmó,* 17, not more.

nír, 20, nir, 4, 5 × 2, = ni-ro, not.

nir',* 12, 31, = nir-bo, nirb, it was not, would not be.

nirb, 5 × 2; nirbo, 11, 30, it was not.

nítha,* 6, *gs.*, of battle, of wounding.

no, 7 (*written* ɫ), 11, 18, or.

no, 9, 14, 25, 34, 41, 46, 51 (= *dno*, *dano*), too, then, *autem*, *LL.* 79 b.

no, 11, 22: no co n-, until, unto; no cot, 7, unto thy.

noco, 5, 23; nocho, 22; nocho n-, 22, not (*is* was sometimes understood).

nói, 11, nine; 53.

nói-chrutchaige, 53, *gsf.* of nói-chrutchach,* nine-formed (of beauty) or ship-shaped (?), *LU.* 103 b.

northmannia, 7.

nós,* 25, 26, *ns.* glory; *g.* nuis, *LU.* 40 a; árd nós, high honour, "Harl. Glosses," 1802; nós: nodh :: luas: luath. *Cf.* nos, nosmar, "B. of Fen." 228.

ó, 11, 17, from.

ó, 17, from whom = ó + a n-, whom.

ó, 57, since.

oc, 45, 46, 48, at; idiom. with *infin.*, and after gabaim, 45, 48.

óca, 34 × 2, *npm.* of óc, young; *dp.* ócaib, 14, youths, warriors; ócu, *p. voc.*, 31, 32, 33; óic, 4, *np.*

ocainni, 17, at, with, of us.

óc-bad,* 34, *gs.* or *pf.*; ocbad n-, 38 *gp.* Cf. findbad, gl. *beatitudo*, *Ml.* 14; *np.* ócbaid, warriors, "Magh Lena," 40; *dsf.* ócbaid, "Ann. of Loch Cé, I. 400.

óclách, 11, (oc-) 49, (óc-) 49; *ns. gp.*, young warriors.

ocht, 48, eight: ocht cét.

óen, 35, oen, 4, 25, 59, one.

oenach, 6, fair, assembly. *Cf.* ní hindbad oenaig ind indbad garb gemrecta so, "Mesc. Ul." 18.

oen-fecht, *ds.*, 25, 57, 57, one time, the same time: i n-oenf., together.

oengus, 8; *g.* Oingusso, *LA.*

oenláma, 8, *gs.* Oenláme, *LL.* p. 94; father of Oengus.

oenur, 38, one man, a single person, in *phr.* m'oenur = I myself alone.

oesam, 38, 42 (*ds.*), protection; oesum, 40, 41, *das.*, protection, defence; *see* aesam; for foesam, "B. Hymns," ii. 131, = faesam, *LL.* 268 b; *gs.* faésma, adoption, "Sench. M." iii. 16.

óil, 11, 13, *gsN.* of ól, drinking; ól, 8, *gs.* or *np.*, or an adjective; *as.* so-óla, pleasant to drink, *LL.* 58 ab.

ólaib, 7, King of Norway.

oll, great, 3, 15, etc.; uille, more, "B. of Magh Lena," 140.

oll-chóiceda, 3; oll-choiceda, 15, *ap.* or *np.*; *dp.* oll-choicedaib, 16, 17, great provinces.

ólnecmacht, 11, *g.*, old name of Connacht; *g.* olnecmacc, *LU.* 34 b.

omna,* 18, *gs.*, tree, oak, spear; here a man's name; omna ibair, *Tl.* 218.

ón, 17, 25, 44, that (thing).

ón, 19, from the.

or, 7, *gp* for orc (?), the Orkneys.

or, 55, *as.*, brink, margin; *ds.* ur, 26, 27.

ór, 4, gold; *g.* óir, 5, 57.

orc, 7, *g.* of Orkney; possessed by the Galian, "Nennius," 50; *LU.* 112 b.

or-fáiltius,* 18, *as.*, great joy; th'-[f]orfáiltius; forfáilid, overjoyed, *LA.*

orgenamár,* 17, 33; *see* notes.

ós, 16, 27, 56, over, above.

piscarcarla,* 7, 10, *gsf.* A town of the Faeroe Islanders.

póc,* 8, kiss, *ap.* for póca (?); *as.* póic, *Fled. Bricr.*, 50.

phopa, 3, *voc.*, master, friend; .i. maighistir, *O'C.*; phobba, *LL.* 119 a; o mo phoba, *Nen.* 90.

praind, 23, 24, *ns.*, a meal, dinner; proind 7 tomailt, *LL.* 57 a.

pupla, 11, 20, 20, 23, 24, *gas.* and *np.* of pupall, tent.

purt, 3, *ds.* of port, place, port.

ra, 2, 3, 6, 8, 12 × 2, 15, 19, 26, 27, 40, 48, 54, = fri, *q.v.*, for, during, against, towards, in order to, *passim.*

ra-, = ro; see *infra.*

ra, 26, 27, for la (in the opinion of).

rá bar, 46; ra bar, 46, = fri, la bar, with your, towards your.

raba, 4, 34; rabi, 19, was.

rád, 3, 5, 6, 14, 20, 26 (act of) saying; *see* raid.

ragat, 25 × 2, 26 × 2, 27, I will, shall go; 3 *sg.* raga, 17; 1 *pl.* ragmait, 21.

ra-glan, 19, very neat; (ra = ro).

raib, 20, it might *or* may be; raibe, 45, *depend. pret.*, he was; *see* bad.

raid, *imper.*, 14; *pret.* 3 *sg.* raid, 14; ro-ráid, 28; ro-raid, 55; 3 *pl.* ro-ráidsetar, 12; ro-raidsetar, 2, 19; say, declare; *verbal noun*, rád. *supra.*

railge,* 34, *npf.*; *g.* ralach dirge, *LL.*, p. 108 a; *nom. sing.* rail, oak; ruad-daire 7 railge ruada, *LL.* 33; *gp.* ralach, trees, "Mesca Ul." 14; *n.* rail, in the mod. version.

raind, 10, *gsm.*, part; *gf.* rainni, 7.

raind, 13, 54, *asf.*, dividing, carving.

ro-raind, 51, *pret.* of rainnim, it split; *perf. pass.* ro-rainned, 10, was divided.

ránic, 25; ranic, 51, he reached; 3 *pl.* ráncatar, 22.

rannair,* 13, *np.*, for rannairi, distributors; *np.* rannaire, "Mesca Ul." 12; *see LL.*, pp. 29, 30.

rarmetairne, 5 (?), that has troubled us (?). *Cf.* rarmeallais, thou hast deceived us, "Frag. of Irish Ann." 14; rarmarnestar, has betrayed us, *LL.* 59 aa.

ratha, 22, *np.* of rath, forts (*or* fortresses ?); *gsf.* ratha, *LL.* 109; *as.* Cruachan-ráith, 16, *Tl.* 236.

na-ra-t-ruibther,* 54, lest thou be cut off; = ra-t-ro-fuibther; condrubaim, fuibnim, *LL.* 124 a.

rap, 36; rapa, 57, was; *see* bad.

recartaib,* 16, *dp.*

reog,* 5, furious, = reogach; *np.* rig reoga, *H.* 2, 16, 919; "C. M. Rath," 278; reog, fury *or* mad cow, *O'Cl.*; reog, powerful, "C. M. Rath," 98; a beog, no reog, no lua, no saebleim, *from* start, *or* bit, *or* kick, *or* false spring, "Laws," iii. 180; Reog is Ailill's jester in the "T. B. Cualnge"; ropo talcair a thrénreog, *LL.* 129 a.

ro-redigsetar,* 37, *pret.* of réidigim, they made ready *or* even, fixed.

réir, 14, 19, 53, 54; reir, 15, *dsf.* of riar, will; dom réir, in submission to me.

reme, 3, 11, 12, 15, 23, 25, 45.

remi, 12, 16 × 2, 25; reime, 48 (before him); rempu, 10, 19, 21 (before them), forward, onward.

resna, 36, *dp.*, before the; ria n-, 37, 39, before their; riam, 4, 18, 20, before, ever.

rem-thús, 36, front; remtus, preface, "B. of Fen." 372.

rémur,* 11, *ds.*, preparation (?).

renaib* (na bóinne), 18, *dp.*, waterways; rian, gl. muir, span, space, *O'Cl.*: see il-rianaib; rén, gl. *torrens*, *Ml.* 134 b; Mend macc Salcholgan ó renaib na bóinne, *LL.* 99, col. 2; rén, span, "Stokes' Metr. Gloss." p. 90; "S. na Rann," l. 6788; raoin, paths, "C. M. Lena," 76.

rí, 5 × 2, 16, 19, 22, *ns.*; *ns.*, 19, a king; ríg, *gs.*, 7, 10, 15, 20, 57; *da.*, 38, 46, 2, 7; *gp.*, 1, 13, 20, 54.

ri, 1, 6 × 4, 39 × 2, 55, = fri, for, during, with, against; rib, to you, 5.

rib, 5, to you.

rígdacht, 27, majesty.

rígdaide,* 34, royal; usually rígda. *Cf.* rignaide, queenly, *W.*

ríg-filid,* 46, *np.* of ríg-fili, royal poets.

rigi, 52, *gs.*, reach, stretch (?).

rige lagen,* 52, *ns.*, the Rye, which joins the Liffey at Leixlip; dar Rige dar Mag Nuadat, "B. Balymote," 295 a; ó Rige co rig bóinn, "C. M. Lena," 80.

rig-thech, 15, royal house, *asm.*; *gs.* ríg-thigi, 28.

rind, 56, with us (in our opinion) (?).

ris, 17, with, to whom.

ris, 44, 52, 55, towards, against, concerning him, it; *ap.* riu, 14, 14.

risin, 8, 17, 18, 19, with, on the; risin, with that, on that, 19; *pl.* risna, 14, 51, to the, against the.

ristí,* 55, with him who.

rith, 22, 39, *ds.* (act of) running.

rithalma,* 9, *gs.* of frithálam, preparation.

riu, 14 × 2: towards, against them.

rocht,* 48, *t-pret.*, he arrived; roacht, *W.*; *fut.*, roisset, 22, they will reach; ni roisse, ni roisset, *Sg.* 229, *Ml.* 74; roissam, may we reach, "B. of Fen." iii. 310; ruacht, he reached, "F. Mast." *an.* 1121, *Tl.* 30.

róen, 55, 56, way, course of battle, defeat; r. 7 ruathar, *LB.* 206 b.

rofir, 7, rafir, 10, *gsm.*, strong man. *Cf.* *g.* Rofir oenbero, *LU.* 64 b.

ro-gasta, 19, very sprightly.

róin, 10, *np.* of rón, seal.

romi, 25 (before him), forward; romaind, 22, before us; rompu, 8, 15, 18, before them; romom, 26; romum, 25, before me.

romda,* 56; ruamda, magnificent, O'Reilly; glosses uasal, noble, in the "Felire" Index.

ro-móir, 25, 25: see ro-mór.

ro-mór, 15, 34, very large, very great, very tall; *gs.* romóir; *npf.* romóra, 34.

romra, Romrach, 7, 10, *gs.* *Cf.* Trachte Romra, "Adamnan," xlv.

ropo, 36, it was.

ros, 20; ross, 23, 29, a wood, *das.*; *g.* ruis, ruiss, 1, 22; is *neuter*, *LL.* 297 b, 298 b; *N.* Ros n-Dairbrech, "B. of Lismore," 147 a.

ros na ríg,* 20, 23, *ds.*, the wood or wooded promontory of the kings; Rosnaree; Ruiss na Ríg, 22, *gs.*

rosa ruaid,* 16, 57, *gsm.*, Ros Ruad, father of Cairpre, Ailill and Find, and King of Leinster.

rosbae,* 56 (that was for him?).

ROSC-BÉIM,* 34, *asN.*, a sudden rush; rusgaim, "Coneys," do rúsgfainn, I would smite, E. G. an amarám, l. 206; rethait rithrosc, "S. na Rann," p. 116.

ROSC-LETHAIN,* 15, *gs.* of rosc-lethan, large-eyed.

ROSC-LETHNI,* 27, *dsf.*, of largeness of eyes.

ROSS NA RÍG, 23: see Ros na Ríg; "ross imtheit bóind," 29.

ROSSAIL, 10, *np.*, walruses (?) *Cf.* ro-sualt, a sea animal; .i. mur-iasc mór, *LL.* 118 a; ainm dobeist bis is ind fairrci, *LU.* 11.

ROUT N-, 51 × 2; *as.*, a cast, a throw; ród, a cast, *O'Cl.* = ro-fut n-urchair, *LL.* 60.

RÚADA, 34, *npf.* of ruad, strong; .i. trén, *O'Cl.*; *or* red.

RÚAD-DAIRE, 34, a strong oak-grove (?). *Cf.* ruad-fer, "Harl." 348.

RUANAID, 5, mighty, strong, "C. M. Rath," 120; r. rigthend trén, *LL.* 68; 266 a; but = red (?), *LU.* 115 b; .i. calma, "O'Dav." 113.

RUC, 4, brought; ras-ruc, 7, that took it; rucatar, 47, 3 *pl.*

RUCAD, 3, was taken.

RUCAIT,* 13, ructha, 7, were brought.

RUCHT,* 39, 48, *nas.*, noise, shout, groan, *O'Cl.*

RUDRAIGE, 14; rudraigi, 16, 27, 35; *gs.* *Cf.* Loch Rudraigi, Dundrum Bay, "MS. Mat." 429.

RUIND,* 54, against us, = rind, frind.

RUIS, 1: see ros (I.).

RUISC, 39; *np.* of rosc, eye.

S, them: rosceastar, 12.

SA, 3, 6, 14, 15 × 2, 18, 44; *demon. suffix* following *noun*, preceded by *article:* = this, these (*adj.*); not repeated after 2nd noun, 15.

SA, 3, 4, 5, 8; *emph. suffix* following *pers. pron.* or *poss. adj.* 1 *sg.*

SA, 11, *emph. suffix* following a *vocative.*

SA, 5, *emph. suffix* attached to forms of *verb* is. *Cf.* a fhir Diad má-sa thú.

SAEB-LÉIM,* 25 × 2, *asN.*, false leap.

RO-ṠAIDSET,* 20, *s-pret.*, they pitched; 3*rd sg.*, saidis, *Ml.* 55; saidis a claideb, *LL.* 268 b; ro-saittea,* 24, were thrust, stuck; *perf. pass.*, sáitted,* 23, let them be pitched.

SAIFITER,* 22, *fut.* of so-im (?), they shall be turned.

SAIGET, 40, arrow.

SAIGID, 14, 18, 38, 43, 44, 51, *ds.*, act of approaching, in phrase d'a saigid, &c., towards him, &c.; do s., to seek, visit, *LL.* 71 a: see in-naigid, insaigid.

SAIN, 13, 17 × 3, 18 × 3, 19, 21, *demon. suffix* following *noun* with *article* = that, those (*adj.*)

SAIN, 3, 11, 16, 23, 43, 45, *demon. pron.* = that.

SAIN, 10, *emph. suffix* 3 *p.*

SALCHA, 6, *pl.* of salach, dirty.

SAL-CHOLGAN, 18, *gsm.* of salcholcu; *n.* colcu; *g.* colgen, colggen, "Adamnan"; "F. Mast." an. 613; "An. Ult." 617.

SÁM, 1 × 2, pleasant leisure, *LU.* 58.

SAMAIL, 34, *ns.*, likeness (equal); *np.*; samla, "B. of Fen." 276.

SAMLAID, 1; saml(aid), 1, 2; *asm.*, so; perhaps for is-amlaid.

ṠAMRATTA, 6, summer (*adj.*); grenda no Samrata, *O'Cl.* v. samrun.

SAXAN, 7; *gp.* of Saxain, Saxons.

SCÁILTER, 54, *pres. pass.* of scáilim, (which) is spread.

SCEINNIS, 8, *s-pret.* of sceinnim, he leaped.

SCÉL, 54, *nsN.*, tale, story; scéla, 21, scela, 8, *nap.*, news, tidings.

sciath, 35, 45 × 2, 48, 52, *nda.*, a shield; *gs. np.*, 17, 35, 45, 48, .i. ditin, "O'Dav."; sciath dar long, 52, rear guard, 52. *Cf.* "C. M. Lena," 18.

sciathrach, 17, *ns.* for sciath-rech; *cf.* cuim-rech, shield strap, trappings of a shield, "Man. & Cust." iii. 162.

sciggire, 7; sciggiri, 10, *gsf.* or *gpm.*

scithia, 7, *gs.*

ra-scuich, 39, *perf.* of scuichim, he departed; roscáich, *W.*

se, 5, *demonst. suff.*, this.

se, 5, 6, 8, *emph. suff.*, 1 *sg.*

sech, 36, past (*prep.*)

secha, 51, past them.

sechoind, 21, past us.

secht, 7, 53, seven.

sechtair, 7, 12, away, by, outwards.

sechtmad, 7, 10, seventh.

sechtmaine, 53 × 2; sechtmaini, 55, *gsf.* of sechtmain, week.

sed, 2, *demonst. pron.*, this: better read iss-ed.

seilb, 43 × 2; *ds.* of selb, possession, property.

seimne, 9, Semni, 10 (Inber); *gs.* Inber, at Larne, Co. Antrim; inis Seimne = Island Magee.

sein, 40, that, = sain.

séitrig,* 6, *np.*, strong, robust, "Frag. Ir. Ann." 200; "F. Mast." i. 562; "C. M. Rath," 156, 182, 214, 54; potent, "L. na gCeart," 200.

sél,* 22; *recte* scél, tidings.

sel, 57. *Cf.* sel iarsin, a little after; cach la sel . . . in sel aile, now . . . again, *Wb.* 15 a.

selais, 39, *s.-pret.*, he drew (a sword); ro-selach, I attacked, *LU.* "S. Charpat Con C." 384; = selastar, *Z.* 465.

sell,* 12, forth (?), look!

sen, 54, *gp.*, old (persons, ancestors).

sen-athar, 53, *gs.* of sen-athair.

sencha, 11, 12, 52; *nsm.*, son of Ailill, son of Culcan, "Sench. M." i. 150.

sen-charpait, 15 × 2, *np.* of sen-charpat, old chariots.

sen-eich, 6, *np.* of sen-ech,* old horses *or* chargers.

sen-gabra, 15 × 2, *napf.* of sen-gabair, old horses.

sen-laich, 15, *npm.* of sen-laech; *gp.* senlaech, 14, veterans.

senoraig, 15, *npm.* of senóir; *gp.*, senorach, elders.

sénta, 51, charmed; blessed, *O'Cl.*

seo, 13, *demonst. suffix*, = this.

sergg,* 1, *ds.*, sickness, decline, withering.

serraig,* 6, *npm.* of serrach, colts.

sescind* (Dun), 4, *gs.* of sescend, a marsh.

sét, 11, 27, *gp.*, precious things.

-si, 5, *emph. suffix*, 3 *sf.*

-si, 11 × 2, *emph. suffix*, 2 *p.*

siar, 7, westwards.

sib,* 11, 46, ye.

síblanga, 11, *ap.*, long boats.

sibthib,* 56, *dp.*, sithbe, pole of a chariot, "Man. & Cust." iii. 597; sithbe, in the 2nd version at foot of p. 56; a general, *O'R.*, *W.*

síd, 27, 55, peace; *gs.*, sída, 52, and *LL.* 111 a.

-side, 23, -side, 48, *emph. suffix*, 3 *sg.*

side,* *as.*, a dash, a rush, as of a wind *as.*, sidi, *LL.* 87 a.

sin, 1, 7, 8 × 3, 11, 12, 14, 15, 16 × 2, 17 × 3, 20, 52, 56, *demonst. suffix*, = that, those; sair sin, above that, 7.

sin, 8, *emph. suffix*, for sium.

sin, 6, *nsf.*, weather, storm; *nd. Mil.* 1.

sin, 25, = issin, in the.

sír-galar, 1, *ds.*, long illness *or* distress.

sír-glan, 4, *asN.*, long-renowned.

-siu, 5, 7 × 3, 12, *emph. suffix*, 2 *sg.*

siugraid* soga, 7 (a Dane, Sigurd ?). *Cf.* Siugrad m. Imair, "Wars of the G. & G." 233.

siúil, 11, *gs.* of seól, a sail.

slaide, 34, 45, 47, 52, *ds.*, (act of) smiting, hewing; 1 *fut.*, slaidfet, 44; ra-slaidit, 34, *perf. pass.*, were cut down.

slainnid, 19 × 2, 22, *imperat.* 2 *pl.* of slainnim, name, particularize, relate.

slána, 6, *pl.* of slán, whole.

slataigecht,* 7, (act of) plundering.

slechta,* 22, *ap.* of slicht, track, accounts. *Cf.* sliucht, gl. *cognitio*, *Sg.* 200 a.

slechtad, 34, 45, 52, *ds.* (act of) cutting down, smiting; slechtait, were cut down, "Four Masters," I. p. 6.

sleg, 51, spear, *nsf.*, *read* [cruad] sleg; *as.* cruadlann, hard lance, "B. of Fen," 220.

ro-slemun-chirtha,* 24, *perf. pass.*, were smooth-combed.

slicht, 56, *das.*, race, stock; .i. buiden, *O'Cl.*

sliged, 28, *gs.*; *gp.* 7, road; *as.* sligid, 23; *ap.* sligeda, 6.

slúag, 51, 25, 25; sluag, 5, 22, 26; *nds.*, army; *g.* slóig, sluaig, 23, 23, 47, 52, 52, 26, 26, 26; *dp.* sluagaib, 36, 39, 40, 44; *np.* slúaig, 22, 26; *n.* for *acc.*, 26.

sluaged, 14, 15, 57; sluag(ed), 15, 17; sl(uaged), 15 × 2; *nas.*, military expedition; *ds.*, sluagud, 17; sluaged, 14, *cognate acc.* *Cf.* rachaid ccthri echtra, "B. of Fen," 282.

sobairge,* *gsm.*, from whom Dun Severick; *g.* Sobairgi, "B. of Armagh.

so-berla, 27, good speech.

sochaide, 56, multitude.

solus-trath, 13, *ds.*, bright hour, dawn.

-som, 2, *emph. suffix*, 3 *pl.*

són, 44, son (?), 11, *demonst. pron.*, = that.

sond, 17, *g.* suind, 17, a bawn, wall; pole, *O'Cl.*, *O'Dav.* 118.

sortadbud* sort, 7; *cf. sort*, Cornish for "hedgehog," *Z.* 1075.

sosad, 20, 23; *as.* sossad, 11, 14, 20; *np.*, sosta, 23, 24, station; sosad in duine, the rampart of the fort, *LU.* 19 a; sossad 7 forlongphort, 14; sosad, rest, "B. of Fen." 398; it also means "cessation" or truce.

sruthair, 10, *das.* of sruthar, stream, current.

sruthar* na máile chind tiri, 10, The North Channel; Sruth na Maoile idir Eirinn 7 Albain, "Ch. of Lir," p. 132.

-su, 4, *emph. suffix*, 2 *sg.*

suail, 5, 15, a trifle, a little; suail nach, almost; suail, .i. beag, *O'C.*; suail nach, "B. of M. Rath," 188.

súdiam, 7, *gs.*, Sweden (?).

ro-suidigthea, 24, *perf. pass.*, were set; suidigter, 23, *imperat. pass.*, let them be set.

-sum, 2, 8 × 2, 12, &c., -sum, 8, &c., *emph.* 3 *s.* and 3 *p.*, iat-sum, 32.

sund, 19, 29, hither; 22, 45, here.

suntaich,* 6, *np.* of sonntach, joyful, active, *O'Cl.*

th', 18, 38, 40, thy.

tá, 11; *see* atá.

tabairt, 36, 38 (*ds.*), (act of) giving, putting.

thaeth, 5, he will fall; toetsat, they will fall; do saeth, he fell, "B. of Fen." 174, 406; da taetsad, he would fall, *LL.* 57 ab; do saethsat, they shall perish, "F. Mast." ii. p. 1158.

táin, 8, *asf.*, cattle(-raid, -driving); *g.* tana, 1, 17; tanad, 6; *n.* táin, driving, "Laws," i. 264; *g.* tanad, *LL.* 104 b.

ταρ, 54, in the east.

ταιρις, 25, over him.

ταιρνριτhιρ, 22; see *fut. pass.* of ταιρνιm, he shall be lowered, bowed down; ταιρνιδ, it ends, "B. of Fen." 238, 282; τορnem, to bring down; *nsf.*, or *dat.* (?) ταιρinnuδ, gl. *dejectio*, *Cr.* 33 d.

ταn, 11, time.

τάnιc, 10 × 2, 12, 23, 25 × 2, 31, 45 × 2, he came; 1 *pl.*, τancamar, 19; 3 *pl.*, τancαταρ, 8, 10, 15, 18, 19, 37, 57; see τιc; τancαρ, *ventum est*, *LL.* 112.

τάρ, 7, *ns.*, disgrace, blemish; τάρ, .ι. ταρcuιρne, *O'Cl.*; *as.*, ταρ, "B. of Fen," 238.

ταρb, 5, *gpm.*, bulls; *g.* ταιρb, 22.

ταρbgα,* 5, bull-spear (?); ταρbgα, "MS. Mat." 492. *Cf.* ταρb-léne; a leather shirt, and ταρbgαe, *LL.* 70, 103, 166; rendered cowshed by some; I think it was a pet name for ταρb. *Cf.* τhαccτ-τlαchτgα, Liath-ga, Cu's horse, *LL.* 103; mαg ταρbgα, *LL.* 166 b; 199 a.

ταρmchιllenδ,* 11, *depend. pres.* of ταρmchιllιm, surrounds; ταιρm-chell, .ι. τιmchell, *O'Cl.*

ταρlα, 51, *depend. perf.* (for δο-ραlα); it fell, fell out, happened.

ταρlαιc, 51 × 2, *depend. pret.* of δο-lέιcιm, he let go, cast.

ταρραsαταρ, 52; ταρραssαταρ, 13; 3 *pl. perf. depon.*, they tarried; δο-n-αιριssιδ, gl. *quod perstatis*, *Wb* 14 c.

ταsτel,* 7, *ds.* (act of) journeying.

ταulαιg, 27, = τulαιg, 26, τιlαιg, 28; *dasf.* of τulαch, a hill; *dp.* τιlchαιb, 57. *Cf. LL.* 97 a, 115 a.

τech n-, *nsN.* 11; τech, 13; *ms.*, τeg, 17, house; *d.* τιg, 22; *g.* τιgι, 17.

τecαιτ, 22, *pres. pl.*, they come; see τιc.

τechιδ, 38; *gs.* of τecheδ, flight, retreat.

τechτα, 27, (act of) going; *cf.* τechτ, δolα, and δol.

τechτα, 8, 9, 14, 17, 19, 22 × 2, 29; τecτα, 7 × 2; *npm.*, envoys; used in the *np.*; *gp.* τechτ, *nuntiorum*, *Ml.* 129 a.

τechταιρechτ, 18, 19, τecτ-, 8, *na.*, embassy.

ι τegαιδ, 23, for ιτ-δegαιδ, after thee.

τeιchριτhe, 36; 2*ry. fut. pass. sg.* of τechιm, I fly, used *impersonally*.

τeιgeδ, 18, let him go; ρα-τheιgre-ταρ, 26, they came, went.

τemαιρ, 57, *dsf.*, Tara; Τemραch, 16, 23, 46, 47, 48, 54; Τemραch, 56, *gs.*; τemραιg, 16, 18, 19, 53, *das.*

τemραιg lυαchρα, 16, *as.*, on the slopes of Slιαb Luαchρα, which divides Limerick from Kerry, "Mesca Ulad," iv.

τenδ, 54 × 2, *nas.*, tight, stiff; mighty, "B. of Fen." 352.

τenτα,* 11, *ap.*, bonds, securities.

τenτι, 24, *np.* of τene, fires; *ap.* τenδτι, "Fled Bricr." 54.

τeoρα,* 29, *np. fem.* of τρí, yet used before cατhα, 29; *gp.*, 1, 3; *ap.* τ. póc, 8.

τeρnα,* 5, *subj. pres.* 3 *sg.* (?), that she should escape, *or* escapes; ní τeρnα, he escaped not, "B. of M. Rath," 318; "Nenn." 54; co nαch τeρno, "B. of Fen." 254; co ροτeρno, that he may escape, "Fragm. of Ir. Ann." 82; τheρnαm, 5, (act of) escaping; go τheρnó ιn α chοτlα, .ι. δο chuιl, *O'Cl.*; nι eρnα, *LU.* 98.

τess,* 36 (in the) south: τess bοιnδ, south of the Boyne.

τéτ,* 53, *gp.*, cords.

τeτιmnech,* 53, *as.*, cord-creaking, twanging.

τιαchταιn, 14; *asf.* of τιαchτu, to come.

ρο-τhιb, 25, *pret.* of τιbιm, it laughed.

tibrimmis, 33, *2ry fut. depend.* of dobeirim, we should give (battle); 1 *sg.*, tibrind, *LL.* 115 a.

tic, 22, *pres.* of ticim, he comes; ticed, 21, let him come; ticfad, 11, *2ry fut.* 3 *sg.*; ticfait, 25; ticfat, 22, 29, *fut.* 3 *pl.*

tí, 5, 22, *s-fut.* 3 *sg.*; 3 *pl.*, tisat, 30, 31; corostí, *LL.* 168 b.

tidacht, 36 (act of) coming, to come.

tigardail,* 40, 41, 42, 43, 46, 49; *asf.*, combat (?); t. 7 buraig feirge; for tig-ḟardail, *cf.* tig lecht, last bed, *LL.* 59 a, "B. of Fen." 264; tiugdal, last meeting, "Adamnan," 266; tigradus, .i. imáin, "R.I.A. MS." 35, 5, pp. 16, 17.

tigerna, 11 × 3; tigerna, 46, *ga.* and *voc.*, lord.

tigernais, 26, 27, *gsm.* of tigernas, rule, command, "B. of M. Rath," 106.

tigernmais, 30, 31; *npm.* of tigernmas, chiefs.

timchell, 57, around.

tinlucun, 27, *ds.* for tindnacul, bestowal, = tidnacul, *LL.* 106.

ra-thinóil, 4, *pret.*, he assembled them; tinól, 2, 8; tinol, 5, *infin.* (act of) gathering, a gathering; tinólfaider, 22, *fut. pass.*, tinólaim; it shall be assembled.

tír, 8, 53, 57, *nasN.*, land, country; *gs.* tíri, 10.

thís, 11, below (*adv.*)

tlachtga, 28, *gs.* or *gp.*, garb, vesture; tlacht, a cloak, *O'Cl.* *Cf.* tarb-ga.

tobuch, 7, *ds.* of tobach (act of) levying (taxes, &c.); co fult tobach, with cut hair, *LL.* 68, 266 a. *Cf.* topacht; toibges, who levies, "B. of Fen." 294.

tochostul, 2, 8 (*N.* tochurstal n-ulad, *LL.* 94), assembling, muster. tinól 7 tochurstul, *LB.* 227 b; "MS. Mater," 508.

thoirm, 8, noise, tramp; in toirm 7 in torann, *LL.* 58 a; *g.* túirm, *LL.* 58 aa.

tóisig, 30, 31, *npm.* of tóisech, leaders.

ra-tholathar,* 1; -tholathar, 1, 2; *pret. depon.* of tolaim, which pleased him (?); rontolomar, "Colman's Hymn," and "Bk. of Hymns," II. 129; toltanagud, *complacere*, *Ml.* 74 d.

tomaltus, *ns.*, 23, 24, eatables.

tond, 16 × 2, 25, 35 × 3, *nsf.*, wave; *np.* tonna, 16, 35; *g.* tuinne, 8; Tond Cliodna, T. Rudraige, T. Tuage Inbir, 16.

ton-topacht, 46, *t-pret.* 3 *sg.*, and cut off; from do-bongaim; = reaped, *LL.* 353 d, 58 a.

tora, 22, he will come; 3 *pl.* torset, 22, 22, they will go. *Cf.* totoraig, he comes; *see* dororset.

torchair, 26, he fell.

torchratar, 45, 47, 48, they fell; *perf. depend.* of do-crenim (?).

torrian, 7, *gs.*, The Tyrrhenian Sea (?). *Cf.* Fiac's Hymn.

torset, 22 × 2, *fut.* 3 *pl.* of doroichim, they will reach, arrive; *see* dororset, tora, *LL.* 97; co torracht cobair, so that help came, "Nennius," 100, 40; cotoraig, he comes, from do-rigim (?). *Cf.* tairrsid, *enclit.* *2ry fut.* of do-airicim.

tra, 10, 12, 34, *quidem*, *autem*, now, yet.

tráig, 10; traig, 11, *as.*, strand.

tráig* báile meicc buain, 10, 11, the strand below Dundalk, now Trawvally, = Dundalk.

traigid, 38, *np.* of traig, a foot.

trebairi, 11, *ap.* of trebaire, guarantees; "Laws," I. 254.

ro-thregd, 51, *pret.* of tregdaim, it pierced.

tremsi, 1, 2, 3, *as.*, a division of time, period.

trena, 6, *np.* of trén, strong; tresriu, 13, 44, mightier.

treóin, 30, 31, *npm.*, strong men.

tres, 57, third.

tress, 54, *as.*, conflict; tres, *g.* tresa, "B. of Fen." 378, 282; *dp.* treasaib, "L. na gCeart," 243; *ap.* tressu, "Bodl. Cormac," 38.

tressi, 10, might, *ns.*

trethan-glassi, 8, sea, gl. *gurges*, *Sg.* 66 b, a raging sea *or* gulf; trethan, power, "B. of Fen." 228.

trí, 11, 14, 16, 30, 35, 38, 46, three (*num. adj.*) [46, trí, *n.* and *acc.*]. trí, *g.*, 49; tri, *g.*, 31, 49.

tri* n-, 57, trib (?), *dp.*; trí, *af.*, 14, 35.

trí, three (*num. subst.*), 10.

tri, 7, through.

trian, 10 × 3, 33, *nm.*, a third part: in trian.

triar, 30, 47, three persons, trio; *gs.* thrir, 13.

triasin, 34, through the; trirna, 51, *dp.*

tríath,* *vs.*, 11 × 2, 15, &c.; *as.*, 46, chief = rí "Man. & Cust." III. 514; .i. tigearna, *O'Cl.*; .i. *rex*, Stokes' "Bodl. Cormac," 26.

troit, 5 × 2, a fight, struggle.

trom-choblach, 10, 12, *ns.*, a great fleet; trom, .i. mór, "O'Dav."

trom-longes, 57, a great exile *or* sea-voyage, *or* group of exiles.

tuage* inbir, 16, 35, *gsf.* tuag* inbir; cf. *LL.* 152 b.

thuaid, 9, 57, in the north; tuaich, 56, 57 (?).

ra-tuairced, 35, *perf. pass.* of tuaircim, was struck (do-ro-orced); *pret.* 3 *sg.* *deponent*, thuairgertar, 48.

tuaith, 56, *dsf.* of tuath, a country, region.

tuarascbáil, 27, *asf.* of tuarascbál, description; *gs.* tuarasgbála, quality, "M. Rath," 268.

tuargabtar, 15, 37, 50, *pret.* of tuargbaim,* they raised, lifted, carried away; re tuargabáil gréine, *ante ortum solis*, "Nennius," 82.

tuasciurt, 25, *ds.*, the north quarter *or* division.

tuathbil, 25, lefthand-wise *or* north; tuathbel, *LL.* 114 b, seems *genitive*, but *d.* deisiul, righthand-wise, "B. of Fenagh," 254.

tuc, 5, 25 × 2, 51, *s-pret.*, he brought, gave, = tucastar, 45; 3 *pl.* tucsat, 15; tuca, 54, *pres. conj.*

tucad, 14, 55, was brought; tucait, 13, and tuctha, 3, 17, *perf. pass.*, were brought.

tuir, 5, *ns.*, lord, *O'Cl.*; multitudes, "S. na Rann," 153; tuir, captain, "Ode on Br. O'Rorke," 294.

tuirsech, 3, sad, weary.

tuitt,* 5, he fell; *s-pret.* con-tuta,* 6; tutta in Fac-simile; tuta or tuda in *LL.* It seems for con-tuitea or con-tudcha, contudchad, till summer season may fall *or* come to us; *subj.* of tuitim or *sec. pres.* of tudchim or dodechud.

hua, 7, 10; hua, 18 × 2, grandson.

uachtur, 36, *asN.*, upper part; i n-u., above.

úad, 47; uad, 8, 9, 51, from him; uaim, 3, from me; uait, 7 × 3, 14, from thee; úan, uanni, 29, 22, from us.

uair, 13 × 2, 35, 51, hour, time: in (n)uair, *as.*, when; *g.* huaire, 12, 34, 36.

uair, 17, 18, 46, for (*conj*), seeing that.

uait, 7 × 3, 14; *see* ó (I.).

úaitecht,* 26, *as.*, pursuit, following; *cf.* fuatecht.

uamun, 20, *nsf.*, dread; *d.* ar m'uamain, *LL.* 67.

uathmar, 47, terrible.

uathnib,* 57, *dp.* of uathne, pillar; uatne in *W.*

ucht, 40, 51, 53, *dasm.*, breast; re hucht, against, "B. of Fen." 402.

uile, 4, 35, 48, all, all things, 6; *np.* 48; uili, 2.

ulad, 2, 34, 36, 48; ul(ad), 8 × 2, 9; ulaid, 4, 9, 22, 52 × 2, 25, 53, *np.*, the Ultonians who occupied a region co-extensive with the Diocese of Down; *dp.* ultaib, 1 × 2, 2, 9, 18; ultaib, 1, 2, 8; *voc. pl.* ultu,* 25, 30, 48.

ulc, 11, 18, *ds.* of olc, evil, ill, wrong.

hurbada,* 3, 15, *nap.* of urbad, cuttings, ravages: urbada 7 airgni; urbad no gearrad, "Book of Lecan," 175 a b.

urchair, 51 × 2, *gs.* of urchor, a cast, throw, shot; aur-chor, *LL.* 59, 61.

urgnam, 24; irgnam,* 23, preparation, dressing, cooking.

huscida,* 6, *ap.* of usce, water.

út, 17, 26, there, yonder, *istic.*

uthechair, 9, *gsm.* *Hennessy* and *Dr. Atkinson* read uthidir, uthithir; he was Celtchar's father; *g.* uitheochair, "Gen. Chorca Laidhe," 62; *gsm.* uithichair, *bis* full, *LU.* 103 b.

INDEX*

OF THE

MORE IMPORTANT WORDS OF THE MODERN TEXT.

* See Notes on page 264.

ceaċtarḋa, adj. 29, 29.
céad-lúṫ, ns. 32.
ċeana, adv. 17, 28.
cearcaill, ns. 5.
ceas (móir-), ds. 1.
ceasnuiġṫear, pass. pres. 17.
ceaṫa, ap. 23.
ceaṫair-ċiuṁsaċ, adj. 27.
ceilioḃraḋ, as. 13.
ċinġ, pret. 3 s. 23.
ciniḋ, (-nn-?), pres. 3 s. 35.
cinnioṁ, 27.
cíoraċ, adj. 27.
cíoraḋ, verbal noun, ds. 21.
cíorr-(ḋuḃ), 26.
ciorrḃaḋ, verbal voun, ds. 21.
ciorrḃaiḋ, pret. 3 s. 37.
ciort, ds. of ceart, 9.
clas-(lonnraċ), 23.
cleaṫaċ, (díoċonair-), adj. 28.
clí, ds. 26.
cliaiḃ-ionar, ns. 27.
clisiḋ, 35.
clóḋ, gp? 32, (-ḃuilleaḋa) 30.
clóḋaḋ, pass. pret. 29.
cloiḋṁṫiḃ, dp. 25.
cneis, ds. 23.
coḃsaiḋ, (coṁ-), vsm.? 38.
codroma, gsm.? 38.
cói(ṁ)-meata, adj. 25.
coṁ-ṫuargain, verbal noun, ds. 35.
coinġeonam, fut. 1 p. 27.
coirr-(ġéara), 25, (-leaṫan) 26.
collaḋ, ns. 32.
collaṁuin, np. 29.
colpaḋaiḃ, dp. 29.
coṁaiḋ, ds.? 14; 32, ap. 11, coṁad, gp. 9, 15.
comairc, ds. 29.
coṁ-ḋáil, ds. 17.
coṁ-ḟosaḋ, verbal noun, 26.
coṁ-ḟosuġaḋ, verbal noun, 40.

coṁ-ḟuaiḋte, ns. 27.
coṁ-maoiḋṁe, gs. 46.
co(ṁ)-móra, npm. 29.
coṁragaċ, adj. 27.
coṁraiġṫeaċ, adj. 23.
coṁraṁaċ, adj. 29, 35, -aiġ, vsm. 33.
coṁ-ruaṫar, ds. 35 (see ruaṫar).
confaḋ, vs. 33, (cruaḋ-) ns. 43.
confaḋaċa, npm. 29.
connla, npm. of connail, 35.
corrac (read -aċ), adj. 25.
corcra, adj. or gs., (daṫ) 24, (lean-) 16.
ċosgair, pret. 3 s. 36.
cosgar, ns. 43, as. 22, (-ċon) 32.
cosgraċ, (dian-), adj. 27.
cosṁailios, ds. 23.
(craoiseaċ), gs. -iġe, 26, ap. -ioċa, 30, dp. -ioċaiḃ, 29.
créaċtaċ, (loinn-), adj. 24, -aċa, npm. 28.
créaċtaiḃ, (úir-), dp. 20.
cró, ds. 38, (-fairsinge) 29.
croḃ, ds. 21.
croiḋeaḋa, np. 40.
crú, ds. 3.
cuaċ-ṡnaiḋm, 16.
cuḃaiḋ, adj. 9.
cuid, as. 22 (idiomatically).
cuingeas, hist. pres. 38.
cuinne, ds. 46.
cuire, (ban-), ds. 33.
cuma, adv.? 3.
cuṁdaiġṫe, part. 25, as. (caoṁ-) 27.
cúplaiḋeaċ, adj. 27.
cur, *champion*, ns. 35, 39, gs. curaḋ, 16, g. dual tréan-ċuraḋ, 40, np. -aiḋ, 28, saor-ċuraiḋ, 37, gp. -aḋ, 29, 29, ap. -aḋa, 17, 39, dp. (as np.) -aḋaiḃ, 5.
curata, adj. 27.

earraḋa, ap. 28.
easargain, verbal noun, ns. 33.
easargas, hist. pres. 43.
eaṫruiḃ, dp. 15.
eidir, adv. 9.
eidir-ġleoḋ, ds. 16.
éidríoṁṫa, apm. 21.
eileaphaint, gs. 27.
éin-ġil, gsm. 23.
et, read agas, *passim*.

faḃra, ns. 5.
faċain, ds. 3.
fágḃar, subjunc. (= fut.) 1 s. 4.
faġ(ḃ)ar, subjunc. (= fut.) 1 s. 4.
ḟaiḋ, pret. 3 s. 21.
faiḋreanna, 35.
faiġleannaiḃ, dp. 31.
fain-ḟeaḋa, gs. 35.
fairceiona, gs. (= adj.), 5.
fairḋinge, np. 29.
fannaiġ, np. 29.
faol-ċú, as. 21, gs. -ċon, 20.
faoṁaim, pres. 1 s. 32, 33, 1 p. -am, 33, pret. 3 p. ḟaoṁsad, 45.
faon, adj. 43, (-luiḋe) 35.
feaḋ, 46.
feaḋaiḃ, dp. 29.
feaḋm-ṁar, adj. 16.
feaġaḋ, verbal noun, 38.
feall-óglaoiċ, np. 42.
féiġ, adj. 38, npm. féiġe, 28.
féine, (ríġ-; read -nniḋ?) ns. 8.
féinneaḋ, as. 19 (read -nniḋ?)
ḟeiseaḋ, imperf. 3 s. 18.
féiṫreannaċ, adj. 16.
feoċair, adj. 38.
fiallaċ, ds. 29.
fian-sgor, ds. 27.
fillios, hist. pres. 22.
fíoċ-da, adj. 42.
fíoċ-ṁar, adj. 37.
fíoḋḃaḋ, ds. 35.
fionn-ċoire, ns. 26.
fionndruinne, gs. 27.
fios, verbal noun, ds. 20, 21.
fitte, part. 27.
fobairt, as. 37(see fuabairt).
fó-ċlár, ds. 43.
fo-ċuasaiḃ, dp. 29.
fo-ġa, gp. 35, -ġaiḃ, dp. 29.
foġar, ns. 35.
foġlaiḋ, (fear-) ds. 39.
fóir-(neart), 31, (leaṫan) 25.
foir-ḃfir, np. 42.
folṁaḋ, pass. pret. 29.
fo-luaimneaċa, npf. 29.
fo-luamna, dpm. 29.
fonn-(ġlasa), 17.
foránaċ, adj. 42.
foras-da, adj. 19, 24.
ḟorbair, pret. 3 s. 37.
for-ḃfaoilte, gs. 1.
for-(ḋonn), 23, (ġona) 22.
formna, ds. 27.
fosaiḋ, adj. 25, -a(i)ḋ, 19, pl. -aiḋe, 28.
fosg-(ċnocaiḃ), 17.
fosgaḋ, as. 19, ds. 35.
fó-ṫrarsna, adv. 43.
foṫrom, ns. 35.
frais-, fras-, in comp.—
diuḃracaḋ, 35.
diuḃraicdís, 23.
néallaiḃ, 29.
ḟaoḃar, 27.
garḃa, 29.
fraoċ-(drong), 25, (ġruama) 38.
fraoċḋa, adj. 23, 38.
frasa, np. 29.
frasaċ, adj. 5.
freasdal, ds. 17, 18.
fria, prep. 39.

tul-amair, gs. as adj. 29.
ṫúr, pret. 3 s. 38.

uaine, ns. 34.
uaiṫneaḋa, np. 29.
uallaċ, (mór-), adj. 25.
uaṫaḋ, ns. 23.
uaṫ-ṁar, (daor-), adj. 27.
uċḃaḋaċ, verbal noun, 35.
uċt, ds. 1.
úḋṁall, adj. 20.
uille, adj. (compar. ?) 5.
uilleann-aċ, adj. 26.

uillionn-uiḋe) (ceaṫar-), gsf. 26.
úir-, úr-, in comp.,—
ċréaċtaiḃ, 20.
éargaḋ, 20.
ḟéaċain, 20.
ṫimċioll, 23, 27, 28.
árda, 29.
ġranna, 42.
noċta, 28.
spraicṫeaċ, 23.
ṫosaċ, 23.
uṁaiḋe, adj. 26.
úr-, see úir-.
úrlaḃra, ns. 23.

INDEX

OF

PROPER NAMES OF THE MODERN TEXT.

The corresponding names in *LL.* version appear in italics. Names not found in the *LL.* text are marked (*). The figures refer to the sections of the Modern Text.

NOTES

TO

SOME WORDS IN THE FOREGOING INDEX.

(*Vide Pages* 251 *to* 263.)

---

aḋċíu, M.; the variants aḋċiḋ, iḋċiḋ = he saw, *MS. Materials*, 474, *Tl.* xlix.

aḋnaiġ, "he kindled," may be the same as aḋnaiḋ, he puts, from acnaim, *Cormac*, 20; but cf. rohaḋaintea, were kindled, *LB*. 210*a*; or aḋnaiġ may be for acraiġ, rises, *Bodl. Cormac*, 12.

aimiarmurtaḋ, furious, *C. M. Lena*, 138.

aimḋreanḋa: ḋreanḋ .i. ḋebaiḋ, *unde* ḋrennaḋ; .i. ġarḃ, unde aimḋreanḋ, *O'Dav.* 15.

aimrġleaḋ: aimrcle .i. ġleo ir imrra no ir anrra, *O'Dav.* 55.

aiḃle: tromaiḃle teaċt fola: cf. aiṫle .i. aṫfola, ar merra hí olḃar fola, *O'Dav.* 3.

aireaḋ, cf. aireaġ, aireċt, staying, *L. na gC.* 4.

aiṫġleannaiḃ, faiġleannaiḃ, arġleannaiḃ, anġleannaiḃ; see notes, p. 89.

airġeana: airġenn .i. ġuin, *O'Dav.* 52.

altaiḃ ḋéaḋ: calġḋet .i. arambiat na halta ḋét .i. ḋét míl móir a imḋuirn, *O'Dav.* 72.

anam: a m'anam! cf. a ċuirle mo ċroiḋe! ror é Mac Néill a hanam, Mac Neill was the darling of her soul, *Circ. of Ireland*, l. 44; m'anam irtiġ ṫú, you are my soul within, *Neilson's Grammar*.

arairm = errairm of *LL.*

bacaiḃ: ocur baco ir baḋall, *O'Dav.* 6.

beiṫir: applied to a warrior, *LL.* 247*a*, *L. Lecan*, 635; g. beṫraḋ, *LL.* 247*a*. See maṫġaṁna.

bíoġarnaiġ, joined together? cf. ġarneal, catch, hook, *O'R.*

ḃolġraḋ: cf. bailiġuḋ, to gather, collect, *MacCurtin's Dict.* p. 250.

brioċt-ḃeilġneaḋ, staff-thorny? briċt .i. baḋall, *O'Dav.* 6.

brosgar, crashing; cf. brosg .i. torann, *O'Don. Suppl.*; brusgar, broken ware, mob, *O'R.*

bruasṁór, bruaḋtṁór: cf. bras .i. mór, *O'Dav.*; bres .i. oll, *LL.* 395; bruaḋ .i. mór, bruaḋda .i. mór, broġda, céimniġṫeaḋ, *O'Clery.*

buaile boḋḋa, hedge, = buailiḋ, *qv.*

buailtib: buailib mbodbai, formidable or warlike hedge, *LB.* 207 *a.*

caiṫċrios, battle-belt or noble belt: caiṫ .i. uasal, *O'Dav.*

caobaiḋ: caib, layers of the brain, *Bodl. Cormac*, 32.

Celtċar: his six sons are named in *G. Corca Laidhe*, 62.

ceṫern (*LL.* version) should be translated as plural, or rather collective. Singular ceṫernaḋ.

clár-ḋaingne, 25; cf. clar-daingen, strong-cased (helmet), *C. M. Rath*, xiv.

clas-lonnraḋ; cf. clais-leitreḋ, letter-graved sword, clais-réiḋ, smooth-bladed, *C. M. Rath*, xiv.

Cloċra, cf. cloċra, little bell, *O'Dav.* 67.

coirr-ġéara, -leaṫan; corr, smooth, *G. Corca Laidhe*, 342.

corr-gabla, sails? cf. corrgabul .i. craiceann gabair, *O'Dav.* 63.

costud, to steady, *C. M. Rath*, 182.

culpaiḋeaḋ, 27, *variant*; culpait .i. coimet air ḟuaḋt, *Cormac*, 10.

dáiġ, fire, *or* cause.

diongnaḋaiḋ: raṫa ⁊ rodindgna, *LL.* 162β; dindgnaib ⁊ cnocaib, *LU.* 28β.

díorġaḋ, for díreccra, unanswerable, irresistible?

diorma .i. buiḋean, *O'Clery.*

dísgire, quick, restless: eiḋ díscirí, unbroken steeds, *Tl.* 252; precipitate, *Ann. L. Cé*, i., 412, *LB.* 215β; dian díscir, *LB.* 218 *a.*

dumaḋ .i. duma, mound.

fairdinge, great impact? cf. dinge, to push, *C. M. Rath*, xiv.

féiṫreannaḋ, smooth-pointed, feiṫ, smooth, *O'Dav.* 93.

fobairt, fuabairt: do ḟuabradar, they attacked, *Frag. of Ir. Ann.* 236.

forránaḋ, furránaḋ: said of a bull, *LL.* 247 *a*; fergaḋ forránaḋ, *H.* 2, 12.

furruamanta; cf. ruamnaḋ, reproving, *Bk. of Fenagh*, 248; cf. ruaiṁniġṫe.

iaḋtaḋ; iaḋtaḋ .i. éiġeaṁ, *O'Clery.*

imḟníoṁ, fatigue, *MS. Mater.* 515.

ionnsma, indsma sleġ, to set spears, *Frag. of Ir. Ann.* 3.

iorraḋ = erraḋ, erreḋ.

lábrann: ns. labar .i. laoċ, *O'Dav.* 84.

leagaiḃ, 16, means perhaps leagues.

leargа, 34; cf. lifi lerg-móir, wide-sloped Liffey, *Man. & Cust.* 484.

longaḋ; longuḋ, eating, *LU.* 103 *a.*

lomann; asf. lomain, a cord, *LL.* fo. 79 *aβ.*

lúṫṁar, nimble; lúṫ, lúḋ, velocity.

mall-ḃruaċaiḃ; cf. mall, modest, *MS. Mater.* 5 i 5.

oiririor; cf. for anaḋ ⁊ for airirem, *W.*

raḃarṫa; cf. roborta .i. imaḋ, *O'Dav.* 113.

riṫleарg; cf. riṫléimneaċ, extemporaneous verse, *O'R.*

ró, S-future of roċim.

ruiġe; go ruiġe ro = go ró ro, 45, = corrici ro, till this, up to this.

rgor, lámrgor; rcor = yoke of two horses, *Tl.* 244; rian-rgor, warlike plain; rcor .i. maġ, *O'Dav.* 115.

ronn-ċaṫa: cf. ruinn caṫa, *Frag. Ir. Ann.* 76.

taiġle: the M variant taiḃleaḃ is better.

taiġleoireaċta; better taiḃl-; cf. dorn-aiḃlibea, *eos visitabit.*

teaċt-fola for tiugfola, thick blood; cf. tiuġ-bainne, *O'Dav.* 77; *tyuch* = tough, thick, in Ulster; or from téaċtaḋ, congeal, *Mac Curtin's Dict.*

SUPPLEMENT

TO THE

INDEX VOCABULORUM OF THE "GRAMMATICA CELTICA."

[WHILE searching for Irish neuters in the Grammatica of Zeuss I discovered that about six hundred and thirty-two words, or word-forms, and a great number of useful references have been omitted in the Index of Drs. Gütterbock and Thurneysen. I give here only the word-forms which they left out; cf. *supra*, p. xxii. The numbers refer to the pages of Z^2.]

REFERENCES, NOT GIVEN IN THE INDEX, WHICH MAY PROVE USEFUL TO LEXICOGRAPHERS AND LINGUISTS.

(*See line* 18, p. xxii. *of my Preface.*)

THE END.

CPSIA information can be obtained at www.ICGtesting.com
Printed in the USA
BVOW06s2246210915
419042BV00018B/226/P

9 781165 924622